Waterloo and the Romantic Imagination

Waterloo and the Romantic Imagination

Philip Shaw

© Philip Shaw 2002

All rights reserved. No reproduction, copy or transmission of this publication may be made without written permission.

No paragraph of this publication may be reproduced, copied or transmitted save with written permission or in accordance with the provisions of the Copyright, Designs and Patents Act 1988, or under the terms of any licence permitting limited copying issued by the Copyright Licensing Agency, 90 Tottenham Court Road, London W1T 4LP.

Any person who does any unauthorised act in relation to this publication may be liable to criminal prosecution and civil claims for damages.

The author has asserted his right to be identified as the author of this work in accordance with the Copyright, Designs and Patents Act 1988.

First published 2002 by
PALGRAVE MACMILLAN
Houndmills, Basingstoke, Hampshire RG21 6XS and
175 Fifth Avenue, New York, N. Y. 10010
Companies and representatives throughout the world

PALGRAVE MACMILLAN is the global academic imprint of the Palgrave Macmillan division of St. Martin's Press, LLC and of Palgrave Macmillan Ltd. Macmillan® is a registered trademark in the United States, United Kingdom and other countries. Palgrave is a registered trademark in the European Union and other countries.

ISBN 0–333–99435–3

This book is printed on paper suitable for recycling and made from fully managed and sustained forest sources.

A catalogue record for this book is available from the British Library.

Library of Congress Cataloging-in-Publication Data
Shaw, Philip.
  Waterloo and the Romantic imagination / Philip Shaw.
    p. cm.
  Includes bibliographical references.
  ISBN 0–333–99435–3
  1. English literature—19th century—History and criticism. 2. Waterloo (Belgium), Battle of, 1815, in literature. 3. Napoleonic Wars, 1800–1815—Literature and the wars. 4. Napoleonic wars, 1800–1815—Art and the wars. 5. Waterloo (Belgium), Battle of, 1815, in art. 6. Romanticism—Great Britain. 7. Battles in literature. 8. War in literature. I. Title.

PR468.W38 S53 2002
820.9′358—dc21   2001059842

10 9 8 7 6 5 4 3 2 1
11 10 09 08 07 06 05 04 03 02

Printed and bound in Great Britain by
Antony Rowe Ltd, Chippenham ,Wiltshire

Contents

List of Illustrations	vii
Preface and Acknowledgements	ix
Abbreviations	xiii

Introduction: the Return of Waterloo   1
    States of War   6
    Victory sublime!   9
    The Wound   19

1 Walter Scott: the Discipline of History   35
    The Vansittart of verse   35
    The wounded horseman   39
    The spirit of contested lands   48
    The dance of death   53
    Coda: forging *The Antiquary*   61

2 Exhibiting War: Battle Tours and Panoramas   67
    The regimented gaze   71
    Unlimiting the bounds of painting   78
    'The perfect disciplinary apparatus'   83

3 Southey's Vision of Command   92
    La Belle Alliance   92
    A poet's fame   97
    'Upon the field of blood'   101
    'Now, said my heavenly teacher, all is clear!'   105

4 Coleridge: the Imagination at War   114
    Beating the retreat   114
    Strange explosions   120
    A state of peace   130

5 Wordsworth's Abyss of Weakness   140
    The pleasures of war   140
    The pure intent   144
    Poetizing the political   147
    Contesting visions   155
    Binding the work   162

6 'For Want of a Better Cause': Lord Byron's War with Posterity 165
Napoleon's farewell 167
The trumpet of a prophecy 172
Glory's dream unriddled 175
The spoiler's art 178

Conclusion 192
Contested pleasures 194
Women in war 196
Beyond Waterloo 203
War! What is it good for? 209

Notes 212

Bibliography 242

Index 253

List of Illustrations

1. J. M. W. Turner, *The Field of Waterloo*, oil on canvas, 1818. Copyright © Tate, London 2001. — 23

2. J. L. H. Bellangé, *La Garde meurt et ne se rend pas!*, oil on canvas. Cliché Bibliothèque nationale de France, Paris. — 27

3. Sir Charles Bell, soldier with missing arm, lying on his side, grasping a rope, inscribed 'XIII, Waterloo ...', watercolour, '11 Aug.' 1815. Copyright © Wellcome Library, London, by kind permission of the Trustees of the Army Medical Services Museum. — 40

4. Sir Charles Bell, soldier suffering from a head wound, part of his scalp shaved, watercolour, 1815. Copyright © Wellcome Library, London, by kind permission of the Trustees of the Army Medical Services Museum. — 41

5. Sir Charles Bell, arm wound, 1815, inscribed 'XII Waterloo', watercolour, 1815. Copyright © Wellcome Library, London, by kind permission of the Trustees of the Army Medical Services Museum. — 42

6. Unattributed, *Bonaparte's Observatory, To View the Battle of Waterloo, June 18, 1815*, engraving, London 1819. Christopher Kelly, *History of the French Revolution*, 2 vols. London: Thomas Kelly, 1819. University of Leicester Library. — 69

7. J. C. Stadler, after E. Walsh, *La Belle Alliance, taken on the Spot, June 25th*, hand-coloured aquatint, London 1815. *The Repository of Arts*, 14. London, 1815. Plate 20: 'La Belle Alliance'. Yale Center for British Art, Paul Mellon Collection. — 70

8. Robert Mitchell, *A Section of the Rotunda, Leicester Square*, coloured aquatint with etching and engraving, London 1801. Robert Mitchell, *Plans and Views in Perspective of Buildings Erected in England and Scotland*. London 1801. Plate 14: 'A Section of the Rotunda in Leicester Square'. Yale Center for British Art, Paul Mellon Collection. — 84

9. Jeremy Bentham, *Section of an Inspection House*, watercolour, 1787, Bentham Mss. 119. University College London Library. — 86

10 John Burnet, after Henry Aston Barker, *Explanation of the Battle of Waterloo, painted by Mr. Henry Aston Barker*, woodcut, London 1817. Yale Center for British Art, Paul Mellon Collection. 87

11 Bell [?], *Entrance to Hougoumont*, engraving, London 1816. Robert Southey, *The Poet's Pilgrimage to Waterloo*. London: Longman, 1816. 104

12 George Cruikshank, *Making Decent!!*, engraving, London 1822. Copyright © The British Museum, London. 198

Preface and Acknowledgements

> *July 17th, Monday, Brussels.* A very hot morning... Departed at a quarter past eleven for *Namur* by the way of Waterloo... the wide fields were covered with luxuriant crops, – just as they had been before the battles, except that now the corn was nearly ripe, and *then* it was green. We stood upon grass, and corn fields where *heaps* of our countrymen lay buried beneath our feet. There was little to be seen; but much to be felt, – sorrow and sadness, and even something like horror breathed out of the ground as we stood upon it! ... The ruins of Hougamont had been riddled away since the battle, and the injuries done to the farm-house repaired. Even these circumstances, natural and trivial as they were, suggested melancholy thoughts, by furnishing grounds for a charge of ingratitude against the course of things, that was thus hastily removing from the spot all vestiges of so momentous an event. Feeble barriers against this tendency are the few frail memorials erected in different parts of the field of battle! and we could not but anticipate the time, when through the flux and reflux of war, to which this part of the Continent has always been subject, or through some turn of popular passion, *these* should fall; and 'Nature's universal robe of green, humanity's appointed shroud', enwrap them: – and the very names of those whose valour they record be cast into shade, if not obliterated even in their own country, by the exploits of recent favourites in future ages.[1]

As historical commentators are fond of reminding us, the battle of Waterloo, fought on 18 June 1815, brought to a dramatic close one of the lengthiest periods of conflict in the history of Western Europe. When a few days later news of the Allied victory over Napoleon reached London, the effect was electric: heads of state wept, official business was suspended and crowds thronged the streets; some, like the artist Benjamin Robert Haydon, read and reread Lord Wellington's *Despatch*, hoping to find, in the words on the page, a focus for their wildest imaginings. The battle had brought to an end some 22 years of conflict, a period which forged the idea of the nation, as Linda Colley observes. Yet, like many an ending, the long anticipated relief – from the labour of antagonism, the effort of defining oneself against the hostile Other – was accompanied by unexpected feelings of grief, disappointment and melancholy. In the wake of Waterloo, one might say, the nation was forced to confront the possibility that wartime alone supplied the conditions for the assertion of unanimity; the peace, as Haydon and countless other commentators were to discover, did not mark the restoration of civil society, because the idea of civil society, as the revolution debate confirmed, could not be substantiated. Understood in this way, the war against France was precipitated and sustained by a legitimation crisis.

So what of the aftermath of war? The melancholy that Waterloo arouses in its Romantic commentators is evident in Dorothy Wordsworth's account, quoted above. Visiting the field with her brother in 1820, Dorothy is struck by how time and nature conspire to erase the specificity of Waterloo; five years have passed and an event premised on the cessation of conflict and the establishment of pacific or 'normal change' shows every sign of giving way to the flux and reflux of war.[2] As Dorothy attests, war, like Nature (the quotation here is taken from *The Excursion*), abhors a vacuum; the end of history is thus from a Romantic point of view unthinkable and perhaps undesirable. Faced with this problem at the close of the campaign, British observers registered equal amounts of pleasure and pain; the battle was Sublime – this was to become a frequent figure in Waterloo discourse – precisely because it exceeded, even as it generated, the ascription of narrative closure.

The sublimity of Waterloo was felt at numerous levels: from the bewilderment of the radical press to the triumphalist bellows of Lord Castlereagh and the Waterloo 'bards'. Only, it seems, by rereading and representing, could the significance of the event be brought into the purview of symbolic understanding. Yet something of Waterloo remains to trouble this endeavour, prompting a number of writers and artists – from the pro- establishment Scott and Southey, to the oppositional Leigh Hunt and Lord Byron and the equivocal Turner – to give voice to the fragility of the post-bellum consensus. The question that is posed by the end of war, and to which these writers and artists respond, is this: how does a wartime state, parlayed into unanimity through mutual distrust of the enemy, address the exposure of the absent or impossible totality that is pre-war and postwar society? How, in other words, should we live in the aftermath of victory/defeat?

In postwar British culture the anxiety on which this question is founded exhibits itself in a number of ways, from the ambivalent presence of the dead and wounded soldier in paintings, sketches and guidebooks to the unbidden melancholy of the first official 'thanksgivings'. But it is in the work of the Romantic poets that ideas of nationhood, authority and the relations between violence and identity are most severely tested. It is the argument of this book that the Waterloo writings of Scott, Southey, Coleridge, Wordsworth and Byron speak volubly of the impossibility of private and public imaginings; to hear this voice again we must reflect in turn on our current preoccupation with the limits of culture and the ends of war.

It is always difficult to give due acknowledgement, not least when the debts one owes are so numerous and run so deep. My sense of indebtedness is compounded by my sense of the quirkiness of this book's evolution. The idea of Waterloo as a subject for inquiry emerged during the final stages of a PhD thesis at the University of Liverpool in the late 1980s. It was not, however, until 1994, following an informal conversation with Nicholas Roe, that the idea of writing a book about *Waterloo and Romanticism* began to take shape. I am grateful to him for accepting publication of an exploratory essay on this topic in the first issue of *Romanticism*. During this period, I benefited considerably from the inspiration and guidance of Vincent Newey; his work on the Romantic poets is never far from my thoughts. I am thankful to him for support at every stage of the way. I wish to extend thanks to the following colleagues and friends at the University of Leicester: William Myers, Mark Rawlinson and Greg Walker of the Department of English for reading and commenting on parts of the manuscript; Alison Yarrington and Geoff Quilley of the Department of the History of Art for helpful contributions and generous assistance; Susan Pearce, past Director of the Department of Museum Studies, for guidance on the material culture of Waterloo. I am grateful to the contributors of *Romantic Wars*, especially Simon Bainbridge, David Collings, Diego Saglia and Eric C. Walker, for pointing my thoughts in the right direction. I would like to thank Steve Boulter, in particular for help and advice during the preparation of the final version of the text. Peter Foster, of the National School Hucknall, guided me at a time when I began to think seriously about the study of literature: with patience and good humour he taught me how to read. In this respect I am grateful also to Geoff Ward: discussions with him at the University of Liverpool helped shape my appreciation of poetry and taught me much about critical thought.

My research was supported by travel grants from the Department of English and the Faculty of Arts at the University of Leicester. I acknowledge this assistance with gratitude, and wish to extend my thanks to the staff of the following libraries and institutions: the Bibliothèque nationale de France, Paris; the British Library; the Department of Prints and Drawings at the British Museum, especially David Rhodes; Leicester University Library; University College London Library; the staff of the Yale Center for British Art, especially Scott B. Wilcox; the Library of the Wellcome Institute; the Prints and Drawings Rooms at Tate Britain; Captain (Retd) P. H. Starling of the Army Medical Services Museum. I want especially to thank Eleanor Birne and Becky Mashayekh at Palgrave Publishers for easing the transition from MS to print with efficiency and care. I also thank the anonymous Palgrave reader for his thoughtful evaluation of the manuscript. Parts of the introduction and parts of Chapter 5 appeared as 'Leigh Hunt and the Aesthetics of Post-War Liberalism' in *Romantic Wars*, ed. Philip Shaw (Aldershot: Ashgate, 2000), pp. 185–207 and 'Commemorating Waterloo: Wordsworth,

Southey, and "The Muses' Page of State"', in *Romanticism*, I, 1 (1995), 50–67. By permission of Ashgate Publishers and the editors of *Romanticism*. A version of Chapter 3 was published as 'Displacing Waterloo: Southey's Vision of Command', in *Placing and Displacing Romanticism*, ed. Peter J. Kitson (Aldershot: Ashgate, 2001), pp. 106–28. By permission of Ashgate Publishers.

Thanks are due to the following colleagues and friends whose kind support and advice have buoyed me along: David Amigoni, David Appleby, Ashley Armstrong, Bernard Beatty, Stephen C. Behrendt, Adrian Berry, Fred Botting, Gordon Campbell, Ashley Chantler, Stephen Cheeke, Michael Davies, M. C. Drak, Steven Earnshaw, Nicholas Everett, Timothy Fulford, Jerome de Groot, Martin Halliwell, Keith Hanley, Clare Hanson, Angie Kendall, Peter J. Kitson, Jacqueline M. Labbe, Sue Lloyd, Ian Maclachlan, Philip Martin, Elisa Milkes, Jeanne Moskal, Brian Nellist, Stephen Prickett, Sharon Ruston, Joanne Shattock, Peter Smith, Jane Stabler, Martin Stannard, Helen Stoddart, Mark Storey, Elaine Treharne, Timothy Webb, Mark Weber, Nigel Wood, Duncan Wu.

Above all, I want especially to thank my wife Louise and our daughters Betty and Olive, a loving family whose shared eccentricities help me stay on the good foot. This book is dedicated to them, and to my parents Keith and Sybil Shaw, who made it all possible.

Abbreviations

BL	Samuel Taylor Coleridge, *Biographia Literaria or Biographical Sketches of my Literary Life and Opinions*, 2 vols, eds James Engell and W. Jackson Bate, Bollingen Series. London: Routledge and Princeton University Press, 1983.
BLJ	*Byron's Letters and Journals*, 12 vols, ed. Leslie Marchand. London: John Murray, 1973–82.
CL	*Collected Letters of Samuel Taylor Coleridge*, 6 vols, ed. E. L. Griggs. Oxford: Clarendon Press, 1956–71.
CN	Samuel Taylor Coleridge, *The Notebooks of Samuel Taylor Coleridge*, 6 vols, ed. Kathleen Coburn. New York: Pantheon Books, 1957–73.
EoT	Samuel Taylor Coleridge, *Essays on His Times – in The Morning Post and The Courier*, 3 vols, ed. David V. Erdman, Bollingen Series. London: Routledge and Princeton University Press, 1978.
F	Samuel Taylor Coleridge, *The Friend*, 2 vols, ed. Barbara E. Rooke, Bollingen Series. London: Routledge and Princeton University Press, 1969.
HCW	*The Complete Works of William Hazlitt*, 21 vols, ed. P. P. Howe. London: J. M. Dent, 1930–34.
LCRS	*Life and Correspondence of the Late Robert Southey*, 6 vols, ed. Rev. Charles Cuthbert Southey. London: Longman, Brown, Green & Longmans, 1850.
LoL	Samuel Taylor Coleridge, *Lectures 1808–1819 on Literature*, 2 vols, ed. R. A. Foakes, Bollingen Series. London: Routledge and Princeton University Press, 1987.
LoPR	Samuel Taylor Coleridge, *Lectures 1795 on Politics and Religion*, eds Lewis Patton and Peter Mann, Bollingen Series. London: Routledge and Princeton University Press, 1971.
LS	Samuel Taylor Coleridge, *Lay Sermons*, ed. R. J. White, Bollingen Series. London: Routledge and Princeton University Press, 1972.
LWS	*Letters of Walter Scott*, 12 vols, ed. H. J. C Grierson. London: Constable, 1932–57.

MY I	*The Letters of William and Dorothy Wordsworth: The Middle Years, Part I, 1806–1811*, ed. E. de Selincourt, 2nd edn revised Mary Moorman. Oxford: Clarendon Press, 1967.
MY II	*The Letters of William and Dorothy Wordsworth: The Middle Years, Part II, 1812–1820*, ed. E. de Selincourt, 2nd edn revised Mary Moorman and Alan G. Hill. Oxford: Clarendon Press, 1967.
NLRS	*New Letters of Robert Southey*, 2 vols, ed. Kenneth Curry. New York and London: Columbia University Press, 1965.
SiR	*Studies in Romanticism*
TWC	*The Wordsworth Circle*
W	Samuel Taylor Coleridge, *The Watchman*, ed. Lewis Patton, Bollingen Series. London: Routledge and Princeton University Press, 1970.

Introduction: the Return of Waterloo

> Nothing in ancient or modern history equals the effect of the victory of Waterloo.
>
> *The Times*, 29 June 1815[1]

> Moral reflections on the Grand Interposition of Waterloo, are forever conflicting in the mind, and forever injuring its power of discriminate and satisfactory consideration. The thought by far the most prominent, is the speed of the course which has been run – 'a fell swoop' which in an instant, like the judgements of heaven when punishing by miracle, has made *such* an enemy to vanish, and wrought *such* a change in the face of human affairs.
>
> James Simpson, *A Visit to Flanders in July, 1815*[2]

It is a curious aspect of modern culture that Waterloo is best remembered as a tragic defeat rather than as a glorious triumph. In newspaper headlines the name is synonymous with rapid failure and collapse: 'The Japanese stockmarket meets its Waterloo', 'England team heading for Waterloo'. And in a popular Euro-hit (everybody knows it) defeat is not only remembered, it is also turned into a paradoxical affirmation: 'I feel that I'll win if I lose.'[3] If, as Jacqueline Rose has argued, our interest in celebrity turns on the inevitability of loss, one can understand why Napoleon, solitary, tragic and glamorous, wins out over the 'pure good' of Wellington. Too much stultifying rigour is bad for the soul. Crucially, if love of Napoleon the failed adventurer represents a form of perversity, an 'impulse [that] is more or less undesirable for the smooth running of our...affairs, it is no less the precondition of our participation in the so-called civilized world'.[4] In sum, we are predisposed to enjoy the sight of titanic failure because we are drawn to scenes that repeatedly play out our desire to overcome the limits of the possible. This is why, I think, the Duke of Wellington never ceased to remind his public that the battle of Waterloo was a 'near run thing', so near in fact that the British nation would glimpse, in the spectacle of the retreating French Empire, an image of its own, potential dissolution.

The fascination with loss provides one explanation for the enduring appeal of Waterloo, but it fails to explain why, throughout the last two centuries, the battle was represented, with very little equivocation, as a resounding British triumph, symbolic not only of the defeat of French tyranny but also of the inevitable rise to power of a non-aggressive, anti-expansionist and, most dazzlingly of all, anti-Imperial mode of Empire. Linked to the bluff facade of a nation secure in its right to govern the world is the critical role played by the Duke of Wellington. In contemporary biographies, as Iain Pears has noted, the Duke was consciously constructed as a pedestrian foil to the irascible genius of Napoleon.[5] Where the latter displayed the lightning flash of genius with none of its virtues, the former was singled out for his 'moderation and sagacity' as well as his military skills.[6] It was in fact Lord Castlereagh who, in his thanksgiving address of 1815, singled out the Duke, 'the greatest Captain of his age', for his 'innate modesty' – an epithet frequently invoked in public discourse of the time to excuse the anti-climacteric tone of the notorious Waterloo despatch.[7] With the arrival of the Victorian cult of self-discipline, the patrician virtues of 'patience', 'simplicity' and 'good sense' had become firmly entrenched in the English psyche. Wellington was presented then as the living embodiment of a nascent sense of national character, a man celebrated for his modesty and restraint, as well as for his ramshackle, pragmatic approach to the attainment of ends. Where English writers stressed Napoleon's professionalism, what Pears has termed his 'Cartesian devotion to grand plans' (p. 228), Wellington's equal proficiency in the field was played down in order to emphasize his gentlemanly qualities. By 1852, the year of his death, Waterloo had come to symbolize the contest of 'order against revolution... of method against madness (or caution against genius)... of modesty against ambition, of civilization against anarchy and even of gentlemen against players'.[8]

Yet for all the emphasis on Wellington's superiority of character (a trait that we will have reason to address elsewhere in this study), something of the Regency spirit – its love of theatricality and display, its curious amalgam of melancholy and exuberance – survives in English culture. Here again it is Waterloo, the climacteric event of 'an age of scarlet and steel', that provides the public with a focal point. In the romance novels of Mrs Gaskell and Colonel Maxwell, the battle is celebrated for its 'inherent picturesqueness'.[9] In the poetry of Scott, Byron and Southey, stirring dactyls and galloping iambs sought to recapture a sense of rapid motion and stylized glamour – a quality epitomized in the prose-poetry of De Quincey's 'English Mail Coach'. Thackeray's *Vanity Fair*, Leigh Hunt's *Captain Sword and Captain Pen* and, later still, Hardy's *Dynasts* also embody fleeting glimpses of the erotic charge of battle. A recognizably romantic impulse is detectable in these works, a desire that eschews abstinence and order in favour of indulgent fantasies of violent becoming – indeed, the very stuff of Napoleonic identity.[10]

At another level, and in a sense that is not confined to the short period of time with which this book is concerned, roughly the 12-month period from June 1815 to June 1816, Waterloo was depicted as an event of peerless even transcendental significance. Thus Castlereagh again, on the day the news was delivered to Parliament:

> It was an achievement of such high-merit, of such pre-eminent importance as had never perhaps graced the annals of this or any other country till now... it must be felt that it opened to our view a prospect so cheering, and so transcendentally bright, that no language could do justice to the feelings it must naturally inspire.
> (*Parliamentary Debates*, XXXI, col. 980)

Similarly the battle was documented in the *Annual Register* as the most important happening not only of the year 1815 but also of the entire history of modern warfare.[11] Waterloo was perceived therefore, from the outset, as a mythic event occurring outside the texture of documentary or annualized history – the history that James Chandler traces, via Habermas, to the emergence of the public sphere.[12] When we speak, therefore, of the battle's potential to excite the imagination, it is important that we attend closely to the ways in which it is used or, to be more precise, *cited* in subsequent moments of historical and cultural crisis. For having uncoupled itself from the annualized account, Waterloo takes on the status of a supersensible Idea, ungraspable from the point of view of conventional historiography yet able to inform or legitimize the ideological text in which it is invoked.

To illustrate this idea let us consider the significance of a representative sample of historical recollections. At the close of 1815, the *Annual Register* followed its hyperbolic praise of the battle with a note urging those who felt disappointed with the aftermath of war – rising taxes, unemployment and national debt – to keep in mind the achievements of the previous summer. In 1816 the *Anti-Jacobin* noted that 'notwithstanding the distresses of the times, the enthusiasm of public feeling was nobly displayed' in Ipswich at a dinner to commemorate the first anniversary of 'the sublime victory'.[13] In 1835 a group of Scottish conservatives held an anniversary dinner to celebrate the defeat of 'restless republicanism' and to warn against continuing calls for 'revolutionary change in the [British] constitution'.[14] Later, in 1852, the year of Wellington's death, Tennyson and Sir Edmund Creasy, as a means of preparing the nation for a healthy dose of 'war for war's sake' in the Crimea, invoked the battle.[15] Still further, in 1915, patriots writing in *The Nineteenth Century and After* used the Waterloo centenary as an occasion for extolling the 'naked truths of a war for high ideals' and, more prosaically, as a call for the enacting of conscription.[16] More recently, the novelist Bernard Cornwell, creator of the highly popular 'Sharpe' series, represents the battle as a testing ground for Thatcherite assaults on the immobility of a class-bound society; his hero is a self-made man at odds with an over-determined army bureaucracy and the ossified traditions of the *ancien régime*.[17] Common to all these events is the way in which Waterloo is cited at a moment of social crisis.[18] In each case the battle is invoked as a means of validating a claim to authority: as guarantor of national unanimity; as symbol of the triumph of the 'martial spirit' over the vitiating effects of commercialism; as a key stage in the rise of middle-class individuation. Yet, at a structural level, it is clear that the oppositions mentioned earlier have yet to be resolved. Waterloo is meant to confer a sense of stoical grandeur and epic stability; the overcoming of 'angry and turbulent passions' (Napoleon) and the triumph of 'established character' (Wellington).[19] In reality, however, the event also brings with it a recollection of a period of bewilderment, shock and insecurity, a time when the concept of the nation was exposed to the most rigorous scrutiny.

Thus Tennyson is at his most perceptive when he describes Waterloo as 'that world-earthquake', for in many respects, coming hot on the heels of the collapse of the Emperor's miraculous escape from Elba, the battle brought with it a pervasive sense of the instability of things.[20] When Castlereagh asserted that Waterloo was beyond expression he was speaking not only of the grandeur of the event but also of its fundamental impossibility: the very idea than something could occur which would bring the history of Britain's relations with its violent other to a 'decisive' end. What I am suggesting here is that the termination of Britain's twenty-year engagement with the enemy had repercussions that went beyond conventional ascriptions of stability and security, as if the attainment of victory exposed a fundamental *lack* in the idea of the nation. There is, for one thing, something peculiarly unsettled about the tone of public discourse in the months following Waterloo. True enough, the public is assured that Waterloo signals the end of a lengthy and debilitating state of war, but for every memory of the 'consummate and transcendent glory' of the victory of 18 June, there is also the concern that such affirmations will lead to the return of torpor, depression and collapse.[21] In the light of my reading of the culture of 1815 I would propose that Waterloo also captures a moment of life-threatening fragility, the point where dreams of national perfection teeter on the edge of impossibility.[22]

There is an indication of this feeling in a statement from a gentlewoman's diary, written at the height of the postwar celebrations: 'I begin to be afraid, like the frog in the fable we shall all burst with national pride, for never, to be sure, did we stand so high before.'[23] The comment is a throw-away, part of the chatter of everyday life, but it may be taken, I think, as representative of a pervasive sense of unease – with the spoils of victory, with the end of war and with the loss of the other.[24] To explain the relevance of this notion it is helpful to consider the insights of an ontological approach to the study of war and the structure of nationhood. Hegel, whose *Phenomenology of Spirit* and *Philosophy of Right* may be seen as foundational texts for a philosophy of war, is an obvious point of contact.[25] Let us begin then, by thinking about the problems of state antagonism, the relations between states and the suggestion that, at a certain level, war may be necessary for the creation of national identity. Why is it that nations might fear the cessation of war?

The judgement of the unnamed diarist is reciprocated in the midst of an otherwise effusive passage from the journals of Benjamin Robert Haydon (a text that we will consider in more detail later on):

> Perhaps in this glory may be the seeds of ruin & commotion, perhaps the effort may be so great and the strain so violent that it may be long before the [country] may attain solidity, peace & real prosperity after it. But let her be ruined if she must fall. Can she bring destruction on her head in a nobler way than by a glorious struggle for the liberty & intellect of the earth? No. Who would not be whelmed by the ruins of such a result?[26]

There is, doubtless, something very English about the fear of hubristic displays of triumph, in the sense that the attainment of victory is less attractive than the pleasure of defeat. Haydon, for one, would gladly sacrifice the well-being of his nation for a *frisson* of tragic glamour. The statement carries with it the implication that the desire to substantiate the ideal of 'the nation' is haunted by the spirit of its negated other, as if, in Hegel's terminology, a 'healthy' identity were dependent on the continued existence of antagonism. In the absence of such conflict, Haydon suggests, the nation at the height of its triumph may justly extinguish itself.[27] The state's experience of war is therefore a macrocosm of the process by which individuals encounter the possibility of their own extinction; in both cases the system 'discovers' its autonomy and coherence by taking on the other. Yet war is, at the same time, the means by which the individual overcomes the descent into selfishness and corruption. For Hegel in *The Philosophy of Right*, war is principally a social system, the means by which self-consciousness is realized through the capture of the desire of the other. By discovering itself in the place of its antagonist, each party is ideally bound to the other, turning 'unrest' away from the internal to the external world: 'Successful wars have checked domestic unrest and consolidated the power of the state at home.'[28] In the English tradition, De Quincey takes this further, arguing that state conflict is necessary not only to the health of the nation but also as a means of defending the modern civilized state from a return to its origins in barbarism: 'Banish war as now administered, and it will revolve upon us in a worse shape, that is, in a shape of predatory and ruffian war, more and more licentious.' The end of war would, in De Quincey's view, promote 'precisely the retrograde or inverse course of civilization...an interminable warfare of a mixed character...infesting the frontiers of all states like a fever'.[29] The supposedly peaceful realm of civil society is therefore 'impossible' without reference to conflict as a vital principle of negation.

Perhaps now we can begin to understand why the end of the Revolutionary and Napoleonic wars prompted its observers to reflect on what was at stake in the sense of an ending. At once the symbol of national perfection and the point at which symbolization fails – for henceforth the shape of the nation is hazy and undetermined, open to contestation from within – we might do well to conceive of Waterloo as a wound or fissure in the text of historical memory. As I will go on to explain, there is something overdetermined or unassimilable about the significance of this event, such that one might be tempted, along with countless nineteenth-century witnesses, to refer to it as Sublime.[30] In the pages that follow I will argue that the sublimity of Waterloo far exceeds the dictates of a conventional Kantian understanding. As we shall discover when we come to look more closely at the texts and paintings of Waterloo, the effects of the Sublime are such that nothing in reality can ever match up to its presence, hence the victory is turned into an impossible object of desire, a measure of the limits of imagination and crucially of the lack at the heart of the nation state. I would suggest further that something of this impossibility is traceable in even the most untroubled of postwar recollections.

States of war

As I have indicated, the core of this study centres on writing and painting produced in the wake of Waterloo. Its main concern, however, is with poetry and the efforts made by Romantic poets to negotiate the Scylla and Charybdis of public celebration and private reflection. I will go on in the next section to outline the parameters of my argument. Before doing so, however, I would like to comment briefly on the theoretical underpinnings of this project.

It might be objected by critics of a more strictly historicist persuasion that my analysis pays rather too much attention to the ontology of war and not enough to concrete historical particulars. The work of Michel Foucault would appear to offer notional support for this view. As Foucault asserted in an interview from the 1970s: 'the history which bears and determines us has the form of a war rather than that of a language: relations of power, not relations of meaning.'[31] By which he means that critical analysis is mistaken when it seeks to reduce historical processes to the 'great model of language (*langue*) and signs' (p. 56). The forces that prompted the Napoleonic wars, Foucault would claim, are best understood 'in accordance with the intelligibility of struggles, of strategies and tactics. Neither the dialectic, as the logic of contradictions, nor semiotics, as the structure of communication, can account for the intrinsic intelligibility of conflicts' (ibid.). Characteristically, Foucault's respect for the raw materiality of events, what he calls 'the always open and hazardous reality of conflict', prompts him to reject the 'Hegelian skeleton' of dialectics and semiology (p. 57). Yet, as Joan Copjec has argued, Foucault's notion of 'intrinsic intelligibility', when properly conceived, is as reified and abstracted as the theories he condemns.[32] To state that the cause of war is immanent within the field of its effects and cannot be conceived beyond the realm of positive appearances is to ignore the extent to which wars develop out of a desire to realize 'the nation' as a meta- or transcendental principle.[33] Why, after all, does a nation concede to risk its integrity? As Elaine Scarry points out in her classic study *The Body in Pain*, the 'structure of feeling of being eager to go to war' arises when a population acknowledges that its country has become a 'fiction' and that it no longer has recourse to 'benign sources of substantiation'.[34] We might add, however, with a glance towards Lacanian theory that nation states, like individual consciousnesses, are founded precisely on the fiction that they are unified and autonomous. When the dream of integrity collapses it is because the nation, as subject, is unable to avoid an encounter with 'the Real', that which makes every assertion of identity 'for ever "not all"'.[35] To modify Scarry, therefore, I would propose that we regard the desire for war as a deeply neurotic attempt to protect the illusion of unanimity. Lacan's description in the mirror-stage of the split between the ideal self and the physical self is apposite here. The sense that the immature body fails to match up to the image that is 'out there' produces a 'narcissistic fear of damage to [the] body', 'a neurosis of self-punishment',[36] and images 'of... mutilation, dismemberment, dislocation, evisceration' – just what the nation can expect when it engages in war.[37] We can hear something of this in the text of Coleridge's 'Fears in Solitude' (examined in Chapter 4). For too long, Coleridge avers, the English have protected themselves from the material effects of war. Content to wage war by proxy, the nation has established its identity on the basis of an unjustified (and untested) assertion of moral superiority. There is, in effect, a gap at the heart of the nation that is structurally comparable with the gap at the heart of self-consciousness. For Coleridge, to adapt the words of Stephen Heath, 'the stake is clear': war is 'a division that joins all the same', as a 'stand-in' for national solidarity war names a 'lack in the structure but nevertheless, simultaneously, the possibility of a coherence, of the *filling in*'.[38] The solution that Coleridge proposes to assuage his nation's guilt is thus truly perverse: to heal the wound in the nation, to fill the gap in the Real, the war must be brought home.

This leads me to consider the role of the enemy or, more precisely, the relationship between 'the nation', conceived as an ideal object, and its antagonistic other. Let us take the example of Britain's entry into the war against France. As the historian Eric Evans has pointed out, while the September Massacres, the declaration of a French republic and the execution of Louis XVI were not in themselves pretexts for war, the decision to contest the ambitions of an aggressor in an area sensitive to British interests – Evans has in mind the French invasion of the Low Countries and the legal claims of the Triple Alliance – acted on an ideological plane as a symptom of the nation's desire to defend itself from the spread of revolutionary fervour.[39] From a Lacanian point of view, the threat of the revolutionary other is exactly represented by the concept of the Real: that ultimate 'unspeakable' truth concealed by the 'legitimacy' of the 'Glorious Revolution' of 1688. The threat of this encounter explains, I think, the vital importance of Edmund Burke. What the *Reflections* provided was nothing less than a national fiction of incalculable legitimizing force. In its pages the English Constitution took on the characteristics of a unitary, organic body. The French Revolution, by contrast, was described as an incoherent, viral body, a 'plague' that threatened to spill out of its national boundaries to infect the 'heart' of England.[40] To counter this contamination, Burke urged the government to engage in a 'religious war', conducted on a scale unprecedented in the history of European conflict.[41] Thus, as Paine reminded his audience of the more prosaic reality of war – sustained foreign conflicts meant high taxation and increased revenue for government under the 'old style'[42] – Burke converted the fight against France into a principle of heroic individuation, all material considerations were to be subsumed in the missionary zeal to 'extirpate' the 'evil' of Jacobinism 'from the heart of Europe'.[43] He predicted that the ensuing struggle would be 'long' and 'total', and in this, as in so many respects, Burke was right. What, after all, was the nation fighting for if not the right to project its fears onto the image of a hostile disordered other?

The success of conservative ideology in authorizing the acceptance of war at all levels of society can be gauged from a fugitive comment of 1811. Speaking of the ineffectual nature of the peace petitions, an associate of William Strutt observed that his countrymen regarded war 'as an evil inseparable from the very constitution of social life'.[44] Conflict had fictional powers that went beyond the practical considerations of social and economic stability. As *The Times* noted in 1812: 'We are engaged in a war – a war of no common description – a war of system against system, in which no choice is left us, but victory or extirpation.' It was impossible to engage in such a struggle, 'without sweat', and crucially, 'without a wound'.[45] The Burkean rhetoric of apocalypse was a critical element of government propaganda. That it was opposed by radicals eager to expose its fictional foundations in no way detracts from its overwhelming success. The war against an overtly hostile other, as Linda Colley observes, encouraged the British to forge themselves as a coherent national body. Consensual loyalism would be the yield of conflict; Waterloo would be its endgame and its hypostasis.[46]

The contest between Britain and France was therefore imagined, on one level, as a form of total war, of system against system predicated on the inevitability of a decisive outcome. But warfare unbound, whether this is imagined in the origin or in the tendency of society, was regarded by many as a principle to be resisted. Moreover, for every assertion of the inherent value of violent confrontation there were many more from those who wished to transform the progress of history once and for all. Following Wellington's victory in the Peninsula in 1813, the British government initiated a system of alliances that would establish settled relations between the major European states for the next forty years and facilitate the emergence of 'great power' politics. In these negotiations Britain was led by Lord Castlereagh, whose diplomatic aims may be summarized as follows: first, to keep the allies together long enough to bring about a total defeat of Napoleon; second, to create a system of 'mutual checks to expansionism' that would satisfy the territorial aspirations of all nations, including France. Following Napoleon's first abdication in 1814 the new rhetoric of 'balance', 'congress' and 'settlement' appeared to herald a new age of peaceful coexistence.[47] Yet even as Europe adjusted itself to the affectless conflicts of economic competition and colonial expansion, there were signs that the bellicist culture of the past was due for an unfortunate return. Shortly after the treaty of Fontainebleau in 1814, the Marquis Wellesley remarked that the government had treated Napoleon 'as if he were a sovereign and therefore an equal ... there was no arrangement whatever to provide against the resurrection of Bonaparte, the affair was left entirely open'.[48] Waterloo was meant to put an end to this fudge. Once again Napoleon was depicted as a threat to legitimacy: there was to be no negotiation with the 'outlaw' and no attempt to represent the restoration of Louis XVIII as anything other than the return to the French of their rightful monarch. Waterloo was to be presented therefore as a 'settling of accounts', the accomplishment of symbolic destiny, a form of narrative closure.

Victory sublime!

In practice, however, the news of the event provoked a very different response in its recipients. To explain how Waterloo exceeded the simplistic desires of the state I would like to turn now to a discussion of some representative reflections. We shall begin with an early contribution to the philosophy of history. There is, as Carlyle perceived, a difference between an act and a representation. Where the former 'bodies itself from innumerable elements' the latter is 'by its nature, of only one dimension; only travels towards one, or towards successive points: Narrative is *linear*, Action is *solid*'.[49] On 18 June 1815 Waterloo entered the public sphere with all the appearance of solidity: its status as an 'action' was incontrovertible. What was less certain was the place it occupied in a Christian model of progressive and providential history. In the months preceding the Emperor's defeat the bodying forth of action often exceeded the ability of narrative to work in concert with this model. When, referring to the abdication of 1814, Robert Southey remarked that the 'sudden' and unexpected 'termination' of the conflict had 'brought with it an awful sense of the instability of things', he was referring to the *failure* of that event to 'bring down the curtain on this tragedy of twenty-five years' (*LCRS*, IV, 68–9). Less than a year later, the equally unexpected and no less 'decisive' defeat of Napoleon induced similar feelings of delight and dismay. True, the victory was 'brilliant and complete' – Scott described it as a 'grand finale' (*LWS*, IV, 74) and Byron as 'a devil of a finish' – but the assertion of narrative closure masked an underlying feeling of incredulity, as if, to adopt a Hegelian figure, Waterloo had revealed itself as a moment of rupture rather than as an instance of self-definition.

A frequently cited passage from the diary of Haydon provides us with a clue to the structure of this feeling:

> How this Victory pursues my imagination! I read the Gazette four times without stopping... I read the Gazette again, the last thing [before] going to bed. I dreamt of it & was fighting & waking all night. I got up in the morning in a steam of intense feeling. I read the Gazette again, ordered a Courier for a month, called at a Confectioner's shop, & read all the Papers till my stomach aked. The more I think of this Glorious Conflict, the more I glory in it...
>
> There is something to me infinitely imposing, sublime, & overwhelming in the present degraded state of France & Napoleon Buonaparte... One's imagination is oppressed with [Waterloo's] brightness, one's faculties dulled by [its] remembrance.[50]

Like the passage quoted earlier, Haydon's support for the victory is accompanied by a feeling of imaginative instability – a feeling that was to haunt the painter for the remainder of his life. In this case, even as reason attempted to qualify the sublime 'shock' of Wellington's triumph, every presentation of an object designed to 'make visible' this absolute greatness would prove to be painfully inadequate. Likewise, for the painter James Ward, commissioned by the British Institute to create an 'allegorical representation' of Waterloo, the significance of the battle could realize itself only in the paradoxical form of the unrealizable project.

Despite the risible nature of the painters' attempts to give form to Waterloo, the experience of radical negativity, of the radical inadequacy of all phenomena to the Idea, provided a useful support for governmental attempts to elevate the battle to the status of a peerless event, beyond the reach of public representation. In the state-sanctioned press, victory over the detested French other was presented as an incomparable event in national history, its sublime import derived not from its tendency to crush the imagination, but rather from its ability to enhance a supersensible Idea of collective genius. Thus, in Parliament, the concept of 'transcendent' victory was deployed by Castlereagh as a means of silencing the opposition. At the conclusion of the minister's vote of thanks Sir Francis Burdett stood up to announce 'he thought it was not fair in the noble lord to hold such language with respect to that which he knew such different opinions prevailed'. Those who 'denied the justice of the case must either seem to acquiesce in the description thus given of it, or be compelled to appear unwilling to assent to the motion for a vote of thanks where it was so deemed'.[51]

For those outside Parliament the disciplinary effect of this positioning, as William Cobbett describes it in his 'historical notice' for Saturday, 24 June, a mere two days after the initial announcement, would prove to be overwhelming:

> The *Times* newspaper says, that the campaign has opened with 'a great and glorious victory; that Bonaparte's reputation has been wrecked, and his last grand stake has been lost in this tremendous conflict; the fabric of rebellion is shaken to its base.' The *Morning Chronicle*, that pink of hypocrisy, tells us, that it has been 'a brilliant and complete victory, which will for ever exalt the glory of the British name; that it is the grandest and most important victory ever obtained.' The *Courier*, in the height of its frenzy, declares, that there could not have been 'a greater victory in point of glory, more vital to the real interests and safety of Europe, big with more important political consequences'. – Of course, as this same *Courier* says, 'the city is a scene of complete confusion; business is entirely neglected; the immortal Wellington is the universal theme; the streets and Exchange are crowded to excess – all anxious to hear the details of the glorious victory obtained by our noble countrymen.'[52]

It is worth looking at Cobbett's text in detail. As the passage proceeds, the radical's qualifying language – 'that pink of hypocrisy', 'in the height of its frenzy' – is overwhelmed by the inflationary rhetoric of greats, grands and grandest. The deployment of state-sanctioned hyperbole suggests the creation of a new and seemingly indisputable consensus, one that Cobbett, as a representative of the counter-public sphere, seems powerless to critique. By the time the final sentence is reached, the passage has turned into a performance of the very power that the radical must 'speak through'. What he is faced with, however, is the incontrovertible force of a 'universal theme' – in this case the sublime fiction of the 'immortal Wellington'.

Unlike Haydon, however, Cobbett's encounter with the textual sublime found its check a week later through the reimposition of the rational language of socio-economic critique. In the following passage it is satire that establishes a clearer perception of the effect of Waterloo:

MY LORD, – The intelligence of this grand event reached me on Saturday last, and in the following manner. I had been out very early in the morning, and, in returning home to breakfast, I met a populous *gang of gypsies*... upon a nearer approach to them, I perceived the whole caravan decorated with *laurel*. The blackguard ruffians of men had *laurel* boughs in their hats; the nasty ferocious looking women, with pipes in their jaws, and straddling along like German trulls, had *laurel* leaves pinned against their sides. The poor assess, that went bending along beneath the burdens laid on them by their merciless masters, and that were quivering their skins to get the swarms of flies from those parts of their bodies which the wretched drivers had beaten raw, had their bridles and halters and pads stuck over with *laurel*. Somewhat staggered by this symbol of victory, I, hesitating what to do, passed the gang in silence, until I met an extraordinary ill-looking fellow, who, with two half-starved dogs, performed the office of rear-guard. I asked him the meaning of the laurel boughs and he informed me, that they were hoisted on account of the *'glorious victory obtained by the Duke of Wellington over Bony;'* that they were furnished them by a good gentleman, *in a black coat and big white wig*, whose house they had passed the day before, between Andover and Botley, and who had given them several pots of ale, wherein to drink the Duke's health. – 'And, to be sure,' added he, 'it is glorious news, and we may hope to see the gallon loaf at a *grate* again, as 'twas in my old father's time.'[53]

To Cobbett, the victory of Waterloo stood for the triumph of the establishment over the people. Since a sizeable portion of that people had been slaughtered in the campaign, the muted reception of the news among the labouring classes seems entirely credible. In this aggressive parody, Cobbett implies that to wear the laurel is to rescind one's claim to true nationality. The gypsies are a feckless race, duped into acting the part of 'rude mechanicals' by a ruthless aristocracy, intent on transforming the nation into a picturesque backdrop as a distraction from the effects of invidious economic policies.

Despite Cobbett's best efforts, London at the close of June 1815 was widely depicted as a scene of universal celebration. On the morning of the 22nd, Edward Smirke reported that he 'had been to the Park, and found the People [we may speculate over the composition of this group] everywhere rejoicing at the intelligence'.[54] The following evening illuminations, reminiscent of those seen the previous year, appeared at the Public Offices and at houses on the north side of Oxford Street. In such an atmosphere it was difficult to imagine any form of constructive questioning. As Wellington's sublime status was proclaimed over London, literally so in the form of a giant illumination depicting a mounted figure, sword held aloft, in pursuit of a fleeing dwarf, the best that confirmed Napoleonists such as Whitbread, Byron and Charles Blagdon could register was a form of blank astonishment.[55] In the

Examiner for 2 July, Leigh Hunt offers the following reflection on the state of unreality: 'The changes that now take place in the world have really more the look of pageants or shews than anything else.'[56] Successive articles struggle to get behind the 'vacant airiness' of the times: 'the daily events of our time are like the wildest dreams of a century back. *Dartineuf*, the epicure... never had a nightmare more oddly compounded in its visions.'[57] 'For some time we have been fed with astonishments; the last eighteen months have fairly surfeited us'. But, in an 'age which has seen Kings and Emperors made and unmade... in the twinkling of an eye, – and, in short, has been familiar with infernal machines, massacres, revolutions, restorations, revolutions again, and all sorts of great and remarkable changes', perhaps Hunt could be forgiven for failing to perceive the distinction between the virtual and the actual.[58] So 'oddly compounded' was the present state of affairs that all but the most dogged ideologue would be disturbed, as Cobbett himself came to realize: 'While this delirium continues at its height, it would be useless in me to attempt to bring the public back to reason... I might as well expect that a drunken man could discuss, with calmness and perspicuity, an argument in mathematics or moral philosophy.'[59] The effects of the 'great exhibition of political things', as Bagehot was to express it, had permeated the whole of society.[60]

How does a society that has experienced the ecstasy of the Sublime, and thus the fictional foundation of its being, learn to return to the everyday world of experience? Quite simply by supplying representations – romance, tragedy, satire, comedy and epic and so on – that would suggest the possibility of binding Waterloo within the inclusive fabric of narrative historiography.[61] But given the political connotations of these representations – in the words of Hayden White modes of emplotment involve 'ontological and epistemological choices with distinct ideological and even specifically political implications' – the choice of genre was by no means an innocent one.[62] Whether Waterloo was to be seen as a victory for constitutional freedom or turned into a catalyst for social revolt depended as much on the form in which it was to be presented as on the content that it must assume. It is useful, in this light, to consider the concluding stanza of an address delivered at the close of the first anniversary dinner held in Ipswich:

> Spirit of PITT! if, yet, thou hoverest near –
> If, yet, thou viewest this dull terrestrial sphere –
> If they dear land, to which thy all was given,
> May claim one thought within thy happier Heaven –
> O, bless the proud result, through THEE obtained!
> A world in peace! – PARADISE REGAINED![63]

By incorporating Waterloo and the history it concludes within the providential fabric of Milton's epic verse, the writer is unequivocal in his belief

14 *Waterloo and the Romantic Imagination*

that the battle can be approached as an object of knowledge. With Satan defeated and the old order restored the world can indeed look forward to a period of blissful serenity.[64]

For other poets, however, especially those writing in the immediate wake of the battle, the ascription of narrative form was by no means easy. As an example of such a response let us consider briefly the work of William Thomas Fitzgerald, whose extempore poem 'The Battle of Waterloo' was printed in six journals and is representative of the vast number of pro-battle verses published in the period. Like the Ipswich address, its central statement is blithely triumphalist. At first sight it is the sort of work that yields little or no pressure to the touch of analytic criticism:

> But where's the BARD, however grac'd his name,
> Can venture to describe GREAT WELLESLEY'S fame?
> Such Bard, in strength and loftiness of lays,
> May soar beyond hyperbole of praise,
> And yet not give the tribute that is due
> To BRITONS, WELLINGTON, led on by you!!
> For to the plains of WATERLOO belong
> The magic numbers of immortal song.[65]

The opening statement of this extract captures the dilemma facing a majority of Waterloo bards. The very fact that the victory was indescribable placed enormous pressures on the power of art to capture its significance. In stating that Wellington's fame would outface the 'hyperbole of praise' Fitzgerald crisply defined an agenda for all subsequent songs: the Aristotelian privileging of poetry over history was to be redefined. Since Waterloo was already a poem of sorts, bardic representations were all but redundant: the event had manifested itself as a poetic universal, distinct from the ordinary particulars of history, a notion reinforced by the reference to heaven having 'decreed' the event. The verse may well 'fail' as a piece of complex verbal art but it speaks, nevertheless, of a dilemma that is all too recognizable: the collapse of the oppositional relation between culture and politics. Fitzgerald's poem is shot through with the insistent voice of legitimacy and yet its docile acquiescence, its clichéd admission of artistic inadequacy remains implicitly critical of the social order from which it springs. This negative knowledge only emerges, however, when the rhetorical question addressed at the start of the poem is answered, in all seriousness, by a far greater poet.

Writing in the 'Advertisement' to his 1816 collection of 'Thanksgiving' poems, Wordsworth states that the moral 'splendour' of Waterloo is threatened by a darkened veil of 'present distresses' – economic, social and political.[66] Under such circumstances the hasty application of narrative form would serve only to alert the public to the disparity between historical actuality and aesthetic form: resulting in a vision of national unity *in propentia* rather than in actuality. In order, therefore, to divert attention from this 'overpressure of the times' Wordsworth presents the battle in terms reminiscent of the disciplinary strictures of the Kantian Sublime:

OCCASIONED BY THE SAME BATTLE
February 1816

The Bard, whose soul is meek as dawning day,
Yet trained to judgments righteously severe;
Fervid, yet conversant with holy fear,
As recognizing one Almighty sway:
He whose experienced eye can pierce the array
Of past events, – to whom, in vision clear,
The aspiring heads of future things appear,
Like mountain-tops whence mists have rolled away:
Assoiled from all incumbrance of our time,
He only, if such breathe, in strains devout
Shall comprehend this victory sublime;
And worthily rehearse the hideous rout,
Which the blest Angels, from their peaceful clime
Beholding, welcomed with a choral shout.

'From all this world's encumbrance did himself assoil.'

Spenser[67]

The opening presents an idealized bard figure, freed 'from all incumbrance of our time' so that he may 'pierce the array / Of past events' and prophesy the 'aspiring heads of future things' (lines 5–7). Within this scheme, those events that threaten to veil the splendour of victory must be neutralized by means of a civic totality: the propensity for sublime feeling that resides in the concept of a 'national mind'.[68] The problem is, however, that as a recent event in the history of the English, Waterloo as yet has no 'figure'. Its pains and sufferings are still felt as material wounds in the body of the nation, too overwhelming to be sublimated 'by the tie of sweet and threatening harmony'.[69] In the terms of the Sublime, such is the magnitude of modern warfare, in the sense of its ideological promptings, human effects and political consequences, that the creative mind is unable to activate a power of understanding sufficient to overcome its subjection to the overburdened imagination. Since its effects remain heterogeneous, it becomes impossible to reduce Waterloo to the status of a historical object. Consequently those poetic treatments which attempt to assimilate the immensity of battle to a mental economy of loss and return risk the accusation of bad taste.

Such objections, voiced at the time by dissenting critics such as the Methodist Josiah Conder, went for the most part unheard in the rush to make sense of the significance of what had recently occurred. The battle may well have thwarted the efforts of rational understanding to gain a purchase on its meaning but this did not prevent writers from both sides of the political divide from making the attempt. For non-establishment liberals, in particular, the victory presented an unusual challenge: how to support the overthrow of the perverter of liberty while addressing the undesirability of its means and the uses to which it will be put. Leigh Hunt's response to this problem is set out in an editorial from the *Examiner*, which takes as its opening premise the idea that Waterloo was not won by aristocratic 'individuals' such as the Duke of Wellington but rather by the collective efforts of the people:

> ...It is truly the *English* who have won this great victory, and not one man of merit among them nor one hundred... let us hope that good will come out of the evil, though of a different complexion from what the Allied Sovereigns may contemplate.

By replacing the name of Wellington – or, for that matter, Napoleon, which a Foxite Whig such as Byron might have preferred – with 'the solid strength of the [English] national character, and of [its] constitutional causes', Hunt can look forward to a period when 'civil power, intellect and rights of the community at large, [may] be heard and felt in their own cause'.[70] Put another way, even as Hunt gestures to a time when the despotic simulacra of pageants and 'shews' will give way to the democratic reality of the ideal speech situation, the time, that is, when a poetics of justice and understanding replaces the degraded forms of tragedy and sensation, he is unable to imagine this community on the basis of anything other than a civil or military conflict.

This much is shown in Hunt's patriotic poem, the 'National Song', first printed in the *Examiner* for 25 June 1815:

> Hail, England, dear England, true Queen of the West,
> With thy fair swelling bosom and ever-green vest,
> How nobly thou sitt'st in thine own steady light,
> On the left of thee Freedom, and Truth on the right,
> While the clouds, at thy smile, break apart, and turn bright!
> The Muses, full voiced, half encircle the seat,
> And Ocean comes kissing thy princely white feet.
>   All hail! all hail!
> All hail to the beauty, immortal and free,
> The only true goddess that rose from the sea.
> Warm-hearted, high-thoughted, what union is thine
> Of gentle affections and genius divine!
> Thy sons are true men, fit to battle with care;
> Thy daughters true women, home-loving and fair,

With figures unequalled, and blushes as rare:
E'en the ground takes a virtue, that's trodden by thee,
And the slave, that but touches it, starts, and is free.
   All hail! all hail!
All hail, Queen of Queens, there's no monarch beside,
But in ruling as thou dost, would double his pride.[71]

According to Hunt, the poem was written, not as Cobbett thought 'in allusion' to Waterloo, but rather 'in contemplation of that general character of the natives, which keeps our country altogether the freest in Europe, and is the true secret why it is victorious even when it may not be on the best side of the question'.[72] It is important to keep in mind Hunt's own estimation of his poem for it goes some way to correcting a persistent reading of the work which sees it as unambiguous 'celebration' of victory. In fact, the poem's real concern is with the recovery of the popular rights won during the Civil War and placed in contempt by the wanton authority of the Regency. Thus, Hunt's England is not the land of Castlereagh and Croker, but of Hampden, Milton and Sydney: 'On the left of thee Freedom, and Truth on the right.' As the poem proceeds the language struggles to contain its prior investment in internal strife by foregrounding images of national unity. Thus, in a return to the idealized merry England of the Elizabethan period, England becomes the 'true Queen of the West', at whose feet the unity 'Of *gentle* affections and genius divine' (my emphasis) is sanctioned by a universal 'hail!' This 'gentle genius' is not only a figure of an anti-Romantic creative power (though, for that matter, it is antipathetic towards virtually all hegemonic ideas of genius), it is also symptomatic of an attempt to redefine the political significance of nationhood: away from the bellicose nationalism of the Regency and towards a restitution of the unifying ideals of the Constitution, albeit filtered through the ubiquitous image of the hearth and home (line 14). But, in a sense, the poem falls victim to the author's indefatigable meliorism, rendering Waterloo the means by which Napoleon, the perverter of liberty, is thrown into 'obloquy'. Therefore, while it is possible to read the 'National Song' as a fulsome response to the victory (and clearly this is what Cobbett believed), to do so one must overlook not only the immediate context of Hunt's politics, but also the extent to which the poem presents Waterloo as an essential element in the *telos* of universal happiness.

Hunt is therefore brought to the uncomfortable recognition that violence is indeed 'endemic to the very constitution of society'. The attempt to assimilate the magnitude of Waterloo, to reduce it to a key stage in the gradual progress of enlightened humanity brings with it a recollection of the impossible origins of civilized society, the very 'thing' that Hegel and De Quincey warn against. What Hunt fails to realize, however, is that it is the antagonism between state violence and civic debate that constitutes the rational society he wishes to bring into being. As Habermas has argued, the public sphere is the product of a provisional settlement between aggressive expansionism and the interests of the commercial sector. Yet the 'founding controversy' of the public sphere does not disappear; indeed, as Mary Favret observes, it is liable to re-emerge in times of social stress when state interests prevent the legitimate expression of dissent.[73] In order for the nation state to exist, therefore, it must continue to provide channels for the filtering of dissonance. In the absence of such channels, violence returns to mark the failure point of symbolization, what Lacan would term the impossible traumatic origins or the real of the state's desire.

This is why Hunt's evocation of a democratic, united England bore with it a reminder of ancient, constitutional issues that the official dogma of a United Kingdom sought desperately to quash. When in 1816, the *Anti-Jacobin Review* noted in a review of a Waterloo poem that 'there are some subjects on which the mind so delights to dwell, as never to be fatigued by continuance, and never to be sated by repetition', the note of enthusiasm was tempered by the observation that the poet, a Scotsman named Henry Davidson, had avoided 'that display of *nationality* which, unless managed with extreme delicacy, becomes revolting to the natives of other countries, by wearing a strong semblance of assumed superiority'.[74] The previous December, the same magazine gave its approval to Edmund Swift's *Waterloo*, noting that the poem contained 'abundant proofs of Mr. Swift's loyalty as a subject'. Swift, an Irishman, had included in his volume a note on the correct meaning of 'national': 'as Irish nationality is systematically perverted into imperial separation, the author did not chuse to contribute his strings to the harp of discord.' Instead his work celebrates the power of music, 'softly and sweetly sublime' to unite countries in the imaginative space of song.[75] What the *Anti-Jacobin* discovers, however, is that fantasies of blending and containment are insufficiently strong to prevent a recollection of the unstable conditions of national unanimity.

My point here, in dwelling on the occasional verse issued in the wake of the victory of Waterloo, is to suggest that questions of genre and narrative form went hand in hand with anxieties about the state of the nation. Whether the battle was represented through the medium of the sonnet, the extempore effusion or the lyric 'song', the idea that Waterloo was as yet too big for the imagination to comprehend its sublimity was a notable feature of these early attempts at representation. More often than not, local crises in the form and content of these verses were related to larger questions concerning the nature of the nation state and the authority of the poet.[76] As we have seen, the attempt to impose form on the heterogeneity of Waterloo rebounded on its chief practitioners. The effect is not confined to the writers of occasional verse. As we shall discover, Waterloo places into abeyance the smooth and easy transition from history to myth, whether this is seen in the fractured form of Scott's and Southey's romance, or the breakdown of authority that is a manifest feature of Wordsworth's 'Thanksgiving' poems and of Coleridge's *Zapolya*.

The wound

As a final example of how symbolization breaks down in representations of the battle I would like to conclude this introduction with an exploration of matters that ought, by rights, to take the central place in any serious study of the relations between warfare and culture. I speak, of course, of the 'reciprocal activity of death and injury' on the outcome of which victory or defeat is raised. For Elaine Scarry, the soldier's body – wounded, maimed and destroyed – is the real thing that ideology absorbs in its efforts to give substance to the state's desire for cohesion. One would expect that direct contact with this primal reality would result in the unveiling of ideology: a notion written into all manner of anti-war texts, from *The Red Badge of Courage* to *Catch 22*. It is instructive therefore to turn to Stendhal's version of the corrective powers of experience. The Waterloo section from *The Charterhouse of Parma* focuses on the efforts of an impulsive ingénue, the incongruously named Fabrizio del Dongo, to achieve distinction in the service of the Emperor Napoleon. Above all else he wishes to experience a real battle at first hand. Armed only with his knowledge of Ariosto and Tasso and the noble enthusiasm of youth, Fabrizio stumbles through mud and smoke and finds himself unable 'to distinguish anything'.[77] Disappointed with his experience he turns to his jaded, more experienced fellows and asks 'is this one a real battle?' (p. 60). Not even the 'spectacle' of the dead and wounded makes much of an impression on him. Fabrizio is so intent on finding the object of his desire – 'So I have missed seeing the Emperor on a field of battle, all because of those cursed glasses of brandy' (p. 62) – that the reality of battle passes him by. When finally, exhausted and abandoned, he admits to himself that 'war was no longer that noble and universal impulse of soul devoted to glory that he had figured it to be from Napoleon's declarations', it seems that the youth has been chastened. He has learnt that the banal and recalcitrant reality of war is far removed from his dreams of heroic endeavour and knightly comradeship. Yet still Fabrizio persists in his questioning: 'was what he had seen a real battle? And, if so, was it the battle of Waterloo?' (p. 59). The fact that the content of the event consistently fails to fulfil its symbolization means that the return to lucidity, as Victor Brombert has noted, is at best provisional. Indeed, 'far from undermining the lyric illusion, the elements of parody' in the novel 'serve to protect it. They reveal an oversensitive hero who is forced by the world's coarseness to withdraw into himself' and who is thus impelled to set out in quest of 'that undefinable "something"' that will fill his 'inner emptiness'.[78] Fabrizio, in other words, is in search of the missing object that will allow him to suture the breach between the ideal I and the symbolic. Brombert goes on to call the battle a 'special therapy destined to cure Fabrice of his illusions' (p. 158). But the hero's progress does not result in his assumption of the 'prosaic view', an awakening to reality. Rather, as therapy, the experience of battle forces Fabrizio to go off in search of a stronger, more resilient fiction, a nameless 'something' that will allow him to subsume the pain and terror of the Real.

Stendhal's insight into the relationship between fantasy and reality will serve here as an introduction to the themes addressed in this section. To begin with let us consider the ways in which the 'truth' of Waterloo was communicated to its audience. When the *Morning Chronicle* reported on 21 June that the 'encounter' had been 'dreadful in carnage', its readers were as yet unaware of the unprecedented ferocity of its climax.[79] Within an area of land measuring just less than three miles from east to west, and less than a mile and a half from north to south, over 40,000 were about to be killed.[80] The ensuing struggle lasted a little over eight hours; at the end of this period – short even by modern military standards – an empire lay in ruins and the destiny of Europe had been secured. The victors, the nations of Britain, Prussia, Holland and Belgium, would each go on to claim the battle as their own. To this latter end, even the dead could be brought to account; the fantasy of honourable sacrifice – lives are not wasted when offered in the service of their country – saw to it that the gross fact of human loss would be absorbed by the ideological fantasy of national coherence.[81] But even as the work of translation took effect, something would remain of these bodies to trouble the smooth workings of the system. With only a thin covering of soil to protect them from exposure, the dead had an uncanny knack of returning. Yet, with the exception of a handful of paintings and poems (Byron is possibly the only poet in this period to convey a genuine sense of moral revulsion), the impact of such sights was, for the most part, easily adapted to the task of national aggrandizement. As the Waterloo bard Henry Davidson conveys, the passage from sorrow to enchantment is all too brief:

> Is there no one to sing the brave?
> Is there a tear to steep the grave
>   Of those who fought and fell?
> O if there be, here grudge it not –
> For ne'er was triumph dearer bought,
> And ne'er was a field so desperate fought, –
>   So sternly and so well.
> Dark field of sorrow, WATERLOO!
> How silent are thine echoes now;
> How still the scene, – how deep, how dread
> The slumber of thy thousand dead!
> No stir, how faint soe'er, to quell
> The magic of thy potent spell,
> That binds, as to enchanted spot,

Each sense, each passion, and each thought;
And mingles grief and feeling high
In one deep thrill of ecstacy.[82]

The thrill of the Burkean sublime, described by the favourable reviewer of the *Anti-Jacobin* as 'a mingled sensation of hope and awe, arising out of a consciousness of the approach of something awful, something portentous, of which no definite idea can be formed', is used here to facilitate the shift from fixated mourning to 'joyful exultation'.[83] This 'deep thrill of ecstacy', when combined with the more prosaic current of Malthusian thought which argued that wars – like famines and pestilences – were natural (i.e. divinely sanctioned) means of disposing of excess populations, saw to it that the dead would be put to work as the cannon-fodder of victory sublime.

To explain this notion more fully let us examine a work that offers an unequivocal challenge to the ideology of sacrifice, Turner's *The Field of Waterloo* (Figure 1). The painting depicts the ruined shell of Hougoumont, a defensive position regarded by Wellington as crucial to the outcome of the battle. In the background, to the left of the still burning manor house, the sky is lit up by a rocket, its sulphurous glare in marked contrast to the feeble glow of the women's torches. The torchlight directs the viewer towards the open face of a woman, attending to her child, a reminder of peaceful, generative forces in a destructive setting. This, in turn, leads us to consider the mother and child, positioned in the immediate foreground of the painting. Turner's 'message' is clear: the sense of sublimity, suggested by the rapid shift from light to darkness in the night sky, is placed against an image of suffering femininity, as if the painting itself were questioning the very grounds on which the distinction between the Sublime and the Beautiful is raised. For even as the viewer considers the pathos of this representation, there is a nagging feeling that the composition has exceeded its rubric, that the juxtaposition of terror and pity, violent masculinity and caring femininity, has exposed something fundamental about the portrayal of peace and war.

There are good reasons to suppose that Turner had intended his painting as a critique of the ravages of Waterloo. In 1818, when *The Field of Waterloo* was first shown, the exhibition catalogue had printed alongside the number given to the picture stanza 28 from Canto III of *Childe Harold's Pilgrimage*. Byron's poem offers a verbal equivalent of the scene Turner was trying to describe:

The thunderclouds close o'er it, which when rent,
The earth is covered thick with other clay,
Which her own clay shall cover, heaped and pent,
Rider and horse – friend, foe, in one red buriel blent![84]

Byron's 'other clay' looks forward to a central trope of contemporary war poetry – one thinks especially of the sculptural motifs of Tony Harrison's 'A

Cold Coming'. In Byron's case, however, the face of war is not 'an armature half-patched with clay' but an indistinguishable mound of flesh and soil.[85] The image of the red burial mound is also in place in Turner's image, but where the painting goes beyond its poetic inspiration is in the attention it gives to the ontological subtext of this theme. Dismissed by J. W. M. Hichberger as compliant with the postwar logic of sacrifice, *The Field of Waterloo* nevertheless presents us with a powerful commentary on the links between warfare, wounding and national identity.[86]

I want to begin with a closer look at Turner's treatment of the wounded soldier. Why is it that images of the body in pain are so elusive in this period? In the light of Elaine Scarry's persuasive analysis it may be that the reality of warfare must remain, for epistemological reasons, strictly unthinkable to its passive observers. In the context of the Revolutionary and Napoleonic wars, however, the reasons for this lack of comprehension are also significantly political. For one thing, as Favret has argued, the conflict with France was channelled for the public 'through institutions and verbal conventions that filtered and altered its content...in several senses war could not enter the public sphere. Like the unnamed soldier whose body was injured or destroyed by warfare, war itself was labelled "private".'[87] In so far, however, as the ordinary citizen could be parlayed into a defender of 'the polity and protector of those – women, children, the elderly – who allegedly cannot protect themselves', – his new identity made manifest the relations between state and public sphere. This relationship could be exacerbated, moreover, when the allegedly omnipotent and immortal form of the citizen-soldier is recognized to be a wounded or dying body, in need, that is, of protection himself. At such moments the state runs the risk of exposing the fundamental deceit on which the process of corporeal transformation relies. To prevent this occurring, the soldier must, as Favret argues, be 'translated [back] into a private body, identified with the feminine, and distanced from our vision of the public man' (p. 542). It is this last notion that bears on our reading of *The Field of Waterloo*. The presence of women and children alongside the dead and wounded soldiery serves to conflate the separation on which the fiction of national identity depends: the idea, that is, that the mortal body of the 'private' can be abstracted from the collective and immortal body that he is meant to defend. By allowing the domestic and the military realms to merge, as it were, Turner is able to display that 'other body' of the soldier, the vulnerable body that can be maimed and killed. As such, the painting disturbs the ideology that perpetuates war: that it will keep violence – in the form of invasion or civil strife – from 'coming home' (p. 547).

My claim that this painting questions the logic of sacrifice ought, however, to be viewed in the light of some more orthodox representations. One of the most celebrated myths of Waterloo concerns the actions of Magdalene De Lancey, the young wife of Sir William, Wellington's trusted Quartermaster

Figure 1 J. M. W. Turner, *The Field of Waterloo*, oil on canvas, 1818

General who, at the height of the fighting, had received a desperate wound. Lady De Lancey's diary describes how she tended her husband in a hovel on the edge of the battlefield. For six nights she hardly slept; the surgeons repeatedly bled the dying man. She applied the leeches and blisters they supplied, bathed him and combed his hair, tore up the gown she was wearing to make bandages, and contrived to find food and blankets while providing constant love and encouragement. Eventually, when the end came, she climbed into the back of the narrow wooden bunk her husband lay in and held him as he died. The account moved Dickens to tears and was generally taken to be a fitting tribute, both to the courage of the man who suffered in the cause of his country and of the woman who demonstrated such constancy.[88] In a similar vein, Fanny Burney describes the charitable actions of the women of Brussels, whose selfless care for the injured of both sides was also held up as a model of feminine virtue.[89] With Turner, however, the comfort that femininity offers to the dying man is placed in the context of the greater wound suffered by the family and thus, by extension, the nation. Far from being a precursor of the angel at the hearth, the women in *The Field of Waterloo* are shown to be no less damaged than the citizen-soldiers they support.[90]

I will return to the significance of Turner's vision in a few moments. For now I would like to place these comments in the light of some further reflections on the significance of the wound. I offer, as an illustration, one of the most quotable accounts of Waterloo: the story of Lord Uxbridge's leg. In countless histories, the description of Wellington and Uxbridge's insouciance in the face of battle is presented as something of a set piece, indicative of the stoical disregard and 'pluck' of the English aristocrat. Thus, in David Howarth's account:

> Lord Uxbridge came galloping up and joined the Duke. 'For God's sake, Duke, don't expose yourself so,' he shouted – advice a good many people had wanted to give that day. 'I'll be satisfied when I see those fellows go,' the Duke answered, indicating the squares of the Garde. And a moment later Uxbridge was hit by a ball that had passed over the neck of Wellington's horse. 'By God, sir, I've lost my leg,' he is said to have cried. 'By God, sir, so you have,' the Duke replied.

A footnote in Howarth's text adds that the 'source of these famous exclamations is unknown. It is not likely this is exactly what they said, if they said anything, but whoever invented the story succeeded in epitomizing their characters.' What this story occludes, apart from the confusion over what was actually 'said' in this exchange, is the nature of Uxbridge's wound: the physical transformations that occur when a cannon ball travelling at high velocity impacts on the knee bone. The leg is not haplessly 'lost' but rather shattered, disintegrated or destroyed. Uxbridge himself seems to have taken an active role in erasing this event. As an aide-de-camp notes, on being taken to the rear, 'He told me immediately he must lose his leg & then began conversing about the action & seemed to forget his wound in the exultation for the Victory.' To the surgeons he only said:

> 'Well Gentlemen... if the amputation is to take place the sooner it is done the better'... he never moved or complained, no one even held his hands. He once said quite calmly that he thought the instrument was not very sharp. When it was over his nerves did not appear the least shaken, and the Surgeon observed his pulse was not altered. He said smiling 'I have had a pretty long run, I have been a Beau these 47 years and it would not be fair to cut the young men out any longer'; and then asked us if we did not admire his vanity.[91]

It is easy to admire the convoluted logic of this banter. As a lesson in wounding the story is an exemplary one – not least for a Monsieur Paris, the owner of the house where the amputation was performed. Paris quickly saw the value of 'the relic' and with the permission of the 'owner' he placed it in a coffin and buried it in his garden. The grave containing Lord Uxbridge's leg became something of a tourist attraction and was visited by generations of Waterloo pilgrims, including Scott, Southey and, in later years, Uxbridge himself, who insisted on dining at the table 'he had been carved on' (p. 220). The effect of the anecdote on British cultural life was immediate. Within three weeks, Uxbridge returned to London, where an adoring crowd unharnessed the horses from his carriage on Westminster Bridge and drew it through the streets. For this lesson in wounding the Lord became a Marquess. And so it goes, as Vonnegut might add.

The history of Waterloo contains many such anecdotes. What these stories share is an almost total disregard for the inner experience of wounding; bodies *en masse* are pierced, maimed, dismembered and crushed but descriptions of individual suffering are blandly erased, as if, to adapt Scarry's analysis, the body had been emptied of personal and civil 'content'. To make this clear let us consider two further examples: the first a poem by Wordsworth, the second a painting by Bellangé.

Published in February 1816 and eventually included in the 'Thanksgiving' volume, the sonnet 'Occasioned by the Battle of Waterloo' invites its readers to view the British troops as 'Heroes! – for instant sacrifice prepared'.[92] Having consented to the violation of their bodies, the material content of death and injury disappears: the dead soldier becomes a willing sacrifice. As with 'The Bard whose soul is meek as dawning day', the Kantian implications of the verse are clear: the desire for national substantiation displaces suffering as 'mortal accident', which allows it to be apprehended 'as sublime with a joy which is only made possible by the mediation of pain'.[93] The wound, that is, has taken on a purely structural role in the construction of victory. In Bellangé's *La Garde meurt et ne se rend pas!* (Figure 2), the viewer witnesses a related act of transubstantiation. The painting focuses on a moment of individual heroism: the defiant response of General Cambronne to the allies' invitation to surrender. What marks it out for special attention is the way it incorporates this focus within a larger pattern of corporate action. Whether the eye follows the diagonal from top left to bottom right or from bottom left to top right the painting depends for its force on the sense of repetition. Thus the steadfast posture of the general – sword held aloft, eyes fixed on a point beyond the frame – is echoed in the attitude of the standard bearer and the Chasseurs to his right. Heroism, then, is not confined to the individual. As the bottom half of the painting shows, Cambronne's resistance is dependent on the literal and figurative support of the dead and wounded. In Bellangé's view, it is not only the leaders of men who support the eagle; ordinary soldiers are actively engaged in the struggle for Napoleon as well. Many of them have given up their lives, willingly it would seem, for the cause of the nation. But as the eye homes in on the centre of the work attention is drawn to a certain amount of artistic redundancy: the soldier clinging to the leg of a wounded officer is a reversal of the figure clinging to the eagle's pole. Both figures echo the attitude of the supporting couple below. The head of a corpse between the officer's legs is a sideways projection of the head depicted at the bottom of the canvas. The faces of the Chasseurs to the right-hand side are the same.

A painting that takes support as its theme, that draws on the homoerotic potentials of group subjectivity and ritual wounding (the right leg of the officer and the head of the crouching foot-soldier testify in some way to the idealized passion of war) jars uncomfortably with that other image of Waterloo described earlier: the sense of mass panic, of terror in the face of carnage. These material realities – 'the body in pain, the body maimed, the body dead and hard to dispose of' – are transformed in Bellangé's work. The wound is 'separated from its source and conferred on an ideology... impatient of, or deserted by, benign sources of substantiation' – in this case, the transcendent fiction of the Empire.[94] The same is true of Wordsworth's vision. In each case, the body is emptied of reference so that it may become the property of the 'nation'. We should not be surprised therefore when the stubborn materiality of the wound returns to haunt the texts of ideology. As Scarry notes, war requires 'both the reciprocal infliction of massive injury and the eventual disowning of injury so that its attributes may be transferred elsewhere, as they cannot if they are permitted to cling to the original site of the wound, the human body' (p. 64). But as with everything disowned, elided or repressed, it is only a matter of time before the forgotten object begins to reappear, albeit in disguised form, in the self-representations of everyday reality.

Introduction: the Return of Waterloo 27

Figure 2 J. L. H. Bellangé, *La Garde meurt et ne se rend pas!*, oil on canvas

To understand this notion let us return now to the example of Turner's *Field of Waterloo*. The painting marks, I have suggested, the point where the sublimity of war exceeds the task of recuperation. Its force is derived from the stark manner in which it presents the effects of death and injury on both corporeal and incorporeal bodies. We have traced these phenomena in the painting's complex representation of the military and domestic spheres. But it is at the level of its reception – the way the work was presented to its viewing public – that the effects of incorporeal wounding are most apparent. This brings us back to a central issue in the present study – the complex interlinking of generical, historical and aesthetic questions and their role in the symbolization of war. Briefly, in the summer of 1815, as Lord Castlereagh moved in the House of Commons that a public monument should be erected in London to commemorate the victory, debates raged between the Royal Academy and the British Institution over the propriety of commissioning an 'official' Waterloo painting. Spurred on by Reynolds's objections to including battle painting in the hierarchy of genres, the argument culminated in the offering of a 'Premium' from the dissident British Institution for a picture that would suitably convey the patriotic significance of the battle. It is from within this context that Turner was to join the Waterloo trail in the late summer of 1817.[95]

The picture he produced, however, was markedly different from the sort of work that either the Institution or the Academy would have expected. In short, the painting failed to conform both to the Academician's ideal of a Great Work and to the British Institution's interest in national elevation. At the picture's first showing in the Academy exhibition of May 1818 *The Field of Waterloo* met with a critical response that can best be described as 'ambivalent'. Battle paintings were meant to be straightforward 'documentary' accounts of the facts of engagement, yet here was a picture that focused on the superfluous details of pain and suffering. Critics would praise the picture as 'solemn and striking' while denouncing it as a 'failure' and an 'error'.[96] The cause of this confusion, to adapt an argument of J. W. M. Hichberger's, can be traced to the belief 'that any battle painting which aspired to the status of "art" must necessarily have abandoned any relation to the historical event and, conversely, that any work which was outside the High Art tradition must be read as a neutral description of the event' (p. 14). Turner's work was an assault on both fronts: by straying beyond the state-sponsored view of war it was untrue; by taking a military subject for a theme it could no longer be considered High Art.

It is here, I would suggest, in the gap between history and art, that the force of Turner's work is most apparent. Since the work satisfies neither criterion it is, in the eyes of Regency culture, non-existent. At once too real and too fictional, a painting that concerns itself with the representation of the dead and injured ends up unmasking the symbolic wound on which the assimilation of Waterloo is based. From a structural point of view, the painting Turner produced keeps faith with the body in pain not by virtue of its unmediated grasp of this noumenal unknown but through its critical intervention in the signifying process. In this respect, the painting has become Sublime in the most radical sense of the word. Instead of functioning, like Fitzgerald's 'The Battle of Waterloo' as an indicator of a higher dimension of transcendent Law' the unrecognizable *Field of Waterloo* marks the point at which the system of national substantiation – identification through conflict with an antagonistic Other – encounters its central impossibility. And it is, I would conclude, in this stronger sense of the word that the sublimity of the battle of Waterloo is best understood: Waterloo presents itself to its observers as an 'unparalleled', 'decisive' and 'transcendent' event, but this failure to capture the grand significance of the battle – whether in verse, prose or painting – is nothing but the failure point of the process of symbolization. It leads not to the beyond of national identity but rather to the radical inadequacy of all attempts to realize this Idea.

A view from the centre

Much of what I have to say about the importance of Waterloo turns, of course, on the idea that the battle retains its status as an indeterminate object of desire. That this status has been neglected in recent years has, I believe, serious implications for our understanding of Romanticism. As readers of Wordsworth and Coleridge, Blake and Paine, we are used to hearing of the tremendous impact of the French Revolution, yet comparatively little attention has been given to its no less dramatic close. Of the few studies to have focused on Waterloo, the majority concede that the battle was appellant to the imagination only as a signal for apostates to display their loyalist credentials; according to this view, the footnotes of English literary history are littered with their bellicist rodomontades among which there is very little to praise and even less to consider.[97] As the Romantic reviewer Josiah Conder noted, the poetry of Waterloo is, in general, 'wholly artificial, armed by no glow of passion and prompted by no definite impulse'. Characterized by 'Loyalty devoid of affection, patriotism destitute of virtue, triumph without joy, and hope without confidence; what can be expected from the inspiration of such feelings, but cold adulation, unmeaning boasts, empty predictions, and commonplace sentiment?'[98] This attitude is repeated in the stance taken by contemporary critics of Romanticism. By virtue of its wish to situate itself at the centre of an ideologically and politically dominant culture (so the argument runs), the Waterloo poem fails to supply material for thoroughgoing critical analysis. There is, in other words, 'no linguistic loss, no crack for the critic to fill, no struggle to detect and explicate by the disturbance it causes'; the calm activity of such writing 'preempts the work of the critic. We have nothing to say because the poetry is so busy saying things itself'.[99] And what this poetry says bears little relation to what we, as critics, wish to hear.

It is this positive embrace of orthodoxy, visibility and centrality that accounts, I believe, for our current indifference to these works. Since our tendency as critics is to pass over writing that fails to communicate a sense of disturbance, we tend to regard Scott's *The Field of Waterloo*, Southey's *The Poet's Pilgrimage to Waterloo* and Wordsworth's 'Thanksgiving Ode', not to mention the effusions of countless minor poets, essayists, painters and travel writers, as in some way insufficiently Romantic. What this type of judgement tells us about our habit of conflating aesthetic and historical categories is itself worthy of debate. But of greater interest, I think, is the idea that criticism shies away from such writing out of a wish to avoid an encounter with a disturbance that lies beyond accepted critical parameters. In short, I am suggesting that it is criticism, not culture, which fails to evoke the requisite sense of loss – the gap, crack or fissure – from which interpretative interest is derived. To return to Conder's evaluation, what could be more lacking, and thus more alluring, than a poetry of emotional indeterminacy, a poetry devoid of affection, destitute of virtue, unmeaning in its boasts and expectant without confidence. The clichés and commonplaces in other words exist to disguise a certain failure-point in the idea of Waterloo, one that invites us to respond, were we to listen, with the voluble stuff of critical completion.[100]

Before proceeding let us consider an example of the sort of practice I have in mind. Exceptionally among poetic responses to the battle, Byron's stanzas on Waterloo from *Childe Harold's Pilgrimage* have been justly celebrated, both for their controlled literary intelligence and for their political indignation. By contrast, following Ruskin's judgement that on the whole the reader will gain more pleasure from Byron's humanity than from Wordsworth's triumphalism, the Laker's response to the battle has been largely ignored.[101] On the face of things, the reasons for this avoidance are obvious. In Wordsworth's 'Thanksgiving Ode', for instance, we are presented with a particularly damning portrait of political and creative disengagement, one that rests uneasily with our privileging of the High Romantic Imagination:

> Imagination, ne'er before content,
> But aye ascending, restless in her pride,
> From all that man's performance could present,
> Stoops to that closing deed magnificent,
> And with the embrace is satisfied.
> (lines 163–7)

If we read these lines, as Simon Bainbridge suggests, as a retroactive commentary on Wordsworth's militant engagement with 'the threat and challenge of Napoleon' then it becomes evident that the poet's satisfaction with Waterloo marks a final withdrawal from the politics and poetics of struggle.[102] Where, in the 'Imagination' passage of Book VI of *The Prelude*, Wordsworth had sustained an 'ennobling interchange' with the Satanic other, in the 'Thanksgiving Ode' the reasons for this conflict have been diffused. The forces of transcendence have entered the plain of history, confirming the poet's faith in the power of the Imagination to see beyond 'the things that pass away' to a 'shew / Of objects that endure' (XII, 35–6).[103] With Napoleon gone, along with the instrumentalism and materialism that he represents, there is simply no need for Wordsworth to continue in his fight. The poet 'stoops' now to place himself at the centre, acquiescing in the right of politicians to appropriate the poetic language of sublimity and transcendence.

While Bainbridge is surely right to emphasize Wordsworth's embrace of orthodoxy, visibility and centrality, the notion that his Waterloo writing marks a withdrawal from the politics and poetics of struggle seems to me to be questionable. For one thing it must assume that the centre – whatever this may be – is necessarily untrammelled by the sort of shocks and disturbances that proliferate on the margins of culture. As I hope to have shown, however, the view from the centre is no less riven than the view from the margins; indeed, by now it ought be clear that the centre is precisely the place where the ideological text encounters its impossibility – meets its Waterloo, in fact. Somewhat controversially, therefore, I would urge the reader of Wordsworth to approach the 'Immortality' ode of 1804 through the lens of the 'Thanksgiving Ode' of 1816, seeing in the latter work a mode of pleasure – specifically the love of 'Carnage' – that is the wayward counterpart, perhaps even the unacknowledged foundation, of the earlier poem's pacific humanism. That access to this pleasure is blocked by a critical inability to see beyond the binaries of Radical and Tory, marginal and central, speaks volumes about the limitations of our own orthodoxy, currently operating under the sign of enlightened materialist or ideological critique but woefully in thrall to romantic fantasy.

To clarify this last point let us pause for a moment to consider the theoretical nature of this orthodoxy. The assumption underlying a number of recent critical readings of the Romantic poets is that the disclosure of indubitable social facts constitutes a point of contact with the 'real' and, by extension, a means of unsettling the effects of aesthetic ideology. But the belief that it is possible to encounter such facts, stripped of the freight that Romanticism deposits on them, is, I would suggest, an illusory one. Interestingly enough, critics are often well aware of the sort of problems that arise whenever ideology is approached as a purely epistemological matter. A cursory view of much that passes for new historicist and cultural materialist readings of Romanticism reveals, however, that there is a discrepancy between what the critics know and what they are doing in practice. As John Rieder has argued, the difference between the clear-sighted history of the ideology critics and the benighted humanity of a poet like Wordsworth is very often moot. Crudely put, whether the text in question is 'Simon Lee' or *Wordsworth's Great Period Poems*, the effective world of social difference behaves like a Platonic form, a transcendental principle going through a series of embodiments. Thus, while the materialist critic knows that history is a property of the particular – that is, of really existing social relations – the problem is that in her practice she acts as though the particular things (the beggars, the war widows, the discharged soldiers and so on and so forth) were just so many embodiments of this universal value.[104] History, in other words, as Alan Liu postulates, has taken the place formerly occupied by a host of displaced transcendental signifieds.[105] But here we may query whether it is indeed possible to conduct a critical practice that makes no reference to transcendentals, quasi or otherwise. The belief that one can sidestep the reification of history by appealing to 'the new empirical evidence', as Jon Klancher advocates, is admirable in intent yet ultimately mistaken, for what is overlooked in the realist thesis is the way the relationship between poem and reality continues to be facilitated and conditioned by ideological fantasies.[106]

Lacan's point about the opposition between dream and reality is apposite here: far from being an evasion of reality it is fantasy itself that constitutes our effective social relations and that 'enables us to mask the Real of our desire'. As Žižek elaborates:

> It is exactly the same with ideology. Ideology is not a dreamlike illusion that we build to escape insupportable [intolerable] reality, in its basic dimension it is a fantasy-construction which serves as a support for our 'reality' itself: an 'illusion' which structures our effective, real social relations and thereby masks some insupportable, real, impossible kernel (conceptualized by Ernesto Laclau and Chantal Mouffe as 'antagonism': a traumatic social division which cannot be symbolized). The function of ideology is not to offer us a point of escape from our reality but to offer us the social reality itself as an escape from some traumatic, real kernel...[107]

If it is the case that the 'only way to break the power of our ideological dream is to confront the Real of our desire which announces itself in this dream' (p. 45) then this should prompt us to reconsider a further aspect of our practice: the habit of regarding texts as masks or veils and not as the site where subjects encounter the reality of their desires. This positive definition of the relationship between texts and reality takes us closer, I feel, to what is really at stake in the discussion of Romantic maladies and cultural crises. When, as Lacan asserts, the dreamer awakes into 'so-called reality it is to be able to continue to sleep, to maintain his blindness, to elude awakening' into the perception of the 'insupportable, real, impossible kernel' (ibid.). And it is the same with texts: the illusions, which support effective social relations in 1815, conceal a fundamental 'antagonism', a traumatic psychosocial division that cannot be symbolized.

Before we go on to examine the representation of Waterloo let us consider one final example of how the battle provoked in its spectators equal measures of joyful ebullience and anxious despair. The myth of Waterloo states that the

Allied victory was greeted with a universal chorus of approval. Yet, as I will argue throughout this book, for every celebratory word or deed – whether this takes the form of the official victory celebrations with their stage-managed processions and *son et lumière* displays or of the spontaneous acts of crowds and individuals – there exists a secret history of apathy, enervation and indifference. The reasons for this disparity are complex and almost impossible to evaluate. Still, there are enough examples of this second-order level of response to justify the assertion that Waterloo was not so much the closing act of a grand drama as the disappointing terminus of a history that, perhaps for the first time, unsettled the identity of form and content. Like the famously bungled suicide scene in *Anthony and Cleopatra*, Napoleon's failure to be himself, to fulfil, that is, the tragic destiny that the Napoleonic script had carved out for him, was perceived by many to be indicative of an age characterized not by heroism but by absurdity.

Appropriately, for a writer who seems to show so little interest in party politics, it is Charles Lamb who provides what is possibly the most representative comment on the times:

> Your boute-feu (bonfire) must be excellent of its kind. Poet Settle presided at the last great thing of the kind in London, when the pope was burnt in form. Do you provide any verses on this occasion?... I cannot muster up decorum for these occasions... Anything awful makes me laugh. I misbehaved once at a funeral. Yet I can read about these ceremonies with pious and proper feelings. The realities of life only seem the mockeries.[108]

The passage is taken from a letter to Robert Southey who, along with Wordsworth, on 21 August would lead the unofficial celebrations on top of Mount Skiddaw. The story of that night is well known. As the victory bonfire blazed, a strange figure grandly dressed like a 'Spanish Don' accidentally knocked over the kettle of boiling water for the punch and 'sought to slink off undiscovered', but revellers identified the villain as Wordsworth, much to the delight of Southey who led his party in a dance round him singing, "'Twas *you* that kicked the kettle down! 'twas you, Sir, you!'[109] Lamb would have enjoyed this story. Not least because it has the flavour of an Elian moment: the dour man of the mountains, the sage of the Lakes, patched and deflated, raised up, if anything, into a figure of fun.

Lamb, though, is a special case. Behind all the kidding there is, as always, a subtle intelligence at work. At first sight the opening phrase becomes a gentle slight at Southey's virulent anti-Gallicism: 'Your boute-feu (bonfire) must be excellent of its kind.' Next, it is a mock version of a profound reality: the French Revolution consuming itself, expiring in flames and ashes. Still further, it becomes a pious comment on British triumphalism, a reminder of just what might be going up into the sky on that late summer night. Lamb recalls the burning of an effigy of the 'pope', attended by 'Poet Settle' – the defeat of papacy and absolutism celebrated by a former poet laureate just as, he predicts, the current laureate will celebrate *this* defeat. But lest we make too much of Lamb's anarchic humour, the conclusion of the passage suggests a more conservative context. Lamb meets the sublime, the tragic and the portentous with laughter and derision, but only in order to restore history to the sober realm of reading and writing. For just as Lamb decries the performance of Shakespeare, arguing that the physical representation of tragedy diminishes its emotional force, so here he undermines the performative aspects of his times. Pious and proper feelings belong to the order of aesthetic detachment, to privacy and self-communion. By contrast, the energies exhibited in a public display, whether at a funeral or a victory celebration, demand psychic unanimity. The former nourishes the ego; the latter, unless punctuated by laughter, threatens to dissolve it. As this book proceeds we will drift further away from the clamour of hyperbole and more towards the quietly troubled zone of interiority. Perhaps Lamb knew already what Southey, Wordsworth and Byron would encounter in their Waterloo poems: that peace is rarely settled and authority never assured.

This book is concerned, then, with the place of Waterloo in the stories that individuals and nations tell about themselves. It takes as a founding premise the idea that success in the war against France had traumatic consequences for the victors as well as for the defeated and that far from acting as – in Wordsworth's phrase – a 'closing deed magnificent' the battle opened up more than it could close. In this sense, I will be suggesting that Waterloo plays a key role in contemporary consciousness, whether this is discerned in the failures of individual poets to insert themselves into an imaginary tradition, or in the inability of the state to domesticate the unsettling termination of 'foreign' hostilities. As will become evident from my discussion, the silence surrounding the battle of Waterloo not only obfuscates a decisive moment in the history of Regency culture; it also marks an evaluative distinction that has serious repercussions for our grasp of the 'historicity' of Regency literature. The attempt to recall the antagonism of representations in this period will, if successful, return Waterloo to its original status as a sublime object: an 'impossible Thing' prior to its domestication as a symbol of national unanimity, of the foreclosure of the international movement for liberty and independence, and crucially of the limits of Romanticism.

1
Walter Scott: the Discipline of History

The Vansittart of verse

In the summer of 1815 a young advocate from Edinburgh named James Simpson sat among the ruins of La Belle Alliance, scene of the famous meeting between Blücher and Wellington at the close of the battle of Waterloo. He brought with him two documents: the Duke of Wellington's 'renowned but controversial' 'Waterloo Despatch', and a text of the speech that Walter Scott had lately made in Edinburgh at the launching of the 'Waterloo Subscription'. First printed in the *London Gazette Extraordinary* the Duke's account of the battle was regarded by many pro-war enthusiasts as an insufficiently celebratory account of the battle. Written, as Elizabeth Longford writes, with the Duke's 'accustomed brevity and restraint', it simply described the four days from 15 to 18 June and when published on the 22nd covered barely four columns in *The Times*. The 'description of troops was reduced to a minimum' and 'a reference to bravery found its way into the text only once (over the guards at Hougoumont)'.[1] Reactions to the despatch ranged from bafflement to outright hostility. Wellington had not only neglected to honour the heroes of Waterloo, he had also failed to address the transcendent significance of the event.

I am tempted to suggest that Simpson was also disappointed with the Duke's account. But the truth is rather more complex. For Simpson, who would go on to write his own account of the battle, the soldier's brevity and the poet's loquacity presented a mutually supportive vision of the British victory. The Duke with his 'steady principle' and 'self-contained' character had described the battle in 'prose' where 'the plainest language of truth is to be preferred to the finest flowers of rhetoric'.[2] Scott, with the bard's eye for transcendent truth, had provided this factual account with its necessary literary supplement. As Simpson went on to write: 'The mind has scarcely buoyancy sufficient to allot to Great Britain a pinnacle of glory high enough for this crisis. The account is too complete as well as too vast, to allow at one grasp a view of all its elements.'[3] It would take a poet to comprehend the veiled sublimity of the 'Waterloo Despatch'. Accordingly, when Simpson surveyed the graffiti on the whitewashed walls of the farmhouse at La Belle Alliance he found himself overcome with the spirit of the moment and proceeded to quote 'on the very spot of Napoleon's final defeat and ruin, and on his *first* trial of strength with "the Wellington"'' the concluding lines from Scott's *The Vision of Don Roderick*. In these lines, the poet had predicted that the victor of the Peninsular campaign would triumph over Napoleon in a single, decisive combat.[4] Possessed by 'the spirit of the moment' Simpson had paid unwitting testimony to the myth of Waterloo as the 'closing act' of 'a deed magnificent'. The final event of the long, drawn-out struggle against Napoleon Bonaparte had proved that providence and poetry were allied.

Scott, who would meet Simpson a few days later in Paris, had an equally keen sense of the relationship between war and representation. Like Simpson, the poet was keen to visit the field where legitimate government had triumphed over the forces of anarchy and despotism. Here at last were 'real' wounds and 'real' bodies that would validate the nation's claims to unanimity and coherence. And here also was the site where Scott could relive his own fantasies of command – by donning the uniform of the dragoon officer that he had worn almost two decades earlier. For Scott, therefore, who had always considered himself 'quite a military man', Waterloo was a valedictory occasion: the poet was saying goodbye to the imaginary conflict that had sustained him since the beginning of his career. But the battle was also seen as a means of closing the 'vacancy' that the abdication of 1814 had opened up. In Scott's view, the sudden, massive absence consequent upon the Emperor's failure to fulfil his tragic destiny was more than compensated for by the recent 'illustrious' feats of Lord Wellington. Not only had Wellington 'taught' his countrymen to 're-establish the renown of Agincourt and Blenheim', but certain of those countrymen, Scott among them, had responded in kind by representing him as a kind of classical warrior: a Scipio to Napoleon's Hannibal.[5]

Shortly after his arrival on the continent, Scott would get his desired reward: a meeting with Wellington, the significance of which will be discussed in due course. This chapter's main concern, however, is with the poet's efforts to relate the sublimity of Waterloo to its romantic precedents. As we shall discover, Scott's celebratory attitude to the defeat of Napoleon disguised a more vexed concern with the survival of verse romance, the very genre that Scott had made his own. In a larger sense, therefore, this chapter touches on the extent to which the conclusion of the war precipitated a transformation in Scott's real 'business': the production and dissemination of literary capital. The concluding lines of a poetical squib printed in the *Morning Chronicle* on 4 December 1815 and therefore well into the period of post-bellum economic depression will serve as a gloss on this theme:

> Then comes Waterloo
> With a *haloa ballou*!
> Of legions disabled and slain;
> But you are not content
> With the blood they have spent,
> Will *mangle* them over again.
> Ah! teaze our good folks
> No more with this *hoax*,
> Which JOHN BULL in a *doze* could not see
> But now broad awake
> This *tax* will not take,
> He's determined to live, Sir; SCOTT *free*.[6]

The object of this satire is *The Field of Waterloo*, the 'minor' poem with which Scott hoped to crown the achievements of a united kingdom while, as I will go on to suggest, bidding farewell to an exhausted form of symbolic command, namely the effort to condition recent history to the pleasurable charms of verse romance. With an ironic echo of Tom Paine's critique of warmongering, the writer reminds his audience of the socio-economic costs of war: 'legions' are 'disabled and slain' in order to support the government's thirst for revenue. In this case, however, the cessation of war has brought with it neither peace nor prosperity. As another 'extempore' from the *Chronicle* pithily comments: 'What is it, after all, the people get? / Why! Widows, Taxes, Wooden legs and Debt!'[7] This chimed with the feelings of a cross-section of British society: from landowners fearing the effects of foreign competition in corn, to manufacturers unable to adjust to the conditions of a peacetime economy. Wellington may have temporarily relieved the political tension, but after Waterloo monetary matters reasserted themselves. The subsequent increases in unemployment, poverty and the poor rate were levelling the nation once again; peace now appeared as the continuation of war by other means.

Scott, whose poetry celebrated and partook of the rhythms and sensations of war, was most easily associated with this 'context'. Indeed for some there is no distinction between the matter of his verse and the fraudulent economy that produced it; for what, as the *Chronicle*'s poetaster wittily conveys, is Scott's burdensome output if not the repeated 'mangling' of public 'taste' (from the Latin *taxare*)? The implication is clear: *The Field of Waterloo*, the profits from which were directed to the fund for the relief of the returning soldiers, was not a poem but an unnecessary form of postwar taxation. In producing this work, the Vansittart of verse had allowed the resistant matter of the poem to be absorbed, like the body of the soldier, by an economy of ruin.

For Scott, as is well known, the fortunes of war and writing were closely aligned. In 1815 the celebrated poet published no less than ten volumes of poetry and prose, a figure that may be compared with Byron's nine and Shakespeare's sixteen. In broad terms, Scott was the most prolific contemporary author of the Waterloo period; his works consistently outsold the less well-known and critically vilified Lakers. Yet this was the year that also marked the decline of Scott's poetic fortunes. When measured against the successes of *The Lay of the Last Minstrel* (1802), *Marmion* (1808) and *The Lady of the Lake* (1810), the sales of *The Lord of the Isles* (published in January 1815) and *Harold the Dauntless* (composed in the autumn of 1815; published in 1816) were comparatively poor. It seemed as if the public was adjusting its taste for Scott's poetry just at the moment when their country's fortunes appeared to be reaching an equivalent moment of crisis. But contrary to the satirist's perceptions, John Bull, for all his complaints against the continuation of the Income Tax, showed little inclination to live entirely 'Scott free'. If anything, the taste for Scott was intensified by the poet's decision to wind down his verse-making enterprise and to capitalize on the spectacular success of *Waverley* (1814). Henceforth, what the public demanded, and what the public would get, would be the serial production of historical novels. If, in 1815, *Harold the Dauntless* marked a farewell to bardship, then the subsequent composition of *Guy Mannering* (1815) and *The Antiquary* (1816) signalled its author's commitment to a literary career that would revolutionize the publishing industry.

Scott's transformation from poet to novelist is, I would suggest, structurally analogous to the changes then taking place in the English economy. The movement from the wartime rhythms of boom and bust, from conflict's ability to stimulate capital growth to postwar attempts to regulate the system in accordance with peaceable and more sustainable means, finds its echo in the refashioning of Scott as a maker of taxable 'things': historical novels that issued in and from a new set of productive relations and that necessitated an entirely new conception of the author. No longer visionary in character, the romantic writer was to adapt himself to the boundary-making forms of contemporary commercial society: to invoke an argument of Jerome Christensen's, the combative nature of the visionary poet was to give way, once and for all, to the self-ironizing, self-conscious yet essentially productive activity of the romantic novelist.[8] Yet Scott's retreat from the visionary imagination was no simple matter; as I argue throughout this chapter, the movement away from poetic identification with the forms of waste and ruin, to novelistic detachment, was born out of a sense of struggle. The site for this struggle was of course the field of Waterloo, for it is here that the writer first experienced the limits of poetic romance. As one of the last poems to be issued under the name of Scott, *The Field of Waterloo* dramatizes the passage from romantic lyricism to historical actuality, and from bardic authority to novelistic anonymity. At times, the verse provides an oblique commentary on its own passage to redundancy, as if the text were lamenting its inability to cast the veil of romance over contemporary events.

Mindful of the fact that *The Field of Waterloo* is preceded by *Waverley* and succeeded, as it were, by *The Antiquary*, in a manner that bears, as I shall explain, more than a superficial resemblance to the relations between Waterloo, the abdication of 1814 and the final surrender of 1815, I want to go on to address the role that violence plays in forging novelistic concepts of individual and national identity. Given that, in the first instance, the significance of the novel is conditioned by a sense of anti-climax – of a peace that fails to satisfy the desire for a decisive clash or arms – and, in the second, by the aftershock of 'a near run thing' – a force of arms that discloses the impossibility of fulfilling such a desire – we must look closely at how these novels set about depicting the effects of war on the minds of its participants. Why, for instance, does Edward Waverley emerge from the battle of Preston a hero despite having failed to strike a single blow against the enemy? Is there a sense in which the treatment of the Jacobites is linked with the dangers and delights of struggling against Napoleon? In the case of *The Antiquary* what complexities of feeling does the memory of 1745 harbour in the mind of a man for whom conflict is a matter both of personal fulfilment and of national calamity? And what is the significance of the threatened French invasion? We shall examine these and related questions in detail later on in this chapter, but for now I want to return Scott's encounter with the field of Waterloo and to the bodies – symbolic as well as material – from which the last gasp of the violent imaginary is forged.

The wounded horseman

Like many other visitors to the field, Scott was inspired by the accounts of those who had witnessed the bloody aftermath of the campaign. One notable correspondent was the distinguished anatomist Sir Charles Bell, head of the recently founded medical school at Middlesex hospital.[9] At Waterloo, Bell reportedly worked for three successive days and nights, with only a few brief periods of rest, until his 'clothes were stiff with blood and his arms powerless with the exertion of using a knife'.[10] While it would be pernicious to doubt the surgeon's courage and compassion it is worth noting that as an anatomist Bell stood to gain a great deal from his labours: in the aftermath of battle subjects were plentiful; the severity of the wounds meant that in many cases difficult or obscure areas of the body were already on display; on foreign soil the practice of dissection escaped legal censure. For Bell, therefore, Waterloo was also a locus of scientific curiosity: a zone of suffering, to be sure, but also a zone of knowledge and observation.

Two weeks after the battle, when the immediate crisis was over, Bell set to work on a series of sketches that were to form the basis of his pioneering study of the human nervous system. On one level the studies are a paradigm of anatomical precision; in each case the unstinting portrayal of the effects of violence on the human body allows the mind to comprehend the 'reality' of wounding as a structural element within a manageable analytical system. The same structure of representation that worked in other fields to contain the 'excess' of Waterloo is detectable in Bell's work on two levels: the scientific and the aesthetic. On the scientific level, the drawings translate the recalcitrant matter of bodies into attributes of a higher reality, in this case the universal cause of medical inquiry. But it is at the level of the aesthetic that Bell's work begins to revolt against its avowed principles. As a talented draughtsman and as the writer of a reputable treatise on artistic treatments of human expression, the surgeon was well versed in the Burkean discourse of painful pleasures. Thus, even as Bell accurately presents the nerves beneath the flesh, at the same time he cannot avoid gesturing towards the sense of sublimity that this operation affects in him (Figures 3, 4 and 5). Reason may well rush in to rescue the scientist from his imaginative fixation but the drawings continue to elicit their own yield of elegiac sensations.[11] As the lines on the page remind us of their subject's origin in the primary reality of death and wounding, Bell simultaneously tempers that experience by containing it within a Romantic aesthetic of fragmentation and decay. For what, after all, do these images remind us of if not the blasted shells of noble buildings? Considered as an architectural ruin, the anatomist's depiction of the wound is perhaps more closely related to the picturesque vision of

Figure 3 Sir Charles Bell, soldier with missing arm, lying on his side, grasping a rope, inscribed 'XIII, Waterloo...', watercolour, '11 Aug.' 1815

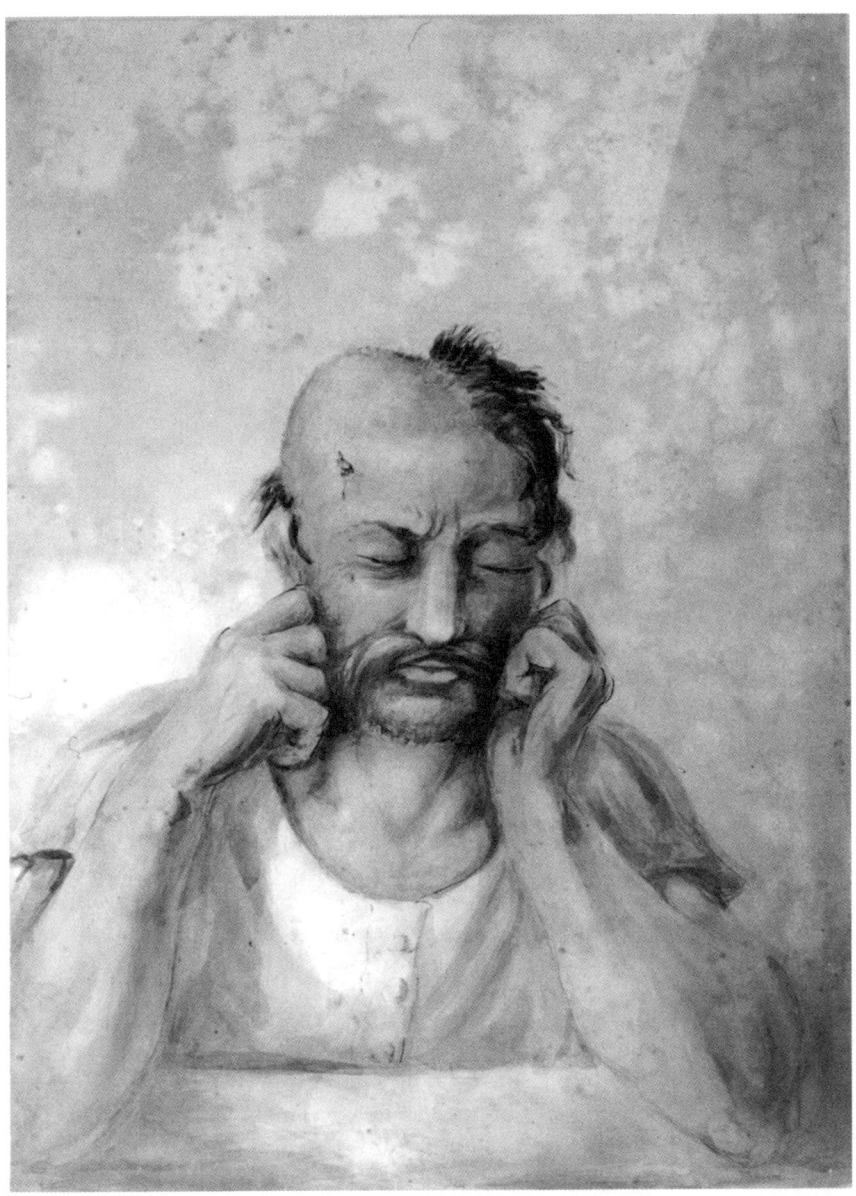

Figure 4 Sir Charles Bell, soldier suffering from a head wound, part of his scalp shaved, watercolour, 1815

42 Waterloo and the Romantic Imagination

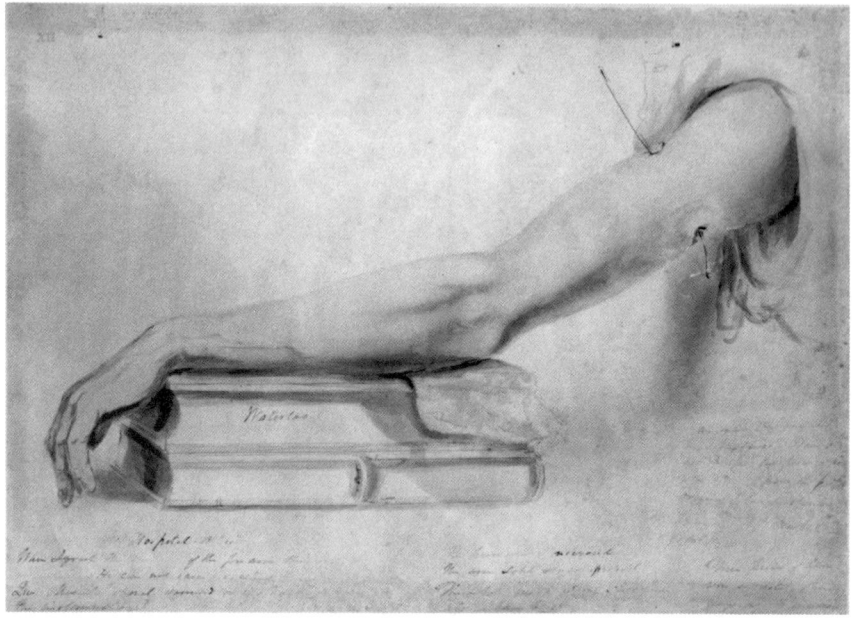

Figure 5 Sir Charles Bell, arm wound, 1815, inscribed 'XII Waterloo', watercolour, 1815

Hougoumont (see Chapter 3) than a totalizing science of pure forms might allow.

In practice, therefore, Bell's depiction of the body *in extremis* serves to reinforce one of the dominant visual strategies of the Napoleonic wars: the fascination with loss and ruination as a Romantic effect. An example from the anatomist's unofficial repertoire – a letter to his brother George Joseph Bell – serves to underline what is at stake in the transition from surgical detachment to aesthetic enchantment:

> I have just returned from seeing the French wounded received in their hospital; and could you see them laid out naked, or almost so – 100 in a row of beds on the ground – though wounded, exhausted, beaten, you would still conclude with me that these were men capable of marching unopposed from the west of Europe to the east of Asia. Strong, thickset, hardy veterans, brave spirits and unsubdued, as they cast their wild glance upon you, their black eyes and brown cheeks finely contrasted with the fresh sheets, – you would much admire their capacity of adaptation. These fellows are brought from the field after lying many days on the ground; many dying – many in agony – many miserably wracked with pain and spasms; and the next mimics his fellow, and gives it a tune,

– *Aha, vous chantez bien!* How they are wounded you will see in my notes.[12]

In common with the anatomical sketches, Bell utilizes knowledge of physiognomy to draw out the internal characteristics of the wounded French. On first sight the Frenchmen are hardy, wild and unsubdued; black eyes and brown cheeks are set against a clean white background. The overall effect is thoroughly picturesque. Yet within a short space Bell abandons this aesthetic view for a more sober, more chastened perspective: 'But I must not have you to lose the present impression on me of the formidable nature of these fellows as exemplars of the breed in France. It is a forced praise' (p. 56). The letter goes on to connect the surface appearance of the soldiers with its hidden mental cause: 'for from what I have seen, and all I have heard of their fierceness, cruelty and bloodthirstiness, I cannot convey to you my detestation of this race of trained banditti' (pp. 56–7). Whereas 'trained' refers to the clinical precision of the Napoleonic system, 'banditti' is a word culled from readings of Byron, Southey and Scott. The overall effect is certainly curious. As Bell closes his sentence, the combination of glacial abstraction and passionate exoticism renders the soldiers repellent at the level of national taste and attractive at the level of fantasy and romance.

To counter the instability of this portrait, the subsequent paragraph centres on the contrasting example of a wounded British officer:

> This superb city is now ornamented with the finest groups of armed men that the most romantic fancy could dream of. I was struck with the words of a friend – E. 'I saw,' said he, 'that man returning from the field on the 16th.' (This was a Brunswicker, of the Black or Death Hussars.) 'He was wounded, and had had his arm amputated in the field. He was among the first that came in. He rode straight and stark upon his horse – the bloody clouts about his stump – pale as death, but upright, with a stern, fixed expression of feature, as if loath to lose his revenge.' These troops are very remarkable in their appearance; their dark and ominous dress sets off to advantage their strong, manly, northern features and white mustachios; and there is something more than commonly impressive about the whole effect.
>
> (*Memoirs of the Life of Sir Walter Scott*, p. 57)

Based around a series of implicit contrasts – the lone horseman's upright posture and fixed expression triumphing over the supine collectivity of the French – the portrait appears to resolve the tension developed in the preceding description. A form of patriotic rectitude, linked with the indefatigable power of the phallus, is shown to triumph over the suffering of history and the lassitude of 'Southern' Romanticism.[13]

Perhaps it was this image that most appealed to Walter Scott: Lockhart reports the poet exclaiming, 'it set me on fire' (p. 55). Doubtless George Bell had an inkling of what would appeal to his literary friend. Scott was probably most struck by the juxtaposition of the northern knight and the southern banditti – a contrast that drew upon and fed back into his own creative work. Like Bell, the poet would have appreciated this image of British fortitude and 'pluck'. To witness the wounded horseman crossing the threshold from history to myth and from louche romance to disciplined sublimity was a signal to Scott that the world had at last been made in his image. The translation of the wound into a symbol of romantic import held, moreover, a deeply personal significance. As early as 1797 Scott was determined to represent himself as an active participant in the war against France. While his lameness made it impossible to serve on foot, on horseback he could, as Edgar Johnson put it, 'cut and slash with any man'.[14] Accordingly, when the invasion scare was at its height, the young militarist set about forming a body of light cavalry, known, by the King's consent, as the Royal Edinburgh Volunteer Light Dragoons. The judgement of Scott's most recent biographer is appropriate here: 'the dragoon officer's gorgeous red and blue uniform and exhausting cavalry exercises were an emotional fulfilment – they erased his disability, the "club foot" as stranger's called it.'[15] Once again, one might add, a recognizably Romantic impulse – the love of display and the theatrical exercise of power – is a means of occluding the visible presence of wounding.

That Scott should have been among the first civilians who hurried over to witness the stage of this 'grand finale' could have surprised none who knew the lively interest he had always taken in the military efforts of his countrymen.[16] A keen observer of the war in the Iberian Peninsula, the poet had, for some time, entertained serious thoughts of going to Portugal 'to see', as he put it, a modern battle. 'But all this', he added, 'is rather a vision than a scheme.'[17] Now, with the threat of Bonapartism at bay and with Europe open, once more, to commercial travel, Scott was at liberty to indulge his interest. Spurred on by the enthusiasm of John Murray, whose firm had commissioned the author to write an epistolary account of his travels, Scott left England on 28 July 1815, accompanied by three companions, all fellow Scots. The party arrived at Hellevoetsluis in Holland on 5 August after an uncomfortable passage in a cutter – one of the many that had been specially commissioned to ferry the army of visitors to Waterloo. As David Sultana notes, the route to the battlefield took the form of an excursion into Romantic lands, a rite of passage where monuments and ruins loomed out as picturesque zones in an otherwise flat and unprepossessing setting.[18] If Flanders was the 'classic land' in European history its significance was not readily available, at least not to the casual eye of the tourist. To the eye of the antiquarian, however, the landscape was charged with mythic resonance. Passing, for example through the tranquil shade of the forest of Soignies, en route to the field of Waterloo, Scott was reminded of the legendary forest of Ardennes and of the immortal landscapes of Boiardo's *Orlando* and Shakespeare's *As You Like It*. Other sites evoked memories of scenes depicted in his own poetry and prose; the castle of Bergen-op-Zoom, the site of a recent siege, presented Scott with a scene that bore an uncanny resemblance to a passage from *Waverley*: the description of the crepuscular eve of the battle of Prestonpans.[19] Waterloo itself, however, turned out to be something of a disappointment. The village was undistinguished, the surrounding area unremarkable. But Scott was determined to encounter the evidence of sublime conflict and, again, this would entail reading beyond the surface of the field to ascertain its deeper, symbolic significance.

How then did the field present itself to Scott? In common with many other visitors, the poet was deprived of the sight of 'the more ghastly tokens of carnage'. By August the bodies of men and horses were either burned or buried, all that remained on the field were the 'cartridges, old hats, and shoes, and various relics of the fray which the peasants had not thought worth removing'.[20] However, in *Paul's Letters to His Kinsfolk*, Scott gives the impression that he saw the field at a much earlier date. 'Had not the ghastly evidences remained on the field,' the narrator surmises, 'many of the blows dealt upon the occasion [of the cavalry engagements] would have seemed borrowed from the annals of knight-errantry, for several of the corpses exhibited heads cloven to the chine, severed from the shoulders.'[21] The incongruous relationship between fact and fiction, history and myth, seems to reach a point of crisis in this image, as if the writer were less concerned with the poet's desire for romance than with the novelist's appetite for the corporeal and the contingent.[22] Yet elsewhere, Scott found plenty to eulogize. All the houses surrounding the field, he noted, displayed 'a most striking picture of desolation'. And here again the poet's fund of quotations – in this case a sensationalist passage from a play by his friend Joanna Baillie – would be called upon to lend shape and significance to the experiences of 'the inhabitants of these peaceful cottages' as 'the loud battle' had raged around them, and as their 'warm and cheerful hearths', where their children had played, had become 'the bloody lair of dying men'.

For the most part, therefore, Scott's knowledge of the more grisly aspects of 'common destruction' was the product of a piecemeal attention to the numerous verbal and written accounts that awaited the 'pilgrim' on his arrival in Waterloo. Scott's immediate source was Jean de Coster, the Flemish guide who had accompanied Napoleon throughout the campaign. Those 'ghastly evidences' therefore were no more real to Scott than the memorandum-book he picked off the field and the buttons, bullets and cuirasses he purchased from the Waterloo 'mart'.[23] As a collector of Highland militaria and old ballads, Scott was on familiar territory. The poet was most struck, however, by the vast quantity of textual material that covered the area. 'The field', he writes, 'was covered with fragments of [soldier's account books]'; Lockhart notes that 'the most precious memorial was presented to him by [Major Gordon's] wife – a French soldier's book, well stained with blood, and containing some songs popular in the French army'. These were the conditions with which Scott felt most comfortable. Picking through the 'fragments' of ballad sheets, muster-rolls, love letters, prayer books, 'illegible songs, scattered sheets of military music, epistles... in praise of l'Empereur' and sullied French romances,[24] the poet becomes a *bricoleur* 'borrowing... concepts from the text of a heritage which is more or less... ruined'.[25] The image of the fractured book introduces, once again, the truth behind the decorous facade of victory sublime. For whether Scott is dealing with the wreckage of history or of romance the result is the same: the ceaseless accumulation of disconnected and discontinuous fragments, without any strict idea of a goal and without any organizing principle. Like the postwar society from which his writing emerges, meaning in Scott is fractured, subject to the whims of a random selection process. In this respect, the bloodied and torn letters of French culture impact not only on the dissolution of the French empire but also on the possible fragmentation of the British. As Coleridge recognized (see Chapter 4), since the health of the state is coterminous with the strength of the poet, the disappearance of a coherent cultural narrative in the field of history entails the loss of any sense of a significant, authoritative centre.

Scott, however, differs markedly from Coleridge in his willingness to entertain this condition. For the author of the *Biographia*, the romantic Bard, as distinguished from the *bricoleur*, is the subject who 'supposedly would be the absolute origin of his own discourse and supposedly would construct it "out of nothing," "out of the whole cloth", would be the creator of the verb, the verb itself'.[26] But for Scott there is no such ambition. Poetic originality meant little to a writer who regarded Waterloo as a jumble of broken signs and his major poems as so many 'soap bubbles'. To Lockhart he confessed that 'my poetry has always passed from the desk to the printer in the most hurried manner possible, so that it is no wonder I am sometimes puzzled to explain my own meaning?'[27] In absolute contrast to the studied efforts of Wordsworth and Keats, poetry for Scott was not a Parnassian grasping at truth and beauty but an attempt to participate in the 'capricious' fancies of commercial society. As a writer for the *Anti-Jacobin Review* put it:

> Mr. Scott is a... poet by habit, we had almost said by *trade*... Hence he has become famed rather for the quantity, than for the quality of his compositions: with good principles, a respectable portion of genius, and no mean talents, Mr. Scott might do much better than he does; but as he fills his purse, he probably thinks he does well enough; and, laughing at our admonitions, perhaps he may say to himself – 'I had better be rewarded for my industry, than celebrated for my merit!'[28]

The scars of Waterloo, gathered together and heaped up in the marketplace as objects of desire for acquisitive tourists, may be said to have reappeared in Scott in a similarly debased form.

And yet this portrait of the magpie-like compositor, sifting through the ruins of Empire in search of the Romantic, is only partially correct. Scott's growing disrespect for the craft of poetry was not prompted by a love of the market so much as by a belief that 'literature ought never to be ranked on the same scale of importance with the conduct of business in any of the great departments of public life'.[29] And the greatest department of all was war. Leaving for now the question of Scott's representation of the field of battle, let us review the poet's attempts to negotiate between these competing spheres.

Debarred from active participation in the struggle against France, Scott responded to the conflict as if it were a form of otherness – something that is always anterior to the subject, that brings the subject into being in the first place, but that always eludes its grasp. As John Sutherland indicates in his discussion of the poet's Volunteer period, there is a sense in which the writing of verse was an attempt to literally thrust his thoughts into violent actuality, as if the sheer mobility, in metrical terms of 'War Songs' such as 'To horse! To horse!' could capture the heroic encounter that Scott so desired.[30] Our concern therefore is with a man who approached verse as a surrogate form of textual combat. If the words themselves seemed hackneyed and threadbare then the force guiding them – literally the motions of the octosyllabic 'light horse' style – would point beyond the fissured texture to the energetic shuttle of command.

A precedent for verse that Scott would go on to write in the aftermath of Waterloo is the 'Bard's Incantation' composed in 1805 at the height of the invasion crisis. The poem has an interesting compositional history. According to Lockhart the poet was returning with his wife from a second honeymoon at Gilsland in the Lakes when he heard of a threatened invasion by the French. The biographer records that he 'was not slow to obey the summons': 'He had luckily chosen to accompany on horseback the carriage in which Mrs. Scott travelled... it was during his fiery ride... that he composed his "Bard's Incantation"... and the verses bear the full stamp of the feelings of the moment.'[31] The following stanzas, from the conclusion of the poem, are representative of the equestrian style that Scott was to deploy, to such lively effect, in the later romances:

> 'By all their swords, by all their scars,
> By all their names, a mighty spell!
> By all their wounds, by all their wars,
> Arise, the mighty strain to tell!
> For fiercer than fierce Hengist's strain,
> More impious than the heathen Dane,
> More grasping than all-grasping Rome,
> Gaul's ravening legions hither come!'

> The wind is hush'd, and still the lake –
> Strange murmurs fill my tinkling ears,
> Bristles my hair, my sinews quake,
> At the dread voice of other years:
> 'When targets clash'd, and bugles rung,
> And blades round warriors heads were flung,
> The foremost of the band were we,
> And hymn'd the joys of Liberty![32]

The poem was eventually published six years later in the *Edinburgh Annual Register*. In this version Scott appends the subtitle 'written under the threat of invasion in the autumn of 1804'. Since in the autumn of 1804 the poet was living only a few miles from Dalkeith where the volunteers assembled, it seems likely that the story given to Lockhart was somewhat embellished. The point is that horsemanship, heroism and composition were so fused in Scott's mind that the event *would have* turned out this way. By infusing the bardic past with the temporal urgency of the immediate now, the poet translates history into myth, rendering the pressure of war into an act of self-dramatization. But, as we shall see, the 'dread voice of other years' was to recede in the face of more urgent developments taking place overseas.

The spirit of contested lands

In his introduction to *The Minstrelsy of the Scottish Border* (1802–3) Scott had claimed that 'the music and songs of the Borders were of a military nature, and celebrated the valour and successes of their predatory expeditions'.[33] Like the war songs of the Volunteer period, the ballad was an inherently martial form. And indeed, the verses included in this collection go some way towards justifying the idea that national and poetic identity is in a state of ceaseless conflict. Just as Scott's border minstrels are perceived against a shifting background of invasion and counter-invasion, so the poet's political *topos* takes on the status of a 'debateable land'. The significance of this status is perhaps more apparent when we consider that *The Minstrelsy* may have been composed as a reaction to the invasion threats and increasing militarism of the 1796–1802 period.[34] With a glance towards his own patriotic activities Scott revealingly adds that '[the Borderers] were wont to assemble 10,000 horsemen in the course of a single day' and that 'the habits of the Borderers fitted them particularly to distinguish themselves as light cavalry'.[35] Thus, even as the poet pledged his allegiance to the national cause his heart was avowedly sectarian. An instinctive Tory, Scott nevertheless fell back on the mythical charge of ancient rebellions to consolidate his cultural and emotional potency.

The spirit of contested lands inflects the vast majority of Scott's early poems, from *The Lay of the Last Minstrel* to *The Lord of the Isles*. But with each successive production, the theme was beginning to seem hackneyed, even to its progenitor. Moreover, the form in which it was expressed, the verse romance, despite the avidity with which the reading public consumed it, was beginning to show signs of exhaustion. When placed in a different light, however, the deficiencies of these later poems are marked by a highly sophisticated – even ironic degree of – authorial awareness. True, the verse continues to immerse itself in a highly stylized version of the Highland past, but we also hear, alongside the clash of sword and pike, a dialogue between the claims of two narrative modes. The first mode is easy enough to identify: it is the romance with its blending (after Johnson) of 'marvellous and uncommon incidents'.[36] The second mode, however, is more difficult to pin down. In 1813 it is loosely identified with the epic, which Scott defines, in its earliest Homeric form, as a 'vehicle...of historical truth'.[37] Later on, as the novelist supplants the poet, it is the novel that takes on this burden.[38] In the 'Essay on Romance', written in 1824, the novel is defined as 'a fictitious narrative, differing from the Romance, because the events are accommodated to the ordinary train of human events, and the modern state of society' (p. 65). Scott's acceptance of the 'inevitable "ordinary train"' is bound up, I would suggest, with the author's resignation to the stereotypical forms of the modern publishing industry that we read about earlier. In both cases, Scott acknowledges the fundamental significance of the mundane and the everyday. Yet, even as romance is 'accommodated' to the discipline of history, the author remains enchanted with its legend-creating potential.[39] He is moreover enamoured with its capacity to evoke a purer code of behaviour, one that predates the 'advent of the system of modern manners predicated on the systems of commerce and jurisprudence'.[40] As the narrator of *Waverley* states: 'The wrath of our ancestors...was coloured *gules*; it broke forth in acts of open and sanguinary violence against the objects of its fury: our malignant feelings, which must seek gratification through more indirect channels... may be rather said to be *sable*. But the deep ruling impulse is the same in both cases.'[41] If modern manners are characterized by the transformation of violence through 'indirect channels' then there may well be, as James Chandler claims, good grounds for aligning Scott with the rise of the public sphere. Nevertheless I would maintain that Scott could never reject entirely the pure passion of and for romance; for just as modern society remains fixated with the spectacle of its fundamental impossibility, so Scott returns to the genre where the collapse of integrity is most apparent.

As specimen, we may take *The Vision of Don Roderick*, published in 1811, the year in which Napoleon came closest to blocking Britain's trade links with Spain and Portugal. The poem divides Spanish history into three periods. The first of these represents the invasion of the Moors, the defeat and death of Roderick, and closes with the peaceful occupation of the country by the victors. The second period depicts the conquests of the Spaniards and the Portuguese in the East and West Indies. The last part of the poem opens with the state of Spain prior to the invasion of Napoleon and concludes with the arrival of the British saviours. From a formal point of view the poem is an attempt to relate the two narrative modes outlined above. Scott, who was well aware of the perils involved in mixing epic and romance, states in a footnote that 'the transition of an incident from history to tradition, and from tradition to fable and romance, [becomes] more marvellous at each step'.[42] Elsewhere, he notes that contemporary history 'neither requires nor admits of the aid of fiction'.[43] Yet, in poetizing the Peninsular War, this is precisely what Scott goes on to attempt. Nor was the gesture in any way remarkable, for the cultural resources for the romanticization of the Iberian conflict were already available, and were widely accepted as a legitimate form of expression. It was not uncommon, for example, to refer to the Peninsular Campaign as a repetition of the 'holy' war that Roderick waged against the Moors. Buoyed along by the rhetoric of romance, the leaders of the British expeditionary force were described as 'Knights' defending the ancient hierarchies of the *ancien régime* as well as the contemporary claims of national liberty and independence.[44] That the romance was widely accepted as a narrative mode for describing the Iberian war becomes clearer when we consider the following extract from George Ellis and George Canning in their résumé of Spanish *affaires* for the first issue of the *Quarterly Review*:

> In surveying the transactions recorded or referred to in these papers, we are almost tempted to doubt whether we are reading the events of real history... [the conflict] presents a spectacle, certainly, not less improbable than the wildest fictions of romance.[45]

'As enthusiastic as the other *Quarterly* reviewers about the Iberian campaign, Walter Scott meticulously followed the evolution of events in the Peninsula and kept a record of the battles fought by the British army on a map. Yet,' as Diego Saglia continues, 'in order to place these events in a cultural frame, he also removed them to a fictional dimension', noting in a letter to Thomas Scott that 'to have all the places mentioned in Don Quixote and Gil Blas now the scenes of real and important events... sounds like history in the land of romance'.[46] Properly conceptualized, the concerns that Scott voices about the relationship between history and romance seem rather unnecessary, for history itself appears to its participants as a form of romance.

Scott, however, recognizes the limitations of this point of view. His 'Essay on Chivalry', begun in 1815, notes, with some pathos, the difference between chivalric 'theory' and military 'practice'. From its inception in the tenth century to its demise in the fifteenth, the chivalric ideal was qualified by actual social corruption and violence. Still, for all his scepticism, the historian maintains that 'real circumstances occurred, of a nature nearly as romantic as the achievements which Don Quixote aspired to execute... Unquestionably, in many individual circumstances, knights were all that we have described them.'⁴⁷ Some years later, in the 'Essay on Romance', Scott returns to this theme in order to show how 'real history' is determined by the 'fabulous' sentiments of chivalry and romance: 'So high was the national excitation in consequence of the romantic atmosphere in which they seemed to breathe, that the knights and squires of the fourteenth and fifteenth centuries imitated the wildest and most extravagant enterprises of the heroes of Romance.'⁴⁸ As a scholar of romance, Scott was well aware that the culture to which it belonged was irrecoverable. But he also acknowledges the critical role that fictional extravagance plays in facilitating the legitimization of a state of war.⁴⁹

As the hardships and political fears of 1811 dampened public support for the war against Napoleon, Scott entered the fray with a poem that would seek to restore a sense of national unity and purpose. The challenge was to create a poem that would do justice to the violence and complexity of modern warfare without precluding the indulgence of the fancy. The search for a form that will combine romance elements with historical detail is therefore the subject of the *Vision's* opening movement. Beginning with some conventional praise of Wellington, the eulogy turns rapidly to a meditation on the vexed relationship between fable and actuality. Keeping in mind his reverence for martial prowess, the poet searches for a 'strain, whose sounds of mounting fire / May rise distinguished o'er the din of war' (I, i). We are only two lines into the *Vision* and already questions have been raised about the inadequacy of literary expression. All this may seem nothing other than formal deference, but as the verse progresses the questions become more frequent and more urgent. In the lines that follow, contemporary bards are dismissed as 'weak minstrels' of an 'exhausted age' (I, iii). Lacking the strength of Homer and Milton, the romancer draws on a dwindling reserve of Celtic inspiration only to find that the 'old traditionary lore' has 'Decay'd' (I, viii). The border 'ravag[es]' and 'rugged deeds' (I, viii) of the *Minstrelsy* period have given way to the pastoral calm of shepherd's song, and the poet is advised to search 'romantic lands' (I, ix) for the 'meed to warrior due' (I, vii).

The Iberian Peninsula is a contemporary version of the old, contested land. Here, it is not only 'warriors' but poets who wield renewed fire in the service of their country. The alliance between history and romance is fragile, however; Scott may have discovered a new source of inspiration but his commitment to this 'meed' is matched only by his consciousness of its artificiality and it is this last sense that bears upon the formal aspects of the poem. Significantly, the topographical shift from the Scottish Highlands to the plains of Spain and Portugal coincides with the rejection of the octosyllabic ballad in favour of a pseudo-Spenserian form. Scott describes his stanza as a hybrid form, combining the 'wonders wild of Arabesque' with 'Gothic imagery of darker shade, / Forming a model meet for minstrel line' (I, xii). Just as, in the language of British martial policy, history is blurred into romance, so, in the poetry, oriental culture is blended with Northern European gothic. But it is at the meeting point between these terms that the real interest of Scott's work lies. To quote Stuart Curran, 'Scott is fascinated with the meeting grounds between cultures and epochs'; and also, we might add, between poetic genres and forms, for the meeting ground, or contest, covers the mutual illumination not only of time periods but also of modes of understanding, specifically the contest between history and romance. The sense of formal instability is echoed in the numerous commentaries that punctuate the fading of the poem's visions. Towards the end of Canto II, for example, the narrator questions whether 'fond fable' should 'mix with heroes' praise?' (II, lxi). Lines such as this display a heightened sense of authorial self-consciousness, as if the poet were aware of the disparity between history and the 'fair fields of romance'.

Elsewhere, however, Scott seems content to allow romance the upper hand, even to the extent of distorting historical truth. This is evident in the way the poem emphasizes the gallantry of the Highland regiments at Fuentes d'Honoro and Barossa at the expense of their lowland compatriots. The decision to all but ignore the decisive role of Sir John Moore, the martyr of Corunna and a popular national hero, was seen by many to be both ill judged and inaccurate.[50] From a poetic point of view, however, the climactic valorization of the Highlanders is in tune with a narrative that derives its vigour from the patriotic and 'savage' passions of the Spanish guerrillas. And so, *The Vision of Don Roderick* turns out to be a border romance after all. At the same time, Scott's identification with the Border regiments allows the poet to insert himself within history. Thus, where we might have expected the *Vision* to conclude with a paean to the victorious Lord Wellington, it is Scott himself, presented bizarrely in the guise of Spenser's Red Cross Knight, who is the true commander of the field.

But what, if anything, has Scott achieved by this imitative act, as benighted as the 'fabulous' gestures recorded in 'The Essay on Romance'? Spenser, as I shall argue in Chapter 5, is an icon of self-marginalization as much as a guarantor of poetic and political legitimacy. For Scott, therefore, the desire for a 'verse of tumult and of flame, / Bold as the bursting of their cannon sound' (III, xiii) ought to be set against the resigned tone of 'How shall a bard, unknowing and unknown, / His meed to each victorious leader pay...?' (III, xii). The latter is more attuned to the solitary, inward Spenser than it is to the Spenser of civic recognition and bardic command. In addition, therefore, to reinventing itself as a border ballad, the *Vision* also turns out to be a form of Romantic crisis poem. Yet unlike Wordsworth and Keats, the crisis is apparent only in brief moments of self-contestation and doubt, specifically where the symbolic pressure of war prevents the assertion of an ideal 'I'. Unable to capture the military real and unwilling to 'accommodate' itself to the 'ordinary train' of history, the poetry opts instead for a compromise formulation. Scott's declaration that he is 'unknowing and unknown' (III, xii) may well smack of false modesty but it also recalls the poet's disparaging view of literary fame. By aligning himself with that other Spenser, the poet of official neglect and patient suffering, Scott fashions himself in relation to a poetic type: that of the meek, yet authoritative sage. But unlike Wordsworth who, as we shall see, derives succour and strength from this image, Scott seems unable to convince himself that the role of the poet, as mystical seer, is anything other than a clever, literary contrivance. In conclusion, *The Vision of Don Roderick* allows the romance and historical modes to collide. In doing so, I would suggest, it ironically exposes the relativity of our notions of cultural and political authority as well as the complexity of an alternative mode of Romantic subjectivity.

The dance of death

> He might have said with Malvolio, ' "I do not now fool myself to let imagination jade me," I am actually in the land of military and romantic adventures, and it only remains to be seen what will be my own share in them.'
>
> (*Waverley; Or, 'Tis Sixty Years Since*, p. 72)

The disparity between Romantic and historical views of the world is the pervasive theme of Scott's next major work of contemporary battle narrative, *The Field of Waterloo*. Considered from the point of view of its publishing history, *The Field of Waterloo* is a remarkable achievement. Conceived and written during Scott's brief tour of France and the Netherlands, the poem attained rapidly a circulation above what had been reached by either *Rokeby* or *The Lord of the Isles*. Its influence is detectable in the Waterloo rhymes of Southey and Byron and in the compositions of numerous minor poets. In light of this success it is a salutary experience to consider the poem's early reception history. Contemporary reviews are ubiquitously damning of the work's structure and versification. The *Anti-Jacobin Review* considered the poem to be 'dull, tame, and uninteresting. Here and there a glimpse of genius is observed, but by no means sufficient to compensate us for the barren heath of insipidity over which we are compelled to travel. The grammatical errors... are of such a description, as almost to raise a doubt as to the author's education'.[51] Even Lockhart found it difficult to excuse the 'weak pomposity of movement': 'The descent is indeed heavy from Bannockburn to his Waterloo: the presence, or all but visible reality of what his dreams cherished, seems to have overawed his imagination.'[52] This, however, is a telling criticism, one that alerts us to a central theme of the poem: the poet who 'deems / Of that which is from that which seems'.

The theme is developed initially in 'an odd, wild sort of thing' called 'The Dance of Death'. First published in the *Edinburgh Annual Register* for 1815, the poem marks a return to the customary 'riding' style: 'Night and morning were at meeting / Over Waterloo' (lines 1–2). Here, the galloping rhythm and borderland atmosphere combine to presage much of what is to follow. Like the *Vision*, the poem is concerned with the 'meeting' between a variety of contraries: the symbolic connotations of storm and stress and the reality of the shivering soldier in his 'dreary bivouak' (line 14); the mythical archetypes of 'Wizard, witch, and fiend' (line 20) and the historical specificity of 'Albyn's war-array' (line 27). As the mystical and actual change places the purpose of the poem becomes clear: Scott wishes to reinvest Waterloo with a sense of cosmic significance. To this end, in stanza II, the verse focuses on the visions of one 'Grey Allan', a soldier in the 92nd Highlanders serving under Colonel Cameron, the 'Valient Fassiefern' (line 34) of Quatre Bras. As Allan waits for the dawn he 'sees' a 'ghastly roundelay...of the destined dead' (line 71). Like all the other elements in this poem Allan has a dual identity, linking the role of 'prophet' (line 23) with his status as an ordinary soldier and, as we shall see, as a Scotsman. Scott reserves the most telling correspondence, however, for stanza III:

> When down the destined plain,
> 'Twixt Britain and the bands of France,
> Wild as marsh-borne meteors glance,
> Strange phantoms wheel'd a revel dance,
> And doom'd the future slain. –
> Such forms were seen, such sounds were heard,
> When Scotland's James his march prepared
> For Flodden's fatal plain...
>   (lines 54–61)

The implicit comparison between the wreck of Napoleonic France and the extinction of Scotland is typically ambiguous. When, in the spring of 1814, the Allies made their triumphant entry into Paris, Scott was at work on the chapters in *Waverley* describing the victorious English campaign at Culloden.[53] Later on, when the author was calling for the trial and execution of 'the arch enemy of mankind' he was completing or about to complete the chapters dealing with the trial of Fergus by the English at Carlisle.[54] While it would be erroneous to claim that Scott maintained a secret sympathy with the French cause (based on a parallel with the notion that Scott was notoriously ambiguous about the destruction of clan culture) there is a sense in which both *Waverley* and the Waterloo poems display an underlying concern with geopolitical and ideological displacement.

The verse's background in the early border ballads suggests that Scott wished to fashion Waterloo as yet another 'fateful' event in the formation of Scottish national identity. The Highlanders who, like the followers of James, are to meet their death on the field do so out of a sense that history has ordained their sacrifice. In this respect it is worth recalling that *Marmion*

(1808) had already sanctified the defeat of Scotland as a necessary stage on the way to Britishness. Thus, what Francis Jeffrey regarded as a 'neglect of Scottish feelings' was, from Scott's point of view, justified by the sense of a greater duty towards the union.[55] But Scott, of course, was prompted by more than political considerations. In *Marmion* Flodden is celebrated as a zone of epic passions, antique costume and martial glamour. This 'knightly tale of Albion's elder day' (Introduction to Canto I) does little to bring out the tragic or political connotations of the event. The same is true of 'The Dance of Death'. By invoking Flodden in the midst of Waterloo Scott ensures that the romantic view of historical conflict prevails: the death of the poet's fellow countrymen is justified in the service of a higher patriotism towards Britain.[56] At a fundamental level we should also consider that the process of dematerialization could also be applied to the poet's sense of self. To draw out this notion let us reconsider Scott's relationship with the spectacle and reality of the Napoleonic wars. If the poet felt that he had in some way missed out on the public 'department' of war, then Grey Allan is a worthy if perplexing surrogate. By combining the roles of seer and soldier, Allan fulfils the poet's most cherished ideal. That such an ideal cannot be allowed to live, even in the borderland of Scott's poetic vision, is a consequence of the poem's investment in the logic of sacrifice. The trauma that Waverley experiences on the eve of battle, 'he saw the wild dress and appearance of his Highland associates, heard their whispers in an uncouth and unknown language, looked upon his own dress...and wished to awake from what seemed at the moment a dream, strange, horrible, and unnatural', is thus effectively discharged by rendering Allan quite literally ghostly.[57] The death of the Highlander in the service of the union leads not to a rejection of the poet/warrior figure but to its sublimation: as the dream lives on in the oral histories of the soldier's comrades so Scott sustains his belief in the formative role of poetic vision.[58] The power of romance, one might say, has been tentatively restored to its central place in the making and unmaking of individual and national consciousness.[59]

'The Dance of Death' forms, as it were, an adjunct to *The Field of Waterloo*. Like *The Vision of Don Roderick*, the poem is intended as a 'nation's choral hymn'.[60] Yet, as we have seen, the nation that Scott claimed to speak for was far from united. A brief glance at the nationalistic epics published between 1793 and 1815 indicates the lack of consensus concerning both the form and content of 'choral' verses. Milton, of course, was the great precursor for pro- and anti-establishment epic poets, and the need to out-trope his influence is responsible, in part, for the sense of 'crisis' that inflects the works of this period.[61] Scott, alone among the Romantics, shows little interest in this endeavour. Where establishment poets wrestled with the baleful effects of Milton's politics and subjectivism, Scott turned to Dryden, a poet who appealed as a literary model for his 'elasticity' and 'rapidity of conception' and, as a political example, for his distrust of fanaticism, his willingness to support the establishment, and his unabashed commercialism.[62] The poet's influence is detectable in the sheer verbal energy of the piece. Where Miltonic inversion impedes the reader's progress, encouraging a meditation on depth and inwardness, Dryden's heroic verse propels the reader from one linguistic unit to another. As we shall discover, it is this latter quality that Scott utilizes in his descriptions of the chaos and confusion of battle.

The idea that *The Field of Waterloo* is best approached by way of an analysis of its links with the Romantic nationalistic epic requires therefore that we revise our understanding of this tradition. For in addition to the influence of Dryden, we must also consider Scott's abiding interest in German ballads, Scottish folk songs, medieval tales and Spenserian romance. The nationalistic poetics that Scott created owed little to the confessional and republican voice of Milton. Scott's focus was directed outward, away from the self and towards the social. True to the letter if not the spirit of the epic tradition, poems such as *The Lay of the Last Minstrel* and *Marmion* mark a return to the Homeric devices of games, shield, feasting and 'fabl'd Knights in Battels feign'd' – the very themes disparaged by Milton as 'hitherto the onely Argument heroic deemd'.[63] By returning the romantic epic to its origins in the pagan past, Scott not only rejected the political and spiritual progressivism of Wordsworth, Keats, Shelley and Byron, he also turned away from their metaphysical quest for the centred self. Only in the questionable form of paradox does Scott come close to the preoccupations of his contemporaries, for it is at least arguable that the poet's compulsive interest in military conquest, border crossings and territorial instability corresponds with the symptoms of a recognizable romantic malady: the impulse to dissolve the mind in ceaseless activity – the very condition that Byron would diagnose and explore in the permanent exile of Childe Harold. The link between national stability and self-equilibrium rests, therefore, on a strange interweaving of order and chaos. To be more accurate, the desire for cohesion in Scott is unavoidably connected with the passion for destruction. The strength of the British nation, and by extension the strength of the self (strong only because it is a given and therefore not in need of definition) can only be asserted through a relentless return to moments of historical crisis: the border conflicts, the Civil War, the Jacobites. At another level this takes the form of the recurring wish to measure the competing claims of history and romance. In preparing the apparently inconsequential form of *The Field of Waterloo*, Scott, I would argue, was driven to confront the very forces that would undo the complacency of his vision.

With *The Field of Waterloo* we encounter Scott's most revealing commentary on the dispute between fact and fiction. The poem begins straightforwardly enough with a measured section of loco-descriptive verse. As the 'unvaried shade' of Soignies gives way to a 'brighter, livelier scene' (I, i–ii), so the reader/viewer is invited to suspend their historical consciousness and contemplate the beauties of rural life. But just as poetic tradition dictates that pastoral be a preliminary for epic so Scott draws attention to the ironic contrast between the peace of rural labour and the ravages of war. Thus, in stanza IV, a credulous addressee is requested to view the landscape and 'tell of that which late hath been'. To such eyes the material marks on the field appear to signify the beautified reality of pastoral: the 'bare extent of stubble-plain' indicates the peaceable activity of harvesting; 'these broad spots of trampled ground' a space where 'the rustics danced such round / As Teniers loved to draw'; a patch of scorched earth signals the remnants of a feast (I, iv). Scott's first act of demystification is dependent on the resuscitation of a hackneyed metaphor:

> But other harvest here,
> Than that which peasant's scythe demands,
> Was gather'd in by sterner hands,
>   With bayonet, blade, and spear.
> No vulgar crop was theirs to reap,
> No stinted harvest thin and cheap!
> Heroes before each fatal sweep
>   Fell thick as ripen'd grain;
> And ere the darkening of the day,
> Piled high as autumn shocks, there lay
> The ghastly harvest of the fray,
>   The corpses of the slain.
>
> (I, v)

The 'topos of fertilization', to adapt Carl Woodring's phrase, used by Scott to underscore the contrast between vegetative renewal and human mortality is, as we shall see, a pervasive trope in the literature of Waterloo.[64] In *Paul's Letters*, the poet draws on the accounts of earlier eyewitnesses to describe how the plain 'on that memorable day bore a tall and strong crop of corn.' But he also writes of its appearance in the battle's aftermath: 'The tall crops of maize and rye were trampled into a thick black paste, under the feet of men and horses.'[65] By late July the plants had begun to re-establish themselves; as Milton Wilson has written, the 'funeral flowers offer only "vain surmise" and "mockery" to the corpse below'.[66] Scott, however, is unwilling to pursue the elegiac connotations of this contrast; within a few lines the potential for empathy with the dead has been supplanted by a return to the historical or anti-Romantic mode. In the stanza that follows, pastoral illusion is supplanted by pastoral irony. The ironic mode allows the viewer to make the transition from ignorance to knowledge so that, on second view, black lines reveal the 'deep-graved ruts' of artillery tracks and the 'harden'd mud' shows where a dragoon fought and fell (I, vi). The rustic visions of Teniers, Durer and Breughel are therefore displaced by a clear-eyed view of 'that which is' (I, v).

For Scott, however, the acknowledgement of the reality behind the facade does not lead to a heightened sense of pacifist indignation: the horrors of war are regrettable, but then, war, because it is reality, cannot be wished away. The shift from pastoral to epic coincides, therefore, with a commitment to narrating the 'matter' of Waterloo. The ideological appropriateness of this gesture (we shall investigate how Byron uses pastoral elegy to qualify Tory triumphalism in Chapter 6) dovetails neatly with the more sure-footed verse that follows. In many respects the combination of the tactician's transcendent view of war as linear progress from engagement to objective with the soldier's experience of immanent, disassociated events, corresponds exactly with the overall effect of Scott's battle poetry. In turning from the bodies of the dead, the poet avoids a potentially enervating encounter with immobility; in generic terms, pastoral stasis is the antonym of epic progress and must be avoided at all costs. Scott is at his best, therefore, when he is attempting to describe the pace of combat rather than the space of death. In this example leading dactyls combine with galloping iambs and repetitive phrasing to increase the momentum of the verse:

> On came the whirlwind – like the last
> But fiercest sweep of tempest-blast –
> On came the whirlwind – steel-gleams broke
> Like lightning through the rolling smoke...
>
> (I, XI)

The effect of this type of description is eminently impersonal. Lancers, cuirassiers and riflemen are present in the poem only as the grammatical functions of the dominant active verbs: 'The lancer couch'd his ruthless spear'; 'The cohorts eagle flew' (XI). By the end of this section the various ranks – 'Lancer and guard and cuirassier, / Horseman and foot' – have been reduced to a 'mingled host' (XII). Rather than dwelling on the pathos of such moments the poem seems to exist for the sake of its structural transitions: 'Then waked...Then down...Then to...And while' (XII, *passim*). Sense and understanding are hurried over in the rush to convey sensation.

There are, however, at least two significant presences in the poem: Napoleon who is associated with the rhetoric of motion, and Wellington who stands at its centre. The French emperor is 'impatient' and 'eager' (IX). His cry of 'On! On!' and his recourse to a language of command – 'Rush on.... advance...charge for France' (X) – mark him out as a figure connected with the desire for the improbable and hence with the very stuff of Scott's poetry. By contrast, Wellington enters the verse as 'his country's sword and shield', a 'beam of light' who urges his soldiers to 'stand firm' (X). Like the panoramists, whose work is examined in the next chapter, the Duke is depicted as a focal point illuminating the action of the field and thus of the poem. Again, in stanza XIII his presence is linked with the imperative to stand and hold fast. Only towards the end of the battle does he give the command to 'Advance'. The sense of pent-up energy is conveyed through the references to 'the ocean's flood' that falls upon the French (XIII). This larger movement is set against the irregular, 'impetuous' (XIV) energy of Napoleon whose course resembles the turbulent rhythms of a mountain torrent. But if the energy of Wellington and by extension British history is shown to be irresistible, that of Napoleon and France seems more attuned to the equine motions of the poem. One is tempted to say that at a metrical level Scott betrays a secret sympathy with the restlessness of the Imperial commander – a comment that seems less banal when we recall the poet's notorious indifference to advice and criticism.

Scott's contemporaries puzzled over the meaning of stanza XVIII in which the poet counsels an exiled Napoleon to 'triumph' over his 'stubborn soul'. At a superficial level the message ties in with the Christian theme of redemption: Scott, unlike Byron, does not agonize over the Emperor's failure to follow the Roman example. Beyond this, however, we must reconsider the stanza's concluding lines in the light of what has already been said about Scott's engagement with border poetics:

> Hear this – from no unmoved heart,
> Which sighs, comparing what THOU ART
> With what thou MIGHT'ST HAVE BEEN!

Formally, the lines echo the distinction between that which is and that which seems. In this case, however, the power of seeming, analogous with the power of making, is looked upon as a redemptive principle. As the future anterior rebounds on the present so Napoleon is lifted from the disappointing emptiness of his final act to reside in a space outside history. The space that Scott creates for Napoleon, in spelling out this wish, is of course the space of beauty and of romance, of finality without end.

As Napoleon is revealed to be the satanic element in Scott's plot so Wellington becomes his divine antecedent. But lest we be tempted to read this opposition in conventional Miltonic terms, we should consider the poet's inveterate resistance to transcendental arguments. In this respect we have already noted the association Wellington has for Scott – as the agent of history, of all that Scott most admires and of everything he cannot attain, the British leader is linked with the love of the probable and the real. If, as I have argued, Napoleon is linked with the love of romance or the improbable, then Wellington, 'in sentence brief' (X), must surely be seen as its historical or Homeric antidote. Looking back on his Waterloo period Scott recalled that 'he had never felt awed or abashed except in the presence of one man – the Duke of Wellington'. The meeting, which took place in Paris shortly after the journey from Waterloo, presents us with a revealing commentary on the relative worth of art and actuality:

[Scott] said he beheld in him a great soldier and a great statesman – the greatest of each. When it was suggested [by Ballantyne] that the Duke, on his part, saw before him a great poet and novelist, [Scott] smiled, and said, 'What would the Duke of Wellington think of a few *bits of novels*, which perhaps he had never read, and for which the strong probability is that he would not care a sixpence if he had?'[67]

Scott's estimation is probably correct: the Duke cared little for works of literature and even less for professional scribblers. But the statement is more revealing for what it tells us about its author's self-evaluation. Scott's success as a writer of fiction was as nothing to the Duke's success in the field of history.[68] Add to this the sense in which Wellington seemed to be converting his intervention into history into personal myth and we encounter the living embodiment of all that Scott most cherished: the ability to forge oneself as a power in reality.[69]

Wellington's historical romance is different, therefore, from the Napoleonic love of illusion. Like David at the end of *Absalom and Achitophel*, Wellington rises as 'lawful pow'r' to counter the 'artificers of death'.[70] Having marked the beyond of fiction and – by extension, the beyond of commerce – he functions in Scott's work, and life, as an enveloping force, one that ultimately reverses the history/romance opposition, covering the wound in the symbolic order. The lesson bears, at first sight, an uncanny similarity with the awakening of Waverley: '[he felt] that the romance of his life was ended, and that its real history had now commenced' (p. 283). Having traversed the fantasy of war one would therefore expect Scott to make a related passage from the enchantment of poetry to the 'domestic' prose of everyday life (p. 135; pp. 290–1).[71] But Scott's experience of history bears little relation to the disappointed, chastened view of his hero. The point may be illustrated with a further piece of anecdotal evidence. Shortly after the abashed encounter with Wellington Scott attended a 'grand ball' at the Duke's hotel. It was here, surrounded by the most senior British and Allied heroes of Waterloo together with the Prussian Royal family and the Prince of Orange that Scott received confirmation of the ascendancy of the real: 'the romance of the Round Table', he announced to James Simpson, 'is probable in comparison. No romance ever came up to this.'[72] Indeed, no romance could ever compare with Waterloo for all points of comparison had been dramatically erased. History itself has done away with the need for mythopoeic representation; the force of romance is, as it were, immanent within the field of actuality. Symbolization is redundant: the battle of Waterloo acts now as a force of pure presence, a sublime object voiding all attempts at narrative comprehension.

The judgement of literary history, that *The Field of Waterloo* cannot 'come up' to the event it narrates, suggests that Waterloo itself is the great poem that Scott can never write. Yet despite the enveloping force of this newly romanticized history, the *Field* does contain a small but telling trace of stubborn actuality. The trace emerges in the poet's concluding address to the Duke of Wellington. 'Thou too', Scott writes, 'whose deeds of fame renewe'd / *Bankrupt* a nation's gratitude' (xix; my emphasis) is a sly reminder of the debates in the Commons about the sum to be granted as a reward for the Duke's endeavours. Scott, covetous of historical recognition as well as of pecuniary reward, must surely have envied this special status. It is a reminder, moreover, of the central role that money plays in Scott's taxing poetics. To echo Curran once again, in presenting Waterloo as a fit subject for verse, Scott offers 'an unlimited field not just for the creation of romance but for its simultaneous critique'.[73] The space in which Waterloo endures is thus the space of genuine romantic 'song': not ahistorical, not asocial and certainly not benighted. For even as the *Field* concludes with its reference to the 'Gallant Saint George', the poem has touched on too many contradictions for the sense of an ending to be a satisfactory one. Neither epic nor romance, *The Field of Waterloo* is too heterogeneous to support its avowed conclusions.

Coda: forging *The Antiquary*

In Scott's final acts of poetic composition then, we are confronted with a work in which history and romance struggle for dominion. Like the battle itself, the significance of the poem is undermined by the expectations of its audience; a work that ought to provide firm justification of the benefits of war – peace, stability and national prosperity – is unexpectedly pitted with reminders of the primal delights of war and its unfortunate costs. In the aftermath of Waterloo, therefore, what the world required and what Scott devoted himself to providing was a work in which the legend-creating potential of romance would be better accommodated to the requirements of modern times.

Conceived in March 1815, but not begun until December of that year, *The Antiquary* was meant to 'complete a series of fictitious narratives, intended to illustrate the manners of Scotland at three different periods. WAVERLEY embraced the age of our fathers, GUY MANNERING that of our own youth, and the ANTIQUARY refers to the last ten years of the eighteenth century.'[74] The genealogical metaphor should be taken seriously, for *The Antiquary* has an interesting relationship with its natural father. Where *Guy Mannering*, the novel of our youth, is traversed by remnants of the imaginary and is thus, in a special sense, struggling with the symbolic insistence of its literary progenitor,[75] *The Antiquary* takes up a more nuanced stance, as befits the subject who, a generation after the father, is advanced in the process of fathering himself. The 'manners' on display in the novel are accordingly more refined, less barbaric than the manners of *Waverley*. Where conflict forms the nexus of Edward Waverley's identity – in *Waverley* the subject is forged in the rift between discourses, cultures and ideologies – conflict in *The Antiquary* is rarely allowed to spill over into actual physical harm; and when it does, as in the duel between the headstrong Captain M'Intyre and the disinherited hero Lovel, the potential for 'tragedy' is rapidly defused. Unlike *Waverley*, which indulges in displaced representations of *'brute* violence' by transporting its readers back to a time of feuds, abuses, and revenge,[76] *The Antiquary* presents a portrait of a modern 'well-ordered island' dedicated to the promulgation of conflict resolution, respect for property and the restraint of desire.[77] Crucial to this programme is the recognition that extreme ideologies, such as Jacobitism, no longer have any substantive reality. The escape from 'affection' and 'conviction' (p. 193), so crucial to the forging of Waverley's adult self, has ceased to be a matter of concern in this post-ideological society. Thus Sir Arthur Wardour maintains his opposition to the house of Hanover rather as 'a matter of form than as conveying any distinctive meaning' (p. 49). In every 'practical' respect 'a most zealous and devoted subject of George III', Sir Arthur's Jacobitism remains an entirely 'theoretical' affair (p. 50).

In the world of *The Antiquary* the 'rules of modern politeness' (p. 51) are such that the ancestral clash between Whig and Tory, Protestant and Catholic is kept within the boundaries of civilized behaviour.[78] Those characters that would assert a principle of innate superiority are revealed as curious anomalies in a world where conflict is mediated through the unseen agency of discursive institutions. Such is the pervasiveness of the Hanoverian ideal – power is most effective when it is represented as least visible – that the potential for discord is minimized from the very start.[79] Not even a passing, academic interest in violence is allowed to trouble Scott's curiously inert vision of successful government. In a particularly telling instance, Mr Oldbuck, the Antiquary of the title, speculates on one of his pet theories: the location of the final battle between the Romans and the Caledonians. Oldbuck is convinced that the conflict took place on land that is now part of his own property and produces archaeological 'evidence' in support of his argument. At the height of his 'ecstatic description' of the ancient fortifications, a voice breaks in to remind the enthusiast of the 'bigging o't' (p. 41). The professional mendicant Edie Ochiltree explains that the stone bearing the legend 'A. D. L. L' (*Agricola Dicavit Libens Lubens*) was planted by a stonemason a mere twenty years ago to commemorate 'auld Aiken Drum's bridal'. On this reading, then, 'A. D. L. L.' stands for 'Aiken Drum's Lang Ladle' and is a mere 'bourd' or joke.

Yet before we conclude that such prosaic disclosure effectively debunks the inflated claims of antiquarianism we should note that Ochiltree's version of the truth has no surer foundation than Oldbuck's (p. 42). What matters then is not the actual meaning of A. D. L. L. but the opportunity it provides for the puncturing of the integrity of a passionately held belief. Enthusiasm is the enemy of consensus, whether it is displayed in acts of political rebellion or in fervent attempts to refashion the past. Accordingly, comic deflation is welcomed for it serves as a reminder of the absurdity of conviction. The joke must be seen therefore as a conservative force, one that works to prevent unofficial knowledge from disturbing a consensus or 'folk' view of reality. And here make no mistake: the beggar does not operate in the service of truth. As Scott points out in the advertisement, the real demand of society is not for truth but for *'gude crack'* (p. 3). Thus *The Antiquary* describes a society where fiction circulates freely, in defiance of correspondence theories of truth but also, we should note, in ultimate compliance with the overarching wish to avoid bothersome disputes over such matters as history, religion, class and identity. Working on behalf of the agency of the letter, as it were, Ochiltree liberates fiction but only insofar as this serves the needs of a society where the desire for hostility is recognized only in symbolic or ritualized form, of which the joke itself is an obvious example.

If the wounded reaction of Oldbuck risks plunging the episode into sentimental bathos the effect is short-lived. This is a novel not of lost illusions but rather of illusions redeemed and rechannelled in the service of the state. It is therefore only a matter of time before the Antiquary is seen encouraging his protégé to write a 'history' of the illusory conflict:

> 'Let me see – What think you of a real epic? – The grand old-fashioned historical poem which moved through twelve or twenty-four books. We'll have it so – I'll supply you with a subject – The battle between Caledonians and Romans – The Caledoniad; or, Invasion Repelled. Let that be the title – it will suit the present taste, and you may throw in a touch of the times.'
> 'But the invasion of Agricola was not repelled,'
> 'No; but you are a poet – free of the corporation, and as little bound to truth or probability as Virgil himself – You may defeat the Romans in spite of Tacitus.'
>
> (p. 127)

Lovel's matter of factness notwithstanding, Oldbuck persists in his vision of a successful struggle against foreign invasion. For all his 'German boorishness' and 'pettifogging intimacy with dates, names and trifling matters of fact' (p. 53), the Antiquary's love of romance is stronger than his passion for truth. Ultimately his particular brand of enthusiasm may be cherished as it poses no serious threat to an order that has abandoned all notions of truth, principle, or genuine (as opposed to imaginary) interests. Moreover, there is every indication that such blind faith will serve the state well in mustering defence against foreign invasion, the threat of which transcends disputes over the nature of the relationship between truth and fiction.

Amazingly, for a novel set in the turbulent political climate of the 1790s, *The Antiquary* is unusually silent about the threat of dissent. Of particular interest is the treatment afforded rooted notions of national identity. Here again, the maintenance of a strong belief is positively encouraged, as its manifestly delusory nature requires no vigorous answer. To argue, as Oldbuck does with the irascible Highland soldier Hector M'Intyre, over the 'authenticity' of Macpherson's Ossian, is a notable instance of harmless, academic folly. Despite the Antiquary's provocative tone – 'and did you absolutely believe that stuff... to be really ancient, you simple boy?' – Hector stands firm: 'like many a sturdy Celt, he imagined the honour of his country and native language connected with the authenticity of these popular poems, and would have fought knee-deep, or forfeited life and land, rather than give up a line of them' (p. 280). Thus while Oldbuck is right to point out that Celticness is a literary invention of recent date and one perhaps nearing its end, Hector is allowed to continue in his fantasy because, along with his uncle, his obsession has no serious claim on his activity as a loyal member of the Hanoverian state.

The aspect of Hector's character that might be expected to run counter to the official message of the novel, namely his capacity for barbarism, is thus effectively consigned to the realm of theory. But if at times his violence appears to be on the verge of breaching the discursive limit, the novel is quick to ensure that order is restored. This is shown most clearly in the passage describing Hector's part in the attempt to rescue the financially embarrassed Wardour family. If these warders of the land are shown now to have fallen on harder, more commercial times, the fault would appear to be directed at modern systems of jurisprudence and, in particular, at their officious representatives:

> 'The legal officer, confronted with him of the military, grasped with one doubtful hand the greasy bludgeon which was to enforce his authority, and with the other produced his short official baton, tipped with silver, and having a movable ring upon it – 'Captain M'Intyre, – Sir, I have no quarrel with you, – but if you interrupt me in my duty, I will break the wand of peace and declare myself deforced.'
> And who the devil cares,' said Hector, totally ignorant of the words of judicial action, 'whether you declare yourself divorced or married? – And as to breaking the peace, or whatever you call it, all I know is, that I will break your bones if you prevent the lad from harnessing the horses to obey his mistress's orders.'
>
> (pp. 377–8)

The silver tipped baton with its movable ring provides an appropriately fatuous symbol of legalistic authority, one that barely conceals the 'greasy bludgeon' of physical coercion. But just when the scene looks likely to dissolve into an exchange of blows, Oldbuck reminds his nephew of the principle of respect for the law. Significantly, his explanation turns on a recollection of the events of 1745: the 'paltry concern of pounds, shillings, and pence' may have supplanted the 'accusation of high treason' (p. 383) as the prime punishable offence of modern times but the system of law provides a means of 'protecting... patrimonial rights' (p. 388). With Hector's ardour cooled by this urbane explanation of the place of the law, the potential for violence is left to wander in unexpected directions, the most apparent being the vulgar word play of '*phoca*'. Meaning 'seal' in Latin, the word is used by Oldbuck as a witty means of linking his nephew's most recent scrapes (the first with an aquatic mammal, the second with the seal of the law) and by Hector as a means of cursing the undefeated baton wielder: 'D—n the *phoca*, sir' (p. 378). As Oldbuck states subsequently, in a comment that sums up the central problem of the novel: 'the practice of the modern seems... the most prudential, though, I think, scarcely the most interesting' (p. 394).

The climax of *The Antiquarian* is, of course, famously anti-climatic. If Oldbuck's Caledoniad has prepared us for the vacuity of national triumph, then the final scene depicting the rallying of the community in its bid to defend itself against the coming invasion is fittingly empty. ' "The beacon, the beacon! – the French, the French! – murder, murder! – and waur than murder!" – cried the two handmaidens, like the chorus of an opera' (p. 400). This being a tale of our recent past, the fear of invasion is played out entirely as a matter of phobic delusion, itself a product of overzealousness and the desire for unanimity. But in a nation where claims to authenticity are shown to be obscure, groundless or fictional, the behaviour of the community at this time of alarm seems not only consistent but also laudable. Oldbuck calls for the sword which his father wielded in defence of the Hanoverians in '45; the impetuous M'Intyre is transformed into a calm and steady leader of men; 'the ancient military spirit of his house seemed to animate and invigorate the decayed frame of the Earl' (p. 403); even the displaced Edie Ochiltree proves his devotion to the land of his fathers by joining with the defenders. The 'courage and zeal which they had displayed' may have been 'entirely thrown away' but their actions provide 'an acceptable proof of their spirit and promptitude' (p. 404). If proof were needed that behind the petty squabbling over questions of truth and meaning there was indeed an authentic spirit of national unanimity then this has been supplied by the actions of the community in the face of its potential dissolution as, disburdened of their various symptoms – constitutional vagrancy (Ochiltree), an overenthusiastic wish to reconstruct the past in accordance with the demands of a system of antiquarianism (Oldbuck), a seemingly unbridled capacity for random acts of violence (M'Intyre), the sickness of mind and body as a result of the collapse of ancient privilege (the Earl) – the defenders act in accordance with the desires of the nation state.

It is the great lesson of *The Antiquary* that ultimate conformity to the state should be a consequence of war *in propentia* rather than war in actuality. In forgoing the romance of the 1740s, Scott seems to be suggesting that Waterloo has ushered in a new age of hyper self-consciousness where the dangers implicit in outmoded literary, political and nationalistic discourses may be channelled towards legitimate ends. Moreover, like a good postmodernist, he appears to endorse the idea that national allegiance is forged within entirely fictional parameters; at the end of the day does it matter if Hector's sense of identity is based on the works of a fabricated third-century poet? In this respect, *The Antiquary* provides an answer of sorts to the challenge posed by the Duke of Wellington: perhaps a few bits of novels can indeed function as one of the great departments of life, albeit a life purged of violent stimuli by the loss of Napoleon Bonaparte. If *The Antiquary* turns out to be the least successful of the initial Waverley trilogy (though contemporary critics were no less disenchanted with the disjointed *Guy Mannering*), then this may well be a consequence of the attempt to come to terms with this loss. With its scrupulous avoidance of actual physical conflict and its grudging acceptance of the 'protection' of legal and commercial discourse (the denouement provides the 'pacific' Lovel with a legitimate title (pp. 403–5) and Wardour with reimbursement), the novel is indeed a work of our maturity. Keats's comment that a certain passage in *Tom Jones* gave him more pleasure than 'the whole Novel of *The Antiquary*'[80] makes perfect sense in the light of this claim. For at the end of the day, what does the novel leave us with if not a sense of missed opportunities, a disappointment that violence no longer falls 'within the common order of things'?[81] In the aftermath of *The Field of Waterloo* could it be Scott's dubious distinction to have written a novel that reduces the trauma of an encounter with the Real to an instance of self-legislative bathos?

2
Exhibiting War: Battle Tours and Panoramas

> All about lay the melancholy remains of the clothes, accoutrements, books, and letters of the dead. The two last, after the internment, were spread over the field like the rubbish of a stationer's shop.
>
> James Simpson, *A Visit to Flanders in July, 1815*

> The quantities of letters and of blank sheets of dirty writing paper were so great that they literally whitened the surface of the earth.
>
> Charlotte Eaton, *Waterloo Days*[1]

Scott was not alone in his desire to see something of the real face of battle. Although his party set off from Brussels shortly after dawn, they found several other parties already on their journey to Waterloo. Typical of these sightseers were a group who called themselves 'the Brentford lads' – members of the lower professional or shopkeeping class who formed the greater mass of society to which the Duke of Wellington would eventually return. On arrival at Mont St Jean they contracted a guide and bought three pints of brandy and a quantity of snuff to block out the 'stench'. Their journey took them to La Belle Alliance where they fraternized with some women harvesters, close to where a man's leg lay in the stubble looking 'very fresh'. As Elizabeth Longford adds, the peasants 'looked even fresher, having made great sums from plunder. But dinner at the inn was dreadful: fat yellow bacon and almost raw meat. They could not help suspecting it had been cut off the dead bodies.' Two of the lads picked a finger each from a Frenchman's half-buried hand, to be taken home pickled in spirits: grisly souvenirs of a day at Waterloo.[2]

Longford's account of this trip offers a splendid insight into the class politics that continue to inflect contemporary attitudes to the battle.[3] Tourism, along with other leisure pursuits in the Regency period, provided opportunities for members of different classes to socialize in ways that would not be possible in conventional society. At Waterloo, a space was created that recalled the electric heyday of the great public gardens: Vauxhall, Kensington, St James's Park. Here members of the aristocracy mingled with the lower classes, viewing the same sights, participating in the same activities, sleeping and dining at the same inns, purchasing at the same 'mart'. It would, however, be wrong to suggest that such spaces did not contain their own form of class distinction. Even on the field of battle it was possible for visitors to engage in acts of social elevation, experiences that mimicked the real, underlying desires of class society. As illustration, we may consider a further extract from the letters of Sir Charles Bell:

> About half a mile of ascent brought us to the position of Bounaparte ... This is the highest ground in the Pays Bas. A noble expanse is before the eye, and the circumstance of the ground still imprinted with the tyrant's foot, the place where the aides-de-camp galloped to and fro, the whole extent of this important field under the eye, filled the imagination... I climbed up one of the pillars of the scaffolding [a trigonometrical tower, erected by the King of the Netherlands and widely (and erroneously) purported to be the vantage point of Napoleon; see Figure 6] ... The view magnificent, I was only one-third up the machine, yet it was a giddy height. Here Bounaparte stood surveying the field. What name for him but – Macbeth, a man who stands alone! There is something magnificent in this idea; then, exalted to a giddy height; and how much further to fall than to the ground? his friends dispersed, his squadrons broken, all in deroute; and well he knew – for he seems to know mankind well – he knew the consequence... This position of Bounaparte is most excellent; the machine has been placed by the side of the road, but he ordered it to be shifted. The shifting of this scaffold shows sufficiently the power of confidence and resolution of the man. It is about sixty feet in height. I climbed upon it four times the length of my body, by exact measurement, and this was only the first stage. I was filled with admiration of a man of his habit of life, who could stand perched on a height of sixty-five feet above everything, and contemplate, see, and manage such a scene. Already silence dwells here; for although it is midday, and the sun bright and all shining in gladness, yet there is a mournful silence contrasted with the scene which has been so recently acting. No living thing is here – no kites, no birds of any kind; nothing but a few wretched women and old men, scattered on a height at a distance, and who are employed in gathering balls.[4]

The scaffold afforded Bell with an opportunity to indulge in a Napoleonic fantasy of command: to stand in the very place where 'the scourge of Europe' contemplated and managed the partial scenes of reality. As the surgeon's eye monitors the field in a vast panoramic sweep, the dissonant presence of labouring wretches and 'horrid smells' is exchanged for an

Exhibiting War: Battle Tours and Panoramas 69

Figure 6 Unattributed, *Bonaparte's Observatory, To View the Battle of Waterloo, June 18, 1815*, engraving, London 1819

illusory ideological totality. And the point of this description is precisely to expose this fantasy: Bell's elevation, like that of Napoleon, Macbeth, or Satan is predicated on the inevitability of a baleful descent to the material world of wounds, wrecks and Brentford lads (Figure 7).

Figure 7 J. C. Stadler, after E. Walsh, *La Belle Alliance, taken on the Spot, June 25th*, hand coloured aquatint, London 1815

The ascent of Napoleon's scaffold also forms the core of an unnamed 'gentleman's diary'. Visiting the field on 16 July 1815, the diarist records how he climbed the Imperial observatory to nail 'the Royal Arms of Great Britain on the pinnacle'.[5] The gesture is striking, not only as a symbol of the popular appropriation of Waterloo but also as an act of Napoleonic usurpation; like Bell the gentleman allows himself to be subtly Napoleonized. Yet in moving from this vantage point to consider the field at closer range, the gentleman encounters an altogether different view of war, a position that comes uncomfortably close to exposing the difference between the actuality of violence and its more pleasurable representation:

> Returned [from a visit to a hospital] witnessing a shocking sight, i.e. the dead drawn along by fishhooks. They were going to be buried in the fields, by the peasants.
>
> 20 July
>
> Met wagons full of wounded, crying out from extreme suffering. The water every where quite red... swarms of carrion flies, preying on the carcasses of the horses which still lie unburied.
>
> 21 July

[passes] 40 wagons of wounded crying out; and not able to be moved before; many died instantly; others were in a putrid state – a kind of living death!
25 July

(Booth's *Battle of Waterloo*, pp. 122–3)

Since the vast majority of visitors to the field would have surveyed a radically altered prospect to the one described here, we should attend to the structural function of these extracts. For what is genuinely remarkable about this text, apart from the insight it provides into the pain and suffering of war, is the fact that it is presented as part of a gentleman's excursion. As subsequent passages demonstrate, observations of carnage are on a par with details of where the man dined and the quality of the rooms where he slept. Before we rush to conclude, therefore, that the encounter with the materiality of the field qualifies the elevated perspective of the tower we should recall that tourism is itself a structure of being, one that is specifically geared towards the avoidance of permanent shock, whether this comes from the meeting with undesirable facets of class or from the repellent matter of the body.

We will return to the political significance of Napoleonic or Imperial vision later on in this chapter. For now I want to relate the discourse of battle tourism to specific 'ways of seeing', modes of visual comprehension that condition the subject to regard the battle, and its outcome, as a sublime object of ideology. As the epigrams to this chapter suggest, there is a sense in which visitors to Waterloo *always already* perceive the field as a locus of textual significance. Our focus will fall, therefore, on the means by which the scattered fragments of battle take shape within the visitor's authentic account. We will then go on to consider how the discourse of tourism was translated into the domestic sphere by focusing on the example of the Panorama exhibition: a vast 360-degree painting housed in a purpose-built rotunda. The desideratum that Waterloo should appear to its public as a visual totality, impervious to the partial gaze of radical critique, was, as it were, literally built into the encompassing form of the Panorama. Its most obvious analogue is with the Panopticon, the carceral apparatus that Foucault cites as a paradigm of disciplinary space. Drawing on Foucault's model – but only in order to supersede it – we shall look closely at how the viewing subject is fashioned into a willing participant in the universal, totalizing rhetoric of postwar imperial expansion.

The regimented gaze

In total contrast to the Argus-like perspectives of the tower, Waterloo was experienced by the majority of its combatants as a fragmented collocation of narrow vistas in which the sensation of blindness was paramount. To the soldiers on the ground, the battle was shrouded in mist and gun smoke; views were limited, often to no more than a few yards, by tall grains and grasses and by the fact that for long stretches of time, troops were concealed behind opposing ridges and were thus unable to witness events taking place a few hundred yards in front of them. The sense of visual obscurity is central to Cavalié Mercer's experience of the battle:

> Of what was transacting in the front of the battle we could see nothing, because the ridge on which our first line was posted was much higher than the ground we occupied. Of that line itself we could see only the few squares of infantry immediately next to us, with the intervening batteries. From time to time bodies of cavalry swept over the summit between the squares, and, dispersing on the reverse of the position, vanished again, I know not how.[6]

In the field itself, according to Llewellyn of the 28th, the crops of wheat and rye were so high 'that...the Enemy, even in attacking our squares, were obliged to make a daring person desperately ride forward to plant a flag, as a mark, at the very point of our bayonets'. This physical circumstance, together with the smoke from rifle and cannon, not only decreased visibility but it also distorted vision. To Cathcart, one of Wellington's ADCs, the French Imperial Guard appeared as 'black looking columns', which 'loomed through smoke and fog'; to the men of the 1st British Guards, the enemy Guardsmen resembled 'a corps of giants'.[7] No one, it seems, with the possible exception of those who commanded the vantage points on the opposing ridges, could possibly have surveyed the entirety of the field. Strategies and tactics were more often based on informed guesswork; their outcome was frequently decided by chance.

In stark contrast to the opaque, muffled visions of the day, Waterloo entered British culture bathed in light.[8] From historical narratives to guide books, and from poems to prints, the battle was represented to its public as a coherent whole. Intricate maps of the field, displaying the decisive formations of the day, proved to be extremely popular. Of these, the most authoritative was undoubtedly the 'detailed plan' executed by W. M. Craan, the official mapmaker of the King of the Netherlands whose trigonometrical tower had played such a large part in Napoleon's fortunes. Craan's map was notable both 'for the accuracy of its detail, and for the exact positions and respective movements it describes of every regiment during the day'.[9] Readers were thus able to orientate themselves in relation to a truth that could be described as objective and neutral but that was in fact based upon the fictitious view of an ideal observer. In this sense the map did more than simply name, recount and locate. In its assumption of an ideal I/eye it also operated as a form of territorial discourse, reproducing political imperatives in the guise of scientific disinterestedness. The 'silent lines' of Craan's plan encouraged readers to locate themselves above the chaos and confusion of battle and thus to consume the field as (to adopt Foucault's terminology) an object of knowledge/power.[10]

The transformation of the opacity of battle into the clarity and 'sense' of national victory was most fully realized, however, in the expanding field of postwar tourism. When, in the aftermath of the victory, British tourists began to pay homage to the field, they took with them copies of Campbell's *Guide to the Netherlands* (1815), Craan's map and, later, Booth's *Battle of Waterloo* (1815). As we noted in the previous chapter, the 'pilgrimage' to the site of Britain's triumph over Napoleon presented its participants with numerous opportunities for picturesque reflection, a mode that was extended to the visitor's perception of the field of battle. The restorative effects of such pilgrimages are pointed out in the introduction to Murray's *Handbook for Travellers in Holland and Belgium*, a guide popular in the Victorian period. Quoting from Samuel Rogers, the book encourages its readers to perceive themselves as beings who are able to 'proceed' and pass over the 'slightest circumstances' in a way that avoids the ego-fixations of an encounter with the tragic and the Sublime, the cognitive states most readily associated with the aftermath of a great battle:

> [on a tour] All is new and strange. We surrender ourselves, and feel once again as children. Like them, we enjoy eagerly; like them, when we fret, we fret only for the moment: and here the resemblance is very remarkable; for if a journey has its pains as well as its pleasures (and there is nothing unmixed in the world), the pains are no sooner over than they are forgotten, while the pleasures live long in the memory.[11]

The most distinguishing feature of this way of seeing is not immobility but, as Raimondo Modiano puts it, 'infinite mobility'.[12] For just as the map allows the subject to 'read' space as a transparent totality, so the tour confronts the observer with a multiplicity of objects, none of which is allowed to arrest the progress of the eye. Filled with a continuous stream of ideas and objects, the mind, as Murray conceives it, selects only those images that induce a feeling of pleasure: 'Our benevolence extends itself with our knowledge. And must we not return better citizens than we went?' (p. 11). So the cultivated leisure of the tourist is profitable after all. Just as, in Lacanian theory, the subject represses the truth of its lack of being by sliding across a chain of signifiers so, in the discourse of tourism, the pleasures of passing, of glancing over select views and striking vistas, enable the subject to gain knowledge and to become a better participant in his government and culture.

If the discourse of the picturesque added a further dimension to the tour, one might assume that its role in the construction of being would be severely compromised by its contact with the unpleasant traces of war. How, after all, is the tourist expected to convert a space of painful significance into a space of significant pleasure? But the guides effected this conversion with remarkable ease, as the extract from the gentleman's diary, reprinted in Booth's guide, effortlessly displays. Apparently free, the eye of the tourist lent itself well to discourses seeking to condition the subject into a 'detached' or 'objective' view of the field of conflict. By passing over the horrors of war, comparing what had passed with what was now present, the rhetoric of the battle guide succeeded in filtering out violent or arresting imagery. As one 'J. W.' noted in the *Quarterly Review* (quoted in Murray), 'A man must carry knowledge with him, if he would bring home knowledge' (p. 11). Using Booth as a primer, this is precisely what the visitor to the field achieved: the importation of civic codes of understanding facilitated the transformation of pain into pleasure and cultivated leisure into sober industry.

On the visual plane, this labour was continued in the form of a foldout panoramic sketch. Stitched into the binding of Booth's guide, the sketch allowed the tourist to compare the scene before them with a fully annotated 360-degree representation: 'Every house, every bush, every tree, every undulation is distinctly copied from nature. There is not a spot on which the eye can rest, that was not immortalized by some heroic deed of British valour' (p. 19). By folding the two plates together (A joining to A, and B joining to B), the viewer is able to form a 'complete circle or panoramic view of the field of battle' (ibid.), one that perfects an otherwise empty sequence of gaps, breaks and partial views. Seen *in toto* we may begin to apprehend more closely the disciplinary function of this device. Recalling Alan Liu's reading of the politics of the picturesque, what may at first strike us as 'emancipation from discipline' turns out, after all, to be secretly dependent on a roll-call of rules, protocols and commands.[13] Taken to its logical extreme, the visitor in possession of Murray's guide is shunted along a closely choreographed sequence of viewing positions: 'Leave your carriage at the H. du Musee; ascend Mound; walk down to the main road...The Mound of the Belgic Lion is by far the best station for surveying the field' (pp. 170–1). In this 1888 version of the battle tour, the rendering of Waterloo into a meaningful sequence of historicized *topoi* places the subject in a relationship with the truth of post-revolutionary, post-Imperial time. To enforce this position, Booth's guide supplements its panoramic view with a set of detailed historical annotations. As well as providing official knowledge about the conflict, the annotations condition the eye to 'rest' on distinct 'spots' of time. The views depicted in the sketch are thus underwritten by a text that shuts off the potential for dissident readings of the field. Through an act of visual regimentation, the infinite mobility of the tourist's gaze is subjected to specific material constraints; the ground is purged of its connections with arresting images of pain and suffering and is transformed into a site of individual and national resubstantiation.

As the above examples show, the disciplining of the English eye is a major contributing factor in the making of Waterloo. In its initial phase, however, the project was qualified by a troubling disjunction between the visual ideal of the battle and its prosaic actuality. One of the earliest guides to encounter this problem was Charles Campbell's *Guide Through Belgium and Holland*. First advertised in July 1815, the second edition (published in 1817) introduced its readers to the notion that

> Waterloo has become a kind of pilgrimage ... there is scarcely an interval of ground between that place and Brussels which is not consecrated by some event or circumstance of a tendency more or less to interest the feelings of the observer. And, yet, Waterloo, thus immortalized is nothing more than a long straggling, and rather a mean village, about nine miles from Brussels, on the road to Namur and Charleroi.[14]

The task that many travellers faced therefore was the reconciliation of competing forces: on the one hand the fact that Waterloo lacked geographical distinction and was therefore unpicturesque; on the other that it had taken on symbolic significance as the place where legitimacy had triumphed over anarchy and despotism. The references to pilgrimage and consecration, derived from Robert Southey's poem *The Poet's Pilgrimage to Waterloo* (examined in Chapter 3), helped to negotiate this passage. Defined as sacred space, the hitherto unregarded prospect of Waterloo was transformed into a locus of triumphal significance.

Yet even as the rhetoric of pilgrimage allowed the traveller to glide over the 'mean' qualities of the site, certain aspects of the field were to remain stubbornly resistant to aesthetic appropriation, as Charlotte Eaton – the unacknowledged 'author' of Booth's guide – discovered:

> On the top of the ridge in front of the British position, on the left of the road, we traced a long line of tremendous graves, or rather pits, into which hundreds of dead had been thrown as they had fallen in their ranks, without yielding an inch of ground. The effluvia which arose from them, even beneath the open canopy of heaven was horrible; and the pure west wind of summer, as it passed us, seemed pestiferous, so deadly was the smell that in many places pervaded the field. The fresh-turned clay which covered those pits betrayed how recent had been their formation. From one of them the scanty clods of earth which had covered it had in one place fallen, and the skeleton of a human face was visible. I turned from the spot in indescribable horror, and with a sensation of deadly faintness which I could scarcely overcome.

> While I loitered behind the rest of the party, searching among the corn for some relics worthy of preservation, I beheld a human hand, almost reduced to a skeleton, outstretched above the ground, as if it had raised itself from the grave. My blood ran cold with horror, and for some

moments I stood rooted to the spot, unable to take my eyes from this dreadful object, or to move away...[15]

Here, at last – or so it would seem – a writer is brought to the point where understanding and signification fail, the point where, at last, the horror of Waterloo is actually *felt*. At a more cynical level, the moment may be viewed as a preprogrammed disruption, a gothic intrusion built into the psychic economy of the picturesque. Thus, rather than collapsing the account of Waterloo, the skeletal hand seems to upbraid the narrator for lapsing into the habits of a commonplace tourist. To re-establish her sense of commanding identity – to present herself once more as a pilgrim – the writer must therefore survey the field from an elevated perspective – free, that is, from the residual traces of commercial ways of seeing, the attitude most readily associated with 'the Brentford lad'. The problem, however, is that the escape from the inauthentic activity of the tourist can only be achieved by way of the very discourse that Eaton seeks to resist. It is therefore the picturesque that supplies the subject with appropriate models of self-determination and with symbolic strategies for evading the encounter with trauma. To this end what could be better or more appropriate than the so-called 'Wellington tree' – the 'immortal' elm from which the Duke was supposed to have commanded the decisive events of the battle? From this nodal point the viewer is able to regain a sense of visual and moral stability. Just as the panoramic sketch, devised by Eaton's sister Jane, had conditioned the viewer to look, as it were, through the 'eagle-like' eyes of Wellington, so the reader is encouraged to perceive the battle as a unified event, no longer subjected to the fragmentary forms of violent actuality.[16] The success of this visual strategy is manifest: so much so that by the end of the *Waterloo Days*, Eaton's sublime inarticulacy at the dehumanizing effects of mass graves and ash piles has been transformed into sublime appreciation for the individual's contribution to the greater good: 'Every private soldier acted like a hero, and thus individual merit was lost in the general excellence, as the beams of stars are undistinguished in the universal blaze of day' (p. 156).

Among the most significant instances of this mythologizing tendency is the moment when Eaton gains her first panoramic view of the field. Like many observers, she notes a feeling of inarticulacy in the face of the sublime: 'we suddenly stopped – we stood rooted to the spot – we gazed around us in silence; for the emotions that at this moment swelled our hearts were too deep for utterance – we felt that we stood on the field of battle!' (p. 127). From here it is possible to reinvent the battle as an object of imaginative as opposed to rational contemplation. Eaton, of course, was not alone in responding to the field in this manner. From Southey to Scott and from Byron to Croker, all the evidence suggests that most travellers to Waterloo experienced some form of 'strong emotion'. John Scott, who visited the field in the summer of 1815, wrote that the first view of the field 'throws' the observer out of 'his ordinary habits of mind... The great cause of excitement, however, lies in his being on the point of converting into a visible reality what had previously existed in his mind as a shadowy, uncertain, but awful fancy.'[17] The following narrative veers between pathos – at the contrast between the quiet simplicity of the unmarked graves and the devastation from which they derive – and sublime excitement. Thus the village of Waterloo is 'dull' and 'obscure'; the battle, by contrast, is impressive and 'famous' (pp. 205–6). Like Eaton, the crucial moment for Scott occurs on the top of Mont St Jean: 'The ascent is easy: you reach the top unexpectedly, and the whole field of battle is then at once before the eye. Its sudden burst has the effect of a shock, and few, I believe, are found to put any question for the first five minutes.' Scott's pleasing pain is salved by the sight of an 'old picturesque tree' (p. 209). Not surprisingly this is the 'Wellington tree'. As an object of picturesque interest it serves to free the mind from its fixation and to place it within a regimented order of seeing. In visual terms, the eye is directed towards the investigation of surface details: the marks of grape and musket shot; the splintered bark and branches. And as with other accounts of the tree, it is used not only to anchor the subject as the apex of a conic field of vision ('the tree... denotes the centre of our position'), but also as an image of fortitude and endurance. For although the tree is damaged, it still retains

> the vitality of its growth, and will, probably, for many years, be the first saluting sign to our children, who, with feelings of a sacred cast, come to gaze on this theatre of our ancestor's deeds... this venerable tree will remain, a long survivor of the grand battle in which it is no slight sufferer, – a monument of its circumstances, – a conspicuous mark to denote and to impress.
> (John Scott, *Paris Revisited*, p. 209)

Scott has no difficulty in reconciling the cataloguing of destruction with the concept of sublimity: 'I would set him down, at once, as either diseased or dull, who would object, either in the tone of humanity or philosophy, to the gross exhibitions of these scenes.' For Scott, such scenes can work to reinforce the moral health of the witness: 'the external phenomenon is often grand, when the cause is dark and pestilential: – the effects in those who are influenced belong to the highest order of poetry.' And further: 'What genius can do for some by its exertions in literature and art – a battle can do for all, – namely strengthen the action of the faculties, widen the sphere of the sympathies, and encrease the ardour of the passions.' Finally, 'there is on these occasions a grand community of soul, pervading multitudes, who, in all common cases, and on all common subjects, have scarcely a point of contact, or a clue to sympathy' (pp. 224–5). War, in other words, is analogous to the work of art – insofar as it facilitates the extension of our sympathies and the honing of our faculties. But even as war mirrors the structure of aesthetic relations, its significance supersedes that of a painting or a poem. The appeal of a great victory exceeds the consensus values involved in a mere judgement of taste, binding the individual to the nation as a link in an indissoluble chain.

Crucial to all the accounts examined here is the way in which trauma – the meeting with the fragmented body of Waterloo – is built into the experience of pilgrimage. The efforts on the part of Eaton and Scott to elevate themselves above the sickening encounter is, in truth, but one aspect of a wider process, what Freud, in *Beyond the Pleasure Principle*, calls the *organization* of negative experience. The movement from ash pit to assent, hand to height, commerce to communion, thus mimics the subject's dalliance with the death instinct, the little piece of negation that underlies the pleasure principle. By organizing the contact with death into predictable, repetitive patterns the visitor to Waterloo and, by extension, the nation state, gains the illusion of mastery and control over a process that, as ultimate real, is beyond incorporation.[18]

Unlimiting the bounds of painting

Let us pause for a moment to take stock. So far in this study we have noted the extent to which the conceptualization of the Hundred Days as Sublime threatened to convert the linear sense of history into a loose constellation of powers. We have also considered the way in which the shock of this dark upheaval was converted into divinely sanctioned peripeteia. By a process of retrospective narration, Waterloo was rapidly conceived as the long-awaited end; the dissonance of the escape from Elba was 'answered' by the consonance of this grand finale. A related structure of being is evident in the battle tour: in Booth, Campbell, Eaton and John Scott, the subject, to echo Alan Liu, is encouraged to compose the field as a 'single, coherent picture washed by consciousness in which nurturing and chastising, beautiful and sublime elements complement...each other'. Only in such a view of Waterloo 'where all chastisement is born with an awareness of consolation can the sublime transcend mere horror'.[19] Nothing, in other words, is allowed to disturb the harmonious correlation of beauty and sublimity. With the Panoramic screen in place, everything is subordinated to the tourist's circumambient gaze.

To introduce this discussion of the fixed or domestic Panorama I would like to turn to the experience of a more recent chronicler, a witness who brings us face to face, as it were, with the ideological import of this totalizing view:

> A panorama of the battle of Waterloo, painted by the French artist, L. Dumoulin in 1912, can still be seen on the battlefield today. By entering

a round building visitors can experience what it must have been like to have been there on that day, 18 June 1815, in the midst of the cavalry charges and hand-to-hand fighting, wounded horses and dying men.[20]

This is a large claim to make for a battle painting. Like Craan's detailed plan, it blithely assumes that the totality of historical experiences can be recreated in the sphere of aesthetic practice. But if it troubles our sense of decorum, is that because it violates our sense of the primacy of the event or our understanding of the limits of art? The art historian, A. D. Cameron, whose words I have quoted, seems quite secure in his approbation of the importance of this work and its site:

> The victory the allies won at Waterloo was significant because, in bringing a long war to a close, it marked the downfall of Napoleon as Emperor of France and the end of French dominance in Europe. Such a triumph for a British commander, the Duke of Wellington, with British soldiers playing so large a part, produced in Britain, regardless of the high number of casualties, a mood of national euphoria.
> (A. D. Cameron, *The Man Who Loved to Draw Horses*, p. 27)

Rephrased, panoramic art, even French panoramic art, replicates for the British viewer a sense of 'national euphoria', *regardless* of the 'hand-to-hand fighting, wounded horses and dying men' (ibid.). There is, of course, a paradox here: that a picture so replete with images of carnage and suffering should instil, in spite of everything, a sensation that sublimates the visible record it places before us. Yet this is precisely the effect the Panorama creates: a binding of wayward death instincts to the cause of individual and national preservation. And here again, lest this reading seem remote from the material culture of the immediate postwar years, it is worth recalling the words of orator Lewis: 'THE VICTORY OF WATERLOO!... has alternately thrilled with rapture and with pain your patriotic bosoms.'[21] It is precisely as a mechanism for alternating pleasure and pain, mastery and loss, that the Panorama should be judged. With this idea in mind let us look more closely at the Panorama.

According to the materialist art critic, Norman Bryson, the ability to respond to an image 'presupposes competence within social, that is socially constructed codes of recognition'.[22] A painting, in other words, is recognized before it is perceived; to understand a painting as a painting presupposes that the subject is conversant with the dominant visual codes available in a given society at a given time. Although I shall have reason to modify Bryson's sociological account in due course, this seems a useful model for addressing the terms in which the totalizing gaze was produced and consumed in the period. The sheer scale of the canvases displayed in the Panorama may be assessed, on one level, as a development of the vogue for gargantuism in Romantic art. Throughout the Napoleonic period, painters experimented with excessive scale as a means of conveying the sublimity of their themes. In 1814, for example, Benjamin West celebrated the defeat of Napoleon with *Christ Rejected by Caiphos*, a huge work measuring over 38 feet long.[23] Following Waterloo the British Institution, set up to promote contemporary art in opposition to the dominant Royal Academy, offered £1000 for a canvas representing Waterloo in an allegorical spirit. The intended work was to measure no less than 16 feet by 10 feet. The prize went to James Ward, and the finished painting, which took almost six years to complete, was over twice this size.[24] Ten years later a Waterloo picture by Fleming Pieneman was so large that, when taken to London, it had to be displayed in a makeshift housing in Hyde Park.[25] As the capital grew in size, so artists took upon themselves the task of representing a world in the throws of exponential growth. In idealist terms, the Sublime in painting exemplified the power of human understanding to synthesize the discrepancy between reason and imagination, swelling the mind to accommodate the vastness within and without. As I mentioned in the introduction, the grand import of Waterloo often exceeded the creative powers of the artist: the tragi-comic endeavours of Ward are a case in point. For the canvas to succeed in awakening the mind to the sublimity of its object, it was apparent that something more than unprecedented size would be required. For such a picture to work, it would have to erase the boundary between world and frame. This, in short, was the ambitious, one might say impossible, project of the Panorama painter.

The psychological effects of the massive in painting have been well documented, more often than not by reference to a perceptualist account of the relationship between an abstract 'viewer' and the isolated perceptual field of the painter. But taking Bryson's thesis into account we should look carefully at the avowed aims of the Panoramists; by doing so we will be in a better position to judge the political significance of their works.

From its origins in the late 1780s the Panorama was conceived primarily as a means to 'unlimit the bounds of painting'.[26] Yet, from the start, its inventor Robert Barker was to meet fierce resistance to his claims. High Art, as Reynolds, West and Constable insisted, was the domain of truth and authority; by contrast, the Panorama was dismissed as 'unsatisfactory' and 'unpleasant': 'it is without the pale of Art because its object is deception.'[27] The elevated regard of 'High Art' bore no relation to the frivolous gawping of this new form. Like Turner, who experienced similar opposition for his genre-breaking painting *The Field of Waterloo*, the work of the panoramists, if 'true', could not be considered as art. To repel this challenge, Barker placed strong emphasis on the social utility of his work:

> Mr Barker Begs to mention, that as his improvement is genuine and pointed, it may not be understood as an Exhibition merely for emolu-

ment, but being the result of a minute investigation of the principles of art, it is intended chiefly for the criticism of artists, and admirers of painting in general.[28]

If the profit-making invention would not be accepted in the Academy, it could at least be legitimated under the signs of knowledge and experience. Thus, in 1801, Barker announced that he was 'determined to spare no expense or trouble to bring forward scenes of useful information, as well as gratifying amusement; and the public may expect to have the most interesting Views and the most noticed cities in Europe, in due time, laid before them'.[29]

A series of notable cities and sites were to follow: from Paris to Copenhagen and from Lisbon to St Petersburg, all with the express purpose of satisfying the public demand for visual information. Enthusiasts would even claim that the exhibition could provide a substitute for travel, offering not only a vivid impression of a distant scene but also 'an almost palpable sense of its reality'.[30] Thus, for a critic writing in *The Times*: 'There are aspects of soil and climate which... in great panoramas such as those of Mr. Burford, are conveyed to the mind with a completeness and truthfulness not always to be gained from a visit to the scene itself.'[31] In this way the Panorama exemplified a key facet of modern society: the transformation of the differential world of social or lived space into the homogenizing, spectacular form of the commodity. As a writer in *Blackwood's Magazine* explains in 1824, with disarming candour:

> Panoramas are among the happiest contrivances for saving time and expense in this age of contrivances. What cost a couple of hundred pounds and half a year half a century ago, now costs a shilling and a quarter of an hour.

The experience, moreover, can be even better than the real thing, if not the real thing itself:

> There is no exaggeration in talking of those things [the things in the panorama] as really existing... if we have not the waters of the Lake of Geneva, and the bricks and mortar of the little Greek town, tangible by our hands, we have them tangible by the eye – the fullest impression that could be purchased ...[32]

For the *Blackwood's* writer 'visual space', is rendered the property of the individual detached observer. Whether the viewer is confronted with the sight of Edinburgh, London, Athens or Rome, the idea is that space can be consumed in a single gaze. There is here, and I am thinking specifically of David Harvey's account of time-space compression, a connection between 'the accumulation of wealth, power, and capital' and the individual's 'knowledge of, and... command over, space'.[33] As *Blackwood's* puts it: 'the fullest impression that could be purchased' by the eye. By consuming a representation of Milan, Windsor or Paris, so the theory went, the public could exercise a form of symbolic 'command'.

The emphasis on control and assimilation ought, however, to be weighed alongside the very specific sense in which Panoramas functioned as aesthetic experiences. At a very simple level, the experience of stepping inside a Panorama exhibition is very different to that of gazing at a painting in a gallery. As Don Slater reminds us, such exhibitions 'were not so much representations as simulations: spaces of absorbing virtuality' in which 'people paid for a re-creation of the real, not simply a picture of it.'[34] Thus, whether the subject was the Battle of the Nile or Copenhagen in 1801, Trafalgar in 1805 or Waterloo in 1815, in each case the aim was to make the audience 'feel as if on the very spot' or, as an advertisement for 'Lord Howe's Victory' promised, to place the viewer 'on the open sea, in the centre of both fleets'.[35] In the views of foreign cities, in particular, the audience was as infatuated with impressive effects and picturesque detail as with the gathering of knowledge. A representative view is given in this extract from a review in the *Repository of Arts*:

> The first sensation experienced by the spectator on entering this panorama [a view of the Polar regions], is one of extreme surprise at the novelty of the scene, which his eye for the first time traces; and he feels, as it were, a sort of chilliness, a congelation of the blood, at beholding the icy and tempestuous regions by which he is surrounded.[36]

To fulfil the public's desire to efface the distinction between world and representation, the inventors of the Panorama went to great lengths to conceal their artistry. Robert Barker's patent, taken out in 1787, specifies that the illusion should be maintained by means of railings and 'interceptions' to block the view of the top and bottom edge of the painting. Great emphasis is placed on effective soundproofing, lighting and ventilation. A raised platform and rail prevent the viewer from getting too close to the canvas. As Scott B. Wilcox notes, all terms of comparison by which the eye could perceive the difference between representation and reality are to be excluded. In a sense, the ultimate aim of Panorama technology was self-effacement. Paradoxically, as Slater adds, the more technology asserted its power over the world, the more it strove to conceal its own existence, in much the same way as ideology seeks to maintain its grip on 'reality'. For the illusion of omnivoyance to work, and for the object to appear as real, the subject would have to be prevented from perceiving the fiction on which the experience of 'reality' is based. Due to the limitations of early nineteenth-century technology, such preventative measures proved short-lived, however;

before long the audience became aware of the mechanisms sustaining their illusion and 'nature at a glance' could be seen for what it was: a commercial diversion of limited durability. Yet even supposing that members of the public were fully aware of the limitations of their experience, this knowledge does not change for one moment the fact that what the public desires is something to fulfil this lack. Like space, the empty subject of ideology cannot tolerate a vacuum; what it desires is greater than what it is content to 'know'. But the Panorama, precisely because it is a representation of reality and not reality itself, ends up merely confirming the terms by which the subject is duped. And once this particular 'fact' is known the subject sets off, once again, in search of the signifier that will stitch up this inconsistency. Hence the sense in which the Panorama experience adapted itself to serialization, as if by mere repetition the patrons and their public could regulate their encounter with the void of reality. It is with this idea in mind that I would like to consider the political ontology of Barker's Waterloo panorama of 1815.

'The perfect disciplinary apparatus'

Of the military Panoramas, many distinguished patrons (Nelson and Wellington were frequent visitors), Napoleon was among the first to recognize its propaganda potential. Having witnessed an exhibition on the boulevard de Capucines, 'Napoleon engaged the architect Celerier to draw up plans for eight rotundas to be erected in the great square on the Champs Elysees; in each, one of the great battles of the Revolution or Empire was to be shown.'[37] The commission was never completed; the defeat in Russia put paid to this dream. In England, where the effectiveness of this propaganda machine was more fully realized, the Allied victory was an obvious subject for panoramic representation. From as early as July 1815, plans were afoot for a variety of static and travelling panoramic exhibitions, designed for the sole purpose of pleasing and instructing the public in the truth of Wellington's great victory. Before such works could be realized, however, it was incumbent upon the exhibitors to offer their patrons a suitable stopgap. To fulfil this requirement, Barker's Leicester Square rotunda extended its presentation of 'The Battle of Paris' and 'A Panorama of Elba'. As Henry Aston Barker joined the Waterloo trail to survey the field and compose his preliminary sketches, the London public acquainted themselves with his representation of the peripeteiac events of 1814.[38] 'The Battle of Waterloo', described by *The Times* as 'a magnificent view of the Battle of Waterloo at the moment of Victory, painted on the largest scale' was first shown in the Large Circle of the Leicester Square Panorama (Figure 8) from about 13 March 1816 to May 1818.[39] It was re-exhibited (or a new version exhibited) from October 1820 to May 1821. Thereafter, the painting was displayed from 22 March 1842 to 18 February 1843 and again from 17 November 1852 to 12 March 1853. The

84 *Waterloo and the Romantic Imagination*

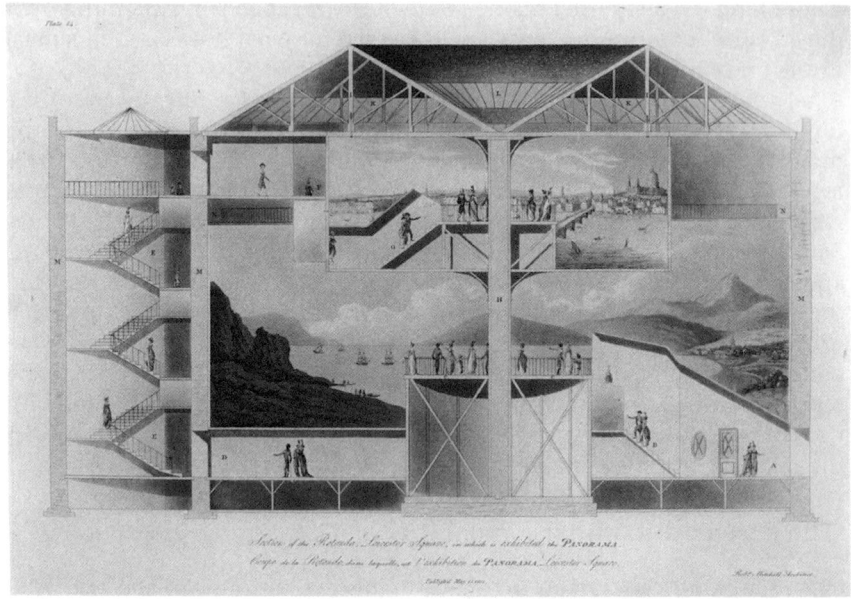

Figure 8 Robert Mitchell, *A Section of the Rotunda, Leicester Square*, coloured aquatint with etching and engraving, London 1801

exhibition was, by all accounts, a tremendous success – so much so that Barker was able to retire on its profits. Other Waterloo Panoramas were to follow, with exhibitors continuously revamping their works to prolong their share of the market. In 1820, for instance, to commemorate the fifth anniversary of the victory, the entrepreneur Peter Marshall exhibited a 'Historical Peristrephic [revolving] Panorama' by H. A. Barker and J. Burford of Ligny, Quatre Bras and Waterloo. Together with a full military band, state-of-the-art lighting, pyrotechnics and other technological effects, the audiences were treated to a revolving display of the main incidents of the battles. As the band played *See the Conquering Hero*, the charge against the French and the appearance of Wellington were met with a rousing chorus of cheers. Most bizarre of all, in Glasgow in 1825, war veterans were offered free admission to celebrate the tenth anniversary of the battle and were requested to come wearing their medals, little realizing that they too had become 'part of the show'.[40]

The sense of 'theatricalization' that Gillian Russell identifies as a key facet of English society during the French wars is especially evident in such examples and, indeed, it might be appropriate to read the Panorama as a form of theatre: a demonstration of the reflexivity of social and military dramatization. What interests me most about the exhibition, however, is the way in which dramatic protocols, such as the relation between audience and spectacle, forum and stage, are apparently subverted. Consider, first of all, the political implications of the move from representation to recreation, or to adopt the contemporary argot, from reality to *virtuality*. If we accept the notion that the Panorama challenged both the hierarchy of genres and the concept of aesthetic distinction (by attempting to negate the visual and ideological function of the frame) then I think it is possible to see the patrons' voracious appetite for the Panorama as part and parcel of a more radical desire for social transformation.

Earlier on I mentioned the democratizing potential of post-battle tourism. In the light of this argument, I would suggest that the Panorama acted in a similar way by encouraging its public to regard themselves as participants in a common experience of visualization. At once a part of society while simultaneously presenting itself as the whole of society, the Panorama achieved uniformity at a number of levels: both in terms of the public it attracted – from the respectable middle-classes, to wealthy loungers – and in the more unsettling area of visual subjectification, the idea being that if all could be seen then all could be the same. In many respects, therefore, the exhibition was a model of the 'spectacular reorganization of power', redrawing the boundaries between social classes as divisions between those who engaged in visual unification and those who did not. But here again, we should note the illusory aspect of the Panorama. What took place within the rotunda was not so much a restructuring of class positions as a form of virtual emancipation, one that temporarily suspended the 'vertical' gradations of society so as to confirm, all the more effectively, their role in the world without.[41]

What is staged in the Panorama, therefore, is nothing less than the spectacular *appearance* of power. The analogy which Alan Liu has drawn between the Panorama and the Panopticon is apposite here (Figure 9): in both spaces the behaviour of the subject is conditioned by the ability of the structure to maintain the illusion of omniscience. What Liu fails to register, however, is the precise nature of the subject's position in the Panorama.[42] While it is tempting to regard the subject as a version of Bentham's all-seeing inspector, possessed of a total plenitude of being, master of all he or she surveys, I would argue that such an approach obscures the disciplinary function of the apparatus. For one thing it seems to neglect a key aspect of Foucault's own thought, that the Panopticon is an architecture of control and that the gaze it constructs has much in common with the Hegelian dialectic of master and slave. Thus, rather than regarding the panoramic subject as elevated and in command, it might be more accurate to think of it as vacillating between the roles of jailor and jailed.[43]

To clarify this notion, let us attempt to place ourselves in the body, as it were, of a visitor to the *Battle of Waterloo*. To help us along with this experiment I would draw attention to the cross-section of the Panorama (Figure 8). For the price of a shilling we (A in Barker's cross-section) enter the rotunda

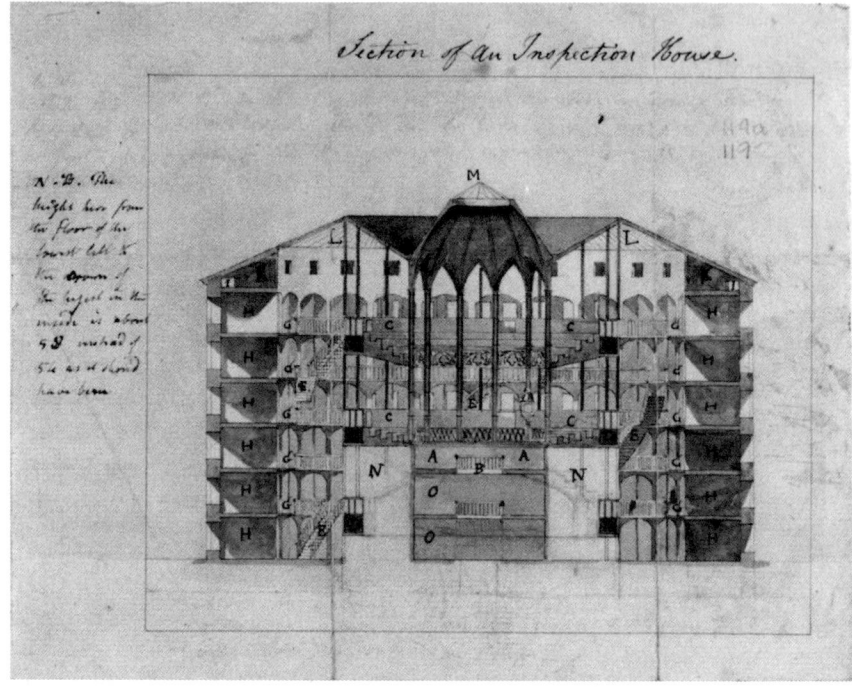

Figure 9 Jeremy Bentham, *Section of an Inspection House*, watercolour, 1787

and our eyes are plunged into darkness. We are greeted by candle-bearing attendants who guide us through corridors and up stairways to the central viewing platform. The light is dazzling at first but in a few seconds the pupils contract. In a cinema the extreme contrast between the darkness of the auditorium and the brightness of the screen helps to promote the illusion of voyeuristic separation. Here, however, we seem to have stepped beyond the darkness and into the screen itself. Gazing at the vastness of the scene before it, the subject experiences, for a second or two, the mind-expanding effect of the Sublime. Now what is gained in this encounter? At a certain naive level, the eye/I has attained a level of scopic command hitherto granted only to the gods: the illusion of seeing all fulfils the fantasy of being all. In this particular example, moreover, the Panorama includes within its fantasy-structure a representation of the very thing that its audience most desires: the Duke of Wellington, designated as number 1 in the accompanying key (Figure 10). The military hero who would go on to give his address as Number 1, London, is depicted holding a rectilinear object in his right hand: is it a baton, a pistol or a telescope? But, at this crucial moment of recognition, something occurs that is not altogether on a par with the comforting logic of narcissistic

Exhibiting War: Battle Tours and Panoramas 87

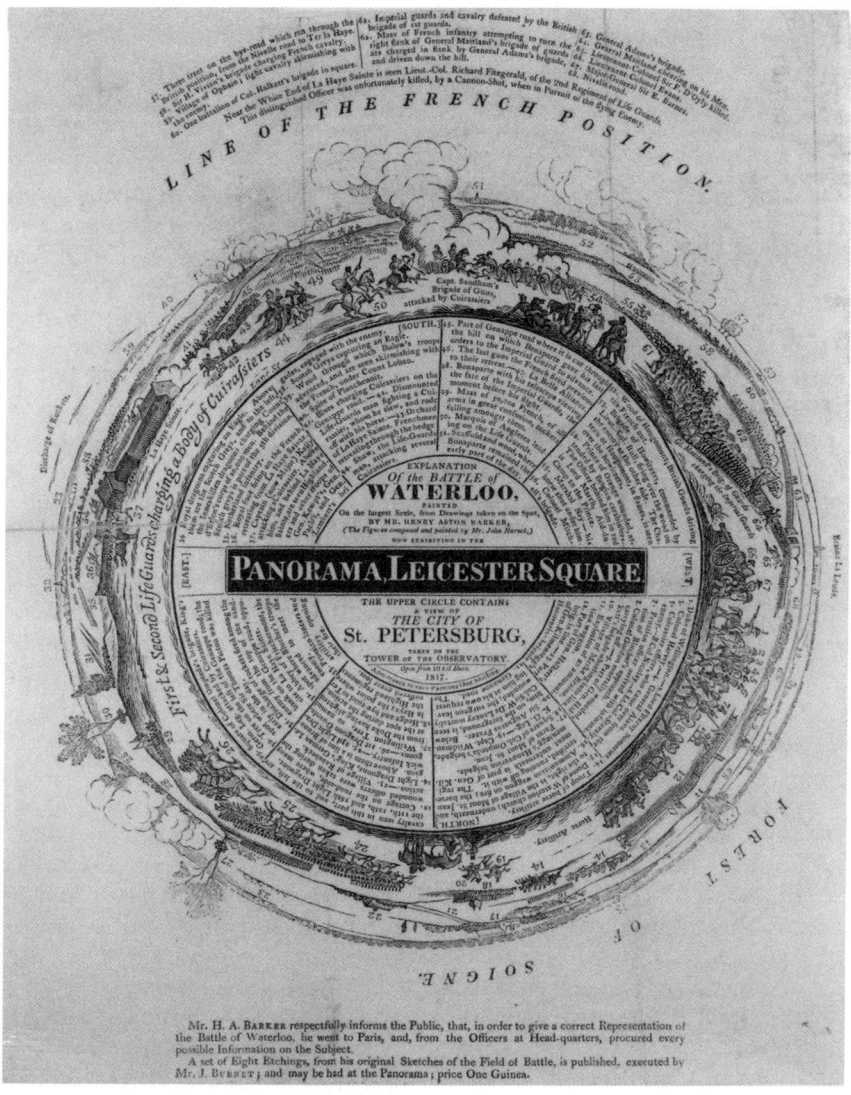

Figure 10 John Burnet, after Henry Aston Barker, *Explanation of the Battle of Waterloo, painted by Mr. Henry Aston Barker*, woodcut, London 1817

identification. Located at the apex of a perspectival cone the gaze of the British commander sees all, including the would-be Argus eye of the viewer. Where we had thought ourselves to be in control and in command we are now reminded of our subservience and subjectification. No longer the master of all we survey, our attention shifts to the omnivoyant eye of Wellington. But where is Wellington looking? The anxiety we feel over the Duke's undetermined object forces us to take up the position of the perceived; faced with a lack, in other words, our instinct is to fill this dark space with our own illusory presence, to become, in short, the prisoner of the Other's gaze. The gaze, therefore, has nothing to do with the image on the canvas; since its range extends beyond the visible, beyond the point that is from which it appear to originate, it comes to occupy the place of the 'fictitious object', an entity without positive existence but with real effects.[44]

To explain this point I want to turn now to a consideration of the accompanying historical key. Containing details of the events of the battle, together with an explanation of the scenes depicted in the painting, the key, as William Galperin argues, encouraged viewers to 'read and thereby control what they could otherwise only see.'[45] What Galperin does not acknowledge, however, is the degree to which the visual effect of the Panorama lent itself quite easily to the politics of submission. To quote the words of a reviewer of Burford's Waterloo exhibit:

> A picture of this description must be, perforce, the representation of a number of different events, many of which did not occur simultaneously; but as the eye can embrace only a part of the subject at once, this forms no drawback to the general effect. All the leading incidents of the battle are faithfully and picturesquely recorded, – and the anachronisms, if such we must call them, escape the attention of the spectator.[46]

According to this viewer there is nothing inherently disorientating about the proliferation of picturesque details in the painting. Through the natural motions of the eye (focusing on a visible part rather than the impossible whole) a potentially fatal identification with the non-existent gaze could (at least in theory) be evaded.[47] It was the eye itself therefore that ensured that the fantasy of seeing all remained on the correct side of the signifying bar, i.e. at a distance from the knowledge of its fundamental artifice.

What the key provided, in addition to this effect, was a means of converting the visual operation into a mode of symbolic understanding. By situating Wellington as the primary figure in the scene, we are trained to view all other images from the point of view of the state. In short, our identification with the guiding lens of the Duke determines not only our subjective coherence but also our ideological response to the scenes around it. Hence, by the time we look at the minuscule figure 48 ('Bonaparte with his telescope viewing... the Imperial Guards, the moment before his flight') we understand that the order of seeing corresponds to the order of history. A sense of the significance of this relation is given in a key passage from Christopher Kelly's *History of the French Revolution* (1817). Here, Kelly returns to the image that inspired Charles Bell and the 'gentleman' to rise above the circumstances of blank actuality:

> Before any of the French troops were placed in the positions that they were to occupy, Napoleon ascended a neighbouring eminence, and carefully examined every feature of the surrounding country. Not an inequality of ground, not a hedge escaped him. He was employed in this preparation during four or five hours, and every observation was carefully noted in a map, which he held in his hand... As the troops of the respective armies advanced to their positions, Bonaparte ascended an observatory, which had been recently erected by order of the king of the Netherlands, preparatory to a trigonometrical survey of the country. From this spot he commanded the whole of both lines. He was particularly struck with the fine appearance of some of the British troops. 'How steadily,' said he to his aides-de-camp, 'these troops take their ground! How beautifully those cavalry form! Observe those grey horse! (the Scotch Greys). Are they not noble troops? Yet, in half an hour, I shall cut them to pieces.'

At pains to qualify the elevated view of the Emperor the writer emphasizes how he is 'struck with the fine appearance of the British troops'.[48] His eye fails to take in the entirety of the field and rests instead on the incidental, fleeting beauties of troop and cavalry formations. The view is detached and fragmented, malevolent yet inconsequential, for the reader knows what is about to happen. Like Satan's fall in *Paradise Lost*, there is a yield of tragic irony in the contrast between the rebel's claim to visual power and the reality of his obscure and ignoble descent. In both cases, the 'wonder' of the divine perspective is belied by 'envy' and isolation, indicating a subject unable to perceive and thus truly command the field in its totality.[49] The moral and ontological shortcomings of Napoleonic vision are contrasted, in the lines that follow, with the divinely sanctioned gaze of the Duke of Wellington. Compared with the stationary French commander, the Duke is a mobile presence in the battle, 'presenting himself wherever the danger was most imminent' (p. 50). He is shown throwing himself into the midst of battle, 'repeatedly exposed to the greatest dangers' (p. 51). Elsewhere, 'while he stood on the centre of the high road in front of Mont St. Jean, several guns were levelled against him' – all of which he observes 'with the coolness of a spectator, who was beholding some well-contested sport' (p. 51).

By 1817, the British leader's impregnability and omnivoyance had become common parlance. In 1815, Booth's *Battle of Waterloo*, described the Duke as 'every where to be found, encouraging, directing, animating... his telescope in his hand; there was nothing that escaped him... and his lynx's eyes seemed to penetrate the smoke, and forestall the movements of the foe'.[50] In visual terms he combines the omnivoyance of the panoramic view without succumbing to the deleterious effects of aesthetic detachment. Critically, it is Wellington's 'penetrating eye' that detects 'the first error' (p. 47). Where Napoleon alights on surface details, Wellington sees to the heart of the matter. Where the former possesses a wider compass of vision, the latter commands a superior depth of field. To draw a further analogy from the world of cinematography, one might say that Napoleon stands for an archaic world of fixed camera shots, able to contemplate from afar but unable to articulate the fragments of the real in a way that would reveal them as being structured by and within the temporal unfolding of the battle. Wellington, by contrast, seems to recognize the contingency of vision; he watches as a 'spectator' but is also present as a visual agent wherever his commanding presence is required.[51] The fiction of Wellington's omnivoyance is predicated, of course, on the detachment of the gaze from its bearer. The eagle eye that saturates the field, at once everywhere and nowhere, more thoroughly animates and inhabits Waterloo than the body from which it derives.

The Duke provides us, then, with a tenable alternative to the usurping eye of Napoleon while, at the same time, standing in as an 'impossible' ego ideal, a Benthamite fiction transcending the field of its effects. But it is in his position at the head of the panoramic key that the Duke plays his most decisive role. This leads us back to the socio-political function of the Panorama. Despite the spectator's fascination with the Marquesses, Dukes and Earls, the ego ideal that the subject identifies with is a superior one and as such it serves to remind the viewer of his or her difference from the body of the establishment. By recalling the subject to the titular superiority of the British command, the key, as Galperin notes, reinforces those vertical gradations that the commercial Panorama threatens to dissolve. At the end of the day, therefore, it seems fair to say that the exhibition was designed to consolidate rather than efface the stratification of Regency society. Through a process of discursive reorientation, literally grounding the omniscient gaze in a mode of symbolization, the exhibit sought to remind the public that in the realm of actuality it is the politicians and generals who underwrite the order of history.

A trip to the Panorama did not, however, end with the descent from the viewing platform. Like all successful exhibitions, the organizers sought to profit from their patrons' curiosity. To this end visitors were given the opportunity to purchase a keepsake (price sixpence) describing the main events of the battle together with some details 'illustrative of the Representation of that great Event'.[52] An epigraph on the title page of the keepsake clarifies any lingering doubts about the genre of the event the viewer has just experienced: 'Rivers of blood I see, and hills of slain, / An Iliad rising out of one campaign.' Rendering the conflict as an epic effectively displaces the primal reality of pain and suffering. On page 4, two passages from Scott's *Field of Waterloo* serve to link this epic sensibility with its visual correlative:

> But on the British heart were lost,
> The terrors of the charging host;
> For not an eye the storm that view'd,
> Chang'd its proud glance of fortitude.
>
> Then Wellington! thy piercing eye,
> This crisis caught of destiny
>   The British host had stood
> That morn 'gainst charge of sword and lance,
> As their own ocean-rocks hold stance,
> But when thy voice had said 'Advance!'
>   They were their ocean's flood.
>   (*The Field of Waterloo*, lines 210–13 and 247–53)

The disciplined gaze, the one that forbears time and change, is the steadfast gaze of Wellington. For a short while the ordinary citizen has mimicked this stance. By maintaining a 'proud glance of fortitude', the subject has withstood the exposure of its impossible constitution; the debt to pleasure has been paid. Now, having learnt that Waterloo lies beyond the scope of the ordinary I/eye, it is time to meditate on the 'growing splendour' of a state that remains permanently out of reach.

3
Southey's Vision of Command

> Me most of all it behoved to raise
>   The strain of triumph for this foe subdued,
> To give a voice to joy, and in my lays
>   Exalt a nation's hymn of gratitude,
> And blazon forth in song that day's renown, ...
>   For I was graced with England's laurel crown.[1]
>   Robert Southey, *The Poet's Pilgrimage to Waterloo* (1816)

La Belle Alliance

In November 1815, Robert Southey, journalist, historian and poet laureate, entered into an unwitting test of wills with a living legend: Arthur Wellesley, the Duke of Wellington.[2] Southey's version of the quarrel, which is set out in a letter to William Wynn (*NLRS*, II, 124–8), is concerned with the veracity of the Duke's account of the recent Allied victory over Napoleon. The revelation that the successful general and hero of the battle of Waterloo should turn out not to be the decorous figure of popular belief, takes its initial force from an editorial dispute. The story can be summarized as follows. In the weeks prior to his visit to the Netherlands – a trip that was to include a visit to the site of the battle – Southey had completed the second half of a laudatory article on the life of Wellington. The article was to have appeared in the *Quarterly Review* for July, but the publication of the July issue was delayed due to Southey's objections to the alterations that John Wilson Croker had made in his text. According to Southey, the Duke of Wellington, through Croker, had interpolated two large passages in which it was claimed that the Duke had not been surprised by the French forces and that no merit was due to the Prussians in the victory. Faced with this wilful intervention in historical truth, Southey risked exposing himself to the full weight of the Duke's indignation and insisted that the papers be returned to him so that the 'falsehoods' could be 'struck out', and the truth 're-inserted'.

The author's version of the *Quarterly* essay was eventually published in November. Wellington was clearly dismayed and, although he did not respond directly to Southey or to Croker, he ensured that his feelings would be known. In a despatch to the Earl of Clancarty, for example, he calls upon the King

> to prevail on his Legislature to pass a good strong law of libel... does [he] not see that he is encouraging and fostering a nest of... libellers in his country, whose object is to overturn his government, and in the mean time to do him and his Allies all the mischief they can.

'The truth', he says,

> regarding the battle of Waterloo is this: there exists in England an insatiable curiosity upon every subject which has occasioned a mania for travelling and for writing. The battle of Waterloo having been fought within reach, every creature who could afford it, travelled to view the field; and almost every one who came who could write, wrote an account. It is inconceivable the number of lies that were published and circulated in this manner by English travellers... this has been done with such industry that it is now quite certain that I was not present and did not command in the battle of Quatre Bras, and it is very doubtful whether I was present in the battle of Waterloo. It is not so easy to dispose of the British army as it is of an individual: but although it is admitted they were present, the brave Belgians, or the brave Prussians, won the battle; and neither in histories, pamphlets, plays, nor pictures, are the British troops ever noticed. But I must say that our travellers began this warfare of *lying*; and we must make up minds as to the consequences.[3]

The passage is notable, not least for the way in which Wellington links the corruption of truth to that dangerously unstable form of Romantic subjectivity, the tourist. The uncontainability of these bourgeois 'creatures' bears visible testimony to the fact that the field of victory can no longer be regarded as a private domain. As the ambassadors of commercial society swarm across the battlefield, set free by economic forces beyond the control of the dukes and earls, the lies begin to multiply: their number is 'inconceivable'; the 'warfare of lying' replaces the war for truth.[4]

Southey, then, is much more than an inaccurate historian. He is, first and foremost, a representative of the mobile bourgeoisie, a middle-class traveller whose claim to distinction rests upon the relentless production of writing. Wellington, as is well known, was notorious both for the disdain with which he held his own despatches – writing was an embellishment, a corruption of the truth – and for his Byronic dislike of professional writers. Unlike Byron, however, he knew which side of the commercial divide to inhabit. His hatred of authors is based on a simplistic distrust of the levelling effects of the public sphere. He had, as he explained later in his life, been 'too much exposed to authors'.[5] One of them, seeking the Duke's guidance for a projected account of the campaign, was sternly advised to leave well alone: 'you may depend upon it that you will never make it a satisfactory work.' To another he cursorily remarked: 'I can refer you only to my own despatches published in the "London Gazette"'.[6] Wellington's hatred of writers is bound up, it seems to me, with a desire to control both the meaning of the battle and his own status as a privatized, autocratic subject. The illimitable spread of writing threatens to undo the discursive hierarchy on which the Duke's idea of individual and national authority depends. To write the battle in defiance of this authority is to stake a claim on an autonomy no longer based on distinction and command but on the tacit acknowledgement that a public sphere exists and that differences and exclusion can be converted, at the level of discourse, to a formal system of equality.[7]

Writing and travel are linked, therefore, to a complex system of deference and consensus. Within this system, as Scott discovered, the accessibility of the field of Waterloo enables the bourgeois traveller to identify with its noble author, to stand on the spot where Wellington once stood and thus to convert an emblem of landed property into the experience of common property. Whether the tourists wrote their names on the walls of La Belle Alliance (after Simpson) or more purposefully converted the field into an abstract space of self-assertion – from Wordsworth's 'Thanksgiving Ode' to Byron's *Pilgrimage* – the site could no longer be regarded as Wellington's own.

Southey's dispute with the Duke touches, then, on a series of questions to do with property, authority and identity. Nowhere is this more apparent than in the controversy over the name of the victory. Throughout his correspondence and in the *Journal of a Tour in the Netherlands*, Southey had expressed his desire that the battle be known by the name of Belle Alliance. In the *Journal* he invokes the voice of the peasant who guided him on the field: 'He was very angry that Waterloo should give name to the battle; call it Hougoumont, he said, call it La Belle Alliance, or La Haye Sainte, or Pepelot, or Mont St. Jean – anything but Waterloo!'[8] Similarly, in the letter he claims:

> One of the passages which I struck out was a sentence saying that the good sense of Europe had rejected the name of Belle Alliance for the battle as being in some degree false. I have since discovered that in the Duke's dispatches he underlined the word *Waterloo*, this for the same mean motive.
>
> (*NLRS*, II, 126)

Southey's preference for the Prussian name emerges out of a vexed contemporary debate. As soon as the news of the allied victory reached England, journals as various as the *Anti-Jacobin Review* and the *Political Register* scrambled for authoritative copy. The editors of these journals, in a bid to satiate public interest, printed Wellington's authenticated despatch alongside its nearest competitor: the more substantial and mellifluous report of the Prussian General Gneisenau.[9] Readers such as Sir John Sinclair were quick to express their disappointment with the Duke's account:

> By its side stands the Prussian Report, like oriental poetry, compared to the firm and vigorous language of the North; it breathes life and fire, all is as it were painted; the feelings are roused, and in the conclusion, there is a species of romantic chivalry...[10]

Such a distinction was anathema to the Duke. Not only had Sinclair violated the law of property in approaching a 'foreign' source – von Müffling but also, in the appendices, the eyewitness account of de Coster, Napoleon's peasant guide – he had also committed the unpardonable sin of poetization. For Sinclair's evaluation of the Prussian and English prose turns on the stock Romantic distinction between the exotic south and the austere North. Rather like Southey, whose work was also invested in this distinction, Sinclair wishes to recast the victory as a form of chivalric romance. And also like Southey, his approach to the battle incurred the wrath of its self-proclaimed author.

Shortly after its publication, Wellington informed Sinclair of his objection to the people of England 'being misinformed and misled by those novels called "Relations", "Impartial Accounts," &c. &c., of that transaction, containing stories which curious travellers have picked up from peasants, private soldiers, individual officers, &c. &c., and have published to the world as the truth'.[11] It is possible that Wellington has a number of such 'novels' in mind – from Simpson's *Visit to Flanders* (1815) to Booth's *Battle of Waterloo* (1815). But given the recent dealings with Croker it is tempting to think that Southey is the real target. The dispute over the name of the battle is a particular sticking point. Wellington had already snubbed Müffling for speaking of the 'Battle of *La Belle-Alliance*'[12] – this too presented a challenge to his authority. Were the victory to be renamed Belle Alliance it would cease to be the sole property of Wellington and the British establishment; an internationalist history would be the result. Moreover, it would legitimate the existence of a non-paternal bourgeois public sphere. In short, the significance of the war against revolutionary France would have been decided not by an autocracy – the political equivalent of Coleridge's 'infinite I AM' – but by an increasingly dominant professional class.

Despite his title, therefore, a writer such as Sinclair places himself in the service of the very forces that were eroding the older, chivalric codes of aristocratic privilege. His appeal to the Burkean rhetoric of chivalry – enacted in his preference for La Belle Alliance over the English-sounding Waterloo – is an attempt to recoup his material losses. Like Sinclair, Southey is also interested in symbolic recuperation. But his passage from tractable bourgeois to poetic page of state has its own, unique contours. Beginning with an early letter to John Rickman, Southey divides his feelings between a private rhetoric of romance and a more social tone of bellicose patriotism: 'The name which Blücher had given it will do excellently in verse – the field of Fair Alliance! but I do not like it in prose, for we gave them such an English thrashing, that the name ought to be one which comes easily out of an English mouth' (*LCRS*, IV, 119). As with Sinclair, prose is equated with Englishness and with Wellington, poetry with the spirit of romance and Blücher.

The Rickman letter was written in July – some weeks before Southey made the journey that is recorded in the *Journal*, and that also provides the inspiration for his verse romance, *The Poet's Pilgrimage to Waterloo*. Looking back on this trip in his December letter to William Wynn, only this time writing with the unofficial knowledge of one of Wellington's libellous travellers, Southey places much more emphasis on Blücher's appellation rather than on the Englishness of Wellington's. But with Southey's literary outpourings in mind, perhaps what is most interesting about this revaluation is the way in which history lends support to the poetry. Once again, the authority of the peasant guide is invoked: 'tell the people in England it ought not to be called Waterloo' (*NLRS*, II, 126). Thus, in a letter dated 19 December 1815, a few days after the letter to Wynn, 'The Poet's Pilgrimage to La Belle Alliance' is the favoured title of his commemorative poem.[13] But here, picking up on the distinction he had made to Rickman, he values the title, not only for the way in which it does justice to the historical fact that the victory is a shared one, but also, quite simply, because it is more aesthetically pleasing.

As befits a composition written in accordance with the requirement that 'A battle can only be made tolerable in narration when it has something picturesque in its accidents, scene, &c. &c', Southey went to considerable lengths to underscore the 'pleasing' loco-descriptive aspects of Waterloo. A chance meeting with the artist Edward Nash, on the road to Waterloo, resulted in the commissioning of a set of engravings to accompany the projected poem. Southey referred to these, perhaps with an attempt at urbanity, as 'all sufficiently picturesque' (*LCRS*, IV, 118). I will have more to say about the relationship between image and text in *The Poet's Pilgrimage to Waterloo* in the next section. For now I wish merely to observe that, for Southey, there is something distinctly unpicturesque about Wellington's chosen name for the battle. Compared with the sonorously iambic La Belle Alliance, Waterloo somehow fails to capture what is most poetic and thus most significant about the event.

In the letter from 19 December, Southey goes on to outline his plans for a national epic on the age of George III:

> The subject ... is nothing less than a view of the world during the most eventful half century of its annals, – not the *history*, but a philosophical

summary, with reference to the causes and consequences of all these mighty revolutions. There never was a more splendid subject, and I have full confidence in my own capacity for treating it.

(*NLRS*, II, 129)

The move from history to philosophy is a telling and not unfamiliar strategy of the Romantic temper. Southey's purpose is to make the significance of the war with France come alive for a national mind preoccupied not so much with history as with its more pressing economic effects. In the *Pilgrimage*, by emphasizing the picturesque through the framework of a philosophical summary, with history invoked as a final arbiter of truth, Southey is exercising nothing less than his right, as poet laureate, to poetize the political, to tell the story of British national history as it *ought* to be and therefore as it *is*. Left to the merely prosaic imaginations of Croker, Wellington and Rickman, the battle risks losing what Byron refers to as 'that undefinable but impressive halo which the lapse of ages throws around a celebrated spot'.[14] Unlike Byron, however, Southey is less equivocal about the attempt to transform the prosody of the present into the poetry of history. If the battle is to survive as a triumphant event in British history, he seems to be saying, it must first of all sublate the chaos and confusion of its linking phrases – the dissonant voices, from Cobbett's stridently materialist *Political Register* to the Whig party's 'history hath only one page' argument – into a politically transcendent proper name. In 1815, La Belle Alliance becomes much more than an empty designator of reality;[15] for Southey it is an index of a more abstract truth: the belief that the antinomies of nation states, classes and ultimately of individuals can be subsumed in a name that is itself a legitimate synthesis of the historical and the poetic.

Behind these public concerns, however, there lies a more personal truth. To validate his own right to distinction at a level beyond that of the abstract principle of discursive equality, Southey must square the Romantic ideal of a heroic, privatized subjectivity with the reality of his social status as a member of the very class that is learning to convert this ideal into a marketable commodity. To address *this* aspect of Southey's work we must consider the context that William Hazlitt created for the reception of the laureate's work in the pages of the *Examiner*.

A poet's fame

In his review of *The Lay of the Laureate*, Hazlitt makes no bones about what he sees as the poet's inveterate egotism: '"Once a Jacobin and always a Jacobin"... every sentiment or feeling that he has is nothing but the effervescence of incorrigible overweaning self-opinion' (*HCW*, X, 139). All of this is worked into a coruscating analysis of the *Lay*'s rhetorical ambition, the Proem of which opens thus:

> There was a time when all my youthful thought
> Was of the Muse; and of the Poet's fame,
> How fair it flourisheth and fadeth not,...
> Alone enduring, when the Monarch's name
> Is but an empty sound, the Conqueror's bust
> Moulders and is forgotten in the dust.[16]

What follows is as psychologically perceptive as it is politically inflammatory. In Hazlitt's view, the impropriety of expressing such thoughts in a poem addressed to the King is only matched by the degree of egotism that it reveals:

> He endeavours to prove that the Prince Regent and the Duke of Wellington (put together) are greater than Bonaparte, but then he is by his own rule greater than all three of them. We have here perhaps the true secret of Mr. Southey's excessive anger at the late Usurper. If all his youthful thought was of his own inborn superiority to conquerors or kings, we can conceive that Bonaparte's fame must have appeared a very great injustice done to his pretensions.
>
> (HCW, VII, 88)

Southey, in other words, is of the devil's party without knowing it. His avowed hatred of the scourge of Europe is prompted by a structure of self-assertion that owes its being to the very imperialism that it denounces. For on what does Southey's claim to greatness depend? Hazlitt asks. If it is on the official symbol of the laureate wreath then it is of no great matter. The crown is not, as Southey contends, an object of great envy. Thus, having first of all set up the poet as a type of inverted Napoleon, Hazlitt makes the further move of identifying his quest for fame with an un-Napoleonic sense of characterless inconsistency: 'Whether he is a Republican or a Royalist, – whether he hurls up the red cap of liberty, or wears the lily, stained with the blood of all his old acquaintance, at his breast, – whether', in short, 'he glories in Robespierre or the Duke of Wellington', in Hazlitt's prose Southey is nothing less than a rhetorical shifter, a paper 'I' caught between violent antitheses, only himself when he is expressing an antipathy to the 'principles' and 'prejudices' of others: 'Such is the constitutional slenderness of his understanding, its "glassy essence"' (HCW, VII, 86).

From a certain sociological point of view, Hazlitt has every right to dissolve his subject in anaphoric vitriol. What this virtuoso display denies, however, is the psychological complexity of Southey's response to the abdication of Napoleon. To John May and Walter Scott, Southey writes of the event as the final curtain on a 'tragedy of five-and-twenty years': 'Much as I had desired [the abdication], and fully as I had expected it, still, when it came, it brought with it an awful sense of the instability of all earthly things.' What the tragedy lacks, however, is a satisfying 'after-piece':

> I thought he would set his life upon the last throw; or that he would kill himself, or that some of his own men would kill him; and though it had long been my conviction that he was a mean-minded villain, still it surprised me that he should live after such a degradation, – after the loss, not merely of empire, but even of his military character.
>
> (*LCRS*, IV, 68–9)

As it is, the 'sudden termination' of the Napoleonic narrative leaves Southey with a peculiar feeling of insecurity: 'it seemed like a change in life itself' (*LCRS*, IV, 68–9) – akin to the discovery that the story of one's life had never, after all, really been one's own:

> For I could not but remember how materially the course of my own life had been influenced by that tremendous earthquake, which seemed to break up the very deeps of society, like a moral and political deluge. I have derived nothing but good from it in every thing, except the mere consideration of immediate worldly fortune, which to me is dust in the balance. Sure I am that under any other course of discipline I should not have possessed half the intellectual powers which I now enjoy, and perhaps not the moral strength.
>
> (*LCRS*, IV, 66)

The material course of Southey's life has been fashioned under the influence of Napoleonic 'discipline'. Now, in the absence of this power – a younger Southey had pronounced the general 'the greatest man that events have called into action since Alexander of Macedon' (*NLRS*, I, 222) – he begins to exhibit uncomfortable signs of mourning. In a special sense, therefore, as much as Byron, Hazlitt or Scott, Southey recognizes his enemy as internal to his own ego, a part of his relationship to himself.[17] But, as we noted earlier, it is the lack of a satisfactory 'after-piece' to the *drama* of this relationship that troubles Southey the most. In the absence of such an act the Napoleonic text remains incomplete, teetering on the edge of a *finale* it can never quite reach.[18] Where, then, is the figure that will take the emperor's place?

By December 1814 the gap is all too apparent: 'We make war better than we make peace... Europe was in such a state when Paris was taken, that a commanding intellect, had there been such among the allies, might have cast it into whatever form he pleased' (*LCRS*, IV, 96). The echo of Coleridge's 'commanding genius' is a reminder that Southey was constitutionally determined to frame the course of his own life and that of European history in terms drawn from the discourse of high Romanticism. To do justice to the enemy, and thus to oneself, all that the drama needed was the intervention of a British genius and a decisive conclusion. At first Wellington and Waterloo would appear to fulfil this aim. But Southey, due to the extent of his investment in the Napoleonic romance, was destined to perpetuate his feelings of dissatisfaction: 'it surprised me that he should live' (ibid.).

In summary, then, both the pusillanimous end of the emperor and the prosaic dealings of the Duke point towards the inability of history to live up to Southey's Romantic script. But if the narrative cannot be completed it can at least be regulated. Like Scott, Southey's response to the gap in the Real is to fill it with his own system of fictional power: the consolidation of his cultural position as a one-man textual industry. Hence the ceaseless production of romances, histories, political essays, definitive editions and, crucially, of laureate pieces. Southey deviates from Scott, however, in the prestige he accords this industry. Weighing up the respective merits of worldly and artistic achievement, he writes that:

> Literary fame is the only fame of which a wise man ought to be ambitious, because it is the only lasting and living fame. Bonaparte will be forgotten before his time in Purgatory is half over... Pour out your mind in a great poem, and you will exercise authority over the feelings and opinions of mankind as long as the language lasts in which you write.
>
> (*LCRS*, III, 144)

Here there is no agonizing over the futility of writing verse, and no regret for the fact that the poet can only represent what the soldier performs. For Southey, the distinction of the poet's activity is quite clear: what the leaders of men sully in the field of statesmanship, the laureate will recoup in the field of culture.

Thus, from the *Lay* through to the *Pilgrimage*, Southey's interest in the significance of contemporary events is prompted by a deeper desire to fashion himself as a power in English literature. Such ambition did not go unnoticed. As Francis Jeffrey remarked, echoing Hazlitt:

> [The poet laureate] has very distinctly manifested his resolution not to rest satisfied with the salary, sherry, and safe obscurity of his predecessors, but to claim a real power and prerogative in the world of letters, in virtue of his title and appointment.

The claim to 'real power' encompasses his relation to literary power – the great poets of the past from Spenser to Milton ('So may I boldly round my temples bind / The laurel which my Spenser wore') – but also to political power: 'it is easy to see the worthy Laureate thinks himself entitled to share in the prerogatives of that royalty which he is bound to extol.'[19] From the letters to the *Quarterly Review* articles, and from the *Journal of a Tour* to the *Poet's Pilgrimage to Waterloo*, what we encounter is the transformation of geopolitical reality into the abstracted space of literature. In what amounts to a virtual remapping of Waterloo, Southey strives to convert a public heterotopia into a private bibliotopia. The one hinges on the other: both the officially sanctioned mouthpiece of a triumphant and newly invigorated nation state *and* the unofficially elected voice of a national poetic tradition.

'Upon the field of blood'

How, then, did Southey substantiate the leading role of the aesthetic in determining the history of Waterloo? To address this question I would like to look in some detail at Southey's contribution to the discorse of post-Waterloo tourism. We have already considered the extent to which the Duke of Wellington viewed the commodification of Waterloo with distrust. No longer a private sphere, the field was open to capture by the mobile bourgeoisie who set about converting the field into an object of aesthetic interest. In the preceding chapter I argued that the alleged 'infinite mobility' of this mode of being was in fact subject to specific material constraints. Through the addition of explanatory guides and keys, the picturesque gaze was brought back into the field of history, albeit a history that had severed its connections with conventional models of signification. Thus for Ann Bermingham, 'what is remarkable about the Picturesque is its demand that surfaces be taken seriously, that they be treated, not in depth, but *as* depth... the Picturesque... complemented an emerging commercial discourse which sought to identify appearances with essence'.[20] As we have seen, the prospect of Waterloo, encountered in the writings of John Scott, Charlotte Eaton and Charles Campbell, offers support for this model. In these texts, the primal significance of death and agony has been absorbed by a gaze that takes delight in reducing history to a catalogue of moving spectacles. Replete with the full panoply of picturesque seeing – from Claude glasses to 'pocket' Panoramas – the battle tourist is 'moved' by the sight of decimation but is crucially free to move on: his pleasing pain is momentary. The shock of the sublime object has been defused by its inclusion within a structure of signification.

To preface this investigation of Southey's depiction of the field of battle let us first of all consider the circumstances that led up to the publication of his travelogue. The year 1815 was something of a watershed year for Southey. As a journalist he had, for some time, been enjoying a comfortable income from his contributions to the *Quarterly* and the *Annual Register*. Both the *Life of Nelson* (1813) and his extensive poem, *Roderick the Last of the Goths* (1814) were best-sellers. On top of the income afforded by his publications, Southey was in receipt of a £100 stipend for the laureateship. By the autumn of this year, a family holiday on the Continent was well within the poet's means. But Southey was no idle traveller. Like his friend and competitor Scott, the poet was keen to ensure that his period of leisure would yield some kind of commercial reward and it is with this desideratum in mind that he set about recording his experiences for the *Journal of a Tour in the Netherlands in the*

Autumn of 1815. The textual journey from prose to poetry was an important one for Southey as it enabled the poet to make sense of both the war and his own part in its cultural reproduction. But taken as a work in itself, the *Journal* offers an interesting commentary on the developing significance of Waterloo. More particularly it foregrounds to an unusual degree the highly politicized significance of aesthetic categories.

Like most Waterloo travel books, Southey's *Journal* begins with an account of the journey from England to Belgium. After a 16-hour crossing (the average being ten to twelve hours), the group disembarked at Ostend from whence they were conveyed by canal to Bruges. The poet's account of the town and its sites are standard traveller's fare, dwelling, for the most part, on descriptions of the major cultural sites and the surrounding countryside. Of special interest, however, is the way in which the picturesque is used to structure an aesthetic response to Waterloo. To begin with, the poet takes delight in detailing his impressions of monuments, galleries and houses, as if he were surveying a work of art: 'the whole city is one series of pictures ...the whole city is in *keeping.*'[21] Important for the present context is the way in which Southey transfers the rhetoric of aesthetic appreciation (in eighteenth-century aesthetics, a successful painting is said to be in 'keeping') to the sphere of history. In a description of a military mass in the town cathedral, for instance, the echoes of the recent war are rendered acceptable by conforming to a containable form of the Sublime:

> After mass, the Belgian soldiers marched in by beat of drum to a mass of their own. Never did I hear anything so dizzying, so terrific, so terrible as the sound... it could not be imitated in a theatre, for no theatre could give the dreadful reverberation which the arches here produced on every side... Mr Nash was almost overpowered by the sound, and he was so shocked by the display, which to his feelings was thus irreverently introduced. It impressed me differently, and I felt what such a ceremony would be worth in a besieged town.

On the canal journey to Bruges the narrative lapses into a series of snapshot impressions: 'a swan plying about... the water alive with fish, water-lillies' (p. 34). Gradually, the poet is lulled into a state of oneiric repose:

> There was something very singular in the silence and solitude of the landscape, for though the agriculture proved the existence of an ample and active population, we saw very few people, and none whatever in the fields; only a few stray travellers...
> (*Journal of a Tour in the Netherlands in August 1815*, pp. 35–6).

Southey's description seems to have effaced the signs of labour in the landscape. Like the Flemish landscape paintings he carries in his memory, fields are considered not for their utility but for their ability to harmonize with a pleasing prospect: 'Trees are not considered injurious to agriculture here... The cultivation seems to be beautiful – no weeds, no waste' (p. 14); 'The country for some distance had the same character of fertility, industry and beauty' (p. 35). In this highly idealized portrait, aesthetic and economic categories are allowed to shade off into each other; the rigidly divided fields and closely cropped wooded boundaries are pleasing to the eye because of their ability to foster Romantic states of inwardness.

We should not be surprised to find the same aesthetic criteria operating on the field of Waterloo. Here, however, instead of ploughshares and peasants, it is the traces of war that are subtly elided. 'Surveying' the field of battle, Southey notes that 'the farm house at La Haye Sainte is well represented in the panoramic print'. It is most likely that Southey is referring to the foldout print often included in copies of Booth's *Battle*. By allowing this mode of response to structure his experience, the poet is clearly eager to make sense of his own sublime encounter; indeed, if anything, the narrative is designed so that a potential moment of self-usurpation is anticipated and neutralized. Thus, as the account proceeds, the description of the landscape and the events that took place in it conforms to the foci and visual field of the Panorama: 'Standing on the chaussee by Mont St. Jean and looking to the field of battle, the forest of Soignes is behind you... La Haye Sainte, and... La Belle Alliance, both straight forward' (p. 83). Having established a cartographic base line, the traveller is now at liberty to recount his emotional and aesthetic responses to the landscape. The chateau of Hougoumont, a scene of fierce fighting, is described as 'the only picturesque point in the whole field, and it is highly so – a sort of oasis, or wood-island, having that beauty which a well-planted spot possesses in bare and open country' (p. 84). In the pages that follow, Southey dwells for an inordinate length of time on this spot, as if it offered some form of protection against the illimitable views of a 'bare and open country' and thus against the more troubling perspectives that the space of Waterloo might present.

I have suggested that Southey deliberately veils the unsightly truth of war. This claim ought, however, to be weighed alongside the feelings that are confessed elsewhere. The poet's first impressions of the field were, on this account, deeply disturbing: 'I had never before seen the real face of war so closely and God knows! a deplorable sight it is.'[22] In *The Poet's Pilgrimage to Waterloo*, the 'open graves, the recent scene of blood' are described as 'morbid images... present to the soul's creative sight' (II, i, 1); elsewhere, the poet is said to be 'possess'd' by the presence of the dead. In the *Journal*, however, it is the tourist's gaze that claims the upper hand, shunting the poet away from a Wordsworthian fixation with the signs of history. Here again, it is the picturesque that holds the key to the poet's deliverance. To consider this proposition we shall return to the ruined shell of Hougoumont. As it appears in Bell's illustration (Figure 11), the chateau offers a

Figure 11 Bell [?], *Entrance to Hougoumont*, engraving, London 1816

lesson in the correct reading of the face of war: a reading informed by the immortal eye of the painter or poet. The swain resting on his spade is lifted from the Georgic visions of Poussin, Palmer and Claude, yet his labour, as the bones in the foreground signify, is not with the propagation of life but with the burial of the dead. In this sense, to recall an argument of Alan Liu's, the Georgic 'is the supreme mediational form by which to bury history in nature, epic in pastoral. Like the tour mode, it is the form in which history turns into the background, the manure, for landscape.'[23] But note that in this version, history is blithely uncovered. Thus, to modify Liu's reading, the swain is engaged in an activity of radical appropriation, representing the bones of the dead as a support for 'history' itself: an 'illusion' which structures the viewer's experience of war and thereby masks its insupportable, traumatic kernel. This notion is carried over to the surrounding trees, which provide the sketch with a framework of cyclical rejuvenation, again rendering the impossible core of social reality all but invisible.

At other points in the *Journal*, the 'ruins' of Waterloo enable the writer to transform an otherwise unremarkable subject into an object of artistic consumption. More so than in Eaton's or John Scott's narratives, the ravages of war are noticeable, if at all, only to the extent to which they afford opportunities for picturesque reflection. For the most part, as Southey observes, 'the surface of the earth [has] lost [the] traces of tragedy – almost, it might be said, as completely and as soon as the sea loses all vestiges of a tempest in which whole fleets are wrecked' (pp. 105–6). What remains is the striking or irregular: a guide rakes out a calcined finger bone from an ash heap; a wall is stained with a five-foot long perpendicular line of blood. Some 'poor fellow', Southey remarks, 'must have been knocked to pieces against it by a cannon ball' (p. 86). Such moments of diversion come to be the ruling strategy of the book, which is to reduce the tragic or sublime connotations of Waterloo to a set of metonymic relays. By substituting the part for the whole, the face-to-face encounter with the violence of war is endlessly deferred.

'Now, said my heavenly teacher, all is clear!'

As shocked as Southey was by the magnitude of suffering at Waterloo, I have argued that his work avoids fixation with the actual human costs of war. The poet, with an eye on the classical hierarchy of genres, knows that his business is not with historical accident but with eternal significance. It is this conviction that underlies the composition of *The Poet's Pilgrimage to Waterloo*. That Southey aimed for something more than the short-term view is borne out in a letter to his fellow Waterloo bard, Walter Scott:

> My poem will reach you in a few weeks; it is so different in its kind, that, however kindly malice may be disposed, it will not be possible to institute a comparison with yours. I take a different point of time and a wider range, leaving the battle untouched, and describing the field only such as it was when I surveyed it.
>
> (*LCRS*, IV, 152–3)

The point of comparison is an apt one. Where Scott indulges his talent for conducting an action – the anaphoric structure of headwords in conjunction with definite articles, imperatives and active verbs – Southey is concerned with the allegorical aspects of battle. Thus, where Scott's poem is passionately factual, Southey's poem is plangently mythical. The former is written within an epic framework, the latter is conceived as a romance. Despite its immediate historical focus, therefore, there is a sense in which the *Pilgrimage* can be seen as a continuation of Southey's earlier quest romances. With its emphasis on the recuperative effects of the journey, the transformation of the intransigent traveller into a steadfast hero and the key intervention of a mythical female guide, the poem is yet another reworking of Book I of *The Faerie Queene* – filtered, of course, through the Puritan matrix of Bunyan. Here, once again, we must mark Southey's departure from Scott. For where Scott confines himself to an historically specific account of the 'matter of Waterloo',[24] Southey, true to the aims of his projected national epic, ranges quite freely through the imaginative realms of time and space.

In one sense, as Simon Bainbridge has observed, *The Poet's Pilgrimage to Waterloo* is conceived as the culmination of the apocalyptic conflict between good and evil depicted in earlier poems such as *The Curse of Kehama*, 'The March to Moscow' and the 'Ode, written during the Negotiations with Bounaparte, in January, 1814'. Despite the wrangling with Croker and Wellington, the poet maintained that the battle 'ought to be considered as the greatest deliverance that civilized society has experienced since the defeat of the Moors by Charles Martel' (*LCRS*, VI, 117). The rhetoric of Christian thankfulness is carried over to the poem's title. Rendered as a 'kind of pilgrimage', the journey alludes to an early modern form of travel, one that precedes the purely acquisitive aims of a Regency vacation. Southey is not only investing his work with sacramental connotations, he is also attempting to filter out the taint of crass commercialism.

In the opening stanzas of part one, the poet again places the battle in the context of the historical struggle of the Christian West against the 'despotic east' (I, i, 2). Beginning with the battle of Platae, when a united Greece had 'smote the Persian's power' (I, i, 1) and moving through the battle of Tours when Martel defeated the Saracens, western history is depicted as the triumph of knowledge and true faith over ignorance and superstition. The terms of this trajectory are extended to the reign of Napoleon. Like the 'Musselmen' who had once threatened to impose on France the 'yoke' of 'misbelieving Mecca' (I, i, 3), a Satanic Emperor has returned to plunge his country into 'sensual servitude' (I, i, 2). With the impiety of Bonaparte established, Southey goes on to affirm his own Christian credentials. The Battle of Waterloo, he writes in the 'Argument', 'was a struggle between good and evil principles'; accordingly its praise must be conveyed in the form of a 'hymn' sung by a man of 'unshaken' faith (I, i, 5). Within the space of a few lines the poet reiterates the idea that the journey, for writer and reader, has become a 'pilgrimage' (I, i, 8), its destination the field of Waterloo, the site of civilization's third deliverance from slavery and error.

In practice, then, the idea that Waterloo has become a sacred place is used to support the larger claim that the battle has secured the peace and prosperity of the civilized West. Images of the 'vicious Orient' (II, iv, 11), invoking comparisons with the age of holy wars, are used throughout to illustrate the contrast between despotism and liberty. Since Christianity is responsible for freedom of conscience Napoleon, in straying from the 'light', is worse than the 'ignorant' Scythian (II, iv, 18):

> Not led away by circumstance he err'd
> But from the wicked heart his error came
> (II, iv, 19)

Southey's meditation on the impiety of the Napoleonic cause substantiates his claim at the beginning of the poem that the pilgrimage will provide 'a store for after-thought' (I, i, 8). Certainly it helps to moderate the poet's reaction to the dead and wounded, first encountered in the hospitals of Brussels:

> Here might the hideous face of war be seen,
>   Stript of all pomp, adornment, and disguise;
> It was a dismal spectacle, I ween,
>   Such as might well to the beholders' eyes
> Bring sudden tears, and make the pious
> Grieve for the crimes and follies of mankind
> (I, ii, 10)

The writer of the anti-war poem, 'The Battle of Blenheim', may well be present in these lines. First published in 1800, the verse was seized upon by Tory supporters of the campaign against France for its unpatriotic portrayal of the horrors of war:

> They say it was a shocking sight
> After the field was won,
> For many thousand bodies here
> Lay rotting in the sun;
> But things like that you know must be
> After a famous victory....
>
> And every body praised the Duke
> Who such a fight did win.
> But what good came of it at last? –
> Quoth little Peterkin.
> Why that I cannot tell, said he,
> But 'twas a famous victory.[25]

But where the younger poet emphasizes the devastation of war, placing it in ironic contrast with the emptiness of the historical point of view, the laureate strives to bring human suffering to account. Fittingly, his opening gesture consists of an act of poetic revision:

> Those wars are a tale of times gone by,
>   For so doth perishable fame decay,...
> Here on the ground wherein the slaughter'd lie,
>   The memory of that fight is pass'd away;...
> And even our glorious Blenheim to the field
> Of Waterloo and Wellington must yield.
> (I, iii, 12)

In this new vision, the transcendental significance of the battle supersedes even the historically redeemed Blenheim. The message seems straightforward enough: the death of men in war, as Wordsworth also affirms, is secondary to 'Heaven-sanctioned victory'.[26] More disturbingly, the reference to 'perishable fame' is a reminder of the distinction made between the infamy of Bonaparte and the 'lasting and living fame' of the poet. Southey's fight to distinguish Waterloo from the 'tales of times gone by' is allied, it seems, with the struggle to assert himself as a transcendent power.

The poet's justification of the waste of Waterloo turns on the shift, in part two of the poem, from material to imaginary space and from historical to divine temporality. Yet here again we find the poet struggling to distinguish his unique vision from socially constructed ways of seeing. In the letter to Scott, quoted at the beginning of this section, the reference to the poem's 'wider range' in connection with the rhetoric of surveying ('describing the field only such as when I surveyed it') recalls the context in which images of Waterloo were produced and consumed in this period. We have observed how Craan's plan encouraged readers to rise above the confusion of war and consume the field as an object of national significance.[27] Southey's act of 'surveying' points towards a similar impulse. With its echo of Cowper – 'I am monarch of all I survey, / My right there is none to dispute'[28] – the rhetoric of command and comprehension has an obvious analogy with the discourse of romantic self-fashioning. But it also suggests the wider equation between literary authority, subjectivity and visual power. In Southey's view the fragmented perspectives of Waterloo have to be monitored by a 'dominant overseeing eye'[29], for the danger of losing the 'wider range' is that of becoming absorbed in the pathos of minute particulars: the 'marks of wreck...for those who closelier peer' (I, iii, 39).

Southey's visual strategy turns, therefore, on a delicate negotiation of topographical power. To elevate the eye above the landscape the poem must recreate the panoramic vision of the mapmaker. To do so, however, is to risk an unfortunate encounter with the structure of false or Napoleonic seeing associated with the popular image of the trigonometrical tower. Southey the journalist refers to this in his *Quarterly* essay: 'In the early part of the day he had reconnoitred the ground, and directed the movements from a sort of scaffolding, observatory, or telegraph, which had been erected from some ichnographical purposes.'[30]

The distinction between false or Napoleonic seeing and the 'penetrating eye' of Wellington was, as I have argued, a stock feature of Waterloo-related literature. Southey, following from Fitzgerald and Scott, locates the Duke's gaze in the centre of the action:

> Deem not that I the martial skill should boast
>   Where horse and foot were station'd here to tell,
> What points were occupied by either host,

And how the battle raged, and what befell,
And how our great Commander's eagle eye,
Which comprehended all, secured the victory.

(I, iii, 32)

In Southey's case, however, the comparison between the task of the historian and the task of the poet also serves as a means of distinguishing one form of surveillance, associated with military command and aristocratic privilege, from another, superior form of seeing: the elevated vision of the bard. Taking an Aristotelian distinction at its most literal, Southey deploys the rhetoric of deference only to assert the 'natural' superiority of poetry over history. Thus, where poets such as Fitzgerald defer to 'Laurelled Wellington', Southey seeks to ensure that poetic laurels take precedence over victory laurels. To do so, however, he must separate his own form of elevation from that of the commanders.

Structurally the poem takes the form of a contest between the cold eye of French materialist philosophy, represented by the duplicitous figure of earthly Wisdom, and the 'scope unconfined' of divine providence, represented by the 'heavenly' guide or 'muse' (II, iii, 48). Here, divinity triumphs over techne. But the assertion of god-like vision is, itself, not without its technical problems. In the Proem, Southey links the transcendental impulse of his hymn with the invocation to *Paradise Lost*: 'what is low raise and support / That to the height of this great argument.'[31] The desire for elevation, detectable at the level of genre and cultural authority, is translated into the description of 'The Field of Battle'. The initial encounter with this sacred site is, in topographical terms, an unpromising one. Waterloo is described as 'a little lowly place', raised by the glory of its recent fame (I, iii, 3). It is only when the poet reaches part II, 'The Vision', that the rhetoric of quest romance is allowed to compensate for the geographical deficiencies of the actual field. Musing in 'solitude' (II, i, 1) the poet travels across an endless plain: a wasteland of dolorous tombs and mouldering ruins, his destination an allegorical representation of Waterloo. It is at this point, in what amounts to a parodic allusion to the melancholic landscapes of *Childe Harold's Pilgrimage*, that the vision of the poet is arrested by the sight of an 'aspiring Tower' (II, i, 8) – the Napoleonic observatory by any other name – upon which resides the figure of earthly Wisdom, the 'Evil Prophet' (II, ii).

The doctrine that Wisdom teaches combines the worst of materialist philosophies: from Voltairian cynicism to Byronic fatalism. Handed a telescope to aid his 'faulty vision', the poet surveys a field of 'darkness'. The creed he is expected to derive from this exercise is straightforwardly egotistic: since there is nothing more to see, and nothing else to do, it is best to cultivate 'pleasure' and 'the Self', 'the spring of all' (II, i, 20–2). This, of course, is not only Byron's creed, it also Napoleon's. Having reached the limit point of Romantic narcissism, Southey's poet counters with an invocation of a well-worn Southeyan theme: the rallying of the martyrs for apocalyptic glory, 'Victorious over agony and death' (II, i, 43). Wisdom replies with a speech that is directly comparable with Byron's 'history hath one page' argument:[32]

> Assuming then a frown as thus he said,
>   He strech'd his hand from that commanding height,
> Behold, quoth he, where thrice ten thousand dead
>   Are laid, the victims of a single fight!
> And thrice ten thousand more at Ligny lie,
> Slain for the prelude to this tragedy!
>
> Thus to the point where it began its course,
>   The melancholy cycle comes at last
>
> The present and the past one lesson teach;
> Look where thou wilt, the history of man
> Is but a thorny maze, without a plan!
>
> (II, ii, 3; 7; 19)

The names of history – Voltaire / Byron / Napoleon – question the values of heroic martyrdom, but it is a questioning that also proclaims the death of tragedy. The field is a 'stage' and war a 'dreadful drama' (II, ii, 10). Here is no catharsis, no relief from the 'vague and purportless' folly of mankind (II, ii, 20). Like the faithless Southey of 1814, Napoleon's mourners gaze on a world of death and defeat, a world that elides the life-giving principles of growth and change. Supremely sterile, the best that Wisdom can offer is a masturbatory round of physical and political entropy.

The denial of heroic death is linked, in part, to Southey's vexed sense of the failure of the Napoleonic drama. But what I want to focus on here is the poem's more problematic visual dynamic, and the politicization of its claims to distinction. The notion of the 'melancholy cycle', of a serial perspective of history, revolving around the focal point of the spectator's eye, is, as we have seen, a key metaphor of the period. No poetry, not even Southey's, could compete with the popular appeal of Henry Aston Barker's Panoramas. It is hardly surprising, therefore, that the *Pilgrimage* should contain so many references to visual elevation and to 'magic' or 'moving' pictures (II, iv, 40), both as terms of disparagement – in the Earthly Wisdom passages – and as terms of appraisal – in the vision of the Sacred Mountain. Indeed, the concluding section is centred on the description of a circular pageant, a panoramic view of futurity in which the 'Hopes of Man' turn around a centred self. Here, in a benign repetition of 'The Tower', the poet gazes 'with scope unconfined of vision free' (II, iii, 48). The world lies beneath him, as it had done for Wisdom, 'like a scroll' or map, as if the distinction between the realms of the visible and readable had been erased: 'so ample was the range from that commanding height' (II, iii, 50).

To relate the Panorama to Southey's view of the melancholy pleasures of Bonapartism is doubtless to do violence to artistic and historical propinquity. In doing so I wish simply to register the sense in which Southey, like Napoleon and Wellington, becomes subject to panoramic fantasies of self-aggrandizement and paradoxical self-abnegation – fantasies that question the very systems on which they depend. It is common to speak of Romanticism's antipathy towards bodily or gross seeing, but in Southey's case we witness a poet whose familiarity with the visual is suggestive of a positive interest in the 'superficial' pleasures of visual consumption. It is an interest that places the idealized notions of command and distinction in jeopardy. For as much as Southey seeks to distinguish his own mountain top perspectives from the artificially simulated vistas of the Panorama, his text is subject to the same contradictions.

Like Barker's painting of the Battle of Waterloo, Southey's *Pilgrimage* is preoccupied with picturesque detail. Part one, 'The Journey', reads like a poeticized version of the *Journal*. The accumulation of curios, irregularities, minutiae and 'rough objects' – from the 'marks of wreck' to the sprouts of corn – are all indicators of the piquant pleasures of picturesque travel. Yet if this part disappoints, it does so because it places its reader / viewer in the role of one of Gilpin's 'disempowered travellers'.[33] While the gradual disclosure of the ruins of Hougoumont has its charms, the love of novelty can only be sustained for a short while. After a time, the disparity between the artist's broken pastoral and the visual totality, which it elides, becomes all too apparent. To satisfy the drive for proprietorial mastery – to signify the shift, in other words, from the voyeuristic gaze of the tourist to the comprehensive eye of the laureate – the poem must move on to other, more lasting scenes.[34]

In part two, 'The Vision', the feelings of insecurity and incomprehension associated with the false perspectives of 'The Tower' are 'countered', as Bainbridge writes, 'by the assertion of a providential and divine schema in the "Reproof" of the Heavenly Guide of (II, iii and iv).' Bainbridge goes on to argue that the contest between these figures is representative of an 'internal debate' involving, on the one hand, Southey's latent sympathy with Napoleon and, on the other, his conviction that the struggle between Republicanism and Legitimacy must be conceived as a battle of Good against Evil.[35] This reduction of complex historical, diplomatic and political debates to a straightforward contest between moral opposites finds its visual correlate in the passage that follows. Unlike the fleeting spatio-temporal sights of 'The Tower', the panoramic visions of the Sacred Mountain are complete and sustained.[36] It is as if the Satanic connotations of Napoleon's 'eminence sublime' (II, i, 12) have been redeemed – a point that is given extra credence when we consider the Guide's penchant for Milton:[37]

> Look now toward the end! no mists obscure,
>   Nor clouds will there impede the strengthened sight:
> Unblenched thine eye the vision may endure.
>   I looked,... surrounded with effulgent light
> More glorious than all the glorious hues of even,
>   The Angel Death stood there in the open Gate of Heaven.
>
> Now, said my heavenly Teacher, all is clear!...
>   Bear the Beginning and the End in mind,
> The course of human things will then appear
>   Beneath its proper laws: and thou wilt find
> Through all their seeming labyrinth, the plan
> Which 'vindicates the ways of God to Man.'
>   (II, iii, 52; II, iv, 1)

For the remainder of *The Poet's Pilgrimage*, the architectonic imagery of *Paradise Lost* is used to convert, as Southey puts it in a letter to Wynn, the 'answering of particulars' into a 'general... picture of the hopes of mankind' (*NLRS*, II, 124–5). The particulars Southey has in mind are the complexities of postwar politics and society. By replacing the ungovernable minutiae of history with the perfected generalities of art, the poet seeks to replace 'transitory doubt' with a Miltonic affirmation 'Of Providence mysterious' and a vindication of the ways of God to men. The ideological force of this gesture is confirmed in the lines that follow: 'Yet rightly view'd, all history doth impart / Comfort and hope and strength to the believing heart' (II, iv, 4). Having learnt, in other words, to conceive of human time as a predetermined, two-dimensional 'picture', the pilgrim is free to address the sacred underpinnings of individual and national identity.

With the contradictions of the false or commercial Panorama consigned to the abject matter of history, the poet gains access to a higher reality of literary or poetic seeing: a 'living picture moved beneath our feet. / A spacious City first was there displayed' (II, iv, 33). The city turns out to be London – a popular feature of panoramic displays throughout the period. In Southey's vision, London forms the focus of a vast perspectival plain. From here the poet's gaze reaches beyond Britain to the fields of Europe and still further to the imperial domains of the East. As the transitory gaze of the tourist gives way to the eternal eye of God, the poet would appear to have attained his goal: the triumph of an encompassing vision and the glory of an integrated and distinctive subjectivity:

> And thou to whom in spirit at this hour
>   The vision of thy Country's bliss is given
> Who feelest that she holds her trusted power
>   To do the will and spread the word of Heaven,...

> Hold fast the faith which animates thy mind,
> And in thy songs proclaim the hopes of mankind.
>   (II, iv, 63)

No longer oppressed by the obfuscated scenes of 'The Tower', Southey is able to link the victory over Napoleon with the affirmation of Christian or redemptive time. Where once the Evil Prophet had questioned 'the fruit of this long strife' (II, i, 2) now the poet proclaims: 'Did ever Victory with such fruits abound!' (II, iv, 60). At this point it seems only natural that the evil eye of Napoleon and the 'eagle eye' of Wellington should be subsumed by the 'commanding height' (II, iii, 50) of the Laureate, he who 'most of all men it behoved to raise / The strain of triumph' (I, i, 6).

It would seem, therefore, that Southey's aims have been achieved: by rewriting Wellington's account of Waterloo through the context of a Spenserian privileging of poetry over history – privatized romance over state-sanctioned fact – and then using this reconstituted history, in turn, as a sanction for his aesthetic ends, the poet has attained the totalizing vision on which high Romantic identity depends. But there is more to this vision than meets the eye. In addition to the uncomfortable reminders of the commercial picturesque, and to false or Napoleonic seeing (*is* there a difference between the 'commanding height' of 'The Evil Prophet' (II, ii, 3) and the 'commanding height' of 'The Sacred Mountain' (II, iii, 50)?), the poem also contains a panoramic 'key' in the form of detailed footnotes. These are mostly concerned with matters of literary elucidation and historical actuality. Here, once again, the peasant guide's complaint is cited – 'call it anything but Waterloo!' – only this time it has been emptied of its geopolitical force. By the time of the poem's publication the name of the battle had become a rigid designator. In the end, therefore, a poem entitled *The Poet's Pilgrimage to La Belle Alliance* has been framed by the politics of deference – to state history, to the marketplace and, ultimately, to the authority of Wellington. Romantic vision, at least in this version, would remain confined, replaced by an autocracy that it cannot quite command.

4
Coleridge: the Imagination at War

> That which does not *withstand*, hath *itself* no standing place. To *fill* a station is to exclude or repel others, – and this not less the definition of moral, than of material, *solidity*. We *live* by continued acts of defense, that involve a sort of offensive warfare.
>
> *The Friend*[1]

>   Peace
> And War are in themselves indifferent:
> The time doth stamp them either good or bad.[2]

Beating the retreat

Thus far I have presented a reading of the victory that places great emphasis on its transcendent or sublime qualities. From the startled evocations of Hunt and Haydon to the elevated rodomontades of Scott, Wordsworth and Southey, a portrait emerges of a nation state desperate to convince itself of the triumphant nature of its recent achievements. Within a few months, however, the great burst of intoxication was to be followed by a protracted period of depression. As Crabb Robinson noted in his diary for 27 November 1815: 'There was an illumination to-night for the Peace, but it did not occur to me to look at a single public building, and I believe no one cared about it. A duller rejoicing could not be conceived. There was hardly a crowd in the streets.'[3] The socio-economic reality that Cobbett wished to expose was now all too apparent. The cost of the wars had been colossal: in 1816 the National Debt stood at £902 million; peace brought with it the promise of an end to hardship. Yet virtually all of the measures introduced in 1815–16 to relieve the ailing economy resulted in further distress. The Corn Laws could not cure the weaknesses of the farming industry; the removal of the hated income tax could not by itself cure the slump in manufacturing; deflation (in 1813 the value of the pound was 30 per cent of its metallic value) brought with it wage cuts, unemployment and a sharp rise in the poor rate.[4] It was with some justification therefore that the *Annual Register* could observe at the close of 1815 that 'all the triumphant sensations of national glory seem almost obliterated by general depression'.[5] The moment of sublime euphoria had come to an end.

As radical reformers agitated against the state, many conservative thinkers looked back to the war years with feelings of nostalgia. Wartime demands had, after all, increased industrial production in certain key areas. The shortage of labour in manufacturing and agriculture meant that employment was plentiful and wages were high. With the onset of peace, however, the return to normalcy required a reorganization of wartime trades. High wages could no longer be sustained and the return of over 300,000 soldiers and sailors caused the labour market to swell. Despite the addition of 17 new colonies, hope of trade expansion was swiftly checked, and the nation was left to face the social consequences of a decline in manufacturing, exacerbated by the threat of foreign competition for corn. Coleridge, in the second *Lay Sermon*, saw in Jeremiah a text for the times: 'We looked for peace, but no good came: for a time of health and behold trouble. The harvest is past, the summer is ended, and we are not saved' (*LS*, 141–2). 'Trouble' came in the shape of renewed calls for political reform. An important article published in the *Quarterly Review*, written by but not credited to Southey, gives an overview of the shapes of dissent, from the address of the Common Council of London to the Prince Regent in which the war is denounced as 'rash and ruinous, unjustly commenced and pertinaceously persisted in, when no rational object was to be obtained' to the 'three-hundred circulars' of Major Cartwright; from the agit-propaganda of Orator Hunt and the cry for 'bread and reform' to the utopian pronouncements of the Spencean Philanthropists.[6] 'Never before' Southey writes, reflecting on the battle of Waterloo,

> had any contest been terminated with such consummate and transcendent glory: – this at least is universally acknowledged ... Yet at this time, when the plans of government have been successful beyond all former examples ... a cry of discontent is gone forth, the apostles of anarchy take advantage of a temporary and partial distress, and by imposing upon the ignorance of the multitude, flattering their errors and inflaming their passions, are exciting them to sedition and rebellion.
>
> (p. 225)

Chief among the reformers' complaints was the iniquitous burden of debt repayment. As Cobbett wrote, in his famous 'Address to the Journeymen and Labourers' (2 November 1816): 'As to the *cause* of our present miseries it is the *enormous amount of the taxes*, which the government compels us to pay for their standing army, its placemen, its pensioners, &c. and for the payment of the interest of its debt.'[7] For workers and owners alike, the Paineite argument that states engage in war to accrue greater tax revenue seemed to make sense: what, after all, had the country gained from its struggles? Faced with the spread of discontent among the manufacturing classes Southey and Coleridge urged their readers to consider the long-term benefits of the National Debt. The argument, that the Debt worked to unite the country in a common cause, is set out in a revised passage from *The Friend*:

> To what then do we owe our strength and our immunity [against Napoleon]?... I answer without hesitation, that the cause and mother principle of this unexampled confidence [in the Bank of England], of this system of credit, which is as much stronger than mere positive possessions, as the soul of man is than his body... the main cause of this, I say, has been our NATIONAL DEBT... as to our political strength and circumstantial prosperity, it is the national debt which has wedded in indissoluble union all the interests of the state, the landed with the commercial, and the man of independent fortune with the stirring tradesman and reposing annuitant.
>
> (F, I, 233)

Taxation, in other words, has had the fortuitous effect of binding the nation's interests together: 'who are a Nation's Creditors? The answer is, every Man to every Man.' No longer restricted in its role as the signified of the nation's interests, the National Debt had become a transcendent signifier, uniting competing claims in the name of an abstract principle.[8] It is profitable to view this argument as a logical extension of the principle of sublimation that Coleridge had previously outlined in the central section of the *Biographia Literaria*. Just as the Imagination 'dissolves, diffuses, dissipates, in order to recreate', so the system of debt and taxation combined to 'idealize and to unify' the conflict of abstract principles and material interests (*BL*, I, 304). In both cases, the system is meant to overcome the effects of uncertainty: contingency, temporality and the world of 'things' in the case of the Imagination; the commercial spirit, individual interests and the nature of the economy in the case of the National Debt.[9]

It is with some irony, however, that what is revealed in the course of these operations is not so much the conflict of competing principles as their structural interdependence. The point becomes clear in the *Lay Sermon* where Coleridge writes that 'the Spirit of Commerce' ought to be 'counteracted by the Spirit of the State' (*LS*, 223). For the state to work in this way it must translate the floating quantity of the National Debt into a symbol of national solidarity – a process analogous to the means by which paper money incarnates itself as property and possessions. The realization that the 'self-power' of the Imagination is related to the instituting power of money leads to some pretty fine distinctions: on the one hand between the giddy madness and self-interest of the 'commercial spirit' (identified with 'the wicked lunacies of the Gaming Table') and on the other 'the hope that is the subliming and expanding warmth of public credit' (*LS*, 168). For all the effort Coleridge expends on elevating notions of Spirit or nationhood above mere economism it is evident that the former must have recourse to the latter if it is to have any effect. The figure that best describes the relationship between the ethico-spiritual promptings of the nation and the amoral system of commercialism is, not surprisingly given its prominence elsewhere in Coleridge's writings, that of chiasmus: the spread of disinterested ideas is diffused through the medium of culture (or education), but clearly that cannot be facilitated outside a system of economic exchange. By the same token, pure economism, if left unchecked, is like the body without a soul. Lose the binding power of a pure idea such as the nation and the result is decrepitude and ruin.

That the uneasy alliance of national and commercial interests was never entirely resolved for Coleridge is evident from other passages in the *Sermon* where he attends to the 'unprecedented prosperity' of the war years:

> It was one among the many anomalies of the late War that it acted, after a few years, as a universal stimulant. We almost monopolized the commerce of the world... and to all this we must add a fact of the utmost importance in the present question, that the war did not, as was usually the case in former wars, die away into a long extended peace by gradual exhaustion and weariness on both sides, but *plunged* to its conclusion by a concentration, we might almost say, by a *spasm* of energy, and consequently by an *anticipation* of our resources... The first intoxication of triumph having passed over, this our 'agony of glory,' was succeeded, of course, by a general stiffness and relaxation. The antagonist passions came into play.
>
> (*LS*, 159)

The conflictual rhetoric of this passage is an aspect of Coleridge's evocation of the unregulated movements of the credit system. Pure economism, like sex, is subject to stimulation, spasms, anticipations, stiffening and relaxation, the outcome of which is exhaustion. The system is energetic to be sure, but in responding to the immediate interests of the pleasure principle rather than the deferred gratification aroused by the philosophical ideal, the nation state is condemned to extinction. As Coleridge continues, in times of prosperity credit soars 'to a certain utmost possible height, which has been different in each successive instance; but in every instance the attainment of this, its *ne plus ultra*, has been instantly announced by a rapid series of explosions (in mercantile language, a *crash*) and a consequent precipitation of the general system' (*LS*, 202). The sentence is notable for its reference to the apocalyptic foreboding of the *ne plus ultra*, a liminal state marking, in Morton D. Paley's words, 'the sense of historically imminent catastrophe – and the expectation of a consequent millennial transformation of society'.[10] Here, however, the promise of the antecedent clause – its status as the 'unrevealable' 'primal scorpion rod' of Night – is discharged in Coleridge's vision of a system dominated by the vagaries of contingency rather than the single, synchronic perspective proper to philosophical reason.[11] In the absence of any accompanying principle of redemption, the crashes of the monetary system serve as a parodic reminder of a world driven by agencies beyond human control. The flimsy barrier separating the mythic sublimity of the cash economy from its bathetic collapse is evinced a few pages later, when Coleridge writes: 'the movements of Trade become yearly gayer and giddier, and at length in a vortex of hopes and hazards, of blinding passions and blind practices, which should have been left where alone they ought ever to have been found, among the wicked lunacies of the Gaming Table' (*LS*, 204). Coleridge is speaking here of a fallible human creation but he might just as well be evoking the idea of a world that has passed from an attitude of unlimited (because disinterested) play to one of unthinking dependency.

The latter allusion is chosen purposefully, for in 1816 the rhythms of capital and the rhythms of war – of alternate boom and slump – fused in Coleridge's mind with the limited returns of a crippling drug habit. His concern with the power of this system prompted a set of distressed antitheses to describe its transformative effects. As the fluctuations of opium addiction teased the boundaries between reason and 'passion', prudence and 'sensual vices', allowing the latter principle to overcome its dependence on the former, so the splendid rewards of the wartime economy constantly threatened to overrun their origins in the 'natural' realm of honest labour and landed interests. Like the system of paper money from which it derived its vigour, the benefits of the wartime economy seemed to be without base or substance. Thus, as early as 1800, Coleridge queried whether Britain's monopoly of the trade of Europe would be a 'real *national* advantage ... would it not give such a superiority to the moneyed interest of the country over the landed, as might be fatal to our Constitution?'[12] Would the pleasures of speculation, in other words, prove fatal to the sobriety of the body politic?

Coleridge's reflections on the stimulus of war and commerce may be set alongside the idealist view that conflict forms the essence of individual and collective growth. In the *Critique of Judgement*, Kant had argued that 'war... has something sublime about it, and gives nations that carry it on in such a manner a stamp of mind only the more sublime the more numerous the dangers to which they are exposed, and which they are able to meet with fortitude.' A 'prolonged peace', by contrast, 'favours the predominance of a mere commercial spirit, and with it a debasing self-interest, cowardice, and effeminacy, and tends to degrade the character of the nation.'[13] The point I wish to make here is that both Coleridge and Kant regard war as destroyer and preserver; an unwelcome disruption, to be sure, but one that is necessary, given certain institutional conditions, for the integrity of the national body. Yet Coleridge's thinking on the beneficial aspects of conflict is far from consistent. In 1799, for example, he affirms the value of peaceful relations, arguing that 'when a nation is in safety, men think of their private interests;

individual property becomes the predominating principle, the Lord of the ascendant: and all politics and theories inconsistent with property and individual interest give way and sink into a decline' (*EoT*, I, 75). In this instance private interests are valuable insofar as they lead to the promotion of national unanimity. By contrast, in times of war artificial theories such as Jacobinism encourage the 'high, and the low' to abandon their individual concerns and to join together in an 'unnaturally stimulated' democracy (ibid.).

I will have more to say about the Kantian aspects of Coleridge's war writing in the next section. Here I wish merely to emphasize the point that the beneficial aspects of conflict are charged with ambiguous reminders of the unnatural and the excessive. The perverse restlessness of the state is such that its idealized object, the principle of national integrity, is submitted to the diminishing returns of the pleasure principle. If the nation is the substance on which the martial imagination plays, then this substance is shown to be nothing more than a *point de capiton*, an empty designator the function of which is to stimulate and maintain the state of war. The picture is complicated further by the arguments that Coleridge explores in his post-Waterloo writings. As I have argued above, Coleridge's uncertainty on the question of the proper relation between war and commerce was tempered by his growing awareness that militarism and monetarism might, after all, be two sides of the same coin. In the absence of genuine millennial expectation, war and money worked in tandem to produce virtual states of social unanimity – states that opened up the possibility of parodic inversion: Jacobinism, in the case of the French Republic, and rampant speculation in the case of an unfettered cash economy. What Coleridge debated in the *Biographia Literaria*, the revised text of *The Friend*, the *Lay Sermon* and in other writings from the postwar period was therefore of crucial importance for his attendant reformulation of the concepts of Nation and Imagination. As we shall go on to see, Waterloo, although not addressed explicitly by Coleridge, nevertheless forms the impetus for a critical reconsideration of the links between the creative power of individuals and that of the nation states to which they belong. Here I take support from Jerome Christensen's recent characterization of the *Biographia Literaria* as 'decidedly a Waterloo composition', as a work that struggles to displace the contingency of wartime with the civic dispensation of 'normal change'.[14] This chapter may be read, therefore, as a paradoxical interlude in the 'story' that is Waterloo and the Romantic Imagination, paradoxical because Waterloo takes shape in Coleridge's writings as an imaginary non-entity, a fictional phenomenon that is never grasped as such but without which both subject and state would collapse.

Before going on, however, to explore the significance of Coleridge's postwar writing I want to dwell on the poetry and prose of the 1795–1803 period, a body of writing that foregrounds the difficulty of reconciling the pacific and violent aspects of the creative imagination.

Strange explosions

In his introduction to *Essays on His Times* David Erdman provides a fitting commentary on the apparent contradictions of Coleridge's political thought: 'he is in truth "ever the same"... he is never single-sided or single-minded but always both Jacobin and anti-Jacobin, Radical and Tory, poet and moralist, intermingled' (*EoT*, I, lxv). To this list of coexistent positions – evidence, perhaps, of an author exhibiting myriad-mindedness – we might add peace campaigner and warmonger. In expounding this idea our attention falls naturally on the writings of the 1790s. For here, whether the subject is the bellicist policies of the Pitt administration or the atrocities committed by the French in La Vendée, Coleridge often betrays a secret sympathy with the sublime or mythic aspects of war. He is able, in other words, to demonstrate an enthusiasm for the epic drama of combat even as he expresses a lyric longing for the restorative powers of peace.

To explain this notion let us recall some of the intellectual currents that informed the writings of the anti-war campaigner in the earlier part of the decade. In recent research by Nicholas Roe, Morton D. Paley and Peter J. Kitson we are reminded that Coleridge's peculiar brand of radicalism was forged out of a deep-seated mistrust of Paineite rationalism.[15] Unitarian theology, Cambridge millenarianism and the stylistic influence of Edmund Burke were the elements that conjoined to place Coleridge in a volatile relation with the more orthodox currents of political dissent. This complex background is reflected in 'Religious Musings', a poem that portrays the horrors of 'scepter'd Glory's gore-drench'd field', as the prelude to divine justice prophesied in *Revelations*. Instead of echoing the call of the London radicals for an immediate end to the campaigns, the verse presents a more imaginative response:

> Rest awhile
> Children of Wretchedness! More groans must rise,
> More blood must stream, or ere your wrongs be full.
> Yet is the day of Retribution nigh:
> The Lamb of God hath open'd the fifth seal:
> And upward rush on swiftest wings of fire
> Th'innumerable multitude of Wrongs
> By man on man inflicted! Rest awhile,
> Children of Wretchedness! The hour is nigh...
> (lines 300–8)

The sentiment expressed in these lines is far removed from the rational critique of war presented by the followers of Godwin and Paine. With his Burkean predilection for the 'sublimer' passages of Milton and Isaiah, Coleridge subjects his reader to a spiralling succession of arresting analogies culminating in the idea that warfare, while deplorable in terms of its human costs and consequences, is nevertheless to be welcomed as proof of the spiritual revelations foretold in the scriptures.[16] The effect of all this is to muddy the ideological clarity of the politics of dissent. With its sights set firmly on the mystical *telos* of human history, the poem regards war as a consequence of human 'progressiveness'. The doctrine of necessitarian optimism leads to the perplexing conclusion that 'Warriors, and Lords, and Priests – all the sore ills / That vex and desolate our mortal life' (lines 215–16) have their origin in the 'restless faculty of *Imagination*'.[17] When viewed from the perspective of divine Providence warfare is merely an extension of man's desire to 'imitate' the 'powers of the Creator'. It is on this basis that Coleridge refuses to protest against the sublime rhetoric of Milton.

As the war continued, however, Coleridge's faith in the 'blest future' predicted by Priestley, Frend and others underwent a severe test. The belief that the war would end with the manifestation of the heavenly throne was dampened somewhat by the realization that the pressures of contemporary historical events forbade the easy application of prophetic analogy. The 'Ode on the Departing Year' published on 26 December 1796 is representative of this mode with its invective against the insularity of a nation content to wage war by proxy:

> for many a fearless age
> Has social Quiet loved thy shore;
> Nor ever proud invader's rage
> Or sacked thy towers, or stained thy fields with gore.
>
> Abandoned of Heaven! mad avarice thy guide,
> At cowardly distance, yet kindling with pride –
> Mid thy herds and thy corn-fields secure thou hast stood,
> And joined the wild yelling of famine and blood!
> (lines 131–8)

The vision of a people in thrall to the tokens of war yet averse to coming into direct contact with its reality is prefaced by lines that make overt reference to the invisible 'agony' of combat. It is clear that Coleridge, labouring perhaps with the memory of an earlier incarnation as a member of the Fifteenth Light Dragoons, identifies with the sufferings of the wounded soldier. But what has greater force than the complaint against war is the sense in which the poet wishes to bridge the gap between self and nation, body and wound. The solitariness of the disaffected radical, the isolation of the island State and the 'fierce solitude' of 'Strange-eyed Destruction' (lines 141–3) are emblems of incompletion radiating from the poem's antagonistic centre. Moreover, there seems in line 138 to be an implicit comment on Coleridge's own tendency to mythologize the war, seeing in millennial discourse an opportunity to transcend topicality. In this respect the conclusion of the poem is especially telling. Faced with the impossibility of resolving the tension between competing representations of the social world the poet opts instead for a form of quietist withdrawal:

> Away, my soul away!
> I unpartaking of the evil thing...
> Now I recentre my immortal mind
>   In the deep sabbath of meek self-content;
> Cleansed from the vaporous passions that bedim
> God's image, sister of the Seraphim.
>   (lines 154–61)

Coleridge's point, that warfare nominates the impossibility of realizing dreams of social perfection, was addressed the previous year during the course of a lecture 'On the Present War'. In this lecture Coleridge remarks how war threatens the integrity of society, melting away the 'beautiful fabric of Love' and replacing it with an 'atmosphere of Imposture and Panic'. In such a climate men are no longer capable of forming spontaneous social ties; the effects of war are such that everyday gestures are perverted through the imposition of an artificial language of social codes: 'our very looks are decyphered into disaffection' (*LoPR*, 60). This last comment gives a clue to Coleridge's underlying concern. The chief evil of war is its negative effect on the constitution of society. It works everywhere as a principle of division: by dividing the ordinary citizen between the private man of the domestic sphere and the public man of the battlefield; by separating the man of conscience from the nation of which he is part; by replacing organic social relations with a network of arbitrary signs. Yet by 1798, the year of Napoleon's threatened invasion of England, the radical connotations of Coleridge's speech have been tempered by an awareness that far from eroding the fabric of society, war may in fact act as a principle of purification. Indeed, this notion is anticipated, structured even, by the pervasive rhetoric of apocalypse. The note accompanying the 1796 quarto of the 'Ode to the Departing Year' gives this scandalous proposition some credence: 'We have been preserved by our insular situation, from suffering the actual horrors of War ourselves ... Such wickedness cannot pass unpunished... God has prepared the canker-worm, and will smite the *gourds* of our pride... "There is no healing of thy bruise; thy wound is grievous."'[18] By acting out the desire for completion in the shadow-play of foreign war, both nation and poet are accused of abstracting themselves from actuality. Somewhat disturbingly, the note ends with the suggestion that the return of war to British shores will bring about the millennial renewal that current practices defer.

War is perceived in the latter half of the 1790s as a perverse means of filling out the void of individual and national subjectivity. If every symbolic identity the state acquires is ultimately nothing but a supplementary feature whose function is to conceal this void, then the appeal to the substantive act of war is a pathological attempt to embrace this emptiness. Coleridge speaks here of a pleasure that exceeds the parameters of the pleasure principle; a kind of inhuman ecstasy or *jouissance* that replaces the comforting dialectics of specular identification with the self-lacerating extremes of historical violence.[19] The desire to found social identity in something other than a network of symbolic relations is thus the theme of 'Fears in Solitude', the central section of which narrates the tortuous course from straightforward denunciation of war to qualified advocacy. Picking up on the themes introduced three years earlier, Coleridge attacks the British public for their passive consumption of war as mere 'animating sport' (line 94), a spectacle to be digested in the paper along with 'our morning meal' (line 107). Once again, the pressure of conflict has brought about a linguistic transformation and with this a corresponding change in ordinary conceptions of the relation between thought and expression. Thus the 'poor wretch, who has learnt only his prayers' becomes

> A fluent phraseman, absolute
> And technical in victories and defeats,
> And all our dainty terms for fratricide;
> Terms which we trundle smoothly o'er our tongues
> Like mere abstractions, empty sounds to which
> We join no feeling and attach no form!
> As if the soldier died without a wound;
> As if the fibres of this godlike frame
> Were gored without a pang; as if the wretch,
> Who fell in battle, doing bloody deeds,
> Passed off to Heaven, translated and not killed...
> (lines 111–21)

War has altered the primal reality of the wound and transferred its attributes to an ideology craving linguistic stability. Coleridge believes, however, that only direct contact with war will 'make us know / the meaning of our words' (lines 126–7). The threatened invasion becomes therefore a curious object of desire. Bringing the conflict home, so the argument runs, will 'force' the nation to 'feel' a unity of purpose, a form of earnest solidarity hitherto masked by the illusion of peace: 'Peace long preserved by fleets and perilous seas... / Secure from actual warfare' (lines 87–8). Coleridge's former objection to war – that it leads to the undoing of society – has undergone a radical reversal. In this new vision, war becomes the means of overcoming a nation's dependence on the artificial structures of signification. As the poet goes on to suggest, rather than mediating violence through signs, direct contact with the substance – with the wound itself – will enable the men of Britain to be themselves, to 'Stand forth!' and become 'pure' (lines 138–9). Warfare, in this scheme, has become a means of filling in the interior lack of the nation, enabling 'Sons, brothers, husbands, all' (line 134) to forge themselves together in defiance of a common enemy. The phallogocentricism implicit in this reasoning had previously been established in 'The Destiny of Nations'. In lines centring on the causes of conflict, Coleridge singles out the moment

> When luxury and lust's exhausted stores
> No more can rouse the appetites of kings;
> When the low flattery of their reptile lords
> Falls flat and heavy on the accustomed ear;
> When eunuchs sing, and fools buffoonery make,
> And dancers writhe their harlot-limbs in vain;
> Then War and all its dread vicissitudes
> Pleasingly agitate their stagnant hearts...
> (lines 396–402)

What was denounced as an artificial stimulant for jaded sexual appetites in 1796 becomes in the later poem a source of vital potency, the antidote to luxury and lassitude, the 'effeminacy' of 'wealth', the solution to the emptiness at the heart of individual and national identity.

It is this support for the revivifying effects of defensive warfare that qualify, in my view, Erdman's belief that the poem is in argument comparable to the Whig speeches made in support of the call for mobilization.[20] For warfare is imagined in the poem as a powerful antidote to what Coleridge calls, in a related article, the 'insensibility of the public temper'. Where in prose, a few weeks prior to the invasion alarm, Coleridge analyses the course of public support for the war from the 'drunken delirium of 1792' to the 'languor and lethargy' of 1798 and calls, in conclusion, for a power to 'mediate' between Britain and France, the poetry invokes a more active force. The erring state will regain its national integrity only on the condition that it actively resists the threat of a foreign Other. But more radically than this, Coleridge suggests that the entry into violence will do away with the need to veil the unthinkable kernel of political experience, the void that the state represses in order to maintain its stagnant, morally bankrupt identity. With its suggestion that history should be lived in close relation with the annihilation of the self, 'Fears in Solitude', poses a fundamental question about the limits of the *psyche* and the *polis*.

To some degree the prose writings of the period 1802–3 may be read as an attempt to respond to this question. In 'The Men and the Times', an essay written in the aftermath of the collapse of the Peace of Amiens, it is now clear that Coleridge views defensive warfare as an opportunity for the English nation to forge itself as an organic unity. Faced this time with a genuine threat of foreign usurpation the English are encouraged to 'be convinced in their understandings that they have a cause of their own; that they must think for *themselves*, and act for *themselves*; for by themselves alone, under the providence of the Supreme Being, must they be saved' (*EoT*, I, 434). This recalls the terms with which, in the autumn of 1802, Coleridge set about rehabilitating Pitt (a significant *volte-face* in itself) as one who 'walks in himself alone' (*EoT*, I, 346). When faced with the choice between the increasingly despotic actions of the French Empire and the unreliability of the Addington regime, Pitt was taken up by Coleridge as the man best qualified to encourage the nation in its defence of the true principles of liberty and justice. When the war was resumed in the summer of 1803, those qualities that Coleridge had previously attributed to Napoleon and Washington, a 'deep sense of internal power, with imaginations capable of bodying forth lofty undertakings' (*EoT*, I, 131), were now conferred on the English nation as a whole. It is worth noting that the concept of the commanding genius was an attempt to synthesize otherwise violent contraries: 'energy' and 'austerity', inwardness and 'visible language', heroism and 'self-subjugation' (ibid., 132). In line with those passages in which Coleridge asserts the inherent value of landed property as a means of counterbalancing the vitiating effects of commercialism, the victorious nation will be the one that most perfectly harmonizes the competing claims of interior worth and external action. Thus, in 1803, more so than in 1798, Coleridge is convinced that the struggle against the French is both 'necessary & just';[21] its fortuitous effect will be the sanctification of a hitherto unworthy cause and the galvanizing of an insensible, undisciplined nation.[22] No longer content to unfeelingly consume the war, the English, it was averred, will become, if not the instigators of a new millennium, then at least the agents of a sublime form of justice:

> Then let France bribe, or puzzle all Europe into a confederacy against us, I will not fear for my Country. I trust, that the words of Isaiah will be truly prophetic, and that, even of this people it will be truly said, 'They trode the wine-press alone, and of the nations there was none with them. – They looked and there was none to help; they WONDERED that there was none to uphold. Therefore THEIR OWN ARM brought salvation unto them, and their INDIGNATION, *it* upheld them.'
>
> (*EoT*, I, 435)

The war therefore has acted on the English as a disciplinary force, binding otherwise intractable elements – party divisions, popular protest and above all the commercial spirit – to the spirit of nationhood. Coleridge's thinking in this period, as Charles De Paolo has noted, is thoroughly inflected with a Kantian sense of 'providential destiny':[23]

> We will tremble at the possible punishment, which our national crimes may have made us worthy of, from retributive Providence; we will tremble

at what God may do; but not at what our enemies can do, of themselves. When were we a more united People? When so well prepared? The very nature of the Invasion will cut off from the French army most of the opportunities of military Tactics – & bring the affair, man to man, bayonet against bayonet. –

(*CN*, II, 1006)

The return of prophetic discourse and the erstwhile support for conflict ought, however, to be viewed alongside those moments when Coleridge appears to withdraw from violent acts. Let us not forget that 'Fears in Solitude' concludes with a return to 'the green and silent' Quantocks (line 1; line 228) and to 'solitary musings' on 'nature's quietness' (lines 229–30) – the very conditions, in other words, of the productive interiorization celebrated in the companion piece 'Frost at Midnight'. War may well provide the grounds for a revivification of national purpose but its potential to place the subject in relation to the unassailable extremes of desire and death is a cause for concern. Coleridge must therefore set about defining the grounds for a non-violent mode of principled identity: one that avoids the fabricated condition of the current nation state while maintaining a distance from the perils of *jouissance*. It is for this reason that he returns to consider the desire for peace.

The distinction between the passive insensibility of a war-fixated public and the creative withdrawal of the poet is the theme of the 'Ode to Tranquillity', a poem written in the summer of 1801 in the period when peace negotiations were underway. In the version printed in the *Morning Post*, Coleridge declares weariness with the 'schemes' of statesmen and soldiers. Reflecting on the turbulence of 1798 he notes that he has come to view 'distant Fights and Treaties crude' with 'quiet heart'; 'the present works of present man' are seen as the 'wild and dream-like trade of blood and guile, / Too foolish for a tear, too wicked for a smile!' (lines 30–3). In this the poet is keen to distinguish his condition of sage-like aloofness from the 'counterfeit' states of 'Satiety' and 'Sloth' (lines 11–12). The peace that Coleridge proclaims on 1801 may be read as an extension of the sentiments expressed earlier in the 'Ode on the Departing Year': the poet's industrious contemplation is far-removed from the general public's mute indifference because, in keeping its sights on matters of principle, it operates beyond the immediate interests of the libidinal economy.

Yet, when viewed from the perspective of the writings Coleridge would produce during the short-lived peace of 1802–3, the affirmation of tranquillity remains structurally dependent on the continued threat of warfare. In 'A Letter to – [Sara Hutchinson] April 4, 1802', the poem that would become the 'Dejection' ode, there is, in the decisive central section, a reference to the incipient violence of the Coleridgean imagination:

What tell'st thou now about?
'Tis of the Rushing of an Host in Rout–
And many Groans from men with smarting Wounds–
At once they groan with smart, and shudder with the Cold!
'Tis hush'd there is a Trance of deepest Silence–
(lines 200–4)

The return of war, albeit at the symbolic level, leads Coleridge to reaffirm his commitment to the productive calm of 'trance-like Depth' (line 110). But the story of 'less Affright' (line 208) that the poem goes on to tell may be read as an infantilized version of the battlefield experience with its 'moans' and 'screams' (lines 214–15). To do so, however, is to ignore the crucial emphasis that Coleridge places on the 'shaping Spirit of Imagination' (lines 310–11). Placed between the 'Indifference or Strife' of the poet's domestic life, itself a microcosm of the extremes touched upon by the warring nation state, the creative imagination combines the hitherto warring contraries of 'strength' and 'joy' (lines 305–18; *passim*) in a productive synthesis: 'This beautiful & beauty-making Power!' (line 311), even to the extent of 'Enveloping the Earth!' (line 303).

And as for individuals so for nation states. The critical role of the Imagination in positing a power beyond the entropic course of empirical existence is closely correlated with the instituting power of the nation. In both cases, through the assertion of an eternal force, set apart from the ordinary realm of chance and change, Coleridge is attempting to liberate the system from its dependence on the warring polarities of the pleasure principle: instant gratification and corresponding annihilation. The distinction between the timeless, untroubled realm of pure reason and the contingent, vexed world of experience and understanding becomes more clear when it is placed in the context of the *Biographia Literaria* with its distinction between the commanding and absolute forms of genius.[24] The argument turns on the assertion that the desire to 'realize' the 'conceptions of the mind' – whether this takes the form of 'a perfect poem in palace, or temple, or landscape-garden; or a tale of romance in canals that join with the sea, or in walls of rock, which, shouldering back the billows, imitate the power, and supply the benevolence of nature to sheltered navies; or in aqueducts that, arching the wide vale from mountain to mountain, give a Palmyra to the desert' – must be subordinated to the 'self-sufficing power of absolute genius'. For when, in times of peace, the former are perceived as humane and beneficent, 'in times of tumult' such men are apt to 'come forth as the shaping spirit of Ruin' (*BL*, I, 32–3). The so-called commanding genius is thus caught in an interminable mirror stage, forever seeking to accomplish idealized images of 'clearness, distinctness and individuality'. The man of absolute genius, by contrast, is able 'to rest content between thought and reality, as it were in an intermundium of which their own living spirit supplies the *substance*, and their imagination the ever-varying *form'* (*BL*, I, 32). When read as a gloss on the 'shaping Spirit' of the 'Dejection' ode we see here again the affirmation of a power that is able to transcend and crucially envelop a world of material change and transformation.[25] Later, and this next point will take on greater force at the close of this chapter, Coleridge will confirm that the power of absolute genius to exist within and for itself is the foundation on which the nation should, ideally, be raised.

But what bearing does this have on the question of war? It seems to me that having once imagined himself a conqueror Coleridge is faced with the problem of having to sever the links between the creative and the commanding imaginations while at the same time asserting a principle of self-sufficiency – an *intermundium* – that does not depend on a dialectical, i.e. antagonistic, relationship with the Other. At first sight 'Our Future Prospects' may seem an unlikely source for the testing of this idea. Published in the *Morning Post* on 6 January 1803, the essay is an attempt to justify the renewal of the war against France on the grounds that nations (and individuals) cannot 'Continue always quiet and unconcerned spectators'. For peace to be restored in Europe, so the argument goes, the creative genius of the Allied states must henceforth impress itself on the world without. In the terms that Coleridge will go on to use in his essay on Rousseau, the absolute truth of Reason must communicate with the world but in such a way that the very act of mediation will preserve Reason in its *a priori* status. Hence the return to the notion of 'a contemplative reserve', a 'tranquil nook or island cove' of extra-discursive authority from which the war can be conducted almost as a thing set apart from the transcendental reality of the philosopher poet and the nation state.[26] For war, as the author admits in private, is a cause for 'guilt & woe': 'Tell Adam, the day after Abel's Death, in 4 square leagues 700,000 men shall be assembled. Possible? – and to murder each other!'[27] In seeking therefore to distinguish himself from both the war mongering of the official opposition and from the conciliatory machinations of the Foxites, Coleridge places the arguments for war in a non-participatory, quasimetaphysical setting. There is no need to wring one's hands over the renewal of hostilities when the collapse of the antagonist is viewed as fact of nature: 'the same law that hurried [the avalanche] from its elevated situation... conducts it .... to the spot where its impelling force is to be exhausted, and it is itself to vanish before a milder temperature' (*EoT*, I, 420). One's role in fostering such an event is, from the point of view of principle, morally negligible.

Nevertheless, as Coleridge echoes elsewhere in *Hymn Before Sunrise*, a mass of snow, loosened by being 'agitated', is at first 'silent'; a single word may tip the balance. In the end the author, and the nation for which he speaks, cannot avoid taking responsibility; the word, like the will of the commanding genius, must act on the world if 'balance' and 'equilibrium' are to be restored (*EoT*, I, 420). We are faced, then, with the unwelcome conclusion that 'cautious powers' cannot 'be kept aloof from the horrors and operations of war' – the very idea that informs the apocalyptic tone of 'The Men and the Times' a few months later (*EoT*, I, 421). The justification for war thus blurs into, and indeed provides support for, the crucial distinction between the state and the nation. For the balance to be restored and for the English to 'stand by themselves', the state must re-engage with the Other while, at the same time, misrecognizing this relation and assuming itself to be wholly self-contained. The state produces itself as a nation, that is, when it transforms lethal, substantive extremes into benign conceptual oppositions. The nation state is born, in other words, when it declares itself aloof from processes that have no significant part in the composition of its being. As Coleridge concludes: 'Every thing in nature has its period... it should not be forgotten, that, when the volcanic matter [of the Revolution] is exhausted, the effects of an eruption are surveyed with wonder and admiration, but cease to be objects of terror and dismay' (*EoT*, I, 422).

With its scrupulous investigation of the fine line separating peace and war, action and withdrawal, 'Our Future Prospects' comes close to exposing the impossibility of the Coleridgean imagination. Governing ideas may well precede empirical nation states, but the former notion must be realized through the necessary contamination of the latter. As the pragmatic, political side of Coleridge would admit, neither side of the metaphysical divide is sufficient unto itself; a balance of powers may only be restored through an act of creative violence. And warfare, that which emerges out of a desire to fill in the void at the centre of the nation (and of the individual), is perhaps the most awful demonstration of this truth.

We are now in a position to regard war in Coleridge's text as a pure fantasy object. For all his apparent insistence on the substantive nature of war and his appeal to its transformative effects, the author's immediate concern is to prevent the state from identifying too fully with the object of its desire. The life of the state, in other words, is preserved by replacing a potentially threatening dependency on the Other with a self-contained, auto-erotic war, a substitutive order of signs in which the state 'is defined and preserved by its turn toward itself and its turn of all else – principles, people, and ministers – into pretexts for its own life'.[28] Strictly speaking, then, there is no peace-making with the Emperor Napoleon – a fact borne out by Coleridge's frequent attempts to define Napoleon as an unjust enemy, outside of ordinary ethical definitions of warfare.[29] For the fight is not against an actual historical personage but rather against an internal form of contestation, a force that violates the constitutive principles of the nation state. What the nation state defends itself against therefore is its own internal self-surpassing: at one extreme, the dangerous pleasures of material conquest, and at the other the feminized lassitude of perpetual peace. If the integrity of the state depends on its ability to mediate a course between these extremes then what better means than to figure identity in the terms of phallic substitution, an endless play of signs in which identity flirts with representations of presence and absence? As we have seen, however, Coleridge does not rest easy with the image of a world in which extra-discursive principles are collapsed into symbolic economies. With Coleridge there remains, I feel, the pathos of having failed to reach the place of the Real in the Other.

A state of peace

Coleridge is well aware that nations turn to war as a means of substantiating a claim to legitimacy. He knows as well that war nominates the impossibility of substantiating this aim. The outcome of war is not identity but discontinuity. By evacuating reason from its proper place, the warring state sacrifices the naked principle of its being to the deadly world of experience. One might say that 'the life of the state' which 'cannot be imagined without a war' renders the existence of a principle that is 'both prior and superior to [the] behaviour' of that particular state inconceivable.[30] Yet this does not prevent the state from orienting its course in accordance with the virtual reality of such ideals. Wars need justification and their life can be maintained only on the strength of their appeal to abstract principles or meta-narratives. But there is no way that such principles can be united with the states they would govern. The passage from nominal to substantive reality is as fraught as that from rhetorical ingenuity to moral conviction. Increasingly, as Christensen notes, Coleridge's war writings come close to exposing the gap between abstract and substantive existence or, to put this in less theoretical terms, the breach between what a nation state would be and what it actually is.

I want to suggest that the implications of this schism are detectable in the work that Coleridge went on to produce in the aftermath of the Napoleonic campaigns. I want to begin, however, with an article written for *The Courier* in the wake of the Peninsular campaign, on the attributes of military as opposed to literary genius. We may approach this topic as an extension of the split between principle and expediency, morality and rhetoric, which motivated the theoretical procedures of the earlier work. Casting around for a loyalist successor to the now detested Napoleon he focused, naturally enough, on the achievements of Lord Wellington. In his glowing account of the victory at Almeida Wellington is represented as a 'commanding genius', on a par with Gustavus Adolphus, Alexander the Great and Scipio. As the natural superior to Napoleon's Hannibal, the Duke has become 'a personification of Great Events', a sublime presence 'Under whose auspices a nation, long degraded, awakes as from a sleep to all its ancestral heroism – like the sun, not only bright in herself, but spreading brightness and vital energy on all beneath him!'[31] An unfortunate reminder of the very forces of Napoleonic militarism to which Coleridge is officially opposed troubles this picture of an apparently benign presence, however. As Coleridge goes on to state, Lord Wellington is motivated by a combination of prudence and aggression; the emphasis is on strategy and tactics with little or no reference to moral qualities. Moreover, the passage suggests a lingering respect for the Satanic power of the Emperor's imagination. Just as the *Biographia Literaria*, conceived in the wake of Napoleon's defeat, betrays its fascination with the shaping spirit of ruin, so the *Courier* article draws energy from a similarly Luciferic source. Wellington as the sun, bright in himself and spreading vital energy to those beneath him, is both 'self-sufficing' *and* 'commanding', sun god *and* Satan, deliverer *and* conqueror. The military and pacific forms of genius are yoked together in a set of warring contradictions that rests uneasily with the fantasy of intellectual and social harmony.

By 1815 Coleridge seems to have tired of searching for a hero to unite the political and poetic forms of genius. On Wellington's prowess at Waterloo, indeed on Waterloo itself, he is virtually silent, seemingly absorbed in the task of separating, once and for all, the 'creative, and self-sufficing power' of the 'absolute *Genius*' (*BL*, I, 31) from the 'Restlessness and whirling Activity' of the 'commanding Genius' (*LS*, 66). Given the poet's visible participation in the peace celebrations of the previous year the reasons for this disengagement are perplexing. On the face of things it seems that Coleridge, like Shelley and Blake, was indifferent to the achievements of his countrymen. And indeed the image of the sage of Calne, assembling in isolation the lifework on which generations of romanticists would form their reading of the literature of the age would seem to preclude all but the most cursory view of 'the greatest event of modern times'. For such readers the insignificance of Waterloo to the development of the *Biographia* would be 'read', if at all, only as the sign of the ultimate triumph of Imagination over the 'ever-varying' world of 'things' – the very world that Wellington and Napoleon, as commanding geniuses, had set out to dominate.

But what is at stake in such a calculated act of withdrawal? The ideology of romantic transcendence, as formulated by Jerome McGann and reiterated with variations in the work of (new) historicist criticism, does not, in my view, provide us with a satisfactory explanation. With its emphasis on significant silences, gaps, aporias or elisions – the non-places where history is said to 'speak' – it encourages readers to ignore those places where history is, in fact, most visible. To illustrate this point I want to explore the text and context of a letter written by Coleridge to R. H. Brabant on 22 June 1815, the day that the Allied victory was first announced in London. The letter is, unsurprisingly, entirely silent on the matter of the crisis in Europe; its aim is simple: to recommend the services of a Mr Falkner, the manager of a theatre company residing in Calne. The letter goes on, however, to focus on the question of the relations between dramatic entertainment and sexual transgressions. Coleridge begins by assuring his correspondent that in 'towns like Calne and Devizes' where plays are performed only on occasion, the risks to the populace are minimal: 'No allurements to vice are held forth; no vicious women collected.' Moreover, in the case of Falkner's company, great efforts are taken to ensure that 'every line that borders on indelicacy, every indecorous or irreverent word is omitted in the acting'. 'I myself', he adds, 'disapprove of the habit of attending theatres in young persons, as undomesticating the disposition, and tending to render them too dependent on foreign and strong stimuli for their amusement' (*CL*, IV, 577). The letter ends with the remark that the company is about to bring out a version of Coleridge's *Remorse*. There are two things to note here. Firstly, it is significant that Coleridge uses the language of 'habit' and 'stimuli', words that appear in the discussion of war and commerce, to describe the ill effects of theatre-going. The drama, it is observed, is a dangerous art form, one that tends towards the 'undomesticating' of the self. If we think back to what has already been said about the relations between individual property, familial affections and the disposition towards peace we can see how the theatre, associated with the loss of domestic control, the promotion of exaggerated feeling and, through the formation of 'habit', with moral insensibility, resembles the vitiating effects of war. It will be Coleridge's task, in the ensuing months to explore these relations and to attempt their negation.

Leaving this discussion suspended, for now, the second thing I would emphasize is the way the concern with theatricality bears upon the dramatic content and political context of the forthcoming production of *Remorse*. Written towards the end of the Peninsular campaigns, the play may be seen as a conscious attempt to query the relation between military expediency and national well-being. It seems fitting therefore, that a production of the play should be staged in Calne in the very month that Wellington, as commanding genius, acted to remove Napoleon from the stage of history. When *Remorse* is read in this context the critique of violence and the endorsement of reflective statesmanship is all the more urgent. For as the play makes clear, deliverance from tyranny is the effect of 'the quiet rhythm of time', not of commanding men.[32] Just as in 'Religious Musings' the course of history is bottomed on notions of divine justice, so in *Remorse* the actions of worldly men are shown to be dangerously precipitous. The play's stress on the superiority of absolute genius extends even to the psychological traits of its central characters. Alvar, the contemplative man, is 'calm', secure in his knowledge that justice will prevail. Ordonio, his structural opponent, is 'restless', a man driven by vengeance and a belief in the power of the sword. In the course of the play Coleridge makes it clear that a nation's health is derived from the inner resources associated with Alvar. Where Alvar's (in)action evokes a mind at peace with itself, Ordonio's violence is shown to be the product of a mind at odds with itself. In this extraordinarily prescient drama, Coleridge points towards the traumatic origins of a nation's lust for war and, in the face of Waterloo, inveighs against the moral shoddiness of triumphalism. The target of the play's critique of violence may well be the French Revolution, but *Remorse* retains enough of its former incarnation as the anti-Pitt, pro-reform *Osorio* (1797) to remind its audience that necessitarianism is the downfall of all nation states. In this sense the staging of *Remorse*, a play that advocates the separation of the contemplative statesman from the man of action, and that emphasizes the role of Providence in securing the reign of the good, may be interpreted as a direct commentary on the culture and politics of Waterloo.

The work that Coleridge went on to complete in the aftermath of *Remorse* is, of course, the *Biographia Literaria*. Enough has been said about the formulation of the contrast between the absolute and commanding forms of genius to warrant the inclusion of this text in the present discussion, but the *Biographia* also includes a reflection on the associative links between war and theatre, one that centres, interestingly enough, on the question of Shakespeare's genius. The passage comes towards the end of a reading of *Venus and Adonis*:

> In Shakespeare's *poems*, the creative power, and the intellectual energy wrestle as in a war embrace. Each in the excess of strength seems to threaten the extinction of the other. At length, in the DRAMA they were reconciled, and fought each with its shield before the breast of the other.
>
> (*BL*, II, 26)

The evaluation of Shakespeare's 'war embrace' and his progress towards a drama of 'reconciliation' might also describe the course that Coleridge wishes to take. In a letter to Southey on the subject of *Remorse*, Coleridge professes that the play is an attempt to address 'the Anguish and Disquietude arising from the Self-contradiction introduced into the Soul by Guilt' (*CL*, III, 433–4). We might regard the play that he goes on to write as an effort to nullify self-contradiction at every level: in the dependence of national (and individual) identity on the drama of war, in the conflict between absolute and commanding forms of will. Above all, however, Coleridge wishes to reconcile the warring opposition between the nation (or the self) and the structures of signification on which the realization of this 'ideal object' depends. In the creation of *Zapolya*, therefore, he seeks nothing less than a solution to the dilemma that has haunted his writing since the beginning of the 1790s.

When we consider that *Zapolya* was originally intended to 'fill the Gap' in volume II of the *Biographia* (*CL*, IV, 703) I think we begin to see how the play might perform a crucial strategic function: as a means of putting theory into practice and as a way of envisioning the interchange between politics and principles. When *Zapolya* is read in this spirit we can perhaps begin to perceive its manifest failings in a different light. And the play is, indeed, a failure. As a drama of (in)action *Zapolya* extends the themes of *Remorse*: its concern is with revolution, legitimacy and the question of armed resistance.[33] As such it offers an implicit judgement on the terms and conditions of the postwar settlement. Moreover, with its stress on the triumph of natural order, seemingly unassisted by violent deeds, it sends a clear message to the commanding spirit of Wellington and Waterloo. For a nation to flourish, its being must be founded on property and domesticity; military genius alone is an insufficient support.

Given what has been said thus far about the war-like connotations of dramatic action we should not be surprised to find the play revolving around the question of performative violence. This seeming obsession with the dangers of 'foreign stimuli' is present even at the level of genre. Published in 1817, *Zapolya* was advertised as a 'Christmas Play' written 'in humble imitation' of *The Winter's Tale*. From its inception, therefore, the work was at odds with a cultural system that required epic or tragic expression. As a 'tragic romance', a 'dramatic romance' or a 'dramatic entertainment' (*CL*, IV, 591), *Zapolya* lacked the sort of gravity that one would expect from historical drama. Indeed, by the time the play was completed Coleridge himself was unsure about its suitability for performance. He told Lord Byron that it would 'not do as a play' but as 'Melodrama with slight alteration' (*CL*, IV, 628).[34] The Drury Lane committee seems to have agreed with this self-judgement and the play was rejected. In late 1817, however, against the author's wishes, *Zapolya* was produced as a melodrama at the Royal Circus Theatre. Thereafter, the play seems to have disappeared from the stage and indeed from Coleridge's oeuvre.

In many respects, however, as the critic Julia Carlson insists, the aesthetics of disappearance – from action, from revolution and from the theatre – is precisely what is at issue here. Staged in the romantic world of Illyria, *Zapolya* is largely concerned with the usurpation of an infant's right to the throne. But the mythopoeic elements of the drama are contained within an allegorical account of the rise and fall of the French Revolution. The allegory centres on the figure of Prince Emerick, a Napoleonic usurper who has wrested power away from the legitimate monarchy. When the loyalist Raab Kiuprili questions his act of usurpation, he is informed by his treacherous son, Casimir, that Emerick is the 'elected king'. Moreover, unlike the legitimate monarch, his right to rule has been tested in martial combat:

> Whence sprang the name of Emperor? Was it not
> By Nature's fiat? In the shouts of triumph,
> 'Mid warrior's shouts, did her oracular voice
> Make itself heard: let the commanding spirit
> Possess the station of command!
> (Part 1, I, i)[35]

Like the tyrants who, in the words of the *Biographia*, 'impress their preconceptions on the world without in order to present them back to their own view' (*BL*, I, 32) Emerick has 'shout[ed] forth his title to yon circling mountains,' and, 'with a thousand-fold reverberation' has caused the rocks to echo back the name of king. Emerick's status as a commanding genius is reinforced by his penchant for 'play[ing] the masker'. Again, rather like the Emperor Napoleon, the usurping King attempts to control his subjects through acts of dramatic deception and deceit. He is the very model of the grand actor – a Kean or a Kemble 'enthral[ling] the sluggard nature in ourselves' (Part 2, IV, i).

In Part 2, the decline of Emerick's power coincides with the failure of his dramatic powers. When the deposed king's son, Bethlen, takes up arms against Emerick, the struggle is heralded by a decisive act of unmasking:

> A king? Oh laughter! A king Bajazet
> That from some vagrant actor's tiring-room,
> Hath stolen at once his speech and crown!
> (Part 2, III, ii)

At this point, the epic and tragic potential of the Emperor's story is undone in a punctual moment of comic irony. Emerick/Napoleon is simply a bad actor. The remainder of the play may be read, on one level, as a battle for fictional authority for as soon as Bethlen has exposed Emerick, the King retorts that he has 'ta'en the mask of rebel!' (Part 2, III, ii). Strictly speaking this is true, for in reality Bethlen is merely asserting his legitimate right to rule and cannot be considered as a rebel, still less as an actor. Yet Emerick, in defiance of this truth, continues to view the world as a stage on which good and bad actors struggle for applause:

> I'll make you
> Find reason to fear Emerick, more than all
> The mummer-fiends that ever masqueraded
> As gods or wood-nymphs!
> (Part 2, IV, ii)

The scene ends with Emerick fooled into thinking that the dead body lying at his feet is that of Casimir, his trusted aide. When Emerick is killed by the real Casimir he has good reason to declare that he has been 'Betrayed and baffled' by his 'own tool'.

The contest between dramatic and anti-dramatic motifs is extended to political and familial relations. Despite Coleridge's claim that the action is 'domestic' and not 'political', it is the family that resists the power of tyranny. But crucially, as with the earlier extract from *The Friend*, the identity of the family centres on the productive opposition between men and women, or rather, to evoke Christensen again, the politerotics of the female state and the masculine nation. Under the rule of Emerick, the distinction between the absolute truths of reason and the circumstanced faculty of the understanding is collapsed with the result that the state exists without reference to an *a priori* principle, a governing idea. Within this order the reign of the phallus appears to be absolute with women routinely subjected to sexual oppression as a means of keeping up the manly state of war. Yet, as Slavoj Žižek points out, it is this 'very lack of an exception to the phallus that renders the feminine libidinal economy inconsistent' and thereby threateningly other.[36] As the play develops and women come increasingly to dominate the action of the play and to pose a challenge to the boundless extension of the phallus, it becomes evident that Coleridge is attempting to restore a line of separation between the revolutionary domain of phallic usurpation and the legitimate field of the desexualized nation state. He is attempting, that is, to restore what Žižek terms, after Lacan, the 'phallic function': '*"phallic" is this self-limitation of the phallus, this positing of an exception*. In this precise sense the phallus is the signifier of castration: "symbolic castration" is ultimately another name for the paradox of "states that are essentially by-products": *if we are to achieve fulfilment through phallic enjoyment, we must renounce it as our specific goal.*' (p. 141) Not surprisingly, the path to renunciation involves some tortuous negotiations with the feminine 'exception'.

Much of Part 2 is concerned with the quest of the hitherto 'Proud' and 'restless' Bethlen to discover his royal name and thus, by extension, the principle that will arrest the unfettered life of the phallus. At first, women seem to have only a negligible relation with this quest. Ignorant of his birthright, Bethlen's wish is for a 'father', so that he may be 'restore[d] to... / A name in the world' (Part 2, I, i). To gain this name, however, Bethlen must first of all encounter the exiled mother, Zapolya, from whom he was separated at birth. In a scene redolent, as Carlson observes, with the ambiguity that Coleridge extends to all his treatments of theatrical women, Bethlen's quest for the mother takes him to a 'savage' mountain wilderness, the haunt of 'war-wolves' and 'vampires' – a fitting domain for the encounter with feminine abjection. Here, at the mouth of the cavern where Zapolya together with her loyal servant Raab Kiuprili are in hiding, the hero prepares for a confrontation with the 'monster'. What he discovers, however, is not some 'fierce shape' but an authoritative 'Voice of command!' – in fact, the speech of the hidden Kiuprili – at whose bidding Bethlen's phallic spear 'trembles like a reed'. The associations between femininity, monstrosity and the transgression of the Oedipal code are thus swiftly checked by the reassertion of the phallic function. War, hitherto associated with the simultaneous preservation and violation of woman is thus displaced by a return to the law of civilization and, by implication, to the acceptance of principle over expediency, castration over fulfilment. With the threat of the hysterical, abject mother removed, Bethlen must 'Retract [his] idle spear' and make 'sacrifice' in the name not of the revolutionary state but in accordance with the disciplinary precepts of 'Patience! Truth! Obedience!' (Part 2, II, i).[37]

The pattern is now set for the reassertion of the family against the solipsistic, sensuous power of the rogue male, Emerick. When, at last, the two forces meet, Bethlen recognizes the ring on Emerick's hand as the 'foul usurping counterpart' of his own. It is at this point that Bethlen decodes the 'secret cypher' on his ring; it is the name of Andreas, the rightful king. Like Coleridge's discussion of *Hamlet*, however, this doubling of the royal seal places a question mark over the authenticity of royal command. For where does authority reside: in the exchange of signs or in the imposition of extra-discursive law?[38] The moral ambiguity introduced by the reproduction of the royal sign ends only with the bestowal, by the royal mother, of the king's name. The potential for vice and violence that Coleridge observes in his women is thus discharged by transforming Zapolya into an ex-centric point of origin. By placing the mother outside the play of signification she becomes a marker of the limits of phallic enjoyment. In this manner Coleridge's play signals the return of 'normal' gender relations. The removal of the mother leads in turn to the resumption of political legitimacy as, in a repetition of Bethlen's acceptance of the phallic function, the weaponry that had previously signalled a threat to normality is returned to men under the aegis of a lawful act of tyrannicide, one that issues from the absolute genius of a domesticated nation, not from a commanding will. In a ritual exchange of swords, old men 'feel in every sinew / A young man's strength returning' and young men 'lift' their father's swords in their 'country's cause' (Part 2, IV, ii). Potency is restored to men, therefore, on the condition that women conceal their fundamental otherness and thereby grant meaning to the substitutive economy of the phallic nation state.[39]

Zapolya may be read then as an 'answer' to the unmanly state of peace. For if, as *The Friend* mistakenly perceives, the stimulus of warfare entails the extension of universal masculine potency, the play is an attempt to correct this error through a reassertion of the phallic function. For Coleridge, then, this is the meaning of Waterloo: the renunciation of endless erotic play and the resumption of symbolic castration. The play ends therefore with a rejection of the unprincipled life of the revolutionary state and a call for 'wholesome laws' to

> embank the sovereign power,
> To deepen by restraint, and by prevention
> Of lawless will to amass and guide the flood
> In its majestic channel ...
> (Part 1, i)

Having embraced the law of the phallus, the 'restlessness' of command must give way to the discipline of domestic 'love' and patriotic 'duty'. The lines bring to mind the concluding part of the *Biographia*'s commentary on Shakespeare. Following the sentence evoking the passage from war-like excess to a drama of reconciliation, the tensions in Shakespeare's works are described as 'two rapid streams, that at their first meeting within narrow and rocky banks mutually strive to repel each other, and intermix reluctantly and in tumult; but soon finding a wider channel and more yielding shores blend, and dilate, and flow on in one current and with one voice' (*BL*, II, 26). It is to the disciplining of the 'animal spirits' of the poet/politician and the excessive emotion of the public that *Zapolya* is addressed. In both cases the will must be channelled, for whether the space in question be that of the theatre or the state, men are

> Least themselves in the mad whirl of crowds
> Where folly is contagious, and too oft
> Even wise men leave their better sense at home
> To chide and wonder at them when returned.
> (Part 1, i)

Fittingly, for a play that resists tragic significance, *Zapolya* ends with the marriage of King Andreas to Glycine, the orphan daughter of Raab Kiuprili. Having secured the symbolic union of sovereign and popular interests, the way is clear for a pacific, non-revolutionary future. The conclusion of the play leads us, then, to re-examine the question of genre and specifically to address Coleridge's earlier reflections on the distinction between romantic and historical time. In his lecture on the 'Origins of Modern Drama', delivered on 2 June 1812, Coleridge had argued that Shakespeare's plays 'are in the ancient sense neither Tragedies nor Comedies, nor both in one – but a different genus... – romantic Dramas, or dramatic Romances' (*LoL*, I, 466). Romantic poetry, like the best Shakespearean drama, appeals to the 'Imagination rather than to the Senses, and to the Reason as contemplating our outward nature'. This explains, I think, why *Zapolya* resists the contingent forms of tragedy and epic. To adapt Coleridge's rhetorical formulation, since reason and imagination are 'independent of Time and Space... – what connection have they with this or that age, this or that Country?' (*LoL*, I, 467). In a similar manner the world of Illyria is timeless and ideal; it stands not for a particular time and place but for *all* time and *all* places. And again it is this principle that marks the difference between fanatical and national genius: the activation of reason that works to destroy all the mediations that make communication possible and the contemplative reserve that maintains its existence both prior and superior to the life of the state. Like *The Winter's Tale*, the play on which *Zapolya* is modelled, significant time is elevated above ordinary temporality. The latter is the plaything of jealous kings and egocentric tyrants; the former is the object of poets, philosophers and the ideal statesman.

There is, however, a further sense in which *Zapolya* seeks to transcend the materiality of time and war. Coleridge associated the 'Dramatic Entertainment' with the 'old comedy' of Aristophanes, of which Shakespeare's comedy was meant to be a direct 'descendant'. He adds that the 'Entertainment, or middle comedy, remained within the circle of Experience... an old Critic said that Tragedy was the Flight, or Elevation of Life, Comedy... its Arrangement and Ordinance.' He concludes by stating that Greek comedy gives a portrait of the 'middle' and 'domestic' classes (*LoL*, I, 458–9). Later on, at the beginning of a lecture on *Hamlet*, Coleridge draws a comparison between the characters of Macbeth and Napoleon. He starts by complementing his 'country on the lead she [has] taken in resisting the attack upon the middle-classes of society; for if the French Emperor had succeeded in his attempts to gain universal dominion, there would have been but two classes suffered to exist – the high and the low' (*LoL*, I, 546).[40] *Zapolya*, therefore, may be seen as a statement of middle-class or 'domestic' identity. In the aftermath of Waterloo, the play's aesthetic, like that of Scott's *Antiquary*, is attuned to an anti-tragic and anti-sublime sensibility – a sensibility that translates, in the political sphere, to a desire on the part of the conservative imagination to formulate the terms of postwar order and restoration. Writing in the conclusion to the *Biographia*, Coleridge would utilize the passage from *Zapolya* in which Kiuprili counsels his audience to 'safelier trust to heaven, than to themselves' to defend himself against the charge of confusing the reader with 'metaphysics' and 'jargon' (*BL*, II, 240–1). The passage had been previously cited by the Drury Lane committee as evidence of the play's 'metaphysical dulness' (*CL*, IV, 721). There is some irony in the fact that a speech uttered in defence of inner reflection, the family and Providence and prompted by the fear of the 'whirling' of 'crowds' and 'the acclamations of the people' (*BL*, II, 240) should be used as evidence of the play's unsuitability for performance. More so than its author perhaps, the Drury Lane committee were aware of the fatal contradiction involved in *dramatizing* the metaphysics of the silent majority. The *Biographia* compounds this irony by placing its defence of *Zapolya* in the context of the 'professedly metaphysical' *Lay Sermon* (*BL*, II, 241) – for what, after all, could be more absurd and thus more threatening to the idea of the absolute national will than the insight that the unanimity of the English middle-classes had been founded on the chimerical growth of the National Debt? In the end, therefore, Coleridge is brought to the unwelcome realization that the National Imagination is linked in a fatal compact with the 'sensual' forms of war, commerce, theatricality and signification, the very 'forms' that in 1796 had marked the course of human progress from its origins in the 'restless faculty of *Imagination*' (*W*, 131) to its end in the coming of a new millennium.[41]

5
Wordsworth's Abyss of Weakness

The pleasures of war

> He said that after he had finished his college course, he was in great doubt as to what his future employment should be. He did not feel himself good enough for the Church...He also shrank from the law...[On the other hand] He had studied military history with great interest, and the strategy of war; and he always fancied that he had talents for command...[1]

>   Divine must be
> That triumph, when the very worst, the pain,
> And even the prospect of our Brethren slain,
> Hath something in which the heart enjoys...[2]

Wordsworth's life-long interest in military history and strategy is matched only by his passion for that 'something' which the heart enjoys in contemplating the spoils of war. *Home at Grasmere* (1800) is unequivocal on this point and interestingly goes on to query the legitimacy of this passion by linking it with the 'wild appetites and blind desires' of the ardent worshipper of Nature, a condition that precedes the self-disciplined aspirations of the philosophic mind.[3] Yet, as Wordsworth confesses, something of that early delight survives to trouble the integrity of 'this great consummation' (line 1004):

> Yea, to this day I swell with like desire;
> I cannot at this moment read a tale
> Of two brave Vessels matched in deadly fight
> And fighting to the death, but I am pleased
> More than a wise Man ought to be; I wish,
> I burn, I struggle, and in soul am there.
>   (lines 928–33)

More than a wise man ought to be, the poet admits his fascination with the 'heroic trumpet' of epic song (line 955), even to the point of glorying in the spectacle of mutual annihilation. That this impulse is never allowed to develop beyond the parameters of the symbolic order tells us something about the poet's participation in a culture of sacrifice, one that finds a perverse form of reassurance, to invoke René Girard's analysis, in rehearsing the spectacle of its own dissolution.[4] The ritualized nature of such displays, designed to reinforce the law during a period of crisis, offers from one point of view a thoroughly restrictive vision of the nature and scope of symbolic violence.[5] Thus, much as culture survives in the mode of its undoing, so warfare persists in the Wordsworthian imagination as the dialectical other of the philosophic self. But problems occur when the mind or nation is seen to derive 'a kind of unspeakable pleasure' in the contemplation of its destructive tendencies, whether this is seen in 'the prospect of our Brethren slain' ('Anticipation: October, 1803', line 12) or in the spectacle of 'deadly fight'. Where Wordsworth differs from Coleridge, therefore, is in his willingness to contest the idea that individuals and nations should keep aloof from the enjoyment of war. While not wishing for one moment to suggest that Wordsworth gloats in the face of destruction – indeed, we shall have good reason to qualify this view – we should nevertheless be alert to the possibility that the representation of conflict is but 'an alibi for the erotics of disorientation, the pleasures of the wound'.[6]

Consider, as example, the critical significance of the discharged soldier in book four of *The Prelude* (1805). Wandering along the public way, the poet's 'self-possession' (line 398) is checked by the sudden appearance of a 'ghastly' figure wrapt in 'solitude', uttering 'murmuring sounds' (lines 411–31, *passim*), a double no less of the rootless would-be poet William Wordsworth. When questioned, the soldier troubles the poet with his sublime indifference. The division between memory and feeling (lines 477–8) makes a mockery of the restorative aims of emotion recollected in tranquility, as outlined in the preface to *Lyrical Ballads* (1800). But more importantly, the soldier's realm of objectivity, of 'hardship, battle, [and] pestilence' remains stubbornly 'sublime' (lines 471–3), suggesting a level of experience that blocks the progress of the originating consciousness to absolute self-consciousness. Small wonder, then, that the listener is unable to rest satisfied with the soldier's tale. The recitation, in 'simple words', of service in the 'Tropic Islands' is remarkable not only for its brevity but also for its lack of tropic energy (lines 445–6), precisely the account of 'Warrior's deeds' that stirred the youthful imagination. What the soldier offers in place of this figural discourse is far more damaging to the soul, for it marks the point at which the listener refuses to recognize 'the ethics of proper distance, of consideration and self-limitation, of avoiding the temptation "to go right to the end."' In seeking to fill the void at the heart of the tale, the poet runs the risk of dissolving the very structure of difference and separation that prevents desire from merging with the 'lethal domain of *jouissance*'.[7]

When, in 'Character of the Happy Warrior' (1806), Wordsworth comes to review the source of his enjoyment, the Coleridgean injunction to maintain a distance from 'Pain, / And Fear, and Bloodshed' is respected. In this poem the warrior is enjoined to 'make... his moral duty his prime care', to exercise a power that 'Controls them and subdues, transmutes, bereaves / Of their bad influence, and their good receives' (lines 11–18, *passim*). Instead of taking pleasure in the unspoken brutality of war, as exemplified in the strange, half-absent words of the discharged soldier, the speaker of this poem is drawn towards an acknowledgement of the moral law. Curiously, however, the submission to authority is couched in the very language that it should ideally disavow. Thus the law *bereaves* violence of its hold on the imagination: the more the warrior is tested in battle the more 'skilful' he becomes 'in self-knowledge'; the more he is 'tempted' the 'more [he] is able to endure, / As more exposed to suffering and distress' (lines 23–5). By not giving way to the temptation of war, the warrior gains in self-knowledge and fortitude but only on condition that he accedes to a Kantian process of division in which an Ego-Ideal (a free being obeying universal laws) is distinguished from its empirical opposite (the soldier as an instrument of the nation state). Having marked this division the warrior is then identified with a 'soul' that feels '*placable*' when 'occasions rise /... that demand such sacrifice' (lines 19–22, my emphasis). Because pacific enjoyment is the province of a transcendental will, guiding the actions of the whole man as he labours to fulfil the moral law, the individual subject or man of fact can no longer be accused of taking sadistic delight in the performance of his duty. The potential for deriving some kind of obscene enjoyment from rendering oneself the passive instrument of the Other's will is guarded against throughout the poem by the rigid separation of duty and desire.

This, then, is the ideal that Wordsworth aims at in his critique of martial pleasure. To avoid proximity with the incestuous Thing (the impossible 'something' on which symbolization founders), the subject must remain faithful to his desire as the Law sustains it. Above all, the military character must keep his enthusiasm for the primal activity of war separate from his identity as subject of the moral law. As an illustration of this maxim we may consider the evidence of a letter, written in 1811 to Captain C. W. Pasley, author of *The Military Policy and Institutions of the British Empire* (1810), in which Wordsworth offers a spirited critique of unbridled conquest. Recalling both *The Convention of Cintra* pamphlet and the Iberian sonnets, the poet asserts that the struggle against Napoleon will only be won if force is 'bottomed upon... notions of justice and right, and... knowledge of and reverence for the moral sentiments of mankind' (*MY* I, 477). Ambitious statesmen may well rely on fleets and armies, and external wealth but a nation's health proceeds from within. Moral health, however, is conditional on the continued presence of enemies to provide an external check on the desire for unlimited expansion:

> Woe be to that country whose military power is irresistible! I deprecate such an event for Great Britain scarcely less than for any other Land. Scipio foresaw the evils with which Rome would be visited when no Carthage should be in existence for her to contend with. If a nation have nothing to oppose or to fear without, it cannot escape decay and concussion within. Universal triumph and absolute security soon betray a State into abandonment of that discipline, civil and military, by which its victories were secured... My prayer, as a Patriot, is, that we may always have, somewhere or other, enemies capable of resisting us, and keeping us at arm's length.
>
> (*MY* I, 480)

Paradoxically, national security is made conditional on the preservation of antagonism. The desire to fight to the death is thus transposed from the imaginary to the symbolic so that it may function as a negative other within a dialectical process of identification. By insisting on the necessity of enmity, Wordsworth thus reasserts the ethics of mutual respect and self-limitation, of avoiding the temptation to reach the place of the Real in the Other.

It is customary to read such documents as harbingers of the poet's alleged decline into political and creative orthodoxy. Yet I think enough has been said about the troubling nature of Wordsworth's interest in militarism to qualify this judgement. These reflections become especially pertinent when we begin to assess the work that Wordsworth produced in 1815–16 as a response to the battle of Waterloo. By now it should come as no surprise that I regard the official message of Waterloo poetry as a screen for anxious meditations on the nature and significance of authority. Where Wordsworth is concerned this crisis becomes especially acute, not least because it is formulated in the aftermath of the so-called 'Golden Decade'. Just as the ethics of war is treated as purposefully vague throughout the entirety of the poet's career, so when we come to assess the poet's attitude to authority we must be careful to observe the persistence of an 'ironic posture' that militates against the submission to orthodoxy, whether this is characterized as 'Duty', 'God' or the postwar state.[8] Once again I would insist that this posture is best characterized as an aspect of the subject's stubbornness when summoned by the call of the Law. To argue that Wordsworth becomes increasingly prone to acquiesce in this authority is to ignore the extent to which Waterloo figures in his poetry as a site of internal contestation, evocative not only of the originary guilt of society but also of the fractured nature of all assertions of integrity, including that of the commanding self. It is, moreover, to elide that aspect of the poetry that presents war as a source of delight. As we shall see, when we come to survey Wordsworth's most controversial statement concerning the relationship between violence and integrity, even carnage must take its place as an object of enjoyment. In line with what has been said about the dangers of conquest, subjects and nations must learn to take responsibility for their pleasures. It is to this troubling aspect of the 'Thanksgiving Ode' that we must now turn.

The pure intent

The popular conception of Wordsworth's place in Waterloo culture was forged relatively early in the critical reception that greeted the volume of 'Thanksgiving' poems. Published in the spring of 1816, the poems were widely regarded as an unnecessary addition to a genre that was swiftly losing its cachet. But something more than mere market saturation was at stake. Many critics, including Josiah Conder, Leigh Hunt and William Hazlitt, took exception to the way in which Wordsworth had presented himself as a cultural spokesman, assuming the vatic tones of 'the Bard' in order to pronounce on the achievements of the nation. Lacking, in Conder's view, the ordinary quality of 'sympathy', the poet had overlooked the terrible costs of Waterloo.[9] Hazlitt's damning judgement on the 'Thanksgiving Ode' with its apparent affirmation of 'Carnage' as the 'daughter' of God set the seal on Wordsworth's fortunes.[10] With the population of England swelled by tens of thousands of returning servicemen, many of whom had been wounded in both the Peninsular and Waterloo campaigns, it was inevitable that such sentiments would jar with the national mood. As Wordsworth admitted in the preface to his poems, a darkened veil of 'present distresses' – economic, social and political – threatened to obscure the moral 'splendour' of Waterloo, transforming its unity into a formless heterology of competing voices.[11] Still, the publication of the volume went ahead and despite the poet's best efforts, something in the 'over-pressure of the times'[12] conspired to prevent the verse from reaching its desired audience. That which Wordsworth had intended as confirmation of his right to pronounce on the state of the nation was decisively rejected, and the volume would have been forgotten but for the tiresome recollection of those lines in which the poet had bestowed divine approval on the all too human business of reciprocal murder.

Let us think about those lines for a few moments. We should recall that Hazlitt's objection to the affirmation of 'Carnage' occurs during the course of his notoriously ambivalent appraisal of *Coriolanus*. If poetry is 'right royal' in its disdain for the measure and proportion of liberal government, such brutal disregard is an indication of its aesthetic excellence. Violence, in other words, is bound up with the affective force of literature. When judged from this point of view, the ascription of mortal destruction to the will of 'Almighty God' makes perfect sense:

> Nor will the God of peace and love
> Such martial service disapprove
> . . .
> For thou art angry with thine enemies!
> For these, and for our errors,
> And sins that point their terrors,
> We bow our heads before Thee, and we laud
> And magnify thy name, Almighty God!
> But thy most dreadful instrument,
> In working out a pure intent,
> Is Man – arrayed for mutual slaughter, –
> Yea, Carnage is thy daughter.
> ('Thanksgiving Ode', lines 260–1, 274–82)

As Carl Ketcham has argued, Wordsworth is trying to convince his audience of the 'darker side of the general thanksgiving... Wordsworth, never one to shrink from an effect because it was startling, halts his readers in mid-celebration, forcing them to inspect the total implications of their rejoicing.'[13] It is this image of arrest that we should keep in mind. Where conventional historiography submits the violence of Waterloo to the discipline of narrative continuity, Wordsworth confronts his audience with a disjunctive, isolated image, one that impresses the reader with a sense of the violent underpinnings of national unanimity. Since the nation 'remains symbolically grounded and secure as long as it keeps itself ignorant of the violence at its foundations' the disclosure of this knowledge precipitates an identity crisis.[14]

That Wordsworth is fully aware of the role that triumphalism plays in sustaining the ignorance around which identity is formed is made clear in the earlier part of the poem. Poets 'Who to the murmurs of an earthly string' recount the conventional tale of 'heroic deeds' and 'martial duties' miss 'the sole true glory' of Waterloo.[15] Where the 'enraptured' voice links the conquest of Napoleon with the wielding of the 'vengeful sword', Wordsworth is keen to qualify this passion with the reminder that 'the sole true glory' of Waterloo is 'not that we have vanquished – but that we survive' (lines 66–91, *passim*). Crucially, the fantasy that sustains the epic view of conflict is associated with those accounts that extol the conduct of a single individual: Lord Wellington:

> Have we not conquered? – By the vengeful sword?
> Ah no, by dint of Magnaminity;
> That curbed the baser passions, and left free
> A loyal band to follow their liege Lord,
> Clear-sighted Honour...
> (lines 56–61)

The unexpected qualifier, 'honour', defeats the expectation that the 'liege Lord' will be granted a proper name. Lacking in 'sympathy', the moral quality that marks out the hero from the conqueror, Wordsworth regards Wellington as, at best, an efficient tool of the state. He certainly fails as an example of the happy warrior, the defender and deliverer 'in whom talents, genius, and principle are united'.[16] Moreover, as Wordsworth makes clear in a letter written in the wake of Waterloo to the pro-Wellington John Scott: 'notwithstanding the splendour of those actions at the head of which he has been placed, I am convinced that there is no magnanimity in his nature... depend upon it, the constitution of his mind is not generous, nor will he pass with posterity for a hero' (*MY* II, 280–3). Wellington's unsteady mixture of contempt, disinterest and aggression marks him out as an unfit subject for the company of English national heroes.[17] Where men such as Alfred, Sidney and Milton acted as selfless representatives of the nation, Wellington is 'led astray by vanity'. Lacking in magnanimity the lord acts in accordance with mean, empirical desires; the transcendental will that would encompass the violence of war and protect the subject from the effective force of carnage is crucially absent. It comes as no surprise that the nation that would identify with such a figure finds itself unable to withstand the disclosure of the truth that this fantasy conceals.[18]

In dispelling the fascination with Wellington, Wordsworth implores his audience to make a related transition from the heedless spirit of epic recitation to the legitimate passion of prayer. This involves, in turn, a corresponding act of submission; the battle is no longer an arena of humanist self-assertion but 'the abyss of weakness' (line 86) in which assertions of pride and integrity meet, as it were, their Waterloo. The question we must now pose is whether the 'chastened sentiment that belongs to the Wordsworthian *via negativa*' can do justice to the senseless, profitless excess of sacrificial violence.[19] If Wordsworth, like Hegel, values the life 'that endures, and preserves itself through... death', that 'gains its truth only by finding itself in absolute dismemberment', then we must be certain that this does not turn on a corresponding act of self-delusion.[20] For true satisfaction cannot be found in a bloodless contest of signs.

As a striking example of the ode's ability to reverse conventional expectations we may briefly consider the moment where Imagination submits to a higher authority:

> Imagination, ne'er before content,
> But aye ascending, restless in her pride,
> From all that man's performance could present,
> Stoops to that closing deed magnificent,
>   And with the embrace is satisfied.
>   (lines 163–7)

Once more, 'Before the eye and progress of [his] Song', imagination lifts itself up.[21] This time, however, its militant energy is disciplined to 'that closing deed magnificent' (line 166): to the hyper-realized subjectivity of national victory, a power no longer corresponding but flatly analogous to the creative mind of man. The sacrifice of Wordsworthian power takes place, then, in recognition of an event that seems, at this point in the poem, to have little connection with the moral offensiveness of Carnage. If the Imagination is 'satisfied' with this 'embrace' could it be because it has not yet faced up to its full participation in war, that it does not yet perceive the illusoriness of the 'closing deed'? When read closely, it is hard to detect a genuine note of submission, for what is most remarkable about the passage is the quality of its conviction: the heavily stressed 'Stoops' is suggestive not of quiescence in the face of higher authority so much as of an act coordinated by a mind as capable of relinquishing control as it is of assuming it. Paradoxically, it is liberty rather than constraint that emerges as the key note of this compelling scene. But what might, at first sight, resemble nothing less than the Hegelian account of the subject, triumphing in its infinity over the sensuous appearance of the objective world, is given a further turn of the screw by virtue of the fact that this triumph is granted in the poem as an illusion, one that obscures the unrecuperable negativity of Carnage.

Later, we will have occasion to consider the exact relationship between Imagination and its participation in the culture of destruction. For now, let it suffice to elucidate the way in which Wordsworth marks poetic form as the arena in which ideas of unity and command are brought into contact with the poetics of negation.

Poetizing the political

The 'Thanksgiving Ode', of course, is not the only poem in which the disclosure of violence runs the risk of preventing the formation of symbolic integrity. Prior to the completion of the ode in late February 1816, Wordsworth composed a series of sonnets reflecting on the significance of the recent Allied victory. Although directed at an object of specific historical note, these poems raise fundamental questions about the problem of articulating the relationship between politics, poetic form and the liberty of the poet. In a recent article, Jonathan M. Hess has drawn attention to the 'mutually constitutive interaction' of aesthetic freedom and political restraint in Wordsworth's *Sonnets Dedicated to Liberty*.[22] Hess's argument concerning the dialectical nature of politics and poetics (aesthetic liberty is a condition of political constraint; formal limitation facilitates political freedom) may be applied to the formal and thematic concerns of the later sonnets. Since, as I have argued, Waterloo figures in romanticism as a dialectical image of self-abnegation and self-authorization, it is worth asking to what extent the sonnet form supports or contests the right of the bard to poetize the political.

Let us begin by looking at an early example from the winter of 1815. In 'Occasioned by the Battle of Waterloo', a subtitle informs the reader that the last six lines of the poem are 'intended for an Inscription'. It need scarcely be said, to adapt the opening of the first 'Essay upon Epitaphs', that an inscription presupposes a monument and, indeed, Wordsworth's poem proceeds as if it were lending itself to the stonemason's art:

> Intrepid sons of Albion! not by you
> Is life despised; ah no, the spacious earth
> Ne'er saw a race who held, by right of birth,
> So many objects to which love is due:
> Ye slight not life – to God and Nature true;
> But death, becoming death, is dearer far,
> When duty bids you bleed in open war:
> Hence hath your prowess quelled that impious crew.
> Heroes! – for instant sacrifice prepared;
> Yet filled with ardour and on triumph bent
> 'Mid direst shocks of mortal accident –
> To you who fell, and you whom slaughter spared
> To guard the fallen, and consummate the event,
> Your country rears this sacred Monument!

The proposed monument was never raised and Wordsworth's paean to the glories of national sacrifice was simply printed, not inscribed. Yet void as this poem is of referential significance, it is nonetheless 'saturated', as Benedict Anderson puts it, 'with ghostly *national* imaginings'.[23] The significance of the verse becomes clearer when we place it in the context of the parliamentary debate about the raising of a national war monument. On 5 February 1816, the day after Wordsworth's poem appeared, Castlereagh proposed that there should be two monuments: one for the heroes of Waterloo; the other for the heroes of Trafalgar. This motion was opposed by William Dundas who argued that the nation 'should show its gratitude to *all* of the soldiers and sailors' who had fought in the war. The contest between Castlereagh and Dundas brought to a head a long-standing argument about the nature and purpose of war monuments. On the day that the news of the Allied victory was received in Parliament, Lord Liverpool asserted that 'the common soldier had only his local duties to perform but the Duke of Wellington was everywhere in the heat of the action and everywhere in the presence of danger'. Accordingly, the national monument should be devoted solely to the genius of England's saviour. Speaking for the opposition, William Wynn argued that the since the battle had not been won by an individual genius but by the will of a nation, the monument should include 'the name of every man' who had fought at Waterloo.[24]

It is unclear what Wordsworth thought about this debate but his poem is in mourning – insofar as it can be considered a poem of mourning – not only for what is 'incarnated' in the monument but also for the monument itself. Wordsworth, that is, attempts not only the negotiation of opposites (life and death, private and public, duty and joy, impiety and the sacred, ardour and self-sacrifice, contingency and eternity), he also endeavours to locate his verse in a field of authority. It remains unclear, however, what form this authority takes; moreover, given Wordsworth's resistance to the aristocratic authority of Wellington and his suspicion of the Whig opposition, it seems unlikely that the public sphere will supply a suitable model. As if in recognition of this dilemma, the poem falls back on a familiar trope: the power of culture to read the carnage of battle according to a carefully fabricated narrative of sacrificial value. But where the 'Thanksgiving Ode' restores the pre-sacrificial sense of carnage in the midst of its affirmation of national unanimity and thus poses an ironic challenge to the post-bellum consensus, 'Occasioned by the Battle' presents a more elusive account of the collapse of authority. Where the sonnet differs from the ode then is in its *failure* to provide a convincing account of the means by which bodies are converted into cultural capital. By placing his inscription 'in close connection with the bodily remains of the deceased' the poet hopes to close the gap that separates him from the national body.[25] Yet, in strict terms, the surface he writes on is two steps removed from the body of the dead: firstly as imaginary monument, secondly as cenotaph. The honoured heroes are not only unnamed in the inscription, they are also elsewhere. The absence of this sepulchral monument – itself a figure for corporeal absence – is a graphic reminder that Wordsworth's national voice is at a double remove from the culture it would govern. Since the liberty of the sonnet is predicated on its negation of the disciplinary constraints of the social world (nuns and hermits 'fret not' at their imprisonment), a poem that proclaims the right of its speaker to negate this negation, to literally inscribe itself on the social body, becomes an ironic reminder of the illusory nature of aesthetic freedom.

When, in 1820, Wordsworth accompanied his sister Dorothy on a tour of the battlefield, the poet was struck by the 'blankness' of the field before him and the sight of 'monuments that soon must disappear'.[26] But even here, in an echo of the poet's qualified distaste for the effects of war, abundant 'recompense' may be found: 'we felt as men *should* feel / With such vast hoards of hidden carnage near' (lines 12–13). Quite how men should feel is left uncertain, however. In one sense the poem attests to Wordsworth's faith in the restorative powers of memory, transcending the contingencies of time and place in defiance of monumental frailty. There is even a sense in which the lines leave open the possibility of deriving secret pleasure from the contemplation of 'hidden carnage' (line 13), the very thing that animates the 'Thanksgiving Ode'. Monuments may succumb to natural processes, the poet suggests, but imagination sustains the 'horror breathing from the silent ground!' (line 14).

It is conventional wisdom to assume that Wordsworth's later poetry defers to secondary sources of authority. We have seen, however, that the assumption of the official view of Waterloo is almost always accompanied by an awareness of its deficiency, particularly when it seeks to conceal its involvement in organized violence. In writing, then, of the significance of victory, Wordsworth wavers between an acceptance of the newly forged consensus and a resistance to or contempt for the lie on which it is sustained. Two poems from the autumn of 1815 add credence to this view. Originally published in Leigh Hunt's *Examiner* in late January 1816, the sonnet, 'How clear, how keen, how marvellously bright', seems an unlikely candidate for inclusion in the 'Thanksgiving' volume. Battle is not the ostensible theme of the poem; instead it takes the form of a meditation on ideas of permanence and tranquillity, focused on the sight of a 'distant mountain's head' (line 2), its snowy beauty 'destined to endure' (line 11). But lest we be tempted into reading this quotidian scene as a figure for the imagination, the final couplet is quick to remind us that it is in fact a work of fancy; the snow will live 'Through all vicissitudes – till genial spring / Has filled the laughing vales with welcome flowers' (lines 12–14). Where, in the opening of the verse, imagination rises like 'another Sun' (line 4) to block the passage from day to night, the closing imagery expressly assaults this vision. The product of imagination is 'but a surface': 'White, radiant, spotless, exquisitely pure', a text unsullied by mortal 'wing', evoking the emptiness of the Sublime (lines 8–12, *passim*). To submit to 'genial spring', therefore, is to rescue the mind from a fascination with a delusory and life-denying form of permanence. Such recourse to the contingent must be seen, however, as one element in a dialectical spiral, moving from self-empowerment through self-abnegation and back to a rejuvenated sense of the precedence of the mind. It is only, in other words, by acceding to a structuralized account of subject and object that the mind is able to cognize the unseen presence of 'Composure and ennobling harmony' as an echo of its own underlying authority.[27]

The political context of this process becomes clearer when one considers its sequel, 'While not a leaf seems faded', again published in the *Examiner* in early February. Here the poet draws upon the image of the 'ripening harvest':

>   this nipping air,
> Sent from some distant clime where Winter yields
> His icy scymetar, a foretaste yields
> Of bitter change – and bids the Flowers beware;
> And whispers to the silent Birds, 'Prepare
> Against the threatening Foe your trustiest shields.'
>
>   (lines 3–8)

As the sonnet continues it is evident that Wordsworth has something other than natural processes in mind: his theme is the retreat of Napoleon from Russia during the bitter winter of 1812. But from this excursion into political commentary the sonnet returns to meditate on the superior force of the poet:

> For me, who under kindlier laws belong
> To Nature's tuneful quire, this rustling dry
> Through leaves yet green, and yon crystalline sky,
> Announce a season potent to renew,
> Mid frost and snow, the instinctive joys of song, –
> And nobler cares than listless summer knew.
>   (lines 9–14)

On one level the sonnet can be read as a song of literary potency, a prayer for the quickening of poetic powers – the production of new 'leaves' – after the listlessness of summer. On another it becomes a homage to the natural force that defeated the advance of the conqueror and thus, by extension, the priority of visionary over military power. Again, the sonnet undermines a mode of deviant authority – the sublime or excursive mode that would position itself in the place of the Other – and asserts the primacy of a creative will working with rather than against the logic of temporality.

In this connection it is instructive to recall that the poem was published by Leigh Hunt, whose fanciful depiction of the cessation of war in *The Descent of Liberty* had provoked a sardonic response from Wordsworth earlier in the summer.[28] The difference between the poets turns on their contrasting relationships with Milton. Where Wordsworth embraces the austere grandeur of *Paradise Lost* and the bracing self-discipline of the political sonnets, Hunt seems doggedly attached to the lesser forms, specifically to the masque and the romance.[29] Hunt's preference for the light and fanciful Milton is reflected in *The Descent of Liberty*. Itself a poetical masque, the *Descent* draws on *Comus* to reconnect the politics of peace (the work was written in the interim period between the Treaty of Fontainebleau and Waterloo) with the poetic example of the early Milton. In an attempt to counter the authoritarian tendencies of high Romanticism, the play looks forward to the time when the tragic cycle of death and renewal is supplanted by the pure pastoral that is the end of history:

> And all this burst of out-o'-door enjoyment,
> Just like a new creation, – Spring and Summer
> Married, and Winter dead to be no more.[30]

Hunt's 'Ode for the Spring of 1814', included in *The Descent of Liberty*, makes similar claims for the levelling of romantic aspirations in the wake of the tyrant's defeat:

> The green and laughing world he sees,
> Waters, and plains, and waving trees,
> The skim of birds, and the blue-doming skies,
> And sits with smile at heart, and patience-levelled eyes.
>
>   (lines 63–6)

While the endorsement of pastoral levity anticipates Wordsworth's 'laughing vales', I would suggest that we bear in mind the elder poet's commitment to the recuperation of authority. If, for Hunt, the return of spring brings the promise of relief from wartime rigour, for Wordsworth the abrupt transition from the illusory permanence of the mountain to the contingency of spring is an ironic reminder of the necessity of time in structuring a vision of the world. When faced with the comfortable encroachment of liberalism's endless summer, the elder poet is quick to remind his genial friend that such states are transient. A submission to 'levelling', moreover, evades the naturalness of temporal hierarchies. Spring may usher in the restoration of peace, but winter takes priority on account of its sublime severity and its indifference to human aspiration.[31]

Shortly after these sonnets appeared in the *Examiner*, Hunt attacked Wordsworth in a leader article entitled 'Heaven made a Party to Earthly Disputes – Mr. Wordsworth's Sonnets on Waterloo'. The sonnets in question, 'Occasioned by the Battle of Waterloo', 'Occasioned by the Same Battle' and the 'Siege of Vienna Raised by John Sobieska', had recently appeared in John Scott's conservative journal, the *Champion*. Overtly political in tone, these sonnets raised the question of the relation between Wordsworth's genius and his political unreliability, a question that, for Leigh Hunt, could be extended to his great precursor, John Milton. Specifically, Hunt's attack centred on 'Occasioned by the Same Battle' in which the Wordsworthian 'Bard' claims the sole power of 'comprehending the victory sublime'. For Hunt, writing in the wake of Waterloo, the lines were proof enough that Wordsworth had perverted the true spirit of Milton: 'We hope to see many more of Mr. Wordsworth's sonnets, but shall be glad to find them, like his best ones, less Miltonic in one respect, and more so in another.'[32] Failing to apprehend the aesthetic-politics of the *Examiner* poems, Hunt believed that he had uncovered a fatal contradiction in Wordsworth's poetry. If the poet of 'How clear, how keen, how marvellously bright' lent himself to the genteel republicanism of the Hampstead set, then his subsequent assumption of that other side of Milton, the bard of 'conscious power' and 'oppressiveness of ambition', signalled a return to the politics of the Sublime.[33]

To explain this point let us look more closely at the sonnet that provoked Hunt's indignation. At first sight, 'Occasioned by the Same Battle' appears confident in its embrace of the grand or vatic view of human history:

> The Bard, whose soul is meek as dawning day,
> Yet trained to judgments righteously severe;
> Fervid, yet conversant with holy fear,
> As recognizing one Almighty sway:
> He whose experienced eye can pierce the array
> Of past events, – to whom, in vision clear,
> The aspiring heads of future things appear,
> Like mountain-tops whence mists have rolled away:
> Assoiled from all incumbrance of our time,
> *He only*, if such breathe, in strains devout
> Shall comprehend this victory sublime;
> And worthily rehearse the hideous rout,
> Which the blest Angels, from their peaceful clime
> Beholding, welcomed with a choral shout.
>
> 'From all this world's encumbrance did himself assoil.'
>
> Spenser

In a passage anticipating the panoramic eye of *The Poet's Pilgrimage to Waterloo*, the bard is freed 'from the incumbrance of our time' so that he may 'pierce the array / Of past events' and prophesy the 'aspiring heads of future things' (lines 5–7). Again, as with Southey, the lines speak of a desire to reimpose the Aristotelian hierarchy, to allow poets to comprehend where politicians and soldiers are blind – to simplify, in other words, historical complexity. As the concluding lines make plain, it is *Paradise Lost* that sanctions this desire. In line 12, for example, the 'hideous rout' recalls several passages describing the defeat of the rebel angels. In the final couplet, the 'choral shout' of the 'blest Angels' suggests that of *Paradise Lost* VI, line 200 where it becomes an anticipation of the defeat of Satan and a hymn of praise to Christ the redeemer.[34]

But where, precisely, is the bard positioned? In *The Poet's Pilgrimage to Waterloo* Southey makes a distinction between the remote, inhuman perspective of the tower and the divinely sanctioned gaze of the poet. Wordsworth, in *The White Doe of Rylestone* (1815), is no less sceptical of the limitations of sublime or elevated perspectives. Offered as a symbol of unlawful assertion, Norton Tower stands 'warlike' and 'single', gazing 'Upon a prospect without bound'.[35] For the landscape to reveal something other than 'waste' and ruin, the poet must ensure that his authority is raised on less worldly foundations. To this end, the doe is offered to the reader as an emblem of consolation, hallowing 'the savage spot' with a vision that is 'first or prime – the first and yet timeless "hour" that organizes history in the poem'.[36] Supplanting the pride of sublimity with the recuperative charm of the beautiful, Wordsworth thus proposes an antidote to the waste of sectarian violence. Such a perspective is humble and timeless; it is certainly the only available alternative to an aesthetic more commonly associated with military usurpation. I want to suggest that Wordsworth effects a similar transition in 'Occasioned by the Same Battle' by qualifying the gothic chiaroscuro of the Miltonic sublime with a reminder, via Edmund Spenser, of the poetics of disengagement. To be '*Assoiled*, from all incumbrance of our time' is thus to withdraw from the folly of false transcendence and to embark on the labour of negation. I am suggesting, in other words, that there is more at stake here than the blithe rejection of earthly freight initially suggests.

Specifically, as Wordsworth explains to John Scott,[37] the line refers to a passage in Book VI, Canto V of *The Faerie Queene*:

> And soothly it was sayd by common fame,
> So long as age enabled him thereto,
> That he had bene a man of mickle name,
> Renowmed much in armes and derring doe:
> But being aged now and weary to
> Of warres delight, and worlds contentious toyle,
> The name of knighthood he did disauow,
> And hanging vp his armes and warlike spoyle,
> From all this world's incombraunce did himselfe assoyle.[38]

Narrating the tale of a warrior who rejects his love of war and renown to take up the life of a hermit, Spenser's poem provides Wordsworth with a meditative counterpart to the epic voice of Milton. In so far as he has given up the pursuit of worldly fame, he functions in the sonnet as a compensatory figure: foregrounding the poet's isolation – the hermit's house is 'like a little cage' – while at the same time drawing abundant recompense for this condition: 'as he the art of words knew wondrous well' (VI, vi, 6). The 'happy prison' is an established trope of Romantic poetry;[39] here it also allows the poet to counsel discipline and self-restraint: 'Abstaine from pleasure... and bridle loose delight' (VI, vi, 14). By foregoing his *jouissance* and acknowledging the disciplinary parameters of self-determination, Wordsworth wins the right to comprehend the 'rout' with an authority beyond that of the official laureate. The hermit, one might argue, functions here as the true voice of Wordsworth's national poetry, enabling the poet to rival Southey's claim to 'the laurel which my master wore' by reminding us of that other Spenser: the poet of official neglect and patient suffering. With its stress on the renunciation of 'warres delight' and the dubious prestige of a military name, the allusion also complements Wordsworth's critique of Wellington. In sum, the sonnet may be read as a qualification of Miltonic command and as a subtle defence of the wisdom of the poet, over and above the functionary status of the warrior.

And yet, as much as Spenser provides Wordsworth consolation for not being the laureate, the fact remains that he wrote as a national poet. At once 'gentle' and 'sweet' *and* 'the Muses'... Page of State',⁴⁰ Spenser cannot help but remind the poet of all that he lacks: civic recognition and cultural authority. This dual image extends to the formal structure of the poem. To avoid an encounter with the *difference* of Spenser, the poet must ensure that his identification with the character of the poet is surveyed as one half of an allegorical structure. Doubling reality in this way, the allure of command is subordinated to the gaze of a self-limiting and entirely fictional other, a hermit whose claim to autonomy is predicated on the abjuration of ambition and the acceptance of disciplinary constraint. Seeing oneself in Spenser, therefore, is made conditional on the internalization of an allegorical structure that keeps the subject ignorant of his relationship with the lack in the Other.

To this extent, 'The Bard' represents a comparatively successful act of repression. By incorporating the 'hideous rout' within a specular structure of identification, one that allows for the dialectical interaction of opposites (peace and war, subject and object, isolation and authority), the poet is able to conceal the emptiness, the absolute negation, that would overwhelm his vision of the world. In anticipation of the counsel offered by the ode, the sonnet resists the pride of the 'earthly string' to find a resource for authority in self-limitation. Again, Wordsworth's divine comprehension is the product of an act of *wilful* submission, supported by nothing more substantial than the acceptance of fictional divisions. We are now in a position to return to the 'Thanksgiving Ode' and to a reconsideration of the relations between poetic form, sacrificial violence and the nature of command.

Contesting visions

In an unattributed review of Southey's *The Poet's Pilgrimage to Waterloo*, the Methodist critic Josiah Conder praises the laureate for avoiding 'heroical descriptions of the battle itself'. In support of his argument he quotes from the poem's opening:

> This were the historian's, not the poet's part;
>   Such task would ill the gentle Muse beseem,
> Who to the thoughtful mind and pious heart
>   Comes with her offering from this awful theme;
> Content if what she saw and gathered there
> She may in unambitious song declare.⁴¹

Southey, therefore, is to be praised for his lack of ambition; his feeling, in other words, that the poet and the historian inhabit separate spheres. For Wordsworth on the other hand, 'trained to judgements righteously severe / Fervid, yet conversant with holy fear.'⁴² 'It is only at intervals that he comes within reach of the sympathy of ordinary readers. We never think of claiming kindred with Mr. Wordsworth as a man of the same nerve and texture as ourselves'. Southey meanwhile, is 'never to be mistaken for any other than a husband, a father, a friend; – a man whose sympathies all link him to his country and his fellow-men' (p. 213).[43] Conder knows the relative status of visionary poetry in an age overtaken by public and commercial concerns. If Wordsworth's poetry does not 'do', it is because its sententiousness is at odds with the suburban conservatism of the 'PUBLIC'.[44]

That Wordsworth wished to distinguish his conception of authority from that of the laureate is clear. In a letter to Southey written in June 1816 Wordsworth refers to the 'Thanksgiving Ode' as 'a poem composed, or supposed to be composed, on the morning of the thanksgiving, uttering the sentiments of an *individual* upon that occasion. It is a *dramatized ejaculation*; and this, if anything can, must excuse the irregular frame of the metre'. This statement of humble intent, distinguishing between individual and collective expression, is bound up with Wordsworth's use of form: 'Had it been a hymn, uttering the sentiments of a *multitude*, a *stanza* would have been indispensable.'[45] As it is, the admission of metrical irregularity along with the claim to have deliberately chosen a non-authoritative point of view contrasts with the more extensive privileges of the laureate, whose recently published 'hymn' had already celebrated a right to proclaim the voice of the national consciousness:

> Me most of all men, it behoved to raise
>   The strain of triumph for this foe subdued,
> To give a voice to joy, and in my lays
>   Exalt a nation's hymn of gratitude,
> And blazon forth in song that day's renown, ...
> For I was grac'd with England's laurel crown.
> (I, i, line 6)

As Curran notes, the hymn is a communal form, one that implicitly acknowledges 'the underlying and mutually binding faith of a congregation'.[46] With the rise of Protestant culture, however, the hymn takes on renewed significance as the occasion of a questioning rather than a consolidation of the values of consensus and communality. More often than not, Romantic hymns act as a means to psychological exploration. In Southey's hymn, however, the impulse to introspection appears to be curtailed by the invocation of two sources of authority. The first is Pindar. In the epigrams to the 'Proem' and 'The Vision' Pindar is used to remind the reader that this is a work of public rather than private consciousness. Thus, while Southey implicates himself in the poem as a bard learning to poeticize the political, the temptation to lapse into romantic self-questioning is forestalled by the knowledge that Southey has, as it were, already come through.

A further point of authority comes from the references to the laurel crown:

> So may I boldly round my temples bind:
> The laurel which my master Spenser wore;
> And free in spirit as the mountain wind
> That makes my symphony in this lone hour,
> No perishable song of triumph raise,
> But sing in worthy strains my Country's praise.
>
> ('Proem', line 24)

Unlike Shelley, whose 'Hymn to Intellectual Beauty' is built around the exposure of the self to patterns of irony, absence and radical doubt, Southey is determined to preserve the traditional hymnal values of sincerity, presence and faith, in this case through an allusion to the poetic precedent and cultural authority of Spenser. But although the *Pilgrimage* is presented as a hymn of praise, the poem itself is actually about the poet's right to compose such a hymn. This idea, as I argued in Chapter 3, is enforced at the close of the work when, having surveyed the works of man from the top of the sacred mountain, the 'heavenly muse' urges the poet to go forth 'And in thy songs proclaim the hopes of human kind' (II, iv, line 61). Southey thus seems to be assured that the poem will survive; he has, after all, been inscribed into a national history. And without irony he can now look forward to the composition of a projected national hymn.

In contrast to Southey's starkly officious claim on Spenserian precedent, Wordsworth, as we have seen, presents a more complex case. Most puzzling of all, however, is the decision to base the 'Thanksgiving Ode' on the unlikely precedent of Spenser's *Epithalamion*. Where Wordsworth's poem commemorates a national victory, Spenser's poem is a lyrical affirmation of love and marriage; where the metre of the Ode is 'irregular', that of the *Epithalamion* is ordered; where the one speaks of actuality the other dwells in the ideal. The only apparent point of contact between the poems is that they are both long lyrical celebrations, in Wordsworth's opinion the longest of the kind attempted in 'our language'.[47] But despite these unpromising oppositions, Wordsworth's comparison is not entirely without significance. As Carol Maddison notes, the author who is commonly given credit for introducing the ode into England is Spenser. Maddison, however, doubts whether Spenser really deserves such credit: 'The *Epithalamion*'s [only] claim to being an ode is that it is an occasional lyric poem, written in an elevated style, celebrating an event generalized to be of vast importance.' The poem should therefore be relegated to a 'historical sub-genre': it is not an ode in the true sense of the word.[48] This is an interesting and significant claim; in the present context it might suggest that Wordsworth's ambivalent treatment of Waterloo is related to a corresponding problem of literary transmission. For if Spenser stands, so to speak, as the false origin of the English ode, then Wordsworth's poem once again signals its status as a literary aberration: a work that belongs not to the centre of a national tradition but to its margins.

This problem is heightened when we consider the form that the Ode actually takes. The irregularity of the poem is derived not from Spenser but from Cowley, the poet credited by Maddison as being the true originator of the English ode and the one responsible for initially investing a Horatian voice in a Pindaric form. The significance of this complex becomes clear when we consider the effect it has in Romantic poems. As Curran writes, through Cowley 'the first generation of English Romantics evolved, or reinforced a recognizable conception of the ode as an inherently dramatic form in which the poet risks the stability of his synthesizing consciousness before universally contrary pressures.'[49] In Wordsworth, therefore, the Pindaric ode of public celebration is continually at odds with the inward pull of a Horatian meditative presence. As the vicissitudes of the poet's private life become the focus of the poem, the gap between poetic understanding and historical experience widens so that, by the time of the 'Thanksgiving Ode', the poet would have to deal with two sets of experiences: one related to the sphere of romantic self-cultivation – the poem as a test of original genius; the other to the sphere of cultural history – the poem as communal discourse. In both cases the result is a collapse of the distinctions between strophe and antistrophe, poetic mediation and external event. For just as Waterloo forces the nation to look within to the 'rapid succession' of events beyond its control, so Wordsworth is drawn, once more, into a confrontation with forces exceeding comprehension.

The 'turns' in the poem illustrate this point nicely. In the first movement the poetry makes a rapid transition from public praise (lines 1–35) to reflections on the bardic powers of the poet (lines 36–56). We then encounter a series of rhetorical questions, corresponding to a pattern of strophe and antistrophe: 'Have we not conquered?' (line 57) and 'Why should the song be tardy to proclaim' (line 93). This section ends with the epode of 'No more – the guilt is banished' (line 125). Again, the question rebounds on itself: whose guilt is Wordsworth addressing here? His own or the nation's? The answer is of course both. In formal terms, no sooner has the antithesis of battle been converted into the uneasy thesis of victory, than the poet finds himself staging these terms as a psychodrama where, to adapt Curran, 'the tensions are both complementary and primary. The logic of the genre reinforces and is reinforced by the logic of internal debate.'[50]

This point is brought home when we recall the terms on which imagination succumbs to the 'closing deed magnificent'. Here self-command is no sooner abandoned than it is taken up again by a subject that concedes the role of discipline in constructing the expressive autonomy, the formal 'irregularity', that distinguishes the subject of the ode. That Wordsworth does not rest easy with the terms of his identification is apparent, it seems to me, in the lines that concede the founding role of violence. It is natural, in respect of this argument, to regard Spenser in his dual role as a source of restoration and destruction: restoration insofar as the poet helps to rescue a sense of dignity and mission from that lethal 'something' which the heart enjoys, destruction in that he serves as a reminder of all the poet must repress if he is to enter the community of men. In this sense we can see the allusion to the *Epithalamion* as an attempt to recast the history of the ode in Spenserian rather than Cowleyan terms. For if the latter is in some sense responsible for the collapse of the poetic persona into the drama of interiority, then an affiliation with the 'gentle' Spenser might appear to offer some form of release.

This idea is reinforced when we consider one of the more literal borrowings from Spenser's poem. The metaphorical continuity of Wordsworth's Ode is based on the passage of the sun in its journey from east to west. This figure has a number of precedents in Wordsworth's own work: from the 'Immortality Ode' to the *Essays: Upon Epitaphs*. It functions, as Paul de Man has observed, as a metaphor for the co-relation of 'origin and tendency', the way in which things pass 'insensibly' from one extreme into another.[51] Here, then, as well as awakening us to a key motif in Wordsworth's poetry, it also serves to alert us to the Ode's origins in Spenser. Thus, the 'universal source of pure delight' that opens the Ode has an earlier birth in the 'Faire Sun' that coordinates the temporal sequence of the *Epithalamion*.[52] But the most overt echo occurs in the wedding scene ('Open the temple gates vnto my loue'). The procession, choristers and 'roring Organs' of Spenser's poem is translated, almost word for word, into a regency setting:

> O, enter now his Temple gate!
> Inviting words – perchance already flung,
> (As the crowd press devoutly down the aisle
> Of some old minster's venerable pile)
> From voices into zealous passion stung,
> While the tubed engine feels the inspiring blast,
> And has begun – its clouds of sound to cast
> > Towards the empyreal Heaven,
> > As if the fretted roof were riven....
> Awake! the majesty of God revere!
> > Go – and with foreheads meekly bowed
> Present your prayers – go – and rejoice aloud –
> > The Holy One will hear!
> > > (lines 321–29; 337–40)

I find it curious that Wordsworth should choose to represent a public, national event through the transfiguration of a private, nuptial occasion. Yet in many respects, Spenser's vision of a world redeemed by the promise of fidelity seems entirely appropriate. For if, as Eric Walker has demonstrated, war is notoriously anti-conjugal, then peace should purchase a matrimonial paradise regained.[53] We have already seen, however, that the claim to redemption is crucially marked by the unwelcome intrusion of Carnage. Framed as it is by religious rites that resonate with Spenserian glee, the ode is nevertheless deeply sceptical about the ability of marriage to hold steady as the sign of victory and peace.

This notion becomes clearer when we consider the relationship between conjugality and war explored in 'Dion', a poem written in the same period as the ode but not published until 1820. Dion is first introduced as a Wordsworthian figure in Book IX of *The Prelude*. In the context in which he first appears, the 'Deliverer' of Sicily leads a 'philosophic war / Led by Philosophers' (IX, lines 423–4). But just as the pure intent of the French Revolution is mired in the retributive justice of the terror, so Dion, the pupil of Plato, yields to the temptation to assassinate his rival Heraclides. Critics of 'Dion' have suggested that Wordsworth is making a point about Napoleon's complicity in the plot to assassinate the Duc D'Enghien.[54] Such a reading must be qualified, however, by the consideration that Wordsworth regards Dion as a good man driven to desperate measures by the villainy of others. The poem is therefore a study in the corruption of virtue rather than a contemporary political allegory. But what is perhaps more compelling about Wordsworth's treatment of the story is the way in which it hinges on the significance of marriage. The published version of the poem draws attention to its source in Plutarch.[55] Here, the exiled Dion is persuaded to wage war after discovering the plan of the tyrant Dionysius to offer his wife 'unto one of his friends'. But there is evidence that the threatened marriage appears less than satisfactory: 'there ranne a rumour abroade (whether it were true, or invented by Dion's enemies) that he liked not his marriage, and coulde not live quietlie with his wife' (p. 145). The lachrymose postwar reunion scene would seem to put paid to all such rumours. Yet the end of Dion's victory is not the restoration of conjugality but rather its warping as the tale descends into a series of violent deaths and personal betrayals. Following Dion's death, the narrative concludes with a bleak catalogue of families and friends devastated as a result of the collapse of civic virtue.

'Dion', therefore, makes overt the contradictions that inhere in the ode's presentation of an antagonistic society redeemed by matrimony. What is more striking is the way Wordsworth relates these contradictions to the theme of cultural marginalization. Plutarch writes that Dion 'by nature had a certeine hawtiness of mind and severitie, and he was a sower man to be acquainted with'. Plato goes on to warn Dion 'that he should beware of obstinacie, the companion of solitarinesse, that bringeth a man in the ende to be forsaken of everie one' (p. 134). In Wordsworth's version, Dion appears to have taken Plato's counsel to heart, so

> That he, not too elate
> With self-sufficing solitude,
> But with majestic lowliness endued,
> Might in the universal bosom reign,
> And from affectionate observance gain,
> Help, under every change of adverse fate.
>
> (lines 31–6)

The humble autonomy, championed in 'The Bard' and in the imagination section of the ode, is shown here to be a vital principle of statesmanship. But Dion is significantly lacking in that other quality that goes to make the philosophic mind: the pacific virtue of a husband. In the lines describing the hero's triumphant return from exile, the hero 'crown'd with flowers of Sicily', in 'white, far-beaming corslet clad' (lines 43–4), is the central presence of an epithalamion. Thus far the commensurability of national and wedded bliss appears to be assured. Yet the vital element, missing in this depiction, is the presence of a wife. Indeed, if anything, it is Dion himself who, in his virginal appearance, most resembles a bride. Such primal narcissism reflects back on the opening lines of the poem where Dion is figured as a majestic swan, 'softly cleav[ing] / The mirror of the crystal flood'. Here, in self-sufficing solitude, 'Winds the creature without visible Mate' (lines 1–16, *passim*).

The link between sexual and moral autonomy is made clear in the conclusion to the poem when, following his descent along the crooked paths of realpolitik, Dion is racked by a terrifying vision of hysterical domesticity:

> A Shape, of more than mortal size
> And hideous aspect, stalking round and round!
> A woman's garb the phantom wore,
> And fiercely swept the marble floor, –
> Like Auster whirling to and fro,
> His force on Caspian foam to try;
> Or Boreas when he scours the snow
> That skins the plains of Thessaly,
> Or when aloft on Maenalus he stops
> His flight, mid eddying pine-tree tops!
>
> (lines 86–95)

There being no genuine felicity in the land of Syracuse it is hardly surprising that the elided feminine sphere should return in Dion's mind as life threateningly Real. Fiercely, vehemently sweeping, the domestic Fury is a symptom of the failure of the solitary character to redeem itself in marriage. And just as the subject of 'Dion' is scarred by its lack of conjugal felicity, so the nation is shown to be absorbed in '*matchless* perfidy and portentous lust' (line 125, my emphasis), modes of solipsism that mark the undoing of postwar reunion.

The 'Thanksgiving Ode' commemorates a ceremony to which the poet was not invited. On the day that civic society paid its respects to the heroes of Waterloo, Wordsworth attended 'humbler ceremonies' in the church at Grasmere (line 330). It is tempting to read this act as a form of atonement for sitting silent 'like an uninvited Guest' as prayers for victory were uttered in the spring of 1793.[56] But I would suggest that alienation is pervasive in Wordsworth's prayers, to the point where public matters of greater importance than the self are transfigured in images of solitude, disunion and dismemberment. The attempts on Wordsworth's part to find recuperation in loss are themselves concomitant with the failure of the state to locate a credible symbol of national integrity and unanimity. What emerges through the terrifying return of the body (the 'Thanksgiving Ode'), the internalization of restraint ('Occasioned by the Same Battle') or violated domesticity ('Dion') is thus 'Proof, for the historian's page and poet's lays, / That Peace, even peace herself, is fugitive.'[57] It is to Wordsworth's credit that this dissonant note is allowed to sound even in the midst of 'zealous passion'.[58]

Binding the work

In a key phrase from the 'Thanksgiving Ode' Wordsworth writes that the dawning flame of the Poet is 'short-lived'. What exceeds this light is the 'holier' splendour of the logos: 'the source is nobler whence doth rise / The current of this matin song' (lines 44–54, *passim*). By securing the origins of his song in something older than the poetic inspiration – that which is, in romantic terms, the property of an individual – Wordsworth seeks to protect his poem from its own internal self-surpassing: the desire, that is, to expose its fundamental illegitimacy. To keep itself as itself, therefore, the originality of the poetic voice must accede to the divine authority of the nation-state. Once again, Wordsworth is caught in a double bind. Lacking the grace of Southey's laurel crown – a title that links him, in notional terms at least, to the hereditary line of Spenser and Milton – he must imagine other sources of cultural subjectification. For this reason the 'Thanksgiving' volume folds within itself and employs a technique of 'self-referencing' in which allusions to previous works abound. It is on this individual basis that Wordsworth attempts to forge his work as a coherent cultural whole. The ode itself, for example, as we have seen, echoes passages from *The Prelude* and the 'Immortality' ode. Other critics, meanwhile, have noted references in the 'Ode Composed in January 1816' to 'I wandered lonely as a cloud' and in the 'Elegiac Verses', the final poem in the volume, to the 'Elegiac stanzas' on Peele Castle.[59]

What is significant, however, is the extent to which these recollections work to rebind the text, the subject and the state to the *telos* of providential history. The argument that Wordsworth tried to create the impression 'that what he did and wrote after the fall of Napoleon was continuous with what he did and wrote in his golden decade'[60] is sustained when one considers the prefatory note to the 'Thanksgiving Ode': 'This Publication may be considered as a sequel to the Author's "Sonnets, dedicated to Liberty"; it is therefore printed uniform with the two volumes of his Poems [i.e. of 1807], in which these sonnets are collected, to admit of their being conveniently bound up together'.[61] We have already seen the extent to which the Waterloo sonnets both extend and qualify the disciplinary poetics and politics of their precursors. What is equally striking is the way the nationalistic idiom of the 'Thanksgiving Ode' is made to chime with the platonic sentiments of the earlier volumes' more famous conclusion. Bound each to each, the 'Immortality' and 'Thanksgiving' odes provided mutually supportive views of the relations between poet and nation, peace and war, liberty and constraint.

Wordsworth's wishes were, in fact, carried out by default as, in 1820, remaindered copies of the ode were bound, together with *Peter Bell* (1819) and the *River Duddon* sonnets (1820), to form the supplementary volume to the *Poems* of 1815. When read together with the 'Intimations' ode, the new end-piece to the composite text does not seem so very remote from its predecessor. In this book, as post-Waterloo readers would become aware, national and individual recuperation could follow, literally, on one another. The filial relation is obvious when one considers the central passage of the first ode:

> Our birth is but a sleep and a forgetting:
> The soul that rises with us, our life's Star,
>   Hath had elsewhere its setting,
>   And cometh from afar:
>   Not in entire forgetfulness,
>   And not in utter nakedness,
> But trailing clouds of glory do we come
>   From God, who is our home...[62]

What follows blends easily into the central preoccupations of the *Essays: Upon Epitaphs*:

> But He beholds the light, and whence it flows,
>   He sees it in his joy;
> The Youth, who daily farther from the East
>   Must travel, still is Nature's Priest,
>   And by the vision splendid
>   Is on his way attended
> At length the Man perceives it die away,
> And fade into the light of common day.
>   (lines 69–76)

There is, however, 'in our embers... something that doth live' (lines 132–3); the memory of the edenic state persists in 'Fallings... vanishings' and 'Blank misgivings' that 'Are yet the fountain light of all our day, / ... a master light of all our seeing' (lines 147–55, *passim*). Indeed the revivifying strength of the 'philosophic mind' (line 189) is conditional on the loss of childhood liberty and innocence ('Shades of the prison-house', line 67). It is at this point that Wordsworth is at his most Hegelian. Buoyed along by faith, the mind can withstand 'all that is at enmity with joy, / [all that] Can utterly abolish or destroy' (lines 162–3). In much the same way, as memory tracks the soul/sun on its journey from material birth to incorporeal death so, in the 'Thanksgiving' poems, the negativity of 'human gore' is finally sublated in the mystery of 'darkness infinite'.[63] Binding the work in this way, Wordsworth prepares for a poetry in which private and national imaginations are 'framed in *subjection*... to the path which God ordains' ('Thanksgiving Ode', lines 16–17, my emphasis).

The frames extend, however, to more doubtful origins in the literature of the past. If the 'Thanksgiving Ode' remembers the *Epithalamion*, it also recalls that poem *through* its memory of the 'Immortality' ode. For that poem also bears the traces of a reading of Spenser's *Epithalamion*. Spenser's evocation of the morning – the birds that 'chaunt theyr laies' (line 78); the 'ioyfulst day that euer sunne did see' (line 116); the 'merry Musick that resounds from far, / The pipe, the tabor... [the] daunce and carrol sweet' (lines 129–35) – all of this looks forward to lines 19–57 of the ode. To a significant section of Wordsworth's post-Waterloo audience, these creative transformations gave more assurance than the arid philosophizing of the 'Thanksgiving Ode' could ever provide. But to those readers of the strange, hybrid text of 1820, the sentiments of the 'Thanksgiving Ode' might not have seemed so very remote from its metaphysical precursor. Where the earlier ode advocates 'Strength in what remains behind':

> In the soothing thoughts that spring
> Out of human suffering,
> In the faith that looks through death,
> In years that bring the philosophic mind...
> (lines 186–9)

the latter offers the 'abyss of weakness'. If the consummation of platonic and martial sentiments, of individual and national consciousness, is a consequence of the life that survives and preserves itself through death, might it be the case that the 'Immortality' ode gains *its* truth only by finding itself in utter dismemberment? But Carnage, as we have seen, sticks in the muse's throat, marking the point at which nations and individuals encounter dissolution. Perhaps this explains why, in 1845, Wordsworth chose to excise the offending line. Only a text purged of the one thing that cannot be negated can truly abide in the world of men.

6
'For Want of a Better Cause': Lord Byron's War with Posterity

> And I shall be delighted to learn who,
> Save you and yours, have gained by Waterloo?
> Byron, *Don Juan* (IX, 4)

On 6 July 1815, a year before Byron made his legendary journey to Waterloo, his friend John Cam Hobhouse was in Paris to witness the English troops taking possession of the gates. The event provoked the following reflections:

> England, who made the exception to the eighth article of the treaty of March 25 in favour of the rights of the French nation to choose their own monarch, now decides that France is to be treated as a conquered nation. The Duke of Wellington behaves with the utmost moderation, the friends of freedom cherish every hope. Lord Castlereagh arrives; the curtain rises at once, and the royal personages appear unmasked. Mufling is made Governor of Paris by Blucher and Wellington, and tells the capital so in a proclamation couched in terms of unrelenting severity. By the side of this appear the addresses of the returning tyrant to his people, denouncing vengeance and restoring at one stroke of the pen the corrupt authorities which vanished on March 20.[1]

There is something here of the paratactical logic of the times. Unable to master the rapid succession of history, the author opts instead for sardonic journalese: Paris is a theatre and Lord Castlereagh is its impresario; liberty is reversed, corruption is restored and hope is foreclosed in dramatic antithesis. The problem for anyone seeking to narrate an opposition line on the restoration was the lack of a suitable narrative precedent. Following the suicide of Whitbread, only Lord Holland, of the so-called 'old opposition', was willing to proffer a coherent challenge to the Establishment. During the Hundred Days he had argued that since Napoleon owed his restoration 'entirely to the love of the French people', any intervention in the affairs of his government would be an offence against the spirit of the English constitution. In the wake of Napoleon's defeat the Whigs were urged by Holland to accept non-intervention in French policy as 'the main, clear and definite object of public policy'.[2] At first, this seemed like a cogent argument; after all, as a matter of principle had not the French a right to elect Napoleon as a constitutional monarch as the British had chosen William III? But the recourse to the ideals of the Glorious Revolution met with little support from the party mainstream. Moreover it was an argument that fell straight into the hands of the government who were eager to claim for themselves the title of *vindex securitas Europae, assertor libertatis Britanniae*.[3]

The link between the decisive events of 1688 and 1815 was taken up again the following year. In his Address upon the Treaties with Foreign Powers, delivered to the House on 19 February 1816, Lord Castlereagh sought to define Waterloo once and for all as a victory 'against usurpation and ... military despotism'. He took this as the occasion to hoist the opposition by its own petard. Foreign support for the return of the Bourbons was justified, he argued, on the grounds that it was conducted not in violation of but in accordance with the precepts of 1688. To drive home his point, Castlereagh alerted his audience to the instrumental role of the Whigs in the triple alliance of 1717. Since the object of the peace of Utrecht had been 'to establish and maintain Protestant succession within these realms, and the succession to the throne of France and Spain' the Whigs had no cause to complain of current government policy. For then, as now, the government had acted 'on the principles of the Whigs of the Revolution'. Castlereagh added, in a brilliant *coup de style*, that Napoleon's military despotism had been founded on precisely that 'state of social disorganization which modern philosophy and modern Whiggism tended to produce'. Now it was the Tories, and not the party of Whitbread, Grey and Holland, who could claim to be the true heirs of the Revolution.[4]

That same day, in the House of Lords, the conservative Whig Lord Grenville gave further justification to the government's address. 'What previously existed in France', he argued, 'was a military usurpation, inconsistent with the rights of man; what was restored was consonant with the liberties and privileges of all classes.' Henceforth, the true 'friend of liberty' would rejoice at 'the destruction of detestable and slavish principles, and in the restoration of social order and representative government'.[5] Just as in 1688 William III had 'come to drive away an odious tyrant', so in 1815 Lord Wellington had fought to deliver the world from an ambitious demagogue. Like William he could justly claim to be the defender of national sovereignty and of the Constitution. As Lord Holland's impressionistic reply confirms, the Foxites were confounded. Denied a cogent relationship with their historical foundations, the voice of the pacificist opposition was effectively debarred from any form of practical intervention. All that remained was personal misgiving, bitterness and despair.

What was enacted in Parliament in the form of Whig division took shape in poetry in the baffled, agonistic voice of Lord Byron. I want to approach Byron's reaction to the politics of Waterloo with some caution, however. In Malcolm Kelsall's influential thesis Byron is portrayed as 'the inheritor of the traditions of one of the main political philosophies which has shaped British history: that of the patrician Whigs'. As Kelsall points out, that tradition was in 'crisis', as was 'the political party that claimed to embody the tradition'. The 'Byronic', he concludes, 'is in part created by the ideology of the Whigs under stress.'[6] It is the 'in part' in this sentence that will be the focus for much of what follows. Like Kelsall I acknowledge the powerful role that Whig politics played in shaping the limits of Byron's imagination. Where I depart from this argument is in the stress I lay on those other pressures influencing the work. For one thing Kelsall seems to hold the poet's literary leanings in contempt. Byron's interest in tragedy, pastoral and commemorative writing is largely passed over in favour of the view that romanticism is a product of revolutionary fervour and attendant disappointment. The aesthetic, in other words, is reduced to a function of the political, leaving Byron no choice but to accede to the limitations of disinherited Whiggery. In the discussion that follows I advance the idea that Byron saw in Waterloo an opportunity to depart from the frustrations of domestic politics to embrace deeper, more personal concerns about the relationship between warfare and identity. In this respect Byron's work is no less political than that of his supposedly more radical peers. The force of this work lies not in its 'consistency' – I do not claim that Byron presents a demonstrable alternative to the politics of his day – but rather in its willingness to weigh up party matters against mythopoeic absolutes. Later, we shall see how those absolutes are, in turn, subjected to the most scrupulous scepticism, but to introduce this theme we will begin with a revaluation of the poet's relations with the Whigs as these stood around the time of Napoleon's final defeat.

Napoleon's farewell

As is well known, Byron was appropriately nonplussed by the news of Waterloo: 'is it true?... But is it true?' he inquired, following this with his most quotable announcement: 'I am damned sorry for it... I didn't know but I thought I might live to see Lord Castlereagh's head on a pole. But I suppose I sha'nt now.'[7] Three weeks later, having recovered from the shock of the Sublime, he penned a more considered response to Thomas Moore:

> Every hope of a republic is over, and we must go on under the old system. But I am sick at heart of politics and slaughters; and the luck which Providence is pleased to lavish on Lord ** [Castlereagh] is only a proof of the little value the gods set upon posterity, when they permit such ***s as he and that drunken corporal, old Blucher, to bully their betters. From

this, however, Wellington should be exempted. He *is* a man, – and the Scipio of our Hannibal. However, he may thank the Russian frosts, which destroyed the *real elite* of the French army, for the successes of Waterloo.[8]

The passage bears the mark of the paratactical logic already detected in Hobhouse's prose. The opening sentence, with its invocation of Paine – 'government under the old system' – seems to locate its author squarely in Radical territory. But the subsequent clause – 'I am sick at heart of politics and slaughters' – betrays a more emotional objection to war than the Radical's concern with taxation and commerce. As rapidly as this tone is introduced the prose undertakes a third 'turn' – this time in the direction of principled flippancy, the tone that Byron uses whenever Castlereagh is within range. The strophic movement of the prose is completed with the rumination on Lord Wellington. He is exempted from the list of butchery and carnage because 'he *is* a man', because, that is, he has behaved as a classical warrior, 'the Scipio of our Hannibal'. The reference is significant because it shows that at this early stage in the history of the reception of Waterloo Byron is largely in tune with the political opinions of Whitbread and Holland. They too were prepared to acknowledge the superiority of Wellington over 'the Greatest Captain of the Age'.[9] In Byron's case, however, it alerts us to a significant imaginative strategy: the relating of contemporary events to a wider, mythopoeic pattern. But the reference to ancient history, as Byron is aware, lends itself well to the rhetoric of the Establishment since, like the Glorious Revolution, the defeat of Hannibal was regarded by both sides as a key stage in the development of constitutional liberty. Add to this the fact that the allusion had already been used by Coleridge in the *Courier* (and would be taken up by Sir Edmund Creasy) and the sentence begins to take on an unfortunate political connotation. Perhaps this explains the final turn of the text, away from classicism and towards the mundane matter of history; since the 'elite' of Napoleon's army had been destroyed by the Russian winter, the conflict was not heroic after all.

Where then does this leave Byron? It would be easy to say that these statements are self-cancelling on the grounds that it is impossible to reduce them to any sort of consistency; in Kelsall's words 'they contradict each other internally by polarizing politics into antithetical extremism' (p. 54). Thus, in its general movement, the passage veers from outrage at the cynical machinations of government to identification with the larger, philosophical patterns of resistance, pathos and heroism that the poet will go on to explore in more detail in Canto III of *Childe Harold's Pilgrimage*. Let us admit then that Kelsall's charge sticks; the passage is contradictory because Byron, like the party of which he is a member, is unable to write himself out of his present dilemma. Yet even if this reading were accepted one would nevertheless have to consider the evidence that the poet continued to speak out against the results of Waterloo. If, at times, the principle underlying these protests is neither consistent nor recognizable this in no way detracts from their actual social effect. In this first section, therefore, I want to turn away from the interiority of Byron's vision to consider its external or strategic implications.

Lord Byron's struggle with the politics and poetics of Waterloo begins with an anonymous and untitled poem, first published in the *Examiner* on 30 June 1815. The poem, which was reissued in *Poems, 1816* under the title 'Napoleon's Farewell (From the French)', may be used to illustrate a critical difference in opposition attitudes to the form and content of political reform. In the *Examiner* the verse is preceded by an editorial note in which Leigh Hunt explains to his readers that 'there are points in the following spirited Lines with which our opinions do not accord; and indeed the Author himself has told us, that he rather adapted them to what may be considered as the speaker's feelings than his own.'[10] As was noted in the introduction to this study, by the summer of 1815 Hunt was especially concerned that the politics of the *Examiner* should not be linked with the Napoleonist sentiments of Lord Byron and the Holland House circle. Favouring liberty over despotism, Hunt was a meliorist who persuaded himself, after the initial shock, that Waterloo could indeed be perceived as a victory for the forces of progress and reform. The defeat of Napoleon, he argued, was vital for the furtherance of national independence and the English Constitution. To reach this position, however, Hunt had to reflect on the nature and extent of his latent Napoleonism. It seems that like Byron, Hunt was unwilling to relinquish his fascination with the scourge of Europe. His decision, therefore, to publish the 'Farewell' was an instinctively poetic act, filtered through a political disclaimer that shields poet, publisher and audience from the threat of unaccountable feelings.

Who, then, is the speaker of Byron's poem? It is conventional to read the 'Farewell' as a conflation of two voices: Byron ventriloquizing Napoleon melts imperceptibly into a personal meditation on fame and exile.[11] But this emphasis often fails to take into account an important political point, one that reflects the conditions of postwar Whig ideology. Consider, for example, the following lines from the poem's concluding stanza:

> Farewell to thee, France! – but when Liberty rallies
> Once more in thy regions, remember me then –
> The violet still grows in the depth of thy valleys;
> Though withered, thy tears will unfold it again –
> Yet, yet, I may baffle the hosts that surround us,
> And yet may thy heart leap awake to my voice –
> (lines 17–22)

In the spring of 1814, Napoleon had promised the French that he would return to France in time to see the violets bloom. In the poem Byron uses this figure to invoke the embattled but irrepressible march of Liberty; like nature the principle may wither away but the 'tears' of injustice guarantee its rejuvenation. The negative side of this equation is that it is impossible to disassociate progressive politics from a cyclical history of loss and return. In lines 21–22, for example, the wish to draw profit from dissolution is severely compromised by the rhetorical insistence of 'yet, yet I may baffle... And yet may thy heart'. As a result, the countervailing force of 'yet... yet' (precisely echoed in 'Yet, freedom! yet' in Canto IV, stanza 98 of *Childe Harold's Pilgrimage*) has been narrowed to the space between the Tory and the Radical, both of whom have claimed the right to speak the genuine language of reform.

If the 'Farewell' poem is a challenge to postwar complacency its effectiveness is compromised by an overall tone of tragic inevitability, the sense in which revolutionary change is best understood as an element of natural rather than of human history. Hunt, I would claim, was well aware of this tendency in Byron's poetry and took steps in his own writing to counter its ideological effects. Between 23 January 1814 and 13 August 1815 Hunt wrote a number of articles on the nature of education and its effects on the development of civilized society. They may be read, in part, as an attempt to provide a sociological context for Hazlitt's autocratic claim that man is 'naturally a lover of kings'.[12] In Hunt's view, the origins of this passion are to be found in the current system of education which promotes 'admiration... for wars and soldiers in general':

> The causes of such men as Bonaparte are not to be found in the viciousness of the individual, nor are their effects to be done away by singling him out for abuse, to the impunity of all others resembling him. The causes are to be found... in that admiration which these very complainers persist in keeping up for their own purposes – in early habits of education – and in books of all kinds, school-books in particular, in Homer, in Plutarch, in Caesar, in Zenophon, and a hundred others which grave Christian divines continue to teach all over Europe. Edifying no doubt were the sermons which these reverend persons preached in all the churches in behalf of the Waterloo subscription, and grievous their denunciations against the lust of conquest and the unbridled violence of the passions... But what then? The next morning these very persons are as didactic as ever in behalf of the Caesars and Alexanders, are giving out themes upon the glories of the Greeks and Romans, and flogging their scholars or their children for not knowing that *virtue* in the Latin language is the same as *valour.*[13]

Against Hazlitt, Hunt argues that the seeds of violence are embedded in our culture, not in our nature. By maintaining a system of education, which places so much value on military achievement, culture has produced, and will continue to produce, Alexanders, Caesars and Napoleons. It is this belief that lies behind Hunt's ambiguous response to Byron's 'Ode to Napoleon Bonaparte', published in the *Examiner* for 17 April 1814. In the form in which it first appeared, Byron's poem was printed alongside an article by Hunt criticizing those who wished to see the Emperor dead, the idea being that public execution or suicide would merely perpetuate the image of Napoleon as a tragic figure. Hunt, however, was sailing against the tide of public opinion. In different forms, and at different times, poets as diverse as Wordsworth, Southey, Coleridge and Shelley would argue for the death of the anti-hero, but the 'Ode' is noticeable for the way in which it incorporates this feeling into a sustained meditation on the suicidal impulse of classical tragedy. Where Satan 'in his fall preserved his pride, / And, if a mortal, had as proudly died' (lines 143–4), or Caesar 'dared depart in utter scorn / Of men that such a yoke had borne' (lines 59–60), Napoleon, by clinging to life, has manifestly failed to be himself; he has failed, in other words, to fulfil the role of sacrificial hero, with the result that a career that ought to be perceived as tragedy can now only be seen as banal: 'To think that God's fair world hath been / The footstool of a thing so mean' (lines 80–1). Henceforth, as the appended epigram from Gibbon makes clear, human history enters the domain of ambiguity: 'By this shameful abdication, he protracted his life a few years, in a very ambiguous state, between an Emperor and an Exile, till – ' As Byron's curtailed quotation indicates, the 'till' of Napoleon awaits fulfilment in a future that may never arrive.[14]

In a gesture comparable to the Hegelian critique of art, what Byron cannot accept in the Napoleonic story is an unforeseen reliance on the irrational and the incoherent. For Hegel, art is an insufficient ground for the realization of self-consciousness; art can never be transparent in the way that pure thought requires. Similarly, in Byron, what occurs in both the life and the poem (as if one could continue to speak of such a distinction) is a form of ambiguity that cannot be converted into profit. Through his failure to die, Napoleon becomes a 'nameless thing', present in the poem only as an unrelenting circuit of exchange: never quite Satan, never quite Caesar, Napoleon is everything and nothing by turns. Not even the promise of a forthcoming Promethean rebellion can compensate for the Emperor's inherent emptiness. Only suicide will provide the strong identity he requires.

Liberal politics, however, would not rest content with such a view: as the *Examiner* makes clear, there is more value to the cause of liberty in the life of a disgraced tyrant than in the death of a romantic hero.[15] Thus, where Byron, first in the 'Ode' and then in Canto III of *Childe Harold's Pilgrimage*, betrays his fascination with the great 'disturbers of mankind' such as Julius Caesar, Augustus and Napoleon, Hunt places more emphasis on the 'great names of wit and *utility*, – with Petrarch, Milton, Shakespeare, Columbus, Bacon, Newton, Voltaire' (my emphasis).[16] The contest is between a tragic and a utilitarian view of history or, at another level, between the aristocratic ideals of the private sphere and the democratic principles of the public.

These writings, together with the 'National Song', discussed in the introduction, can be read therefore as a 'democratic' answer to the patrician poetics of Hazlitt and Byron. By publicly criticizing the demonization of Napoleon, Hunt was able to sublimate the 'essential' tragedy of Waterloo to the happy cause of civilization. His thoughts on the subject also serve as a proleptic response to the agonistic labours of Keats, who gave up his progress poem, *Hyperion*, to concentrate on the fall of the reactionary Titans. Hunt, by eschewing sympathy with the dead fathers, be they of the ancient or the new regime, could incorporate Waterloo into a larger pattern that embraced redemption and made the 'victory' fortunate, *felix culpa*. Alone amongst his contemporaries, therefore, Hunt's view of the conflict is, I would suggest, a potentially comic one; it is certainly the *sensibility* that is most dominant in the narrative poems of this period: from the Spenserian pathos of *The Story of Rimini* to the theatrical extravagance of *The Descent of Liberty*. And it also explains, I think, why his own poetic response would prove to be as inadequate as that of his peers.

The trumpet of a prophecy

The struggles of Hunt and Byron to define and defend a viable opposition response to the defeat of Napoleon should be set within the context of the numerous celebratory verses which appeared in the Tory press. Thomas Fitzgerald, whose poem 'The Battle of Waterloo' was examined at the beginning of this study, provided Byron with a typical straw target. In common with other pro-establishment poets, Fitzgerald placed the battle in the context of Christian theories of predestination. It is possible that Lord Byron had Fitzgerald's work in mind when, in March 1816, he offered an ode, reputed to be 'From the French' to the editor of the Whig *Morning Chronicle*. In the same month Byron wrote to Moore, criticizing Fitzgerald for adopting the 'character of *Vates*' in a verse entitled 'The White Cockade, being an Address to the French Nation'. First published in the *Morning Post* in January 1814, the poem was regarded by Fitzgerald as prophetic of the Emperor's abdication in the following spring.[17] But while it is true that Byron was scornful of Fitzgerald's work it is more likely that the specific target is Robert Southey. Southey's *The Poet's Pilgrimage to Waterloo* appeared a few weeks after Byron's verse, but his intentions to commemorate the battle in verse were widely known and its terms, to some extent, anticipated. So pervasive was the discourse of divine providence that Byron could have predicted the tone the laureate would adopt. And indeed, as I argued earlier on, the author of the *Pilgrimage* is explicit in claiming his right to comprehend the transcendental significance of the battle and to prophecy its influence on the course of English national history. It is with Southey's example in mind, therefore, that Byron set out to subvert a dominant aesthetic strategy of the Tory establishment.

In sending the poem to James Perry, Byron was at pains to distance himself from the claim of authorship. Fearing that poet and editor would be dragged into a legal battle over the subversive content of the verse, Byron advised Perry to publish the poem as a translation from the French. Accordingly, the version that first appeared in print includes the waspish suggestion that the ode was linked with Chateaubriand – disparaged by liberals as a political turncoat. The proofs add, however, that the poem is 'Said to be done into English verse by R. S.—P. L. P. R. Master of the Royal Spanish Inqn. &c. &c.', a clear reference to Southey as poet laureate and author of the history of the Iberian Peninsula. Where *The Poet's Pilgrimage to Waterloo* is a concerted attempt to condition the rhetoric of sublimity within the encompassing logic of the national mind, Byron's counter-prophecy sets out to displace the idea that Waterloo can be owned by a single nation.[18] As the preface notes: 'The French have their Poems and Odes on the famous Battle of Waterloo as well as ourselves. – Nay [possibly a pun on Marshall Ney], they seem to glory in the battle as the source of great events to come.'[19] By providing an alternative national perspective on this 'divinely' sanctioned triumph, the poem dialogizes Waterloo from within, challenging its nationalistic significance through the intervention of an alien voice.

At another level, the ode sets out to unsettle the grounds on which the Emperor was linked, in the Byronic imagination, with the desire for sovereign being. Where 'Napoleon's Farewell' celebrated the deposed Emperor as a symbol of powerful but fated self-assertion, the voice of the ode locates authority with the will of a people:

> France hath twice too well been taught
> The 'moral lesson' dearly bought –
> Her safety sits not on a throne,
> With CAPET or NAPOLEON!
> But in equal rights and laws,
> Hearts and hands in one great cause –
> Freedom...
> (lines 77–83)

This is far removed, I feel, from the tragic romanticism that Kelsall cites as evidence of Byron's political ineffectuality. At a stylistic level, the ode's communal 'we' is a departure from the aesthetic ideology underpinning the 'Farewell' poem. No longer subjected to the maniacal will of the 'Chief', the people refuse to 'curse Waterloo' and thereby secure their release from the circle of tragedy.

Unlike its predecessor, the ode bases its resistance to tyranny on a detailed knowledge of specific historical events. On 20 November 1815, the Allies signed the second Treaty of Paris, an act that sanctified the policies of the 'Ultra-Royalist' French government. Under the new regime, loyal Bonapartists were no longer exempted from public prosecution. But, as Lord Holland pointed out, proceedings against the men in question – Marshall Ney and General Labedoyere – were put in motion before the treaty was signed:

> Up to that time... the inhabitants [of Paris] were entitled to claim political impunity for all political opinions and conduct... A promise of security was held out to the inhabitants of Paris: they surrendered the town; and while Wellington and the Allies were still really in possession of it, Labedoyere was executed [on 19 August 1815] and Ney was tried for political opinion and conduct.[20]

Holland goes on, in the same letter, to attack the conduct of the Duke of Wellington for failing to defend 'a man with whom he had once coped in the field of honourable war'. In Byron's poem, the focus on the deaths of Labedoyere and Ney reflects Holland's belief that the Allies had acted unjustly. Perhaps more importantly, it also announces Byron's departure from the deferential attitude to Wellington that had coloured his initial response to Waterloo. Drawing on this political context, Byron turns once again to the theme of counter-prophecy: the blood of the departed heroes will mingle with the 'crimson cloud' of freedom to 'shake the world with wonder' (lines 11–15, *passim*). In the revised version, printed after the poem's first publication in the *Morning Chronicle*, the bursting of the cloud is linked with apocalypse outlined in *Revelations*, chapter 8: 'The first angel sounded, and there followed fire and hail mingled with blood.' Byron, in other words, makes even more explicit his intention to reclaim the language of prophecy. Unlike 'Napoleon's Farewell', however, the return of freedom is based upon revolutionary as opposed to natural temporality. Released from its association with the tragic cycle of Napoleon Bonaparte, freedom is depicted as an 'ever bounding spirit' (line 100), inspiring the 'voice of mankind' to join in acts of 'proud union' (lines 92–4). Remarkably, therefore, a poem that rises out of Whig disaffection and Foxite despair manages, despite itself, to affirm a progressive view of human history. The achievement of this poem must, it seems to me, be set against Kelsall's belittling of Byron's politics. We may well find just cause to critique the poet's attempts to produce a poetics of coherent protest but the fact that the verse continued to cause controversy – provoking the ire of John Scott's *Champion* and the approval of those radical readers who purchased William Hone's best-selling pirated edition – indicates the extent to which the poem's significance was defined by the circumstances of its consumption as much as of its production.

More so than Hunt, therefore, I would suggest that Byron set out to reconvert Waterloo into a symbol of antithetical resistance – against both the weakened dialectics of the *Examiner* and the consensual loyalism of the Establishment. We have seen, however, that the poet's favouring of tragedy in the ode to Napoleon Bonaparte and of pastoral in 'Napoleon's Farewell' runs the risk of cancelling out the more focused stance presented in 'From the French'. It is in the latter poem that Byron posits an effective form of rhetorical intervention; through the dialogical voices of satire and counter-prophecy Waterloo is effectively drained of its sublime status and repositioned as an object of political contestation. In this limited sense 'From the French' provides us with one of the few effective poetical challenges to the pervasive hyperbole of postwar English culture.

Glory's dream unriddled

> History can only take things in the gross
> *Don Juan* (VIII, 3)

> A fact: see the Waterloo Gazettes. I recollect remarking at the time to a friend: – *'There is fame!* a man is killed, his name is Grose, and they print it Grove.'[21]

There is, in addition to Byron's evident dissatisfaction with the political consequences of Waterloo, a strikingly ethical dimension to consider. So far we have linked the poet's objections to Waterloo to an exclusively metropolitan and party-political context. On visiting the field in 1816, however, Byron's perspective on the battle is sharpened. In addition to satirizing the heads of state whose actions have led to its calamitous outcome, Byron views the event as an occasion to meditate on the elegiac costs of war. In doing so he is brought closer to the traumatic centre of conflict and to the central antagonism of his own work. Before we look at this effect in the romance poetics of *Childe Harold's Pilgrimage*, I want to begin with an analysis of the poem most readily cited as evidence of Byron's antipathy to war: the Waterloo and Ismail stanzas from *Don Juan*.

Stated in summary, were this not itself an illustration of the gross approach to things, Canto VIII of *Don Juan* is Byron's attempt to rescue detail from the emptiness of conventional narrative history. Written in the wake of Peterloo and the postwar consolidation of monarchical power, the poem may be conceived as a war in thought; the chief protagonists are fact and truth, epic and elegy, the gazette and the lyric, the mass and the individual. It is, like all of Byron's works, a self-subverting poem: at its most effective when it is most dissonant, most out of step with the presuppositions of poetic form and cultural value. In the second of the quotations cited above, a man named Grose, an acquaintance from the poet's Cambridge days, is at once an icon for the massive, the palpable and the monstrous in war: 'in one red burial blent!', and an index of its transformative effects. It is nothing more than a printer's error, or a chronicler's oversight, but for Byron the name is the thing. The unfortunate shunting of abject Grose to bucolic Grove, may be taken as evidence of the historical unconscious, a sign of its conspiracy with the aesthetic ideology of postwar commemorative discourse. In summary, then, the military cantos of *Don Juan* state an important truth: history may well take things in the gross, but it is poetics that provides it with the illusion of redemption.

Byron, like the critic Josiah Conder, is well aware of the disparity between ancient and modern conceptions of warfare. Towards the end of Canto VII, for example, he invokes Homer only in order to speak of the gulf separating the art of the past from the concerns of the present:

> But now, instead of slaying Priam's son,
>   We only can but talk of escalade,
> Bombs, drums, guns, bastions, batteries, bayonets, bullets,
> Hard words, which stick in the soft Muses' gullets.
>   (78, 621–4)

The penultimate line, with its alliterative cataloguing, is characteristic of the later Byron. The shock of war is such that matter must get in the way of mellifluousness; to do otherwise would be to collaborate with the process by which history is turned into triumphalist art. The endeavour to blast apart the continuum of classical forms and recent wars is conveyed through a paradoxical revivification of its extinct 'rules'. Thus, Canto VIII opens with a version of the traditional hero's curse:

> Oh blood and thunder! and oh blood and wounds! –
>   These are but vulgar oaths, as you may deem,
> Too gentle reader! and most shocking sounds:
>   And so they are; yet thus is Glory's dream
> Unriddled, and as my true Muse expounds
>   At present such things, since they are her theme,
> So be they her inspirers! Call them Mars,
> Bellona, what you will – they mean but wars.
>   (1)

Like Spenser in *Childe Harold's Pilgrimage*, Byron singles out Homer in order to wrest the classical tradition from state-sanctioned conformity. Once again, the relationship with poetic precedence is an active one; a poetic model is worked upon and transformed rather than slavishly copied. It is of course Walter Benjamin whose thought informs much of what I have to say about the singular quality of Byron's verse. We will return to Benjamin's work later on in this chapter; at this juncture what I would stress is the way in which the satirical poet and the historical materialist are allied in their desire to arrest the seamless flow of causal history. In *Don Juan* this takes the shape of abrupt, specialized configurations, formal effects that crystallize the relationship between ancient and modern into disruptive 'states of emergency'.[22] By juxtaposing the conventional 'blood and thunder' with the factual 'blood and wounds' the dream of transcendent victory is effectively 'unriddled' and returned to its primary reality. Formal dissonance is also present in the slant rhyme Mars / wars. The 'shocking sound' contributes to the thematic contrast of poetic and prosaic combat. Here again it is the juxtaposition of classical and modern, rather than its supposed continuity, that allows the verse, in Benjamin's words, to 'brush against the grain' of predetermined, providential time.[23]

The battle that follows turns on the arresting example of individuals: Juan, Johnson and the Turkish orphan girl. Extracted from the gross their stories exemplify the dictum set out in stanza 3: 'The drying up of a single tear has more / Of honest fame, than shedding seas of gore' (lines 23–4). With the exception of those battles fought in 'freedom's' name (Marathon and Morat), the best that may be extracted from the siege of Ismail is the pathos of 'self-approbation' (VIII, 4, line 1). But it is this 'best' that makes all the difference to the effect of Byron's verse. For in a crucial respect the rhetoric of grief may do little to disrupt the business of war; indeed, at a structural level, it might even be regarded as its necessary other, a co-conspirator in the logic of sacrifice. Suspending, for now, the wider implications of this thought, it should be noted that Byron, of all the Romantic poets, comes closest to conveying a sense of the true cost of war. The effectiveness of *Don Juan* comes from its insistence on the particularity of death. For Byron, the fact that massacres recur does not mean that they are similar; each instance of slaughter and each victim's death possesses its unique history and form. To generalize in the manner of the Waterloo list is to befog death's specificity. Thus, throughout Canto VIII, Byron exhorts his reader to consider 'how the joys of reading a Gazette / Are purchased by all agonies and crimes' (125, lines 993–4). Readerly pleasure and the economy of pain are portrayed as mutually supportive elements within a larger state system, one that transforms civil society into a mechanism for repressing the interdependence of comfort and barbarity. Even poetry is not immune to this civilizing process. With a recollection of Wordsworth's 'Carnage', the poet states that the 'true portrait of one battle-field' is not to be found in the stanzas of the Waterloo bards but in the 'agony' resounding in the individual soldier's 'pang' (13, line 97). Thus, while each individual deserves a 'couplet, or an elegy', the satirical poet leaves this task to the dispatches, for such a 'claim / Would form a lengthy lexicon of glory' (17, lines 134–5). The form that such commemoration takes in the Gazette however, is a reminder of the disintegrative effects of war. As 'fifty-thousand' individuals (17, line 132) are transformed into proper nouns (18) – misspelt ones at that – Byron underscores the pathos of iterability. The fact that a proper noun must be repeatable in any other context – for Grose to serve as a mark of individuation it must take its place within a system of differences and relations – means that it is subject to linguistic displacement. Byron accepts this Derridean logic but only in order to show its ruthless effects at the level of roll calls, musters and lists. Fighting to save the name involves a paradoxical commitment to preserving the sense in which personal identity remains unnamable; just as the 'groan, the roll in dust, the all-white eye / Turned back within its socket' (13, lines 101–2) testify to a depth of suffering that cannot be properly signified, so the misspelt name properly articulates the violent transformation of civic identity. At best, Byron seems to say, poetry can embody a sense of what it might feel like to suffer this violence.

As I have indicated, *Don Juan's* focus on the politics and poetics of commemoration brought to a head a long-standing dialogue with Wordsworth. Notwithstanding Hazlitt's condemnation of the 'Thanksgiving Ode', Wordsworth shares with Byron a commitment to presenting a clear, unalloyed picture of the relationship between individual suffering and national salvation. Neither elegiac, nor epic, Wordsworth's focus on the costs of war differs from Byron's in the emphasis placed on the conflict's 'pure intent'. When judged from such a divine perspective, the affirmation of 'Carnage', as we have seen, makes brutal sense. Where Byron departs from Wordsworth is in the emphasis he places on the inability of writing to raise its authority on the bodies of the dead. The proper relation between *corpus* and inscription is the issue at stake in epitaph writing and it is to the spoiling of this art, with its implicit ideological underpinnings, that Byron turns his attention.

The spoiler's art

'even the dead will not be safe from the enemy if he wins'
Walter Benjamin, Thesis VI

When, in May 1816, Byron rode across the field of Waterloo, he carried with him the memory of a recent debate in the Houses of Parliament about the question of raising a national monument to the heroes of the day. Although it is unlikely that he had read 'Occasioned by the Battle of Waterloo', Byron was well aware of Wordsworth's interest in the property and propriety of epitaph writing. Prior to visiting the field in the summer of 1816, Byron took issue with a passage from the 'Essay upon Epitaphs' in which Wordsworth had singled out the bucolic charm of Turkish cemeteries with their well-placed graves and monitory cypresses, fit emblems of the seamless continuity of life and death. 'This is pure stuff', wrote Byron. In Turkey 'there are no cemeteries in "remote places" – except such as have the cypress and the tombstone still left when the olive and the habitation of the living have perished.'[24] For Byron there is nothing natural about the relation between cypress and olive, tombstone and habitation. Where Wordsworth speaks of the gradation of life into death (and back again) through the associative link with natural, organic processes of engendering and decomposition, the lordly poet insists on their radical difference. Transposed to the field of

Waterloo, only a poetry of antitheses can prevent the dead from being exchanged as values in accordance with a law of general equivalence. It is to the investigation of such a poetics that I now turn.

Lest what I have been describing seems remote from the themes of Canto III of *Childe Harold's Pilgrimage*, it is worth bearing in mind the way in which this verse problematizes the poetics and politics of commemoration. 'Stop! – for thy tread is on Empire's dust!' opens stanza 17 with an arresting appeal to the reader as Waterloo pilgrim. The nameless dead are 'sepulchred below', their shattered bodies unmarked by 'colossal bust' or 'column trophied' (lines 145–8). Suspending for now the discussion of the verse's epitaphic and pastoral connotations let us consider its political implications. As Jerome McGann notes, the stanza itself frames an archaeology of commemoration that goes back to the satirical writings of Lucan and Juvenal. In forging a link with these writers, Byron comments with deft sardonism on the efforts of contemporary ideologues to assume parallels with the great battles of classical antiquity. The line displaces the heroic constellation of ancient and modern concerns by reminding us of their ultimate irreconcilability. Where, as in Tory discourse, the rupture of warfare precipitates the assertion of a historical *telos* in which archaic depths flood into the present to determine a future, in Byron, to adapt Terry Eagleton, 'the present finds reflected back to itself nothing less than its own ineradicable *difference* from that imaginary ego ideal'.[25] The grandeur of Empire, whether this is written in the Childe's encounter with the burial mounds at Marathon or the mass graves of Waterloo, amounts to the same thing: more bodies, more dust, more names to be despoiled. As an index of 'ghostly national imaginings', and as an icon of the irreducible physicality of the body in pain, the unmarked grave displaces the battlefield as sacred place to lay bare its ideological underpinnings; again the poet asks: 'Is the spot mark'd by no colossal bust? / Nor column trophied for triumphal show?' (lines 147–8). Unlike the ideologically charged fields of Wordsworth, Southey and Scott, Byron's space is drained of memorial significance. In this poem there is no monument to mark the transition from material suffering to national resubstantiation, no means by which 'mortal accident' may be allowed to fade into the commemorative discourse of heroic sacrifice. In a space marked by 'ghastly gaps', 'hollows' and effacements, the poet sets out to retextualize the accepted significance of the glorious victory by foregrounding the essentially constructed nature of history. Through a concentration on the politics of fictionality – the investment in myths of origin that allows authority to consolidate its grip on power – Byron, of all the Romantic poets, comes closest to revealing the true nature of war.

His note on the appearance of Waterloo as a field of action is instructive in this respect:

> As a plain, Waterloo seems marked out for the scene of some great action, though this may be mere imagination: I have viewed with attention

those of Platae, Troy, Mantinea, Leuctra, Chaerona, and Marathon; and the field around Mont. St Jean and Hougomont appears to want very little but a better cause, and that undefinable but impressive halo which the lapse of ages throws around a celebrated spot, to vie in interest with any or all of these, except perhaps the last mentioned.[26]

As mentioned previously, Byron, along with Conder, is sceptical of the myth-making surrounding Waterloo. Lacking historical distance, the field of battle, even as it '*seems* marked out for the scene of some great action', is stubbornly resistant to aesthetic sublimation; its material effects – even when these are perceived as significant absences – are all too apparent. Furthermore, time will never permit a comparison with Marathon. *That* battle had been fought to advance the cause of liberty and independence; Waterloo, by contrast, was merely a conflict between one tyrant (Napoleon) and another (the Holy Alliance). In stating this distinction Byron hoped to correct a prevailing view of the establishment: that the classical precedents of Athens and Rome supported a Tory interpretation of the victory. Traditionally, of course, the battle of Marathon had functioned as mythical point of origin for the Whigs. In the terms introduced by Benjamin, however, the nature of Whig opposition prevented the battle from being foreclosed within the symmetrical shape of linear narrative. Consigned to the space of a marginal 'tradition', rather than of homogeneous, causal 'history', the event was used by left-wing Whigs and radicals as a rallying cry for the practice of revolutionary 'beginnings'. While it may be objected that this reading of Whig tradition flies in the face of Marx's critique of the structure of bourgeois revolutions, I would argue there is sufficient evidence in the discourse of official opposition to warrant the extension of this theory. For if, as Benjamin claims, tradition is nothing other than a series of crises and eruptions, then it is possible to regard the Whig reclamation of Marathon, in the wake of Waterloo, as an attempt to establish 'a conception of the present as the "time of the now"'. To this thesis, however, the Marxist thinker must perforce reply that Byron was not a working-class radical; his poetry 'takes place in an arena where the ruling class gives the commands'.[27] As Kelsall maintains, the revolutionary power of a poem like *Childe Harold's Pilgrimage* is defused by the poet's stubborn adherence to the defunct historicism of postwar Whiggism. And yet, when one looks closely at the verse itself it is possible to detect a more constructive principle at work: one that involves, as I have already suggested 'not only the flow of thoughts, but their arrest as well'.

The notion of the revolutionary arrest returns us to Byron's own beginning: 'Stop! – for thy tread is on Empire's dust!' The quotation from Juvenal's tenth satire has been used before: as the epigraph to the 'Ode to Napoleon Bonaparte' and in a footnote to a passage in Canto II of *Childe Harold's Pilgrimage*: 'When Marathon became a magic word' (89). The line has an almost talismanic quality in Byron's work, linking battles and poems in different times and different places. To paraphrase Benjamin again, the recurrence of the figure 'is a question less of history than of certain historical constellations that have an aesthetic interest'. The closing part of this statement may suggest a certain reticence on Benjamin's part to fully grasp the political import of the 'constellation'; the aestheticization of history has disturbing connotations of spatial abstraction such that, on a superficial level, the thesis is open to de Manian tirades against the 'temptation of permanence'.[28] But neither Benjamin nor Byron has this idea in mind when they attend to the structure of this figure. In Byron's case the leap into Juvenalian satire is a version of the dialectical tensions that force history to its crisis. By interrupting the action of the poem, by arresting its flow with a haughty 'Stop!', the constellation is suddenly transformed into a conjuncture or, as Benjamin, terms it, a 'monad':

> Where thinking suddenly stops in a constellation pregnant with tensions, it gives that constellation a shock, by which it crystallizes into a monad. A historical materialist approaches a historical subject only where he encounters it as a monad. In this structure he recognizes the sign of a Messianic cessation of happening, or, put differently a revolutionary chance in the fight for the oppressed past. He takes cognizance of it in order to blast a specific era out of the homogeneous course of history ...
>
> (*Illuminations*, pp. 262–3)

In contrast to the triumphal, homogeneous, continuous time of the victors, historical materialism places emphasis on the broken, suppressed time of those who have failed. Benjamin's thesis contains at this point an implicit theological dimension, for the effort to retrieve the failures of history – and here one might think of the stifling of republicanism – is predicated on the idea that the past is 'open' to 'redemption', ready that is to be appropriated by the oppressed classes at some point in the future. In total contrast, therefore, to Marxist orthodoxy, the materialist surveys the past not as a continuous sequence but rather as a repository of isolated 'monads', danger signs that disrupt the smug luminescence of historical totality. The request that Byron makes to 'Stop!' the flow of history may be read therefore as an attempt to suspend rectilinear time so that the repressed past may be allowed to speak. As we shall see, the revelation of rupture, of discontinuity, involves replacing the notion of diachrony with the synchronicity of the signifier. For it is only by short-circuiting the distance separating past and present that the repressed monad can be made to function as a rallying call for revolutionary action. And such synchronization can only take place in the autonomous network of the text.

To reconstruct the specific 'shock' that Byron generates in his time we must first of all attend to its earliest incarnation. Looking across the Attic plain in 1812 (?), Lord Byron was struck by the sight of Phyle, the ancient fortress from which Thrasybulus journeyed to defeat the Thirty Tyrants and restore democracy to Athens. Wrenching the 'Spirit of Freedom!' from this image the poet meditates on its contrasts with the condition of present day Greece:

> Spirit of Freedom! when on Phyle's brow
> Thou sat'st with Thrasybulus and his train,
> Couldst thou forbode the dismal hour which now
> Dims the green beauties of thine Attic Plain?
> *(Childe Harold's Pilgrimage,* II, 74, 702–5)

In comparison with the grandeur of Greece's heroic past, its present-day inhabitants are 'hereditary bondsmen' (76, line 720), unable to 'uncreate' an 'accustom'd bondage' (73, line 696). History, in other words, has settled into the homogenized, empty time of Turkish rule. Today, the country is unable to boast 'one true-born patriot'; its 'degenerate horde', trapped in powerless resentment, is unable to instate itself in 'that sublime record / Of hero sires' (83, lines 790–1). The past is literally 'shatter'd', but not in the revolutionary form that Benjamin describes. Greece, in this image, can only be renounced, its critical constellation faltering on the edge of a rhetorical question: 'Can man its shatter'd splendour renovate, / Recal its virtues back, and vanquish Time and Fate?' (84, lines 799–800). The question is left tantalizingly suspended, only to be consigned to forgetfulness in the quiet, contemplative stanzas that follow. Since Greece remains 'lovely' in its 'age of woe' (85, line 801), it seems that the pleasures of memory provide adequate compensation for the embarrassment of contemporary servitude. Thus, in what has become, for many critics, a familiar Byronic gesture, the retreat from political engagement is facilitated by a 'romantic' concentration on the relationship between Nature and commemoration. The political charge of ancient Greece is fragmented, awaiting restoration in some remote teleological future; all that remains is the feeble sigh of reactionary nostalgia, crystallized in the gaze of the tourist who lingers 'like me...to sigh "Alas!"' (86, line 818). The failure of political restoration is conjoined with the failure of temples and monuments to triumph over time; only 'well-recorded Worth' survives. Byron seems to have in mind the occasional 'column' or 'half-forgotten grave' (line 814), but it is clear in the stanzas that follow that it is the permanence of writing that is his true concern. Art, like the tomb, may 'fail' (87, line 827) but Nature has taken on its commemorative qualities. Looking towards Athens the poet is struck by the 'haunted' ground of Marathon. It operates in Byron's poem as a repository of 'boundless fame' (89, line 839) and as a confirmation of the Muse's power to defy the effects of wide-wasting time.

Poems, like glorious battles, are the events with which Byron seeks to resist the accretions of time. As he writes in Canto IV, 'When Athens' armies fell at Syracuse...Redemption rose up in the Attic Muse' (16, lines 136–8). But there is another side to the visionary impulse, one that qualifies the redemptive powers of art:

> Such was the scene – what now remaineth here?
> What sacred trophy marks the hallow'd ground,
> Recording Freedom's smile and Asia's tear?
> The rifled urn, the violated mound,
> The dust thy courser's hoof, rude stranger! spurns around.
> (*Childe Harold's Pilgrimage*, II, 90, lines 850–4)

Returning to the immemorial present, Byron presents a very different image of the relationship between history and fame:

> 'Siste Viator – heroa calcas!' ['Stop traveller! You are walking on [the graves of] heroes'] was the epitaph on the famous Count Merci; – what then must be our feelings when standing on the tumulus of the two hundred (Greeks) who fell on Marathon? The principal barrow has recently been opened by Fauvel; few or no relics, as vases, &c. were found by the excavator. The plain of Marathon was offered to me for sale at the sum of sixteen thousand piastras, about nine hundred pounds! Alas! – 'Expende – quot *libras* in duco summo – invenies?' ['Weigh it – how many *pounds* will you find in that greatest of commanders?'] – was the dust of Militiades worth no more? It could scarcely have fetched less if sold by *weight*.[29]

Like the opening statement of the Waterloo stanzas in Canto III, the reference to Juvenal provokes a sequence of indignant, self-baffling reflections. If the present scene lacks the heroic grandeur of Marathon, its poverty reflects back on our nostalgia for the chivalric simplicities of the ancient past. For Marathon too is subject to the spoiler's art, its temporal difference has been blasted by a rapacious modernity, intent on subjecting the historicity of the past to the levelling effects of an exchange economy. By locating Waterloo in the same constellation as present-day Marathon, therefore, Byron underlines the futility of all such epic comparisons. Seen from the point of view of the angel of history all wars are the same; where the ruling-class sees a chain of events, the angel perceives only a single catastrophe: 'as the ground was before, thus let it be; – '; 'Thou first and last of fields!' (*Childe Harold's Pilgrimage*, III, 17, lines 149–53, *passim*). For Byron, in his bleakest mood, there is then no progress, no redemption, only the empty, homogeneous time of harvests, markets and kings.

It is only by placing Waterloo in a conjunctive rather than a comparative relation that the glory of Marathon may be restored:

> While Waterloo with Cannae's carnage vies,
> Morat and Marathon twin names shall stand;
> They were true Glory's stainless victories,
> Won by the unambitious heart and hand
> Of a proud, brotherly, and civic band...
> (*Childe Harold's Pilgrimage*, III, 64, lines 608–12)

The challenge to the Tory's historicization of Waterloo is generated at the level of historical 'textuality'. As the weft of the past feeds into the warp of the present, the poem fosters a critical attitude to the imaginary continuum of past and present. Unlike the battle of Waterloo, Morat and Marathon were fought by a 'civic band':

> All unbought champions in no princely cause
> Of vice-entail'd Corruption; they no land
> Doom'd to bewail the blasphemy of laws
> Making kings' rights divine, by some Draconic clause.
> (64, lines 613–16)

For Byron the allusion works only in a negative sense, for just as Draco authorized an oppressive penal code for Athens (624 BC) so the authors of the Congress of Vienna legitimate the Bourbon throne. Thereafter the comparison breaks down: 'the English and the Prussians resembled the Medes and the Persians as little as Blucher and the British General [Wellington] did Datis and Artaphernes [distinguished leaders on the Persian side] and Buonaparte was still more remote in cause and character from Militiades'.[30] In Byron's opinion it is more accurate to compare Waterloo with Cannae. As Jerome McGann notes, unlike the revolutionary struggles of Morat and Marathon, the battles at Waterloo and Cannae were imperialist in nature. In 1816, the political implication of Byron's comparison did not go unnoticed. As Walter Scott, in an otherwise favourable review of the poem, proclaimed: 'to compare Waterloo to the battle of Cannae, and speak of the blood which flowed on the side of the vanquished as lost in the cause of freedom [was] contrary not only to plain sense and general opinion' but also to the derisory portrayal of Napoleon as 'Gaul's vulture' in canto 1.[31] Scott, believing he had detected a contradiction in Byron's politics, went on to excuse the poet on the grounds that he had no coherent political stance to speak of – a view shared by some of Byron's more recent critics. Yet, as we have seen, the poet is adept at manipulating historical parallelisms to reveal the aesthetic strategies underpinning the politics of dogmatism. Far from being a defence of Napoleon – the Emperor has already been condemned as a 'despot' in stanza 20 and in 64 as an unlikely candidate for the role of Militiades – the allusion to Cannae is a means of undoing the association between Waterloo and Marathon.

The poem works, however, on a more profound level to question the politics of burial and commemoration. The first mention of the battle of Morat comes in stanza 63:

> But ere these matchless heights I dare to scan,
> There is a spot should not be passed in vain, –
> Morat! the proud, the patriot field! where man
> May gaze on ghastly trophies of the slain,
> Nor blush for those who conquered on that plain;
> Here Bergundy bequeath'd his tombless host,
> A bony heap, through ages to remain,
> Themselves their own monument; – the Stygian coast
> Unsepulchred they roam'd, and shriek'd each wandering ghost.

The battle of Morat, fought near the town and lake of the same name in Switzerland in 1476, resulted in the deaths of over ten thousand men in the service of Charles the Bold, Duke of Burgundy. The ossuary in which the bones of the defeated Burgundians were laid 'was destroyed by the invading French forces in 1798, and the bones scattered about and not collected and reburied until 1822'.[32] The 'spot' that Byron describes in 1816 was therefore a charnel ground. But more than this, the poetry depicts a *topos* that we have become familiar with. From the desecrated mounds of Marathon to the shallow graves of Waterloo, the grounds that Byron writes of are alike in their propensity to disinter the matter that ought properly to remain buried. Paul Fry has written of the uncovered remains of the Morat that:

> They show clearly enough what their fate has been; yet they disclose none of the information about their preceding life that a covering epitaph could efficiently remember. Absence alone makes representation possible, and therefore the still-present spirit shrieks inarticulately as long as it is unburied. Whereas an unroofed charnel-scene can be a *memento mori* and remembers death in the midst of life, the covering tomb, provided it be inscribed by man, remembers life by recording its absence.[33]

Art, in this view, is the redemptive force that accounts for the dead by entombing them; hence, as Fry puts it in an elegant formulation: 'Covering is recovery' (p. 173). But if Byron's art is really directed towards the burial and consequent restitution of life then to what purpose does it dwell on scenes of desecration? It is not enough to align Byron's verse with the literary precedent of Virgil's careless ploughmen. In the Georgics the ungraving of the nameless dead is a reminder – a *memento mori* – of death in life as well as a gesture to the unearthing of a repressed literary genre. Unlike Virgil, Byron's act of disinterment seems to me to be directed more towards the uncoupling of historical reality and artistic discourse. Once out of their tomb the dead of Morat are all too present; their inarticulate cry is, we might say, the figure of a historical catachresis, a figure that is unreadable, immemorial, beyond representation.

What, then, can Byron do for the dead of Waterloo? Again we must defer this question to think about Byron's later writing. Like Byron we left Juan 'fighting thoughtlessly enough to win... *one* whole bright bulletin' (*Don Juan*, VIII, 19, lines 151–2). This battlefield, like all Byron's fields, speaks – but not in volumes. Where the graves in *The Excursion* speak of the continuity of past, present and future, *Don Juan* is littered with scraps of inarticulate speech; scraps that function, like the bones of Morat, as their own monument. Towards the end of Canto IX, following a typically digressive tirade against the proliferation of contemporary print culture, Byron takes up his theme only to lose the thread of the argument: 'I have forgotten what I meant to say... *Certes* it would have been but thrown away' (36, lines 282–6). In the wake of Waterloo, print, like bodies, has become expendable, but it is precisely the age's capacity for waste that lays the foundations for future acts of restoration, albeit as the ossified relics of a 'new Museum'. The stanzas which follow comment succinctly on the creation of what Byron calls the 'halo' of the past; following the conflagration of this world a new one 'shall come again':

> Unto the new Creation, rising out
> From our old crash, some mystic ancient strain
> Of things destroyed and left in airy doubt...
> (38, lines 298–300)

Time, in Byron's cosmos, is governed by repetition, such that the archaeologists of the next world, exiled from 'some fresh Paradise' will relearn 'all the Arts at length... Especially of war and taxing' (40, line 318). Museum culture, founded in the philosophy of absence, will see to it that the past remains buried, that its inarticulate shriek is translated into a Romantic poem for 'old, unhappy, far-off things, / And battles long ago'.[34] Such, Byron predicts, will be the fate of his work, the poem in which he has vowed to wage war both in and on thought itself.

Here, we might be sceptical of the line of argument that would place Byron's theses on redemption in the same light as Benjamin's. The dominant picture that has emerged thus far is that of the *soi-disant* radical, unable to supplant the tug of melancholy conservatism with the *jetzeit* of historical transformation. But I would argue that poet and materialist are joined in the ethical perspective they give to the 'end of history'. Byron in these stanzas may well appear to take the jaundiced view that redemption is impossible, that the dead remain lost and failures are buried, but we should recall that this takes place in the middle of the description of Don Juan's rescue of the Turkish orphan girl. It is in this act that Byron finds a principle of just restoration:

> That *one* life saved, especially if young
> Or pretty, is a thing to recollect
> Far sweeter than the greenest laurels sprung
> From the manure of human clay...
> (34, lines 266–9)

It would be easy, I think, to condemn such lines on the grounds that they overlay a mawkish sentimentality on the grossness condemned in the first part of the canto. It is reported by Annie Dillard that Stalin gave words to a disquieting and possibly universal sentiment: 'a single death is a tragedy, a million deaths is a statistic.'[35] Let us apply this notion to Byron. If lyric poetry is on the side of particularity as against history's emphasis on the multiple, then it seems, on this view, to be a woefully inadequate mode of human understanding. Yet the sheer scale of numbers – ten thousand at Morat, fifty thousand at Waterloo – induces, at best, a feeling of awe, at worst, a rational attempt to bring the scale of human suffering under the domain of a concept: Providence, meliorism, the Absolute and so on. The recollection that takes place in stanza 34 must therefore be weighed against the nominal cataloguing of the bulletin and the archaeology of the museum. The artifice of that 'one life saved' is meaningful in a way that the historiographical culture of postwar commemoration is not. The bones of the unnamed dead may well provoke a meditation on the limits of art but in the end only art, for better or for worse, can grant significance to the formless matter of the world.

Commenting on the respective merits of art and nature, Byron wrote of the significance of famous landscapes that:

> It is the '*art*' – the columns, the temples, the wrecked vessels, which give them their antique and modern poetry, and not the spots themselves. Without them, the spots of earth would be unnoticed and unknown: buried, like Babylon and Ninevah, in indistinct confusion, without poetry, as without existence.[36]

Shall these bones live? Looking over the Athenian plain Byron saw the landscape of the ancient poets. Looking over Waterloo he saw dispatches, bulletins and triumphal verses: 'As a plain, Waterloo seems marked out for the scene of some great action, though this may be mere imagination ... [it] appears to want little but a better cause, and that undefinable but impressive halo which the lapse of ages throws around a celebrated spot.'[37] Lacking poetry, in this general sense, Waterloo is 'without existence'. How then does Byron set about recovering significance? How, in other words, does he save the dead from the false burial of empty, cenotaphic verse and the impersonal naturalizing of latter-day Georgic? The answer lays with the recovery of the 'one life' – in this case in the lines from Canto III of *Childe Harold's Pilgrimage* devoted to the memory of Byron's cousin, Major Frederick Howard. Recalling the moment when he stood before the spot where Howard fell, Byron noted that 'the body has since been removed to England. A small hollow for the present marks where it lay, but will probably soon be effaced; the plough has been upon it, and the grain is.'[38] Like Greece in Canto II, the banks of the Rhine in Canto III and Thrasymene in Canto IV, the microculture that was 'gallant Howard' is already ploughed over. Only poetry can grant the existence that time elides.

But poetry, as far as Byron is concerned, has so far failed to distinguish between human significance and covering 'clay'. He writes in stanza 29 that the praise of the dead 'is hymn'd by loftier harps than mine' (line 253) yet the deference to Scott sounds, in the context of the poet's previous pronouncements on commemorative writing, to be somewhat strained, even ironic. As is well known, Byron inscribed the opening lines of his Waterloo verse in the same autograph book that Scott had written in the previous summer. In both cases the lines were extemporized at the end of a day's tour of the battlefield. Byron's verse should be regarded, therefore, from a dialogical point of view. In Scott's *The Field of Waterloo*, as Andrew Cooper observes, 'the fallen "Horsemen and foot, – a mingled host" all belong to the routed French who remain "Objects half seen"; by contrast, the British dead have come to possess "bright careers" that are "Mark'd on [the] roll of blood".' Cooper goes on to note Scott's Conclusion, with its eulogy to the Duke of Wellington and Waterloo, stating 'such havoc brought a name / Immortal in the rolls of fame' and 'serves to "write the moral lesson down" of Tory "constancy in the good cause alone"'.[39] By contrast, for Byron the 'mingled host' is composed of the dead of both sides: 'Rider and horse, – friend, foe, – in one red burial blent!' (*Childe Harold's Pilgrimage*, 28, line 252). Scott, who had been so careful to position Byron outside the conflicts of contemporary political life was dismayed to discover this 'Champion of the English Parnassus' speaking 'of the blood which flowed on the side of the vanquished as lost in the cause of freedom'.[40] In themselves, however, the political force of these lines is directed less at the collapse of republicanism and more at the loss of life itself. The commingling of rider and horse, friend and foe, signified in the exchange of clay for clay, is an erasure of difference against which the vitality of the Byronic imagination protests.

By focusing on an individual the poet does not seek to grant significance to either the Tory or Whig interpretation of the recent war; rather he speaks of a more general absence attendant upon the waging of mutual hostility, whether this is found in the dispute between countries, political parties or within the relationship between poet and audience. Thus in stanza 31, Howard is plucked from the intensely personal focus of the elegiac stanzas to become one of

> thousands, of whom each
> And one as all a ghastly gap did make
> In his own kind and kindred
>
> (lines 271–3)

He leaves behind a 'hollow', a 'gap' that no amount of public rhetoric – the 'Glory' and 'Fame' of noble sacrifice – can fulfil. For Byron, who has already staked his claim on the 'line' with which his family is said to 'blend' (29, line 255), 'the name / So honoured but assumes a stronger, bitterer claim' (31, lines 278–9). Thus heroic death and poetic exile enter into an uneasy relationship as if the poet were using the declivity impressed in the field by Howard's body to locate his own, embittered sense of the costs of literary fame. But the economy of Byron's vision is such that nothing is allowed to go to waste. In deriving perverse strength from his association with Howard, Byron is free to depart from the field and return to his main theme: the absent self and the multiplication of its sorrows (stanza 33). Finding 'a very life in... despair' (34, line 298) Byron is able to redeem a poetics that skirts dangerously close to the undifferentiated matter of death. For the previous stanzas have already introduced a number of 'unreadable' elements that prevent the epitaph mode from covering its subject in lyrical forgetfulness. As an example of Byron at his most knowing, I would draw attention to the stylized pastoral of stanza 27:

> And Ardennes waves above them her green leaves,
> Dewy with nature's tear-drops, as they pass,
> Grieving, if aught inanimate e'er grieves,
> Over the unreturning brave, – alas!
> Ere evening to be trodden like the grass
> Which now beneath them, but above shall grow
> In its next verdure, rolling on the foe
> And burning with high hope, shall moulder cold and low.

A hasty reading of these lines might confirm Byron's place in a litany of postwar romancers. The elegiac contrast between reviving nature and 'the unreturning brave' is, as we have observed, a stock feature of commemorative verse and Byron's contribution would appear to fulfil, triumphantly, the expectations of the genre. Yet on closer scrutiny it is clear that something more is at stake than the reiteration of pure convention. Taken as a whole the stanza is virtually an extended pathetic fallacy, yet Byron is careful to undermine the device even as he utilizes it to the full. The second line refers us to 'nature's tear-drops', only to question this identification in the parenthesis that follows: 'if aught inanimate e'er grieves' (lines 236–7). Like the uncomfortable placing of 'thing' in the fourth line of Wordsworth's 'A slumber did my spirit seal', the function of 'inanimate' – a word signifying the deprivation of voice, is to place in abeyance the positive assertion that nature is in mourning. Looking further back to Milton's treatment of this trope in *Lycidas* one might be tempted to add that Byron is merely continuing the tradition of defamiliarizing an outmoded device in order to naturalize the voice of genuine feeling. But where *Lycidas* remains within the horizon of the pastoral elegiac genre, the lines from *Childe Harold's Pilgrimage* seem less eager to establish a clear distinction between the artificiality of style and the sincerity of feeling. In the latter poem there is no 'Ay me!' to fill in the void left by the dismissal of the flowers of rhetoric; Byron, more so than Milton, extends the scepticism towards poetic restitution beyond the conventional dismissal of 'false surmise'. The process of severing the ties between natural processes and human grief is continued in stanza 30 where, beneath 'the fresh green tree', the poet witnesses the revival of 'fertile promise' only to append the qualification that the Spring 'contrive[s]' 'her work' (lines 264–8, *passim*). There is, in other words, no place, nor force, that has not been touched by the hand of human design. Still we must remember that Byron has already asserted that poetry about the spot, not the spot itself, is existence. If nature takes on the qualities normally associated with human artifice it is only, I would suggest, to place feeling in a locus beyond the facile use of stylistic trickery. Spring may well 'contrive' the return of 'gladness' but poetry is derived from what 'she could not bring'. Poetry begins, in other words, where art fails and in this respect Byron remains paradoxically true to the Miltonic convention he appears to desecrate. Just as the 'tree will whither long before it fall' and 'the ruined wall' stand well after the 'wind-worn battlements are gone' (32, lines 284–5), so the poem 'brokenly live[s] on', its shattered afterlife shows 'no visible sign' yet speaks of 'things . . . untold' (33, line 297).[41]

As I have argued throughout the preceding chapters, that which remains unsaid is central to our understanding of Waterloo. Unlike the idle tourist or the Tory bard, however, Byron will not allow us to lose sight of the fact that significance is sustained on the basis of the *unformed*: just as states produce war to (in)validate their claims to integrity, so poets create works to (dis)confirm their authority. In both cases the symbolic structure includes an element that embodies its impossibility. This element – in his work on painting Lacan calls it a 'stain' – marks the failure point that is the very condition of the subject; for the state it is the dead soldier, for Byron it is the declivity, the burial mound and the broken line. Far from being absences, in the poststructuralist sense of the word, I would argue now that these places do indeed appear as stains or spots in the poetry, as little pieces of the (all too) Real. Still, Byron is right to say that art gives them their existence, only existence must be understood here as that which appears within a system of signification, and for such a system to come into being it must orientate itself around a point that is radically *ex-istent*. By setting style and sincerity constantly against each other, Byron allows us to see that at the heart of every symbolic construction there is a thing that cannot be negated *'because it is already in itself, in its positivity, nothing but an embodiment of pure negativity, emptiness'*.[42] To locate this insight in a more conventional context, I would argue that such an emptiness – one that is crucially insistent and intractable – is detectable in Byron's treatment of a conventional Waterloo trope: the comparison of Soignies with the mythical forest of Arden. Byron's note to the opening of stanza 27 states that 'The wood of Soignies is supposed to be a remnant of the forest of Ardennes... immortal in Shakespeare's "As you Like it".'[43] Lockhart was sufficiently attentive to Byron's authority to use this note as a commentary on the opening lines of Scott's *Field of Waterloo*, but what the editor and the Tory bard neglect is the extent to which Byron stresses the contrived nature of this link. As Laurence Lerner has argued, there are no actual deaths in *As You Like It*: Shakespeare 'removed the violence' from Lodge's pastoral romance to make his own work an ambivalent commentary on the limits of the genre, as if he were saying ' "See what blood would do to my pastoral, it would spoil everything".'[44] Having removed the battle from his play, Shakespeare knowingly contrives the work but in a way that supports our sympathy for the creations of 'frail thought'. Byron, by placing Arden into the context of a battle, also writes of the limits of art but in a way that ultimately points to the subversion of ideology, in this case by highlighting the fictional foundations of postwar triumphalism. To adapt the terms of Lerner's prosopopoeia, it is as if Byron were admitting the potential of blood – the very stain around which postwar identity is oriented – to spoil the work of 'gladness'.

Of all the Waterloo bards, therefore, it is the poet of *Childe Harold* who comes closest to revealing the failure point of individual and national authority. And yet, as we shall see in the concluding pages of this book, the notion that Byron eschews the pleasures of war for a sustained denunciation of its costs and terrors tells only half the story. The poet may well have paused to reflect on the death of his friend, but he also took great delight in riding across the field on horseback. Byron, I would propose, refuses to stay in one place. The writer of *The Corsair* and *The Giaour* knows that war has its vigorous, attractive side, and in his efforts to imitate the equine motions of the cavalry charge he understands the extent of its power to move.

Conclusion

> No equal number of years can be found, during which science, commerce, and civilization have advanced so rapidly and so extensively, as has been the case since 1815. When we trace their progress, especially in this country, it is impossible not to feel that their wondrous development has been mainly due to the land having been at peace... When we reflect on this, and contrast these thirty-seven years with the period that preceded them, a period of violence, of tumult, of unrestingly destructive energy, – a period throughout which the wealth of nations was scattered like water, – it is impossible not to look with deep interest on the final crisis of that dark and dreadful epoch; the crisis out of which our own happier cycle of years has been evolved.
> Sir Edmund Creasy, *The Fifteen Decisive Battles of the World*[1]

So ends Sir Edmund Creasy's history of warfare, an account that begins with Marathon and ends with Waterloo. Written in 1851, the year of Louis Napoleon's *coup de état*, the final chapter of *The Fifteen Decisive Battles* presents a supremely confident account of recent European history. Gone are the doubts and disappointments of the Regency Whigs – that Waterloo crushed the triumph of liberty is a matter of little importance for the conservative Creasy. With the nation secure in the possession of its numerous colonies, the march and progress of universal emancipation may be reformulated as the inexorable rise of British imperialism. In a passage that anticipates current 'end of history' debates Creasy concludes that Waterloo is the last great battle in the struggle for civilization. Henceforth 'the stern excitement of martial strife' is to be replaced by an 'infinitely prouder spectacle':

> We see the banners of every civilized nation waving over the arena of our competition with each other, in the arts that minister to our race's support and happiness, and not to its suffering and destruction... and no

battle-field ever witnessed a victory more noble, than that, which England, under her Sovereign Lady and her Royal Prince, is now teaching the peoples of the earth to achieve over selfish prejudices and international feuds, in the great cause of the general promotion of the industry and welfare of mankind.

(p. 418)

Yet even as Creasy advocates the sublation of war in the 'bloodless' conquests of economic competition and imperial expansion, there is a sense in which the rhetoric of peace is undermined by a desire for the passions of the past. From a formal point of view one might say that *The Fifteen Decisive Battles of the World* is a text haunted by the return of the martial imaginary. Whether its author is writing on Marathon, Blenheim or Waterloo, he remains fascinated with the 'unrestingly destructive energy' of war. More importantly, for our purposes, his script derives its power from a fascination with the cultural products of conflict: with Livy, Homer, Milton and, most tellingly, Lord Byron: the latter even provides the epigram for 'The Battle of Waterloo': 'Thou first and last of fields, king-making victory!' Like most readers of Byron in this period, Creasy pays little attention to the irony of this claim. Since history has diffused the antagonism of the postwar restoration period the reader is free to respond to the verse as a simple statement of fact, in much the same way as western democracies respond to the necessity of an unfettered free market system: that which has become precisely, in Creasy's sense, *the arena of our competition with each other*: a world impervious to irony and critique, almost, one might say, a world impervious to history.

We know that Byron bemoans the spoils of war, or at least we feel the force of his protest against 'king-making Victory!' but in Creasy's text this force is discharged. Instead, the book derives its fascination with war from a more insidious quality in Byron's verse, something that goes beyond the power of political scepticism. Take the following quotation from one of the poet's letters:

> ... there has been a *thirty years war* and a *Seventy years war* – was there ever a *Seventy or a thirty years peace*? – or was there even a day's *Universal* peace – except perhaps in China – where they have found out the miserable happiness of a stationary & unwarlike mediocrity?
>
> (*BLJ*, IX, 30)

The superficial progress of Creasy's new world order has no place in the Byronic imagination. For Byron there is an energy as well as an abyss in warfare that unleashes its own stock of powerful delights. His distrust of 'unwarlike mediocrity' may be set alongside the example of Freud whose first response, on learning of the declaration of war in 1914, was 'one of youthful enthusiasm': 'He was quite carried away, could not think of any work, and spent his time discussing the events of the day with his brother Alexander... He was excitable, irritable, and made slips of the tongue all day long.'[2] The image of the founder of psychoanalysis reverting to the 'military ardours of his boyhood' is, I think, especially instructive. Freud, who would later go on to claim in his paper 'Why War?' that conflict between nations was an inescapable facet of human psychopathology, is shown here to be playing out the very passions he describes.[3] For, rather than bemoaning the futility of war, its waste and ruin, he argues that war plays an essential role in the civilizing process: 'By tending towards the conglomeration of nations, it operates less like death than like eros which strives to unify.' Thus war, like civilization, has its 'advantages and perils'; we owe to it 'the best of what we have become as well as a good part of what we suffer from'.[4]

The point I wish to make is that Freud tells us something useful about the fundamental ambivalence of war: we project onto the alien, or other, the destructiveness we fear in the most intimate relations or parts of ourselves. And because, in war, we are licensed to send our fears abroad, the result can be a tremendous lightening of the soul. Warfare saves us the effort of confronting our self-hatred, it returns us to the 'glad, animal passions of our youth'; it literally carries us away. For the youthful Byron, the link between war and eros is no less explicit: 'I am not insensible to Glory, & even hope before I am at *Rest*, to see some service in a military Capacity.' What prevents the poet from throwing himself into this fantasy wholeheartedly is his knowledge that modern warfare is 'absolutely & exclusively devoted to Carnage'. There is, moreover, nothing glamorous in the life of a mere '*mercenary* Soldier' (*BLJ*, I, 114, 118). It is this latter 'Idea' that provokes the disgust of the Lord. Modernity, with its state monopoly on the body in pain, has subsumed the alterity of heroic action and converted it into a unit of exchange: reciprocal wounding for national substantiation. But even as the political Byron rejects the commodification of war, it is to the ancient, idealized form of combat, conceived as an alternative to the deadly state of *Rest* that Byron pledges a vital part of his imagination. And here, in the conclusion to this book, it is to this aspect of the culture of Waterloo that I now turn.

Contested pleasures

In the introduction to this study I alluded to the Edwardian perception of Waterloo as the culmination of an age of 'scarlet and steel'. This is the image that survives in countless popular works: from Maxwell's *Stories of Waterloo* to Sergei Bondarchuk's 1970 film *Waterloo*. The idea that Waterloo might be conceived as, at some level, a *topos* of desire, is also the subject of Thackeray's *Vanity Fair*. True, the chapter on the battle concludes with a passage of

Byronic pathos (the death of George Osborne), but its central concern is with the erotic qualities of war. Like Creasy, Thackeray derives much of his inspiration from the ballroom passage in the Waterloo stanzas of *Childe Harold's Pilgrimage*. Singled out by the *Annual Review* in 1816 as one of the most memorable passages in poetry from that year, and frequently quoted in subsequent accounts of the battle, the vivid description of the departure of Wellington and his officers from the Duchess of Richmond's ball courted controversy as well as admiration:

> Dear Sir
> Was ever the tenacity of false rumour so illustrated as in the misrepresentations which still circulate of the Duke of Wellington having been surprised at a Ball in Bruxelles.

According to Francis Hart, 'the popular impression of Wellington, the supreme allied commander, unable to tear himself from "a certain ball which a noble Duchess gave at Brussels on the 15th of June", strangely persists.'[5] Although Hart does not mention Byron, the stanzas on the 'sound of revelry at night' did much to promote the view that the Duke had indeed been taken by surprise. Fuelled by rumours that Wellington had committed adultery with the wife of Byron's friend, James Wedderburn Webster, the public accepted the story as part and parcel of the process by which Waterloo was converted from prosaic event into decorous myth. The public may have delighted in the charge of sexual frisson surrounding the ball, the battle and its aftermath but it took a poet to expose its cultural logic.

Byron's presentation of the Duchess of Richmond's ball opens with the 'voluptuous swell' of music and the juxtaposition of 'marriage-bell' and death's 'rising knell!' (*Childe Harold's Pilgrimage*, III, 21). Initially the boundaries between love and death are marked but in a form that suggests their ultimate conjunction. This possibility is developed in stanza 24 where the narrative homes in on the 'tremblings of distress' and

> sudden partings, such as press
> The life from out young hearts, and choking sighs
> Which ne'er might be repeated...
> (III, 24)

Language such as this is of a piece with that overall blurring of category distinctions evident in the sexualized reception of Waterloo. The 'choking' of parted lovers does not so much dramatize the juxtaposition of love and destruction as their uncomfortable association. Whatever pathos is present in these lines is squeezed out by the quickening of pace in the stanza that follows:

> And there was mounting in hot haste: the steed,
> The mustering squadron, and the clattering car,
> Went pouring forward in impetuous speed,
> And swiftly forming in the ranks of war;
> And the deep thunder peal on peal afar;
> And near, the beat of the alarming drum
> Roused up the soldier ere the morning star;
> While throng'd the citizens with terror dumb,
> Or whispering, with white lips – 'The foe! They come! they come!'
>
> (III, 25)

Reading not for the underlying truth but rather for the surface of expression, the anaphoric structure of conjunctions and noun verb formations creates a mounting sense of crisis that culminates perfectly in the vulgar logic of the 'coming' foe. Byron, who utilizes the *double entendre* to vivid effect in *Don Juan*, is well aware of the analogy between sexual and military contests. But beyond this there is also the suggestion that conflict, in itself, may be seen as a displaced form of sexual encounter. The curtailed arousal of the ballroom invites us to make a great deal more of the 'mounting', 'hot haste' and 'rousing of the soldier' than propriety would allow.

Yet propriety is precisely what is at stake here. For where does this tension lead? What pleasure is discharged in the act of war? From a superficial point of view the equation between sexual consummation and violent death is sufficiently supplied by the orgasmic indifference of the 'one red buriel blent!', an image that suggests, via Freud and Bataille, at once a return to an idealized locus of continuity as well as a brutalized curtailment of the discontinuous self. I would propose, however, that such a reading falls at once too short and too wide of the mark. Doubtless the connection between death and sexuality has its place in Byron's thought but our concern, in the present context, will be on the way in which this relation is presented as part of a wider speculation on the militarization of sexual identity.

Women in war

A prevailing image that Byron's poem forces us to reconsider is that of Wellington as the chaste and sober counterpart to the fleshly Napoleon. Linda Colley in *Britons*, reminds us that for many ranks in society the Duke functioned as a powerful object of fascination. (Consider, for example, the homoerotic overtones of figure 13.) The chief group of enthusiasts was upper and middle class women such as Fanny Burney, Charlotte Eaton and Charlotte Brontë. From the age of five, Brontë was an especially ardent admirer of the Duke of Wellington: she collected portraits of him, kept a collection of newspaper cuttings and represented him as a primary character in the fables of Glass Town and Angria. The interest persisted well into her later work. Colley cites the example of the dark and commanding Mr Rochester of *Jane Eyre*, a character who, even today, continues to exert an influence on women readers. In Bondarchuk's *Waterloo* the link between Wellington, romance and sexual fantasy is taken to its logical and thoroughly banal conclusion. We see in the structural opposition between the febrile, hysterical and manifestly corporeal Napoleon (Rod Steiger) and the manly, self-controlled hauteur of the English Duke (Christopher Plummer) a repetition of the fantasies of Regency women. The remoteness of the Duke of Wellington, when combined with his omniscient and omnivoyant qualities – in her description of the battle Fanny Burney gives way to rapture in her attempts to ally the Duke's '*sang froid*' and 'supernatural' energy – presented these women with an attractive and, at the same time, ambivalent image of sexual mastery and exclusivity.[6]

The image took shape in the controversial statue of Achilles, raised in honour of Wellington by 'The Ladies' of Britain. As Alison Yarrington documents, plans for a national monument to commemorate the hero of the Napoleonic wars date back to the successes of the Iberian campaign.[7] Of the numerous triumphal columns, statues and temples proposed in the aftermath of Waterloo, the most significant and one of the few to be realized was the Achilles statue. The idea originated with Lavinia, Countess Spenser, the devout wife of the 2nd Earl of Spencer. In 1814 she launched a public subscription – directed solely at women – to raise funds for the statue. In due course the subscription collected over £10,000 and the commission was awarded to Richard Westmacott, a member of the Royal Academy who suggested that the statue should be a cast of one of the canonical works of antiquity, the *Dioscuri* or *horse-tamers* sited on the Quirinal Hill in Rome. Following the removal of his horse and the addition of a sword and shield, the *Dioscuri* figure was transformed into a colossal 18-foot high representation of the hero of the *Iliad*. It was to be London's first nude statue. Even before it was unveiled the more astute members of the Committee of Taste were concerned that the sensationalist press would misinterpret the statue. In November 1821, when the bronze casting was in its final stages, Earl Spencer circulated a letter to the committee urging the immediate addition of a fig leaf:

> This being the usual covering adopted in Rome and elsewhere, it cannot...be reasonably objected to, neither will it invite criticism or slander...for myself, I can never feel satisfied without entering my solemn Protest against the Statue being delivered from us on the part of the Ladies, without that Covering which the delicacy of the Sex, as well as due regard to the publick Decorum indisputably requires.[8]

For Colley, Spencer's missive is indicative 'of masculine anxieties in the face of unabashed female enterprise'.[9] The contemporary cartoonist George

198 *Waterloo and the Romantic Imagination*

Cruikshank is perhaps even more to the point. In a cartoon dating from 1822 (Figure 12) he depicts an earnest looking gentleman placing his top hat over what had become known as the ladies' fancy. His commentary states that the print 'is inscribed with veneration to that worthy man Mr Wilberforce who with *saintlike* regard for the morals of his country has undertaken to

Figure 12   George Cruikshank, *Making Decent!!*, engraving, London 1822

make the above fig Decent from 10 in the Mg till Dusk'. Wellington as Achilles merely compounds the irony of relating warfare and sexuality. For women in the age of Waterloo, warriors are attractive precisely because of their vulnerability to wounding. It is, after all, Rochester's symbolic castration that finally draws him into the realm of feminine appropriation.

The notion that women pose a threat to the integrity of masculine identity is explored by Byron in his description of the bullfight at Cadiz from canto I of *Childe Harold's Pilgrimage*: the ritualized combat is announced in stanza 68 with a 'Crashing' of 'the lance' and the death of 'man and steed, o'erthrown beneath [the] horn'. The triumph of the phallic bull at this early stage of the game induces a sense of frenzy: 'The thronged Arena shakes with shouts for more; / Yells the mad crowd o'er entrails freshly torn.' In its vigorous enthusiasm for the destructive spectacle, the largely female crowd dallies with the logic of sacrifice, seeking to confirm the potency of the warrior through his ritual dismemberment. When the matador meets his fate it is, tellingly, the 'female eye' that 'shrinks not' from the spectacle of castration 'nor even affects to mourn' (stanza 68). Taken as a whole, the passage suggests that the freedom from affect can only be localized in a body that recognizes the phallus as having no value in itself. As Lacan puts it: 'for the woman it is a castrated lover or a dead man . . . who hides behind the veil where he calls on her adoration.'[10]

The stanzas that follow concentrate on the processional and spectacular aspects of the fight. The chivalric Matadores with their 'gallant steeds' and 'costly sheen' (stanza 73) translate the uncontainable carnage of war into a ritualized form of phallic display. And here again, in an anticipation of the structure of the later Waterloo passage, Byron appears to delight in the confrontation only to succumb to an overwhelming sense of pathos through identification with the suffering bull. The animal's 'mad career' (stanza 76) is symbolic both of Byron's gathering sense of writerly subjection and of the fated course of Napoleon Bonaparte. As emblems of the pure or idealized modes of war and writing, the Lord and the Emperor nevertheless become meaningful only within a system of aesthetic conventions. Poet, bull and militarist are therefore sacrificed to the pitiless gaze of feminized consumption, 'sweet sight for vulgar eyes' (stanza 79). But the real atrocity, the one that remains out of view, 'scarce seen in dashing by', is that of the 'dark bulk'. The material object, the one that is actually sacrificed, whether it is conceived as 'corse', country or corps is strategically *ungraspable* and must remain so if it is to function as an instrument of the Law.

That the psychic economy of the atrocity exhibition is not confined to the Iberian Peninsula is strongly suggested by the juxtaposition of the pagan bullfight with the complacent orthodoxy of the respectable English bourgeoisie. Yet even on Richmond Hill, the anodyne pursuits of the 'smug' suburbanites admit of a significant residue of phallic worship:

> 'Tis to the worship of the solemn Horn
> Grasp'd in the holy hand of Mystery,
> In whose dread name both men and maids are sworn...
> (*Childe Harold's Pilgrimage*, III, 70)

What is mysterious in England is made explicit in Cadiz, but the contrast between sanguine satisfaction and 'dread' lack allows for a more sober point to emerge. The 'fooleries' of the English may well be bloodless, but no society is immune to the theatricalization of pain; for what after all, as Jerome Christensen observes, is the purpose of England's intervention in Europe if not to gratify a taste for sacrificial blood-letting?[11] Byron knows that Spain is the arena into which England projects its fantasies of mastery and loss and that its public desires nothing less than to 'grasp' its dying 'bulk' (stanza 79).

In this, the ascription of artistic form is crucial. Unlike the open field, the arena imposes form on the shapeless event of killing, allowing carnage to be turned towards sacrificial profit. This recalls the means by which death took shape in the epitaph: a genre that Byron deconstructs in the Waterloo stanzas of *Childe Harold* in order to place feeling in a space beyond the taint of spectacular consumption. Above all it is the poetic arena that allows the public to 'gloat on another's pain', be the subject Byron, Napoleon or the slaughtered bull. The unfettered energies of war, as Byron sees it, are always subject to the delusive forms of symbolization. The blame for this, however, is directed at women. Women, as Byron goes on to propose in the battle cantos of *Don Juan* are (after Horace) the '"tererrima Causa" of all "belli"' (IX, 55). The poet, out of respect for metre as well as propriety elides the concluding 'cunnus', but the elision is granted its own form of spectral power as the verse develops. Subsequently addressed as the 'nonedescript', the vagina (Byron is satirizing the war-lust of the Empress Catherine) enters the poem only through the barring operation of the phallus. As negative to the phallus, cunnus becomes a total object of fantasy, elevated into the place of the Other and made to stand for its truth. Even as Catherine, the 'Epitome' of that 'Cause', appears to devour her phallic subjects, she enters the poem only under condition of her accession to the structuring of language. There being, as Lacan insists, no feminine outside language, her existence can only take place through the acceptance of 'phallic' difference.

When Thackeray writes of *Vanity Fair* that 'Our place is with the noncombatants' he is of course encouraging us to look awry at the standard procedures of epic narrative.[12] The author of the novel is not a 'military' man and he is at pains, like the poet of *Don Juan*, to expose the inanities of war. Thus our attention is directed to George Osborne, a man running swiftly to the 'alarm-ground', his 'pulse throbbing and his cheeks flushed', not out of love for his gentle and devoted wife but in eager anticipation of the rout. For Osborne, as for Del Dongo, war is a 'game... a fierce excitement of doubt, hope, and pleasure!'; what 'qualities are there for which a man gets so speedy a return of applause, as those of bodily superiority, activity, and valour?' The sanctifying ground of ordinary familial love is unable to compete with the homosocial economies of 'loss and gain' (p. 311). Thackeray states that his concern is with the non-combatants, with women like Amelia who, stricken with despair, foresee the fatal consequences of their menfolk's ardour: a bullet through the heart in the muddy insignificance of the aftermath. But Thackeray, in the formal arrangement of his couples, is careful to remind us that love and war are correlatives: the same instincts that lead one man to end his life in the great game of war are honed to 'perfection' in the form of Rebecca. Where Amelia grieves for her departed husband, Rebecca, wed to the reformed dandy Rawdon Crawley, a man for whom the 'easy triumphs of the clumsy military Adonis, were quite insipid when compared to the lawful matrimonial pleasures which of late he had enjoyed' (p. 295), is remarkably insouciant. For the calculating Becky, war presents itself as an opportunity to cross the bar of feminine 'ex-istence', to pass that is from the excess of her *jouissance* to the structural coherence of the phallus. Her husband's reluctant departure is thus met with steely-eyed composure and 'a pungent feeling of triumph and self-satisfaction', a response that ought to be weighed alongside the emotional release of her counterpart, George Osborne.[13] For Becky, it is precisely her devotion to plans and stratagems, what we might call her understanding of the art of war, that prevents her from falling into the undifferentiated frenzy of warlust: 'No man in the British army which had marched away, not the great duke himself, could be more cool or collected in the presence of doubts and difficulties' (p. 299).

Becky's mastery of strategy is shown in her dramatic appearance at the Duchess of Richmond's ball:

> She arrived very late. Her face was radiant; her dress perfection. In the midst of the great persons assembled, and the eye-glasses directed to her, Rebecca seemed to be as cool and collected as when she used to marshal Mrs Pinckerton's little girls to church. Numbers of the men she knew already, and the dandies thronged around her...
>
> (*Vanity Fair*, p. 288)

By mimicking the military world around her (the description conflates the personal traits of Napoleon and of Wellington), Becky draws on the valuable lessons she learnt as a child: a woman can only maintain personal power on the condition that she submits to the structuring effects of symbolization. But even at this level there is a case to be made for parodic inversion. Is not Becky's ability to 'marshal' the admiration of the dandies an affectless performance of the 'rapid' returns of the masculine 'game', the very fantasy that lures these men to their ignoble deaths?[14] But here, of course, there is a price to be paid. By not giving in to her 'more than' *jouissance*, by sliding so effortlessly across the signifying chain of her desire – to sustain her coherence she must move from man to man: her father, the Revered Crisp, Jos Sedley, Crawley, Osborne, Major Tufto, the Marquis of Styne and numerous unnamed escorts – Becky's power – such as it is – is at the cost of her personal satisfaction.[15]

Thackeray's novel presents us therefore with a gloomy picture of the restrictive conditions of Victorian femininity. Becky's parody of the 'military Adonis' becomes, in the end, further confirmation of her alienated identity: of her inability to rest content with 'matrimonial law'. The proper place for women, as Dickens and De Quincey aver, is not at the head of the field but rather at the side of the hearth. For De Quincey, in 'The English Mail Coach', warfare is inextricably linked with the pleasures (for men) of domestic fealty:

> Did I tell her the truth? Had I the heart to break up the dream? No... I lifted not the overshadowing laurels from the bloody trench in which horse and rider lay mangled together. But I told her how these dear children of England, privates and officers, had leaped their horses over all obstacles as gaily as hunters to the morning's chase. I told her how they rode their horses into the midst of death, (saying to myself, but not saying to *her*,) and laid down their young lives for thee, O mother England! as willingly – poured out their noble blood as cheerfully – as ever, after a long day's sport, when infants, they had rested their wearied heads upon their mother's knees, or had sunk to sleep in her arms.[16]

This image of suffering motherhood is not incompatible with Byron's *belli causa*: the logic of sacrifice is the same. For De Quincey, however, writing in 1847, the idealization of the mother masks a deeper anxiety. In the age of Waterloo, news was transmitted across the nation by mail coaches, 'like fire racing along a train of gunpowder... kindling at every instant new successions of burning joy'. 'Sublime', in the limited Kantian sense of the word, the horse and coach 'had yet its centre and beginning in man' and moved forward at a pace that could support the idea of 'a grand national sympathy' (pp. 193–4). De Quincey conceives here of a language system centred on the nodal point of woman as phallic object. The absolute 'Otherness' of this object secures for the nation a comprehensible discourse of self-knowledge and truth. But now, with the rise of modern technology, this order is under threat. A 'new system of travelling' with its 'iron tubes and boilers' has destroyed the integrity of 'man's imperial nature': 'Nile nor Trafalgar has power any more to raise an extra bubble in a steam kettle. The galvanic cycle is broken up for ever' (p. 194). More specifically it has led to the exclusion of the mother from the Symbolic. But here, as Lacan would state, the moment of foreclosure entails the return of the mother in the Real. In the case of 'The English Mail Coach' this takes the form of the hallucinatory fantasy of matricide. What the coach crash scene signifies, I would suggest, is nothing less than the psychotic collapse of a system confronting its fundamental impossibility. The fact that De Quincey's fantasy might, after all, be just a dream, does not lessen its power: for here the author confronts the failure point of his symbolization: the realization that the (m)Other does not exist except as a division in language.

Beyond Waterloo

In Leigh Hunt's anti-war poem, *Captain Sword and Captain Pen*, we seem, at first sight, to meet with a radical alternative to the violent imaginings of conventional romantic verse. First published in 1835 together with an accompanying essay, *Remarks on the Duty of considering the Horrors and the alleged Necessity of War*, the poem was conceived as a thoroughgoing response to the cult of militarism. Its targets include Richard Cobden and the Duke of Wellington whose aggressive domestic and foreign policies were in danger of transforming a constitutional monarchy into an oppressive martial regime. Like Shaw's *Arms and the Man*, the subject of the poem is war's 'false romance' and as such it can be read as a backdated response to the irreverent triumphalism of the Waterloo bards. As Edmund Blunden notes, its rhythmic 'swing' is well suited to the debunking of the heroic metricals of Scott, Davidson and Swift:[17]

> And ever and anon the kettle-drums beat
> Hasty power midst order meet;
> And ever and anon the drums and fifes
> Came like motion's voice, and life's;
> Or into the golden grandeur's fell
> Of deeper instruments, mingling well,
> Burdens of beauty for winds to bear;
> And the cymbals kissed in the shining air,
> And the trumpets their visible voices reared,
> Each looking forth with its tapestried beard,
> Bidding the heavens and earth make way
> For Captain Sword and his battle-array.
> (*Captain Sword and Captain Pen*, I, lines 23–34)

The irregular stress on the first syllable of the line creates a form of verbal pulsation. Fatuously grand, the strident metre is an acoustic echo of the Captain's guile, 'As if pomp were a toy to his manly pride' (I, line 36). Hunt places great emphasis on the phallic psychology of war. Like the description of the knight in Tennyson's 'Lady of Shallot', the sun glances off 'bristling steel' (line 9); swords are held 'Gainst the shoulder heavy with trembling gold' (line 12). Most revealing of all, the Captain's horse is a figure of 'shapely potency' (line 16). In the lines that follow 'Glossy black steeds, and riders tall' move with a 'threatening charm':

> With mortal sharpness at each right arm
> And hues that painters and ladies love,
> And ever the small flag blushed above.
> (I, lines 17–22, *passim*)

With the eve of battle comes a gradual decline, expressed in the metre by the languorous iambics of 'But all the next morning 'twas tears and sighs', and the waning dactyls of 'For the sound of his drums grew less and less, / Walking like carelessness off from distress' (I, lines 49–51).

The violence to come is prefaced by a scene of rural peace and innocence, in which nature is depicted,

> Ripening with the year's increase
> And singing in the sun with birds,
> Like a maiden with happy words –
> With happy words which she scarcely hears
> In her own contented ears,
> Such abundance feeleth she
> Of all comfort carelessly
> Throwing round her, as she goes,
> Sweet half-thoughts on lily and rose,
> Nor guesseth what will soon arouse
> All ears – that murder's in the house;
> And that, in some strange wrong of brain,
> Her father hath her mother slain.
> (II, lines 65–77)

The verse, with its perversion of pastoral calm, can be read alongside Hunt's account of the secondary suffering of war. As the comparison suggests, Hunt was haunted by images of female violation, images that account in part for his persistent sickliness and self-feminization:

> How many maimed and blood-saddened men are still suffering in hospitals and private houses; and how much offspring, in all probability, is rendered sickly and melancholy. The author of the present poem believes that he owes the worst part of his constitution to the illness and anxiety caused, to one of the best of mothers, by the American war.[18]

What I would emphasize now is the link the poet forges between feminine innocence and phallic violation. Hunt is saying that war has its origins in domestic violence, that is takes place as a desecration of the feminine space of the hearth and home, imagined elsewhere in his writings as an idealized form of civil polity. Contra De Quincey, therefore, his aim is to undo the ideological contract linking the symbolization of national identity, warfare and matricide. The catalogue of destruction that follows this passage is announced by the 'dark breath' of drums, explosions and 'horse-tempest' (II, lines 81–138, *passim*). Hunt seems preternaturally disposed to dwell on grotesque figures of human suffering: on 'snap burst eyes' (line 105) and the fight that 'grows liquid with lives' (line 114); on the 'mouthless' face 'with eyes on cheek' (line 258) and the charred soldier 'Kneeling, half human, a burdensome sight; / Loathly and liquid, as fly from dish' (IV, lines 304–5). The Boschian intensity of these images seems all the more repellent when one considers the larger body on which these human acts occur. Throughout the battle scene, nature is presented as a kind of meta-body whose physical disturbance reflects the moral and mental disorder of the human. The conflict is a 'storm', a 'tempest' and an 'earthquake' (II, lines 94–123). In its wake, the 'wind is mad upon the moors'; it is 'Stabbing all things, up and down' (IV, lines 194–7). As a soldier dies slowly of a 'wound unutterable', the rain 'mock[s] . . . his homeward tears' (lines 219–40, *passim*); in his 'dreams / The moon looks cruel; and he blasphemes' (IV, line 246).

To return now to the opening passage. All of these images of suffering, I would suggest, occur in the context of the initial murder of domestic quietude and rural bliss with which the section begins. If all is not what it seems in this section it is because nature is always already tainted. Hunt's idealized portrait, a figure for the Rousseauesque state of nature, is troubled by an unstable network of primal desires that work from the outset, as Hobbes might put it, to collapse the cradle of civilization. The maiden, for example, is on the verge of sexual 'ripening', throwing 'half-thoughts on lily and rose' and little guessing 'what will soon arouse / All ears'. The line break itself is teasing, willing the reader to impose his or her own idea of symbolic violence but also recalling, with the reference to 'ears', the pastoral context of ripening grains with which the passage begins. Hunt's idea of symbolic violence is the sexual jealousy of the father. And so the cosy reverie closes, in a nightmare of intra-familial violence, with the death of the mother presaging the destruction of nature by the masculine state of war.

By bringing the war home, so to speak, Hunt ensures that conflict can no longer be kept within a stable symbolic economy. Indeed, as we shall see, the entire poem can be read as an attempt to make 'visible' the violence that the public sphere cannot, for constitutional reasons, recognize. But does this concentration on the violated feminine body imply an idea of sadistic voyeurism? One argument, advanced by Mary Favret, would be that the domestic sentiment evoked by the vulnerable feminine body is itself an instrument of ideological control, deflecting our attention from the 'real' issue of the male body in pain. The fact is, however, that Hunt's poem reveals both sides of war: both the primary fiction motivating the war effort

– that it will prevent war from coming home – and the meta-fiction that allows the domestic or feminine body to function as the symbolic 'other' to the invisible, masculine world of reciprocal wounding. In the world of the poem, the real warfare is always already *here*; so long as human sexuality is *imagined* as a battleground, its effects cannot be fully erased nor contained within the home front.[19]

Hunt extends the desecration of the household to fashion a commentary on the ideological import of the pastoral-elegiac mode. Waterloo, as we have seen, has been described as the exemplification of the agricultural battle. With its imagery of crushed grains and field-grasses it lent itself, from the outset, to poetic accounts of mutability. Whether this takes the form of Southey's sublime identification with the death of nature or Byron's ironic focus on the contrast between natural replenishment and human vulnerability, the poetry of Waterloo underlines the *sentiment* of private and public loss. With *Captain Sword and Captain Pen*, however, the poetry sacrifices pastoral empathy as well as deference to the requirements of brutal, sensationalist imagination. Thus as the bodies 'go down', 'Brains are dashed against plashing ears' (II, lines 106–7). Later on, as female 'vultures' prey upon the dying, 'in an awful parody of ministration', nature is presented as a malevolent force, a maternal superego wreaking vengeance on masculine intrusion. Elsewhere, however, the precedented possibilities of pastoral-elegy are turned to political effect:

> Sneereth the trumpet, and stampeth the drum,
> And again Captain Sword in his pride doth come;
> He passeth the fields where his friends lie lorn,
> Feeding the flowers and the feeding corn,
> Where under the sunshine cold they lie,
> And he hasteth a tear from his old gray eye.
> (IV, lines 327–30)

The formal link with Byron is, at best, superficial. But beyond the apparently unfeeling contrast between 'feeding corn' and 'cold' death, Hunt has a great deal to say about the role such imagery plays in the sentimentalizing of war. The footnote to these lines cites the following lengthy passage from Booth's *Accounts of Waterloo*:

> Every tree in the wood of Hougoumont is pierced with balls; in one alone, I counted the holes where upwards of twenty had lodged. But the strokes which were fatal to human life have not actually injured them; though their trunks are filled with balls, and their branches broken and destroyed, their verdure is still the same. Wild flowers are still blooming, and wild raspberries ripening beneath their shade; while huge black piles of human ashes, dreadfully offensive in smell, are all that now remain of

the heroes who fought and fell upon this fatal spot. Beside some graves, at the outskirts of this wood, the little wild flower, Forget-me-not – ('myosotis arvenis') was blooming, and the flaring red poppy had already sprung up around, and even upon them, as if in mockery of the dead.[20]

More so than Byron, I think, Hunt tips the scales even further in the direction of pastoral satire. Rather than dwelling in elegiac sentiment, the lines from Booth with their emphasis on the 'mockery' of nature allow Hunt to reinforce a didactic point. To understand what is at issue here we must turn to the note that accompanies the passage from Booth:

> The tears of an old soldier for the fate of his comrades are some of the most affecting in the world, and do him immortal honour; far more honour than thousands of things which are considered more glorifying.
> 'They parted: Blucher proceeded on his way – Lord Wellington returned to Waterloo. As he crossed again the fatal scene, on which the silence of death had now succeeded to the storm of battle, the moon breaking from dark clouds shed an uncertain light upon this wide field of carnage, covered with mangled thousands of that gallant army, whose heroic valour had won for him the brightest wreath of victory, and left to future time an imperishable monument of their country's fame. He saw himself surrounded by the bloody corpses of his veteran soldiers, who had followed him through distant lands – of his friends – of his associates in arms – his companions through many an eventful year of danger and of glory; in that awful pause which follows the mortal conflict of man with man, emotions, unknown or stifled in the heat of battle, forced their way; the feelings of the man triumphed over those of the general, and in the very hour of victory Lord Wellington burst into tears'.[21]

The second passage, I would suggest, exists in a dialogical relation with the poetry, for even as the Captain cries, his solitary 'tear' is modified by the unusual choice of 'hasteth'. The ironic contrast between the poetry and the footnote's reference to the tears of the old soldier exists, it would seem, to debunk the myth of the sorrowful Wellington. To Hunt, Wellington is nothing more than a professional soldier whose display of grief has been overemphasized for the purposes of propaganda: 'Small thinking is his but of work to be done' (IV, 332).

This sense of a forceful critique of war elegy is given further impetus in the passage where Hunt engages in dialogue with an imagined reader. Here once again, the effect is to eradicate the distinction between the everyday life of the private sphere and the more abstract, collective being of the public sphere. The passage begins then with a description of the agonized death of a soldier from a sabre slash. Like the 'mockery' of the returning poppy in the note from Booth, the rain 'mocks' the dying man whose 'tongue still thirsts in vain' (IV, 219–20). Hunt's gruesome portrayal of the body in pain is eventually interrupted by the voice of the gentle reader, eager to re-establish the public invisibility of the suffering soldier:

['I will not read it!' with a start,
Burning cries some honest heart;
'I will not read it! Why endure
Pangs which horror cannot cure?
Why – oh why? and rob the brave,
And the bereaved, of all they crave,
A little hope to gild the grave?'

Askest thou why, thou honest heart?
'Tis *because* thou dost ask, and *because* thou dost start.
'Tis because thine own praise and fond outward thought
have aided the shows which this sorrow has wrought]

A wound unutterable – O God!
Mingles his being with the sod.

['I'll read no more.' – Thou must, thou must,
In thine own pang doth wisdom trust.]
                                    (IV, lines 228–42)

Hunt's intervention is designed to shock the reader into an awareness of his own collusion in the war-making process. If gentle readers do not actually cause war, their offering of 'praise and fond outward thought' renders them guilty of promoting its acceptance. In a sense the poem is directed at those who credulously accept the myth-making heroics of Scott and Southey. By dialogizing sentimentality, suffering and heroism from within, as it were, the poem presents a successful challenge to the monologic poetics of Waterloo. It works, moreover, to expose the process by which individuals are transformed into bodies of war. Hunt writes then with an awareness that it is only by revealing the reality behind the show, the body in pain rather than the body as myth, that poetry can resist the naturalization of state war.

I do not wish to dwell for long on the poem's conclusion. It is enough to say that Captain Pen armed only with 'a letter calm and mild' defeats Captain Sword in bloodless combat. The poem ends with an apocalyptic vision of 'weaponless' words circulating in rhythmic homage to the fructifying power of creation. As the 'new-faced world' is 'born', so closes the reign of Captain Sword; the oppressive hegemony of the military state disappears with 'the level[ing] dawn' of civil polity (VI, lines 489–517, *passim*). This version of the Romantic apocalypse has been compared to Shelley, Wordsworth and Blake,[22] and with good reason I feel, for even as the verse asserts the gentle power of literacy, it draws its strength from the rhetoric of military conflict, which emphasizes the point, perhaps, that non-violent revolution is at most a fanciful dream. It is perhaps an unintentional irony of the piece that it should end in an echolalia of sonorous combat:

> A sound as of cities, and sound as of swords,
> Sharpening, and solemn, and terrible words,
> And laughter as solemn, and thunderous drumming,
> A tread as if all the world were coming.
> (V, lines 487–500)

The (s)word that Hunt releases is as violent, in its way, as the sword wielded by Captain Pen. For, as the combat winds down, its descent is in tune with the rhythms of sex, 'Such as Love knows, when his tumults cease' (line 507). Tumult and calm, man and nature, male and female; Hunt cannot conceive of peace in any other terms.

In a sense, however, *Captain Sword and Captain Pen* succeeds where other works fail precisely because it admits violence into its verbal structure. Unlike, say, *The Descent of Liberty* or the sonnets, the poem derives its power from the trope of allegory, the figure that, in Paul de Man's view, 'designates primarily a distance in relation to its own origin, and, renouncing the nostalgia and the desire to coincide, it establishes its language in the void of this temporal difference'.[23] It is in the poem's conclusion that this difference is most apparent, in the way that the poem asserts its dream of peace and in the way that it falls back on the language of destruction. By refusing to close on an image of endless summer or perpetual peace, by maintaining the distance between that which is desired and that which can be achieved, the poem functions as a reminder of the real conditions of separation that stand between the realms of the aesthetic and the political.

A truly liberal aesthetic, therefore, must struggle against the imaginative legacy of high romanticism. Like the mighty instruments of Hunt's late poem, 'The Trumpets of Doolkarnein',[24] romantic verse, at its best, is 'stern' and 'imperious', and when the sound is stopped by 'Nature's least and gentlest courses' we may well 'smile' but there is also disappointment that the 'great' and 'stormy music' has been 'stilled'.

War! What is it good for?[25]

The conventional answer, as the song insists, is 'absolutely nothing'. And indeed when we consider the emptiness of much that passes for Waterloo culture we would be right to agree. But this book's concern has been with a more insistent sense of nothingness: the void that is announced in conceptions of victory sublime; the gap in personal and governmental conceptions of creative authority; the impossibility of submitting the opacity of material conflict to the transcendent lucidity of the panoramic gaze. But the fact that Waterloo frustrates any attempt to render its significance does not prevent English culture from using it as a point of orientation. Take again the example of *The Fifteen Decisive Battles*. The poetic drift of Creasy's prose – that which I have identified as a longing for the constitutive violence of Romanticism – is manifest in the poetry that Alfred Lord Tennyson went on to produce in 1852, the year of Wellington's death and the rise to power of Napoleon III. In his poem 'Suggested by Reading an Article in a Newspaper', the laureate castigates his countrymen for wallowing in a 'commercial mire' (line 50). Disturbed by the growth of capitalism and the resurgence of a hostile Napoleonic empire, Tennyson looks forward to the recovery of 'a manlike God and Godlike men' (line 84). A few months later, in the 'Ode on the Death of the Duke of Wellington', the poet reiterates the phrase, reminding the nation of its debt to the hero of Waterloo. Thus, the poem is more than a work of commemoration; it is also a call to arms. Within a few years Tennyson's wishes would be met with Britain's entry into the Crimean War. The 'long, long canker of peace' had come to an end and the poet was again at liberty to derive inspiration from 'the clash of jarring claims'.[26] But what precisely had Tennyson detected in the jaded rhythms of Creasy's 'happier cycle' and why was he driven to exceed it?

The problem with peace, as the 'Ode on the Death of the Duke of Wellington' makes clear, is its tendency to undermine stable concepts of identity. Where peace unleashes the shapeless form of the mob (line 153), war is directed toward the creation of heroic individuals. Only men such as Wellington, 'moderate, resolute' and 'Whole' in themselves (lines 25–6) can be relied upon to 'keep our noble England whole' (line 161). Hence the call in poems such as 'The Penny Wise' and 'Rifle Clubs!!!' for a return to hostilities:

> O where is he, the simple fool,
>   Who says that wars are over?
> What bloody portent flashes there
>   Across the straits of Dover?
> Four thousand slaves in arms
>   May seek to bring us under:
> Are we ready, Britons all,
>   To answer them with thunder?
>   Arm, arm, arm!
>   ('The Penny Wise', lines 1–9)

The peace of 'sloth or avarice born' ('Rifle Clubs!!!', lines 1–4) is no substitute for the vital engagement of arms; the one involves a slackening of identity, the other its apotheosis. Above all, perhaps, peace entails the effacement of *jouis-sense*, the pathological pleasure that nations experience in the acting out of war.[27] A liberal peace, as imagined by Creasy and Hunt, is therefore nothing, absolutely nothing and for this reason it must be resisted if the nation, as subject, is to recover the grounds of its imaginary coherence. In the end, therefore, as Tennyson states in the concluding notes of *Maud*, the reassertion of identity comes with the exclusion of the hysterical woman – a symptom, no less, of the collapse of the antagonistic grounds of being – and the return of phallic division:

> No more shall commerce be all in all, and Peace
> Pipe on her pastoral hillock a languid note...
> For the peace, that I deemed no peace, is over and done...
> We have proved we have hearts in a cause, we are noble still,
> And myself have awakened, as it seems, to the better mind;
> It is better to fight for the good than to rail at the ill;
> I have felt with my native land, I am one with my kind,
> I embrace the purpose of God, and the doom assigned.
> (*Maud*, III, lines 23–59, *passim*)

But the identity this figure craves is, in itself, also nothing. With the 'I' no longer in thrall to the feminine Other, the stress falls not so much on the inscription of personal identity as on the transcendent will of 'land' and 'God'. For Tennyson, the ascription of heroic identity is born of a passion for 'self-sacrifice' ('Ode', line 41), even unto death.

In socio-political terms the conditions were ripe for a repetition of Waterloo, this time in the Crimea. Unfortunately, for those who wished to see Waterloo repeated in its ideal form, the liaison with Napoleonic France militated against the ease of any further analogies. The impossibility of re-enacting past glories was compounded by the fact that, after the fall of Sebastopol, it was France, rather than Britain, that would emerge with the strongest claim to victory. It would be another half-century before the nation would reactivate, in all seriousness, the sublimity of Waterloo. After the horror of 1914–18 it would be difficult to summon such resources again.

Notes

Preface and Acknowledgements

1. *Journals of Dorothy Wordsworth*, ed. Ernest de Selincourt, 2 vols (London: Macmillan, 1941), II, 29–30. William Wordsworth's response to the field is considered in Chapter 5.
2. For a reading of the transition from war to peace, which bears on this assessment, see Jerome Christensen, *Romanticism at the End of History* (Baltimore, MD and London: Johns Hopkins University Press, 2000), p. 12.

Introduction: the Return of Waterloo

1. Quoted in E. Tangye Lean, *The Napoleonists: A Study in Political Disaffection, 1760–1960* (Oxford: Oxford University Press, 1970), p. 261.
2. James Simpson, *A Visit to Flanders in July, 1815 Being Chiefly an Account of the Field of Waterloo* (Edinburgh: William Blackwood, 1816), pp. 144–5.
3. Abba, 'Waterloo', *Waterloo*, © 1974 Union Songs AB.
4. Jacqueline Rose, 'The Cult of Celebrity', *London Review of Books*, 20, 16 (20 August 1998), 10–13, p. 13. For further information on the psychoanalysis of fame and national identity see Rose's *States of Fantasy* (Oxford: Clarendon Press, 1996).
5. Iain Pears, 'The Gentleman and the Hero: Wellington and Napoleon in the Nineteenth Century', in *Myths of the English*, ed. Roy Porter (Cambridge: Polity Press, 1994), pp. 216–36. For a perceptive reading of Wellington's influence on the mind of a key English poet see Eric C. Walker, 'Wordsworth, Wellington, and Myth', in *History and Myth: Essays on English Romantic Literature*, ed. Stephen C. Behrendt (Detroit: Wayne State University Press, 1990), pp. 100–15.
6. The contrasting 'characters of the great Wellington and the fallen Napoleon' was a frequent theme in public discourse in this period. The orator James Henry Lewis, for example, delivered an address on Monday, 18 September 1815 at which he urged his audiences to meditate on the distinction between Napoleon's 'boundless Ambition!', his excessive 'desires' and the 'spotless virtue' and 'piety' of Wellington, an Augustus to 'This modern HANNIBAL'. See Lewis's *Orations on the Battle of Waterloo and on the rise and fall of Buonaparte* (London: Macdonald & Son, 1815), *passim*.
7. Castlereagh's address was delivered to Parliament on Friday, 23 June 1815. *Cobbett's Parliamentary Debates: The Parliamentary Debates from the Year 1803 to the Present Time*, 41 vols (London: T. C. Hansard, 1813–20), XXXI, col. 983. The Duke's despatch, containing details of the Allied victory and written with his habitual brevity and restraint, was received by Lord Harrowby on the evening of the 21st. I discuss the response to this document in Chapter 1. See Elizabeth Longford, *Wellington: The Years of the Sword* (New York and Evanston, IL: Harper & Row, 1969), pp. 485–6; *Wellington: Pillar of State* (New York and Evanston, IL: Harper & Row, 1972), pp. 8–9.
8. Iain Pears, 'The Gentleman and the Hero', p. 229. Pears adds that by the mid-nineteenth century Wellington had 'become the ultimate definition of gentility, of

social and political position justified by merit rather than as a right, and thus helped modify the concept which, throughout the nineteenth century, was the English ideological answer to the revolutionary notion of equality' (p. 231). Moreover, ' "In him England admires her own likeness" ' (p. 233).
9. The phrases are drawn from Lilian Rowland-Brown's survey essay, 'Waterloo and Romance', *The Nineteenth Century and After*, 78 (July 1915), 103–16, pp. 103–4.
10. In this connection mention should be made of Gillian Russell's excellent study, *The Theatres of War: Performance, Politics, and Society 1793–1815* (Oxford: Clarendon Press, 1995). For Russell the public and military spheres are linked through their immersion in the cultural politics of 'theatricality'. The reciprocal nature of this relation is illustrated in Russell's analysis of a performance of *A Trip to the Nore* at Drury Lane in 1797. The production 'represented an audience watching a topical afterpiece that in turn represented the audience's own participation in the event – a military review rendered as theatrical spectacle – which was itself an example of the theatricalized commemoration of war. (One might go further and claim that Camperdown, governed by the rules of naval engagements, was itself a kind of theatre.) The worlds of war, civic space and the theatre are here synthesized, made inseparable as are the actions of spectatorship and participation' (p. 66). Russell has little to say about the theatrical significance of Waterloo. As will become clear, I think there are good reasons for regarding the battle as a form of representational crisis, a threat not only to the politics of performance but also to the ideological grounds of public and private cognition. While drama is not the primary emphasis of this study (contemporary representations of the battle are surprisingly scarce; the British Library, for example, holds just one play, *The Battle of Waterloo: A Tragedy* by Mary Hornby printed privately in 1819), aspects of theatricality and spectacle come under scrutiny in the discussion of the Panorama (Chapter 2) and in the section on Coleridge's verse play, *Zapolya*, in Chapter 4.
11. See the introduction to the *Annual Register or a View of the History, Politics and Literature for the Year 1815* (London: Baldwin, Cradock, and Joy, 1816).
12. James Chandler, *England in 1819: The Politics of Literary Culture and the Case of Romantic Historicism* (Chicago and London: University of Chicago Press, 1998), pp. 122–5.
13. 'Commemoration of the Victory of Waterloo at Ipswich', *Anti-Jacobin Review*, 50 (June 1816), 572–6, pp. 572–3.
14. 'Anniversary of the Battle of Waterloo', *Blackwood's Edinburgh Magazine*, 38 (July 1835), 112–19.
15. The phrase is Trevelyan's. See his *British History in the Nineteenth Century and After: 1782–1919* (Harmondsworth: Penguin, 1965), p. 296. Sir Edmund Creasy regards Waterloo as the threshold to a new age of bloodless economic competition. See *The Fifteen Decisive Battles of the World* (London: J. M. Dent, 1908), chapter 15.
16. Lilian Rowland-Brown, 'Waterloo and Romance', p. 116; Cecil Battine, 'How to Celebrate the Centenary of Waterloo', *The Nineteenth Century and After*, 77 (June 1915), 1314–19.
17. See Bernard Cornwell, *Sharpe's Waterloo* (London: HarperCollins, 1993).
18. Most recently, *The Daily Telegraph* reported on the 'controversy' surrounding the publication of Peter Hofschröer's *The Waterloo Campaign – The German Victory*. Asked to respond to the author's claim that 'Waterloo was, in fact, primarily a German victory', *The Telegraph*'s defence editor John Keegan states: 'If Mr Hofschröer says Blücher won the battle of Waterloo, he's wrong because he just didn't. Wellington did.' The headline 'We Won the Battle of Waterloo, says German', is

placed beneath an article entitled 'France has "Twisted Facts" on British Beef'. The paper's adversarial stance on the European Union is crystallized, at the level of fantasy, in its vigorous efforts to prevent the Duke's demotion to 'secondary player'. See the *Daily Telegraph*, 14 October 1999, p. 4.
19. 'Anniversary of the Battle of Waterloo', *Blackwood's Edinburgh Magazine*, p. 116.
20. 'Ode on the Death of the Duke of Wellington', line 133. *The Poems of Tennyson*, ed. Christopher Ricks (London: Longman, 1969). Further references to Tennyson's poetry will be to the texts in this edition.
21. The phrase is from an unattributed review article by Robert Southey on calls for parliamentary reform published in the *Quarterly Review*, 16 (October 1816), 225–78, p. 225. The article, which caused considerable controversy at the time of publication, comes under scrutiny in Peacock's *Melincourt* (1817). See *Thomas Love Peacock: The Complete Novels*, ed. David Garnett, 2 vols (London: Rupert Hart-Davis, 1963), I, 172.
22. As a measure of the persistence of postwar anxiety concerning this 'near run thing' we may usefully consider Winthrop Mackworth Praed's counterfactual verse 'Waterloo'. Although intended as a satirical response to a French tourist ('On this spot the French cavalry charged, and broke the English squares!' epigram; 'John Bull was beat at Waterloo! / They'll swear to that in France', line 64), the feverish depiction of the routing of Wellington, the establishment of Bonaparte in Grosvenor Place, Marshall Ney in Parliament, the Pope in St Paul's and the demolition of the Tower of London tells equally of the perverse remainder – the spectacle of loss – that serves as the unacknowledged foundation of national pride. Winthrop Mackworth Praed, 'Waterloo', from *The Political and Occasional Poems* (London: Ward, Lock, 1888).
23. Quoted by Arthur Bryant, *The Age of Elegance, 1812–1822* (London and Glasgow: Collins, 1950), p. 255.
24. The notion that the genteel were guilty of trivializing the suffering of Waterloo in their haste to legitimize the event is taken up by the radical poet R. Shorter in 'On Seeing in a List of New Music *The Waterloo Waltz*':

> A moment pause; ye British Fair,
>   While pleasure's phantom ye pursue;
> And say, if sprightly dance or air
>   Suit with the name of Waterloo?
>   Awful was the victory!
>   Chasten'd should the triumph be;
>   'Midst the laurels she has won,
>   Britain mourns for many a Son.
>   (lines 1–8)

Shorter goes on to juxtapose the violence of battle with the trivial pursuits of the 'courtly ball' (line 13). The close of the poem, with its appeal to the 'softening hue' of historical distance, is surprisingly contrite:

> Forbear till time with lenient hand,
>   Has sooth'd the pang of recent sorrow;
> And let the picture stand,
>   The softening hue of years to borrow!
>   When *our* race has passed away,

> Hands unborn may wake the lay,
> And give to joy alone the view
> Of Britain's fame at Waterloo.
>
> (lines 41–8)

For the gentlewoman, as much as for Shorter, I would suggest, the juxtaposition of 'the enlivening notes of mirth' and 'the pang of recent sorrow' has exposed a fatal contradiction in the nation. Text taken from *Poetry and Reform: Periodical Verse from the English Democratic Press, 1792–1824*, ed. Michael Scrivener (Detroit, MI: Wayne State University Press, 1992), pp. 201–3.

25. Though Kant is a no less obvious choice. See his 'Perpetual Peace' (1785) and 'Metaphysical Elements of Justice' (1797). I look more closely at Kant's contribution to the theory of war in Chapter 4.
26. Benjamin Robert Haydon, *The Diary of Benjamin Robert Haydon*, ed. Willard Bissell Pope, 2 vols (Cambridge, MA: Harvard University Press, 1960), I, 463.
27. See *Hegel's Philosophy of Right*, trans. T. M. Knox (Oxford: Oxford University Press, 1962), section 324, p. 209 and *Hegel's Phenomenology of Spirit*, trans. Arnold Millar (Oxford: Oxford University Press, 1977), section 455, p. 272. There is a cogent and stimulating discussion of Hegel's philosophy of war in Michael J. Shapiro, *Violent Cartographies: Mapping Cultures of War* (Minneapolis: University of Minnesota Press, 1997), pp. 41–3.
28. Hegel, *The Philosophy of Right*, section 324, p. 210. See Daniel Pick, *War Machine: The Rationalisation of Slaughter in the Modern Age* (New Haven, CT and London: Yale University Press, 1993), p. 235. I am greatly indebted throughout this section to Pick's timely account of the conceptualization of war in modern thought.
29. Thomas De Quincey, 'On War' (1854); quotations cited by Daniel Pick, *War Machine*, p. 62.
30. I have followed the definition elaborated by Slavoj Žižek in *The Sublime Object of Ideology*, trans. Jon Barnes (London: Verso, 1989), p. 71.
31. Michel Foucault, 'Truth and Power', in *The Foucault Reader: An Introduction to Foucault's Thought*, ed. Paul Rabinow (Harmondsworth: Penguin, 1991), pp. 51–75, p. 56.
32. Joan Copjec, *Read My Desire: Lacan against the Historicists* (Cambridge, MA: MIT Press, 1994), pp. 4–10, *passim*.
33. Žižek's distinction between 'naïve historicist realism' and 'discursive idealism' is apposite in this respect. In *The Plague of Fantasies* Žižek pits the deconstructive criticism of Paul de Man against classical Marxism. Where Marxism argues that 'every discursive formation is embedded in the context of material practices, and thereby depends on them', rhetorical criticism asserts that the 'direct' experience of reality is an ideological fiction, generated precisely by 'the confusion of linguistic with natural reality, of reference with phenomenalism'. Thus where Marxism would accuse deconstruction of ignoring 'real battles' in favour of the 'staging and playing of rhetorical tropes', the rhetorical critic would regard the 'real battle' as a discursive construct. Despite some recent claims to the contrary (see, for instance, Louis A. Montrose, 'Professing the Renaissance: The Poetics and Politics of Culture', in *The New Historicism*, ed. H. Aram Veeser (London: Routledge, 1989), pp. 15–36), the contest between Marxism and deconstruction does not lend itself to mediation. With its emphasis on reciprocity, interplay and dynamism, the New Historicism fails to register the essential antagonism on the basis of which these schools forge their conceptual integrity. But let us be clear: the nature and

significance of this contest is not a consequence of rooted ideological differences; instead it is due, as Žižek points out, to a failure on the part of both camps to acknowledge their structural similarities. What these positions share then is a suspicion of the 'reified' point of reference, be it the 'transcendental subject' of philosophical idealism which far from positing or mediating reality is in fact a means of concealing socio-historical praxis (the Marxist view), or the concept of 'external reality' which masks the textual matrix in which it is fashioned (de Man). For Žižek, the 'theoretical problem behind these impasses is: how are we to conceive of some "immediacy" which would not act as a "reified" fetishistic screen, obfuscating the process which generates it?' As will become clear, if in this study it appears that I agree with the idealist notion that access to reality is 'always-already "mediated" by the symbolic process' this should not be taken as a sign of my allegiance to any school of extreme 'textualism'. Along with Lacan and Žižek I would maintain that our relation to reality is dependent on an act of 'primordial repression': 'what we experience as "reality" constitutes itself through the foreclosure of some traumatic X which remains the impossible-real kernel around which symbolization turns... the Real as "impossible" is precisely the excess of "immediacy" which cannot be reified in a fetish'. The notion of the Real as an 'excess' of immediacy which, although nowhere present, disfigures (to use a de Manian trope) the work of symbolic representation and thus of the habitual experience of 'reality' is central to the readings that follow. See Slavoj Žižek *The Plague of Fantasies* (London: Verso, 1997), pp. 95–8, *passim*.
34. Elaine Scarry, *The Body in Pain: The Making and Unmaking of the World* (Oxford University Press, 1985), p. 131.
35. Žižek, *The Plague of Fantasies*, p. 216.
36. Jacques Lacan, *Ecrits: A Selection*, trans. Alan Sheridan (London: Routledge, 1993), p. 28. I am grateful to Professor William Myers of the University of Leicester for drawing my attention to this quotation.
37. Ibid., p. 11.
38. Stephen Heath, 'On Suture', in *Questions of Cinema* (Bloomington and Indianapolis: Indiana University Press, 1981), pp. 76–112, p. 86.
39. Eric Evans, *The Forging of the Modern State: Early Industrial Britain, 1783–1870* (London: Longman, 1983), pp. 75–80.
40. Edmund Burke, *Reflections on the Revolution in France and on the proceedings In Certain Societies in London relative to that event*, ed. Conor Cruise O'Brien (Harmondsworth: Penguin, 1968, rpt. 1983), pp. 136, 175, 185, 310.
41. Edmund Burke, quotations from first *Letter on a Regicide Peace* (1796) and *Remarks on the Policy of the Allies* (1793). Cited by Conor Cruise O'Brien in *Reflections on the Revolution in France*, p. 61.
42. Thomas Paine, *The Rights of Man, Common Sense and Other Political Writings* (Oxford: Oxford University Press, 1995), p. 212.
43. Edmund Burke, *Heads for Consideration on the Present State of Affairs* (1792). Quoted by Conor Cruise O'Brien, *Reflections on the Revolution in France*, p. 60.
44. *Leicester Chronicle*, 31 October 1812. Quoted by Clive Emsley in *British Society and the French Wars, 1793–1815* (London: Macmillan, 1979), pp. 162–3.
45. *The Times*, 15 February 1812. Cited in Emsley, *British Society and the French Wars, 1793–1815*, pp. 159–60.
46. Linda Colley, *Britons: Forging the Nation, 1707–1837* (New Haven, CT and London: Yale University Press, 1992), p. 5.
47. Evans, *The Forging of the Modern State*, pp. 86–9.

48. *Parliamentary Debates*, XXX, col. 550.
49. Thomas Carlyle, 'On History' (1830), in *Selected Writings*, ed. Alan Shelston (Harmondsworth: Penguin, 1988), p. 55.
50. Haydon, *The Diary of Benjamin Robert Haydon*, I, pp. 458, 462–3.
51. *Parliamentary Debates*, XXXI, col. 988.
52. *Political Register*, 27, 24 June 1815, col. 783.
53. *Political Register*, 27, 1 July 1815, col. 801.
54. Quoted by Joseph Farrington, *The Farrington Diary*, ed. James Greig, 8 vols (London: Hutchinson, 1922–28), III, p. 12.
55. See E. Tangye Lean, *The Napoleonists*, p. 108. Farrington reports that an associate of Smirke's had said 'The victory, so called, was little more than a defeat', *The Farrington Diaries*, III, p. 13. This may be taken as representative of the Holland House, pro-Bonaparte attitude to the conflict.
56. *Examiner*, 392, 2 July 1815, p. 430.
57. Ibid., p. 417.
58. *Examiner*, 396, 30 July 1815, p. 431
59. *Political Register*, 27, 24 June 1815, col. 783.
60. Walter Bagehot, *The English Constitution* (1867), quoted in Roger Sales, *English Literature in History: 1780–1830: Pastoral and Politics* (London: Hutchinson, 1983), p. 117.
61. Carl R. Woodring, 'Three Poets on Waterloo', *TWC*, 18, 2 (Spring 1987), 54–6, p. 54. Mention should be made here of the sheer number of publications that appeared in the wake of the battle, from commemorative verses to 'dispatches, memoirs, accounts, denials, rebuttals, lists, military analyses, maps, charts, diagrams, guides, anecdotes, caricatures, engravings and journals'. The *Edinburgh Review*, for example, lists at least 32 Waterloo-related publications appearing between July 1815 and March 1817. This, however, is a conservative estimate that does not take into account the numerous ephemera printed in newspapers and periodicals. Francis Jeffrey is perhaps closer to the mark when in a review of Canto III of *Childe Harold's Pilgrimage* for December 1816 he writes that 'All our bards... great and small, and of all sexes, ages, and professions, from Scott and Southey down to hundreds without names or additions, have adventured upon this theme'. Francis Jeffrey, Review of *Childe Harold's Pilgrimage* III, *Edinburgh Review*, 54 (December 1815), 277–310, p. 295.
62. Hayden White, *Metahistory: The Historical Imagination in Nineteenth-Century Europe* (Baltimore, MD: Johns Hopkins University Press, 1972), p. 7, pp. 45–80. For further discussion of the relations between history and narrative during the Romantic period see Lionel Gossmann, *Between History and Literature* (Cambridge, MA: Harvard University Press, 1990), Barton R. Friedman, *Fabricating History: English Writers on the French Revolution* (Princeton, NJ: Princeton, University Press, 1988) and Ronald Paulson, *Representations of Revolution (1780–1820)* (New Haven, CT: Yale University Press, 1983).
63. Quoted in the *Anti-Jacobin Review*, 50 (June 1816), p. 575.
64. The reference to Milton's sequel to *Paradise Lost* is deeply, if unintentionally, ironic given that the poem was written in the teeth of republican defeat. I have more to say about the politics of the Romantic Milton in Chapter 5.
65. William Thomas Fitzgerald, 'The Battle of Waterloo', lines 20–7. The text is taken from *British War Poetry in the Age of Romanticism: 1793–1815*, ed. Betty Bennett (New York and London: Garland, 1976), pp. 592–4.
66. William Wordsworth, *Shorter Poems, 1807–1820*, ed. Carl H. Ketcham (Ithaca, NY and London: Cornell University Press, 1989), p. 178.

67. Ibid., p. 172.
68. Kant proposes this concept in the *Critique of Judgement*, trans. James Creed Meredith, 2 vols (Oxford: Clarendon Press, 1989), I, pp. 112–13 and II, pp. 93–6. For its British equivalent see 'On the Analogy Between the Growth of Individual and National Genius', *Blackwood's Edinburgh Magazine*, 6 (January 1820), 375–81.
69. William Wordsworth, 'Ode: The Morning Of The Day Appointed For A General Thanksgiving, January 18, 1816', line 244. Here, as elsewhere, I use reading text 1 in *Shorter Poems*, ed. Ketcham.
70. *Examiner*, 391, 25 June 1815, p. 413.
71. All references to this poem are to the version printed in the *Examiner*, 391, 25 June 1815, p. 415.
72. Preface to 'Hail England', p. 415. Cobbett went on to attack the poem in the *Political Register*.
73. For further discussion of the impact of the Revolutionary and Napoleonic wars on the English public sphere see Mary A. Favret, 'Coming Home: The Public Spaces of Romantic War', *SiR*, 33, 4 (Winter 1994), 539–48.
74. Henry Davidson, *Waterloo; a Poem with notes* (Edinburgh and London: John Murray, 1816), reviewed in the *Anti-Jacobin Review*, 50 (August 1816), 729–46, p. 729.
75. Edmund L. Swift, *Waterloo, and other Poems* (place of publication unknown: J. J. Stockdale, 1815), reviewed in the *Anti-Jacobin Review*, 49 (December 1815), 471–537, pp. 534–5.
76. The bookseller and poet George Walker, in the advertisement to *The Battle of Waterloo: A Poem* (London: G. Walker, 1815), signals his awareness of the competition from epic bards such as 'Scott, Byron, Southey, Swift &c.' and uses this as a justification for adopting the 'Old English Ballad' with its 'native and simple style', more suited to the expression of modest gratitude.
77. Stendhal, *The Charterhouse of Parma*, trans. Margaret R. B. Shaw (Harmondsworth: Penguin, 1958), p. 88.
78. Victor Brombert, *Stendhal: Fiction and the Themes of Freedom* (New York: Random House, 1968), p. 159.
79. *Morning Chronicle*, 21 June 1815.
80. For further details see the Introduction to David Chandler, *Waterloo: The Hundred Days* (London and Melbourne: Osprey, 1997).
81. This was a common theme of post-Waterloo sermonizing. See, for example, Rev. Peter Roe, *A Sermon, preached in the chapel of Harrogate, July the 30th, 1815, in behalf of the sufferer by the battle of Waterloo* (Knaresborough: G. Wilson, 1815): 'The relatives of the dead, the dying, the mutilated, and the diseased, cannot partake of the general joy, but are obliged to wear in sad silence or agonizing grief, the mournful cypress, whilst we are permitted to wear with delight the victorious palm' (p. 27). A distinction that might serve to recall the audience to an awareness of the irreconcilability of victory and suffering is rapidly displaced by a vision of 'the dead... *translated* to heaven... for ever to celebrate a victory, not of a temporal nature, but over the world, the Devil, and the flesh!' (p. 28; my emphasis).
82. Henry Davidson, *Waterloo: A Poem*, pp. 1–2.
83. Ibid., p. 731.
84. Unless otherwise stated, all quotations from Byron's poetry are from *The Complete Poetical Works*, ed. Jerome McGann, 6 vols (Oxford: Clarendon Press, 1980–91). References to *Childe Harold's Pilgrimage* and *Don Juan* are by canto and stanza. This reference: III, 28.

85. Tony Harrison, *The Gaze of the Gorgon* (Newcastle upon Tyne: Bloodaxe Books, 1992), p. 48.
86. See J. W. M. Hichberger, *Images of the Army: The Military in British Art, 1815–1914* (Manchester: Manchester University Press, 1988), pp. 28–30
87. Favret, 'Coming Home: The Public Spaces of Romantic War', p. 539.
88. Lady Magdalene de Lancey, *A Week at Waterloo in 1815: Lady de Lancey's Narrative*, ed. Major B. R. Ward (London: 1907).
89. See *The Journals and Letters of Fanny Burney (Madame d'Arblay)*, ed. Peter Hughes et al., 12 vols (Oxford: Oxford University Press, 1980), III, pp. 435–6, 447–8. The Rev. Peter Roe, in his sermon for 30 July 1815, called upon the 'females here present to imitate the conduct of the women of Brussels who prepared lint, bandages, beds, bedding for the wounded [by]... giving liberally and cheerfully to the collection this day', *A Sermon, preached in the chapel of Harrogate* (pp. 30–1).
90. Eliza Townsend's 'Lines on a Stone from the Field of Waterloo' (1823), with its depiction of the sanguine effects of mutual 'unlicensed power' (line 15) as witnessed by a 'mute' pebble (lines 21–2), indicates the gap separating the critical consciousness of radical women from the official view of Waterloo. See *Poems and Miscellanies* (place or publisher missing, 1856). The distinction between the victory and the suffering that continues for women is the theme of Louisa Stuart Costello's 'On Reading the Account of the Battle of Waterloo' (1815): 'Those shouts of triumph breath'd from every tongue, / Some anxious heart with agony has wrung' (lines 14–15); from *The Maid of the Cyprus Isle* (London: Sherwood, Neely and Jones, 1815) and also of Charlotte Caroline Richardson's 'To-Morrow':

> Soft Peace our happy land had blest,
>   And Britain's gallant Sons returning,
> Each clasp'd some fav'rite to his breast
>   And fondly hush'd the voice of mourning...
>
> The morn that calls a world to joy,
>   With grateful sounds of triumph swelling,
> Shall see the wretched Anna fly
>   Far distant from her peaceful dwelling.
> I'll seek the turf that Edward prest,
>   There sigh my last adieu to sorrow,
> And pillow'd on his clay-cold breast,
>   We'll wake in happier scenes to-morrow.

In Richardson's verse, the final couplet, with its suggestion of death, either by suicide or as the result of excessive grief is an indication of the emotional trauma suffered by many women in the aftermath of the campaign. The text is taken from *Harvest, a Poem, in two parts; with other Poetical Pieces* (London: Sherwood, Neely and Jones, 1818), pp. 88–9. I am grateful to Stephen C. Behrendt of the University of Nebraska-Lincoln for drawing my attention to this work.
91. David Howarth, *Waterloo: Day of Battle* (New York: Atheneum, 1968), pp. 218–19.
92. See *Shorter Poems*, ed. Ketcham, p. 171.
93. Kant, *Critique of Judgement*, I, 109; translation slightly modified.
94. Scarry, *The Body in Pain*, p. 62.
95. See Hichberger, *Images of the Army: The Military in British Art, 1815–1914*, pp. 28–30 and A. G. H. Bachrach, 'The Field of Waterloo and Beyond', *Turner Studies*,

1, 2 (1981), 5–13, p. 8. For an extensive discussion of monumental art in the aftermath of Waterloo see Alison Yarrington, *The Commemoration of the Hero 1800–1864: Monuments to the British Victors of the Napoleonic Wars* (New York and London: Garland, 1988).
96. For a comprehensive account of the painting's reception see Bachrach, 'The Field of Waterloo and Beyond', pp. 9–10.
97. There are of course a number of excellent exceptions to this rule. These include Simon Bainbridge, *Napoleon and English Romanticism* (Cambridge: Cambridge University Press, 1995), chapter 5; Tim Webb, 'Byron and the Heroic Syllables', *Keats-Shelley Review*, 5 (Autumn 1990), 41–74; Richard Cronin, *The Politics of Romantic Poetry: In Search of the Pure Commonwealth* (Basingstoke: Palgrave Macmillan, 2000), chapters 4, 5 and 6, *passim*; Milton Wilson, 'Byron and the Battle of Waterloo' in *The Mind in Creation: Essays on English Romantic Literature in Honour of Ross G. Woodman*, ed. J. Douglas Kneale (Quebec: McGill-Queen's University Press, 1992), pp. 6–26; Carl R. Woodring, 'Three Poets on Waterloo', *TWC*, 18, 2 (Spring 1987), 54–6; Peter Thorslev, 'Post-Waterloo Liberalism: The Second Generation', *SiR*, 28, 3 (Fall 1989), 437–61.
98. Josiah Conder, unsigned review of *The Poet's Pilgrimage to Waterloo* by Robert Southey, *Eclectic Review* (August 1816), 1–18. Reprinted in *Robert Southey: The Critical Heritage*, ed. Lionel Madden (London: Routledge, 1972), pp. 210–14, p. 212.
99. I have adapted Peter T. Murphy's account of the sort of problems posed by the similarly centred verse of Samuel Rogers. See his 'Climbing Parnassus and Falling Off' in *At the Limits of Romanticism: Essays in Cultural, Feminist, and Materialist Criticism*, eds Mary A. Favret and Nicola J. Watson (Bloomington and Indianapolis: University of Indiana Press, 1994), pp. 40–58, p. 51.
100. Conder's response was not uncommon. In the *Quarterly Review*, for example, J. W. Croker writes of J. Wedderburne Webster's *Waterloo, and other Poems*, that 'the subject of this article belongs rather to mechanics than literature: what Dean Swift ridiculed as a visionary scheme has been reduced, by modern ingenuity, into actual practice'. In the damning criticism that follows, Croker plays on the fact that the poem was printed by M. Didot, the inventor of the *Stereotype*: 'Having words, and even lines, thus prepared, it was a natural yet ingenious thought to endeavour to apply some moving power by which they might be disposed in proper places and forms, without the delay, expense, and uncertainty of human labour.' Wedderburne Webster's claim to authorship, and thus to social distinction, is similarly regarded as a product of commercial engineering. Surveying the spectacle of the mass of Waterloo verse marketed during this period, Croker's satire on Waterloo becomes a lament for the passing of personal, cultural and political authenticity. More generally, the review may be read as a mordant commentary on the waning of Romantic notions of authority and integrity. Again the point is surely that Waterloo marks the point at which readers are made aware of the *mechanics* of celebration. Unattributed Review of *Waterloo and other Poems*. By J. Wedderburne Webster, Esq. *Quarterly Review*, 15 (July 1816), 345–50, p. 345.
101. See John Ruskin, 'Fiction, Fair and Foul' (1880), *The Literary Criticism of John Ruskin*, ed. Harold Bloom (New York: De Capo Press, 1987), pp. 372–3.
102. Bainbridge, *Napoleon and English Romanticism*, p. 176.
103. Unless otherwise stated all references to *The Prelude* are from the 1805 text printed in *The Prelude: 1799, 1805, 1850*, eds Jonathan Wordsworth, M. H. Abrams, and Stephen Gill (New York and London: W. W. Norton, 1979).

104. John Rieder, *Wordsworth's Counterrevolutionary Turn: Community, Virtue, and Vision in the 1790s* (London: Associated University Presses, 1997).
105. See Alan Liu, *Wordsworth: The Sense of History* (Stanford, CA: Stanford University Press, 1989), p. 501. Elsewhere in this book I present a more qualified assessment of Liu's work.
106. The point is made at the end of an elegant, synoptic essay on 'Romantic Criticism and the Meanings of the French Revolution', in *SiR*, 28, 3 (Fall 1989), 463–91.
107. Žižek, *The Sublime Object of Ideology*, p. 45.
108. Charles Lamb, *The Letters of Charles Lamb*, ed. Alfred Aiger, 2 vols (London: Macmillan, 1904), I, pp. 349–51.
109. See the account given by Stephen Gill in *William Wordsworth: A Life* (Oxford: Oxford University Press, 1990), p. 316.

Chapter 1 Walter Scott: the Discipline of History

1. Longford, *Wellington: The Years of the Sword*, pp. 485–6.
2. Simpson quoted by Donald Sultana in *From Abbotsford to Paris and Back: Sir Walter Scott's Journey of 1815* (Far Thrupp: Alan Sutton, 1993), p. 28.
3. Simpson, *A Visit to Flanders in July, 1815*, p. 124.
4. The poet apostrophizes Marsena after the battle of Fuentes d'Honoro:

    > Tell him thy conqueror was Wellington;
    > And if he chafe be his *own* fortune tried,
    > God, and in our cause, to aid, the venture we'll decide.
    > (*The Vision of Don Roderick*, III, xi)

    Text as quoted by Simpson, *A Visit to Flanders in July, 1815*, p. 107.
5. John Gibson Lockhart, *Memoirs of the Life of Sir Walter Scott*, 10 vols (Edinburgh: Adam and Charles Black, 1893), V, 54.
6. *Morning Chronicle*, 4 December 1815.
7. *Morning Chronicle*, 29 December 1815.
8. Jerome Christensen, *Lord Byron's Strength: Romantic Writing and Commercial Society* (Baltimore, MD and London: Johns Hopkins University Press, 1993), pp. 127–31. For a persuasive analysis of Scott's importance as a historical novelist see Chandler, *England in 1819*, pp. 131–51, 303–49.
9. Bell was among the first to treat the wounded at Waterloo, joining an estimated 2500 medical staff working in six hospitals in and around Brussels. For a detailed account of the problems surgeons faced in treating the wounded see John Thomson, *Report of Observations Made in the British Military Hospitals in Belgium after the Battle of Waterloo* (Edinburgh: William Blackwood, 1816).
10. Charles Bell, *The Letters of Sir Charles Bell, Selected from His Correspondence with His Brother George Joseph Bell* (London: John Murray, 1870), p. 247. See also W. J. Bishop, *The Early History of Surgery* (New York: Barnes & Noble, 1960), p. 142.
11. At the conclusion of a letter to Francis Horner, Bell confesses that 'a gloomy, uncomfortable view of human nature is the inevitable consequence of looking upon the whole as I did – as I was forced to do... It is a misfortune to have our sentiments so at variance with the universal impression. But there must ever be associated with the honours of Waterloo, to my eyes, the most shocking sights of

woe, to my ears accents of entreaty, outcry from the manly breast, interrupted forcible expressions of the dying, and *noisome smells*. I must show you my notebooks, for as I took my notes of cases generally by sketching the object of our remarks, it may convey an excuse for this excess of *sentiment*.' *The Letters of Charles Bell*, p. 248. What cannot be conveyed in symbolic representation is indeed the 'excess of sentiment', the unfathomable X, which distorts the analytical depiction of Waterloo. In the illustration shown here, the soldier's attitude and expression are passionate in a very precise sense. A fervent believer in natural theology, Bell's Christianity emphasized the uniqueness of human suffering over medical systematization. In the light of this observation there may be good grounds for arguing that such an image exceeds the limitations of a Romantic aesthetic of fragmentation and decay and thus presents a radical challenge to the official view of battle. For a helpful introduction to Bell's life and work see Ludmilla Jordanova, 'The Representation of the Human Body: Art and Medicine in the Wok of Charles Bell', in *Towards a Modern Art World, For Michael Kitson, Studies in British Art*, I, ed. Brian Allen (New Haven, CT and London: Yale University Press, 1995), pp. 79–94.
12. Quoted by Lockhart in *Memoirs*, V, pp. 55–7.
13. The grounds of this distinction are set out by Marilyn Butler in *Romantics, Rebels, and Reactionaries*, chapter 5.
14. Edgar Johnson, *Sir Walter Scott: The Great Unknown*, 2 vols (New York: Hamish Hamilton, 1976), I, p. 131.
15. John Sutherland, *The Life of Walter Scott: A Critical Biography* (Oxford: Blackwell, 1995), p. 67.
16. For an extensive account of Scott's journey to Flanders and Paris see Sultana, *From Abbotsford to Paris and Back*. See also Johnson, *Sir Walter Scott: The Great Unknown*, I, pp. 495–513.
17. *LWS*, II, 432.
18. See Sultana, *From Abbotsford to Paris and Back*, pp. 4–5.
19. Ibid., p. 8.
20. [Walter Scott] *Paul's Letters to his Kinsfolk* (Edinburgh and London: Archibald Constable and John Murray, 1816), p. 175; see also Lockhart, *Memoirs*, V, 68.
21. Scott, *Paul's Letters*, p. 175.
22. In a letter to Joanna Baillie, dated 10 August – 6 September 1815, Scott admitted that he 'saw few of the more ghastly witnesses of the fray... all the bodies had been burnd and buried before I came there', *LWS*, IV, 91.
23. The impromptu market was soon followed by the construction of a hotel and an 'official' museum curated by Sergeant-Major Edward Cotton. In London, Waterloo memorabilia were shown at the following venues: 1 St James Street (Napoleon's clothes), 97 Pall Mall (Napoleon's horse), Bullock's Museum in Piccadilly (Napoleon's carriage). The desire for contact with the 'real' objects of Waterloo is indicative of a more pervasive shift away from eighteenth-century systems of knowledge with their reliance on taxonomy to a modernist emphasis on the phenomenological 'recreation' of experience.
24. Lockhart, *Memoirs*, V, p. 65.
25. Jacques Derrida, *Writing and Difference*, trans. Alan Bass (London: Routledge, 1978), p. 285.
26. Ibid.
27. Lockhart, *Memoirs*, II, 184–5. Quoted in Sutherland, *The Life of Walter Scott*, pp. 144–5.
28. *Anti-Jacobin Review*, 211 (December 1815), p. 525.

29. Lockhart, *Memoirs*, II, 214. Quoted in Sutherland, *The Life of Walter Scott*, p. 145.
30. See Sutherland, *The Life of Walter Scott*, pp. 64–6.
31. Lockhart, *Memoirs*, I, 452–3.
32. Unless otherwise stated references to Scott's poetry are from *The Poetical Works of Sir Walter Scott*, ed. J. Logie Robertson (Oxford: Oxford University Press, 1904), lines 48–53.
33. *The Minstrelsy of the Scottish Border*, with notes and index by Sir Walter Scott, ed. T. F. Henderson, 4 vols (Edinburgh: William Blackwood, 1902), I, p. 157.
34. See Sutherland, *The Life of Walter Scott*, p. 87.
35. *The Minstrelsey*, I, 130. This passage is quoted by Sutherland, *The Life of Water Scott*, p. 87.
36. Walter Scott, 'Essay on Romance' in *Essays on Chivalry, Romance, and the Drama* (London: Frederick Warne, 1888), p. 65.
37. Scott, 'Introduction and Notes to The Bridal of Triermain', *Poetical Works*, p. 585.
38. For a stimulating discussion of Scott's ambiguous estimate of the rival claims of history and romance see Brian Nellist, 'Narrative Modes in the Waverley Novels', in *Literature of the Romantic Period: 1750–1850*, eds R. T. Davies and B. G. Beatty (Liverpool: Liverpool University Press, 1976), pp. 56–71.
39. Stuart Curran has written in *Poetic Form and British Romanticism* (Oxford: Oxford University Press, 1986) that 'it was Scott's ingenuity, or genius, to recognize that the period offered an unlimited field not just for the creation of romance but also for its simultaneous critique. The simple-minded Scott of his own projection and of subsequent critical history was in fact an artist of subtle deconstructive manipulation. He gives nothing he does not take away, for he is obsessively aware that fiction is not fact, though fact is continually embroidered into fiction' (p. 140). This account seems to me to lay rather too much stress on Scott's imperviousness to the pleasure of the text. By overemphasizing the deconstructive qualities of his writings Curran ignores the extent to which Scott takes clear delight in the satisfactions of romance. 'Romance', as Brian Nellist argues, 'exists in [Scott] as a dangerous possibility' recalling the reader to the presence of a more fulfilling passion denied by the common sense of the novelistic point of view. See 'Narrative Modes in the Waverley Novels', pp. 69–71.
40. Chandler, *England in 1819*, p. 145.
41. Walter Scott, *Waverley; or 'Tis Sixty Years Since*, ed. Claire Lamont (Oxford: Clarendon Press, 1981), p. 5.
42. Scott, *Poetical Works*, p. 612.
43. Ibid., p. 586.
44. For an instructive analysis of the relationship between Romantic poetry and the Peninsular War see Peter J. Manning, '*The White Doe of Rylestone, The Convention of Cintra*, and the History of a Career', in *Reading Romantics: Texts and Contexts* (Oxford: Oxford University Press, 1990), pp. 165–94. For a more wide-ranging but equally stimulating discussion of this theme see Simon Bainbridge, '"Historiographer[s] to the King of Hell": The Lake Poets' Peninsular Campaign', in *Napoleon and English Romanticism*, pp. 95–133.
45. George Ellis and George Canning, 'Affaires d'Espagne', *Quarterly Review*, 1 (February 1809), 1–19, p. 1.
46. For further information on the image of the Iberian war as a fictional contest see Diego Saglia, 'War Romances, Historical Analogies and Coleridge's *Letters on the Spaniards*', in *Romantic War: Studies in Culture and Conflict, 1789–1822*, ed. Philip Shaw (Aldershot: Ashgate, 2000), pp. 138–60.

47. Scott, *Essays on Chivalry, Romance, and the Drama*, pp. 45–6.
48. Ibid., p. 86.
49. The legend of Don Roderick attracted the attention of two other major poets in the period: Walter Savage Landor's tragedy *Count Julian* appeared in 1811, and Southey's 'epic' *Roderick, the Last of the Goths* was published in 1814. The impact of this legend on British Romantic writing is explored by Collete Le Yaounc in *L'Orient dans la poésie anglaise de l'époque romantique, 1798–1824* (Lille: Atelier national de reproduction de thèses, 1975) and by Esteban Pujals, 'La leyenda del Rey Rodrigo en el romanticismo inglés', in *Revisita de la Universidad de Madrid*, 19 (1970), 259–88. I am grateful to Diego Saglia for drawing my attention to these sources in his conference paper 'The Texts of Romantic Rivalry: Collaboration, Friendship, Competition and the "Don Roderick" Legend, 1810–12', presented at the University of Bristol, 10 February 1998.
50. See Sutherland, *The Life of Walter Scott*, pp. 159–60.
51. *Anti-Jacobin Review*, 211 (December 1815), p. 525.
52. Lockhart, *Memoirs*, V, 105–6.
53. See Claire Lamont, '*Waverley* and the Battle of Culloden', *Essays and Studies*, 44 (1991), 14–26.
54. See Sutherland, *The Life of Walter Scott*, p. 172.
55. Ibid., p. 125. Sutherland writes that 'underlying Jeffrey's pique was a Whig distaste for war, particularly in the bloody forms in which Scott glorified it.' Jeffrey wanted Scott to realize that 'there is more in love of country than love of its picturesqueness and more in history than the flash of antique weapons and colourful costume' (p. 127).
56. This sentiment is echoed in the numerous Scottish responses to Waterloo. See Henry Davidson, *Waterloo, A Poem with notes*; David Home Buchan, *The Battle of Waterloo: A Poem* (London: T. & G. Underwood, 1816). In the second edition to his poem Buchan was moved to defend himself against the charge of having copied Scott. With its depiction of Scotland as a 'Romantic land' (p. 19) and its emphasis on Scotland's 'warlike' past excelled by its soldier's prowess on the field of Waterloo the comparison seems justified.
57. Scott, *Waverley*, p. 221.
58. In *Waverley*, a series of events facilitate the hero's growth towards maturity: the impact of the death of Colonel G—, the demonstration of the true military character of Colonel Talbot, the recantation of the ardent Jacobite Flora MacIvor and the death of Fergus. The latter event is of crucial importance as it allows Waverley to overcome his fascination with the political, emotional and sexual immaturity of Jacobitism. As Saree Makdisi has suggested, in recognizing the well-adjusted manliness of Talbot, Waverley discovers his 'true' father-figure. The damaging homoerotic appeal of Jacobitism is thus transformed into acceptable, historicized nostalgia: ' "And this, then, was thy last field," thought Waverley, his eye filling at the recollection of the many splendid points of Fergus's character, and of their former intimacy, all his passions and imperfections forgotten' (p. 281). See Saree Makdisi, 'Colonial Space and the Colonization of Time in Scott's *Waverley*', *SiR*, 34, 2 (Summer 1995), 155–87, pp. 172–3. In the 'Dance of Death' historical distance from the trauma of 1745 enables a related act of poetic restitution.
59. There is powerful evidence to suggest that the historical emphasis on 'Scottish' bravery at Hougoumont and in the charge of the Scots Greys was encouraged by Wellington to foster a myth of union. In fact, relations between the Highland

regiments and British governments were marked by mutual distrust, sporadic rebellions and corresponding acts of oppression. In John Cargill's *Battle of Waterloo; a poem* (Cupar: printed for the author, 1816) Wellington, mentioned briefly in line 189, is rapidly displaced by 'Scotia's far fam'd Grey' (line 193) who are presented as the true saviours of Britain. I am grateful to my colleague, Professor Susan Pearce of the Department of Museum Studies at the University of Leicester, for drawing my attention to this matter.

60. Scott, *The Vision of Don Roderick*, I, ii.
61. For an account of the national epic see Stuart Curran, *Poetic Form and British Romanticism*, pp. 158–79.
62. *The Works of John Dryden*, ed. Walter Scott, 18 vols (Edinburgh: William Miller, 1808); revised George Saintsbury (London: Paterson, 1882–3), I, p. 4.
63. John Milton, *Paradise Lost*, IX, 13–47, *passim*. Here, as elsewhere, I take my text from *The Poems of John Milton*, eds John Carey and Alastair Fowler (London: Longman, 1968).
64. Woodring, 'Three Poets on Waterloo', p. 54.
65. Scott, *Paul's Letters*, p. 178.
66. Wilson, 'Byron and the Battle of Waterloo', p. 22.
67. Lockhart, *Memoirs*, V, 91.
68. Yet consider Ballantyne's reflection on this meeting: 'You are not... to suppose that he looked sheepish or embarrassed in the presence of the Duke – indeed you well know that he did not, and could not do so; but the feeling, qualified and modified as I have described it, unquestionably did exist to a certain extent. Its origin formed a curious moral problem; and may probably be traced to a secret consciousness, which he might not avert to, that the Duke, however great as a soldier and a statesman, was so defective in imagination as to be incapable of appreciating that which had formed the charm of his own life, as well as of his works.' See Lockhart, *Memoirs*, V, 91. Elsewhere Scott remarks: 'I don't know why it is I never found a soldier could give me an idea of a battle. I believe their mind is too much upon the *tactique* to regard the picturesque; just as we lawyers care very little for an eloquent speech at the bar if it does not shew good doctrine.' *LWS*, II, 405. I would propose that Scott's embarrassment was genuine and that his distrust of the Duke's lack of imagination betrays an incipient sense of the irreconcilability of romance and history.
69. Sultana points out that Scott's self-confession may have served as 'model for his later description of Roland Graeme to the Regent Moray in *The Abbot* (1820), in which the former "felt overawed in the presence of the eminent soldier and statesman, the wielder of a nation's power, and the leader of her armies"'. See Sultana, *From Abbotsford to Paris and Back*, p. 69.
70. Quoted from *Dryden: A Selection*, ed. John Conaghan (London: Methuen, 1978), p. 121.
71. At an early stage in the novel Waverley composes a verse in which the 'fairy bliss' of romantic love contends with the 'stern delight' of martial duty. The latter, associated with 'the loud trumpet-call of Truth' bids 'vision pass away' (p. 23). It is of course Waverley's fate to misrecognise war as the antidote to visionary folly. In much the same way he misrecognizes the 'domestic' Rose in his pursuit of the stern, fanatical Flora.
72. James Simpson, *Paris after Waterloo, including a revised edition of A Visit to Flanders and the Field of Waterloo*, (Edinburgh: William Blackwood, 1853), p. 195.
73. Curran, *Poetic Form and British Romanticism*, p. 140.

74. Walter Scott, *The Antiquary* (London: J. M. Dent, 1977), p. 1.
75. In a letter Scott informed his close friend John Morritt that 'I want to shake myself free of Waverley'. *LWS*, IV, 12–13.
76. In 'On the Pleasure of Hating,' Hazlitt argues that civilization has had the curious effect of neutering our capacity for violent acts while leaving the desire for conflict intact: 'We give up the external demonstration, the brute violence, but we cannot part with the essence or principle of hostility.' The man of modernity must therefore resort to symbolic ritual (the burning of Guy Fawkes) and imaginative displacement (the reading of *'Scotch Novels'*) if he is to restore the natural balance of the mind: 'As we read, we throw aside the trammels of civilization... the heart rouses itself in its native lair, and utters a wild cry of joy, at being restored once more to freedom and lawless, unrestrained impulses.' *HCW*, XII, 127–9. As Ina Ferris notes, that 'sense of freedom and unrestrained impulse is, of course, firmly contained by the rational and conservative structure of historical interpretation in the Waverley novels'. This seems to me to be a useful comment to bear in mind when reading *The Antiquary* as a work of imaginative disempowerment. See Ina Ferris, 'Re-positioning the Novel: *Waverley* and the Gender of Fiction', *SiR*, 28, 2 (Summer 1989), 291–301, p. 300.
77. Scott, *Waverley*, p. 73.
78. See Butler, *Romantics, Rebels, and Reactionaries*, p. 111.
79. For an excellent discussion of the issue of political quietism in Scott see Bruce Beiderwell, 'Scott's *Redgauntlet* as a Romance of Power', *SiR*, 28, 2 (Summer 1989), 273–89. For a reading of the passive hero as a hero of a property-based society, see Alexander Welsh, *The Hero of the Waverley Novels* (New York: Atheneum, 1968).
80. *The Letters of John Keats 1814–1821*, ed. Hyder Edward Rollins, 2 vols (Cambridge, MA: Harvard University Press, 1958), I, 200.
81. Scott, *Waverley*, p. 72.

Chapter 2 Exhibiting War: Battle Tours and Panoramas

1. Simpson, *A Visit to Flanders in July, 1815*, p. 132. Charlotte A. Eaton, *Waterloo Days: The Narrative of an Englishwoman Resident at Brussels in June, 1815* (London: George Bell & Sons, 1888), p. 135.
2. Longford, *Wellington: Pillar of State*, p. 9.
3. Consider, as an example, the implicit class politics of *Sharpe's Waterloo* and Bondarchuk's film, *Waterloo* (1971). The latter is discussed in the conclusion to this study.
4. From *The Selected Letters of Sir Charles Bell*, pp. 234–6.
5. Extracts from this diary are cited in Booth's *Battle of Waterloo: Circumstantial Details of the Memorable Event: illustrated with an Original Plan, Views. & co[...] by a near observer, previous to & after the Battle*, 2 vols (London: J. Booth, 1851), II, 121.
6. Cavalié Mercer, *Journal of the Waterloo Campaign* (London: Peter Davies, 1927). This reference is cited by John Keegan in *The Face of Battle: A Study of Agincourt, Waterloo and the Somme* (Harmondsworth: Penguin, 1978), p. 130.
7. Keegan, *The Face of Battle*, pp. 130–1.
8. Major J. Pratt of the 30th Regiment wrote: 'I think you will readily agree with me that a young Subaltern Officer, such as I was at that period, harassed and fatigued after two day's previous marching, fighting, and starving (for by our mismanagement our Division was not provisioned), was not likely to take particular notice of the features of the ground over which he was moving or to direct his observations

much beyond the range of what was likely to affect himself and the few soldiers immediately about him.' Pratt is writing in response to a request from Major-General Siborne who had been engaged to construct a 'faithful and authentic record of the Battle' 'at the moment (about 7 p.m.) when the French Imperial Guards, advancing to attack the right of the British Forces, reached the crest of our position'. Despite Siborne's declaration that the model would not be 'dependent, like a pictorial representation, on *effect* for its excellence' letters such as the above indicate the extent to which personal experience qualified the omnivoyant perspective of the modeller. See *Waterloo Letters: A selection of original and hitherto unpublished letters bearing on the operations of the 16th, 17th, and 18th June, 1815. By officers who served in the campaign*, ed. Major-General Siborne (London: Cassell, 1891), p. 325, ix–xi.
9. Advertised in *The Times*, 6 January 1817. For further details see Willem Benjamin Craan, *An Historical Account of the Battle of Waterloo... intended to elucidate the topographical plan, executed by W. B. Craan*, trans. Captain Arthur Gore (London: Samuel Leigh, 1817).
10. J. B. Hartley offers a penetrating analysis of the relations between maps and power in his essay 'Maps, Knowledge, and Power' included in *The Iconography of Landscape: Essays on the Symbolic Representation, Design and Use of Past Environments*, eds Denis Cosgrove and Stephen Daniels (Cambridge: Cambridge University Press, 1988), pp. 277–312.
11. *A Handbook for Travellers in Holland and Belgium* (London: John Murray, 1881), pp. 10–11.
12. Raimondo Modiano, 'The Legacy of the Picturesque: Landscape, Property and the Ruin', in *The Politics of the Picturesque: Literature, Landscape and Aesthetics Since 1770*, ed Stephen Copley and Peter Garside (Cambridge: Cambridge University Press, 1994), pp. 196–219, p. 198.
13. Liu, *Wordsworth: The Sense of History*, pp. 61–137, p. 95, *passim*.
14. Charles Campbell, *The Traveller's Complete Guide Through Belgium and Holland* (London: 1817). Cited by Bachrach in 'The Field of Waterloo and Beyond', p. 8.
15. Eaton, *Waterloo Days*, p. 137.
16. Eaton, *Waterloo Days*, p. 152.
17. John Scott, *Paris Revisited in 1815, By way of Brussels: Including a Walk Over the Field of Battle at Waterloo* (London: Longman, 1816), p. 201.
18. Sigmund Freud, *Beyond the Pleasure Principle* (1920), in *The Standard Edition of the Complete Psychological Works*, ed. James Strachey, 23 vols (London: Hogarth Press, 1961), XVIII, 3–84.
19. Liu, *Wordsworth: The Sense of History*, p. 373.
20. A. D. Cameron, *The Man Who Loved to Draw Horses: James Howe, 1780–1836* (Aberdeen: Aberdeen University Press, 1986), p. 27. For an insight into the transformation of Waterloo into a museum site see Sergeant-Major Cotton, *A Voice From Waterloo: A History of the Battle Fought on the 18th June 1815* (London: B. Green, 1889). For more recent evidence of the relationship between Waterloo and tourism see F. De Hondt, *Promenade 1815: On Foot or by Bicycle around the Battlefield at Braine, L'Alleud, Genappe, Lasne and Waterloo* (Brussels: Fédération Touristique de la Province De Brabant, 1987).
21. Lewis's *Orations on the Battle of Waterloo*, p. xi.
22. Norman Bryson, 'Semiology and Visual Interpretation' in *Visual Theory: Painting and Interpretation*, eds Norman Bryson, Michael Ann Holly and Keith Moxey (Cambridge: Polity Press, 1991), pp. 61–73, p. 65.

23. Hazlitt, in a review of West's 'Picture of Death on the Pale Horse', quotes the following extract from an advertisement in a morning paper: 'in completion of [West's] having devoted a year and a half to its completion, and of its having for its subject the *Terrible Sublime*, it would place Great Britain in the same conspicuous relation to the rest of Europe in arts, that the battle of Waterloo had done in arms!' For Hazlitt, hyperbole in paintings and battles goes hand in hand. See 'West's Picture of Death on the Pale Horse' in *HCW*, XVIII, 136.
24. For a description of the painting see James Ward, RA, *The Battle of Waterloo in an Allegory... painted for exhibiting at the Egyptian Hall Piccadilly* (London, 1821). A useful account of Ward's work on this painting is given by C. Reginald Grundy, *James Ward, R. A.: His Life and Works* (London: Otto, 1909), pp. xli–xlv.
25. For further details see Paul Johnson, *The Birth of the Modern: World Society, 1815–1830* (London: Orion, 1992), pp. 160–4.
26. *The Diary: or Woodfall's Register*, 9 April 1789. Cited by Scott B.Wilcox in 'Unlimiting the Bounds of Painting', in *Panoramania! The Art and Entertainment of the All-Embracing View*, ed. Ralph Hyde (London: Trefoil Publications, 1988), pp. 13–44, pp. 23–4. Wilcox's study remains by far the most detailed and scholarly account of the Panorama to date.
27. *John Constable's Correspondence*, ed. R. B. Beckett, 6 vols (Ipswich: Suffolk Records Society, 1964), II, 34 and VI, 134.
28. *Morning Chronicle*, 14 March 1789.
29. *Morning Chronicle*, 21 April 1801.
30. See Wilcox, 'Unlimiting the Bounds of Painting', p. 38
31. *The Times*, 27 December 1861.
32. 'Pompeii', *Blackwood's Edinburgh Magazine*, 15 (April 1824), 472–3.
33. David Harvey, *The Condition of Postmodernity: An Enquiry into the Origins of Cultural Change* (Oxford: Blackwell, 1989), p. 244.
34. Don Slater, 'Photography and Modern Vision: The Spectacle of "Natural Magic"' in *Visual Culture*, ed. Chris Jenks (London: Routledge, 1995), pp. 218–37, p. 218.
35. *The Times*, 1 June 1795. Cited by William H. Galperin in *The Return of the Visible in British Romanticism* (Baltimore, MD and London: Johns Hopkins University Press, 1993), p. 46.
36. *Ackerman's Repository of Arts*, 22 (1819), p. 38.
37. Paul Virilio, *The Vision Machine*, trans. Julie Rose (London: BFI Publishing, 1994), pp. 40–1.
38. The exhibit was visited by the Cambridge undergraduate Alexander d'Arblay in May 1815. See *The Journals and Letters of Fanny Burney (Madame d'Arblay)*, eds Peter Hughes et al., III, 236.
39. The following information has been kindly supplied to me by Scott B. Wilcox of the Yale Center for British Art.
40. *Description of the Periphrestic Panorama... illustrative of the principal events that have occurred to Bonaparte, commencing with the Battle of Waterloo... and ending with his funeral procession at St. Helena (Thirteenth edition)* (Exeter: R. Cullum, 1822). For further discussion of this exhibit see Cameron, *The Man Who Loved to Draw Horses*, pp. 34–5.
41. See Terry Eagleton, *The Function of Criticism: From* The Spectator *to Post-Structuralism* (London: Verso, 1984), pp. 12–13.
42. See Liu, *Wordsworth: The Sense of History*, pp. 210–18. Foucault's account of the Panopticon can be found in *Discipline and Punish* (New York: Vintage Books, 1979).

43. The analogy between the Panorama and the Panopticon was first proposed by Stephan Oettermann in *Das Panorama: Die Gesichte eines massenmediums* (Frankfurt: Syndikat, 1980). See *The Panorama: History of a Mass Medium*, trans. Deborah Lucas Schneider (New York: Zone Books, 1997), pp. 40–4.
44. Jeremy Bentham, *The Panopticon Writings*, ed. and introduced Miran Božovič (London: Verso, 1995), pp. 20–1. For more on the distinction between fictitious entities and imaginary non-entities, see Bentham's *Theory of Fictions*, introduced by C. K. Ogden (London: Routledge & Kegan Paul, 1951). The relevance of Bentham's theories to Lacanian thought is the subject of Slavoj Žižek's *Tarrying with the Negative* (Durham, NC: Duke University Press, 1993), pp. 83–9.
45. For an extensive discussion of the relations between the Panorama and Romantic visual culture see Galperin, *The Return of the Visible in English Romanticism*, p. 43. Regrettably, Gillen D'Arcy Wood's *The Shock of the Real: Romanticism and Visual Culture, 1760–1860* (Basingstoke: Palgrave Macmillan, 2001), part of which focuses on the panoramas of Leicester Square, appeared too late for consideration in this study.
46. *The Art Journal*, 20 November 1852, p. 1274.
47. Though consider the argument of Maekawa Osamu that 'the reaction called sea-sickness = see-sickness' has its origins in the Panorama's excessive attention to detail, creating a crisis in perspective. Osamu is correct to argue that 'The cause of dizziness is not found in the impossibility of return from illusion to reality but, rather, in the failure to construct reality, made apparent by excess presence and fragmentariness, and deviatory movement. It is possible that these characteristics were actually points of contradiction contained within the panorama which should function to maintain reality'. To qualify this point, I would argue that by limiting perception to discrete views of the individual scenes depicted within the cylinder, the I/eye is able to mask the cleft in 'reality' exposed by these points of contradiction. See Maekawa Osamu, 'The Panorama and its Subject', *Aesthetics*, 9 (2000), 37–49, 46–7.
48. Christopher Kelly, *History of the French Revolution*, 2 vols (London: Thomas Kelly, 1819), II, 47.
49. Milton, *Paradise Lost*, III, lines 542–3.
50. Booth's *Battle of Waterloo*, I, p. 63.
51. The links between visual technology and warfare have been explored by Paul Virilio in *War and Cinema: The Logistics of Perception*, trans. Patrick Camiller (London: Verso, 1989). In *The Vision Machine*, Virilio makes an explicit reference to the Panorama as a forerunner of the cinema. See also John Grundy, *Thomas Hardy and the Sister Arts* (London: Macmillan, 1979) on the panoramic and cinematic analogues in Hardy's *The Dynasts*, pp. 106–33.
52. *Description of the Field of Battle and disposition of the Troops engaged in the Action fought on the 18th June 1815, near Waterloo* (privately printed, 1816).

Chapter 3 Southey's Vision of Command

1. Robert Southey, *The Poet's Pilgrimage to Waterloo* (London: Longman, 1816), I, i, 6. All further references to this poem will be to the version printed in this edition.
2. The analysis of the relationship between Wellington and Romanticism has been somewhat overshadowed by discussions of the 'commanding genius' Napoleon. That Napoleon should continue to appear as a centralized object of power in

Romanticism is symptomatic of a dominant tendency within Romantic criticism to reify the politics of the past. For a notable exception to this rule see the following essays by Eric C. Walker: 'Wordsworth, Wellington and Myth' in *History and Myth, Essays on Romantic Literature*, pp. 100–15, and 'Wordsworth, Warriors, and Naming', in *SiR*, 29, 2 (Summer 1990), 223–40.

3. *Supplementary Despatches, Correspondence and Memoranda of Field Marshal Arthur Duke of Wellington*, K. G., ed. by his son the Duke of Wellington, 15 vols (London: John Murray, 1858–72), XII, 155.
4. The Duke guarded the site of his greatest victory with jealous pride. When, on revisiting the field in 1821, the Duke saw the Lion Mound erected by the Dutch he is reported to have exclaimed: 'They have spoiled my Battlefield.' See Longford, *Wellington: The Years of the Sword*, p. 79.
5. Wellington, quoted in Longford, *Wellington: The Years of the Sword*, xv.
6. Wellington, *Supplementary Despatches*, X, 509.
7. For a useful introductory discussion of Habermas's concept of the 'public sphere' see Terry Eagleton, *The Function of Criticism: From The Spectator to Post-Structuralism*, p. 9. A more detailed analysis of the relation between deference and consent in the 'growth of early bourgeois society' can be found in Eagleton's *The Ideology of the Aesthetic* (Oxford: Basil Blackwell, 1990), p. 23.
8. Robert Southey, *Journal of a Tour in the Netherlands in the Autumn of 1815* (London: Heinemann, 1902), p. 91.
9. The brief reference in the British despatch to the 'timely assistance' of the Prussians was regarded as discreditable even at the time, prompting more than one observer to criticize the Duke for his lack of beneficence. (See Longford, *Wellington: The Years of the Sword*, pp. 485–6.) Wellington, however, remained unrepentant. As late as 1842 he felt able to refer to his own despatch as the definitive account of the battle: 'The report of the battle made at the time by the Duke of Wellington to the British and the Allied governments of Europe has long been before the public. In that report he does full justice to the exertions made by his colleague the Prussian commander-in-Chief and by the General officers and troops to aid and support him, and to the effectual aid which they gave him.' Following a long extract from the text of 1815 he adds: 'Historians and commentators were not necessary.' Wellington, *Supplementary Despatches*, X, 529–30.
10. F. C. F. von Müffling, *History of the Campaign of 1815. Introductory observations and appendices by Sir John Sinclair*, ed. Major-General B. P. Hughes (Wakefield: S. R. Publishers, 1970), vii.
11. Wellington, *Supplementary Despatches*, X, 507.
12. Quoted in Longford, *Wellington: The Years of the Sword*, p. 484.
13. Letter to Grosvenor Bedford, 19 December 1815. See *NLRS*, II, 128.
14. Lord Byron, *Childe Harold's Pilgrimage*, footnote to Canto III, stanza 29. *The Complete Poetical Works*, ed. Jerome J. McGann, II, 303.
15. For the theoretical background to this discussion see Jean-François Lyotard, *The Differend: Phrases in Dispute*, trans. Georges Van Den Abbeele (Manchester: Manchester University Press, 1988).
16. Robert Southey, *Poetical Works of Robert Southey, Collected by Himself*, 10 vols (London: Longman, 1838–40), X, 139.
17. See Jacqueline Rose, 'Why War?', reprinted in *Why War? – Psychoanalysis, Politics, and the Return to Melanie Klein* (Oxford: Blackwell, 1993), pp. 15–40.

18. For further discussion of Napoleon's failure to satisfy the narrative requirements of Romanticism, see Jerome Christensen, *Lord Byron's Strength*, pp. 127–32.
19. Francis Jeffrey, Unsigned Review of the *Lay of the Laureate*, *Edinburgh Review*, 26 (June 1816), 441–9. Reprinted in *Robert Southey, The Critical Heritage*, ed. Madden, p. 216.
20. Ann Bermingham, 'The Picturesque and ready-to-wear femininity', in *The Politics of the Picturesque*, eds Copley and Garside, pp. 81–119, p. 87.
21. Southey, *Journal of a Tour in the Netherlands in August 1815*, pp. 26–7.
22. Quoted in Geoffrey Carnall, *Robert Southey and His Age: The Development of a Conservative Mind* (Oxford: Clarendon Press, 1966), p. 210.
23. Liu, *Wordsworth: The Sense of History*, p. 18.
24. The phrase is Simon Bainbridge's. See his perceptive essay 'To "Sing It Rather Better": Byron, The Bards, and Waterloo', *Romanticism* 1, 1 (1995), 68–81, p. 72.
25. Text from *British War Poetry in the Age of Romanticism: 1793–1815*, ed. Bennett, pp. 245–7.
26. Wordsworth, 'Emperors and Kings' (composed 1816?), line 7. Text taken from *Shorter Poems*, ed. Ketcham, p. 153.
27. See J. B. Hartley, 'Maps, Knowledge, and Power', in *The Iconography of Landscape*, eds Cosgrove and Daniels, pp. 277–312.
28. William Cowper, 'Verses Supposed to be Written by Alexander Selkirk, During his Solitary Abode in the Island of Juan Fernandez', lines 1–2. Text taken from *The Poetical Works of William Cowper*, ed. H. S. Milford (Oxford: Oxford University Press, 1926), pp. 311–12.
29. See Michael Charlsworth, 'The Ruined Abbey: Picturesque and Gothic Values', in *The Politics of the Picturesque*, eds Copley and Garside, pp. 62–80.
30. Robert Southey, 'The Life of Wellington', *Quarterly Review*, 13 (April and July 1815; second edition 1816), 215–75; 448–526, p. 517.
31. John Milton, *Paradise Lost*, I, lines 23–4.
32. This point is made by Malcolm Kelsall, *Byron's Politics* (Brighton, Harvester Press, 1987), pp. 78–9.
33. The distinction between Gilpin's picturesque of dispossession and the proprietorial 'drive to mastery' of Price and Payne Knight is explored by Kim Ian Michasiw in his article 'Nine Revisionist Theses on the Picturesque', *Representations*, 38 (1992), 76–100.
34. It should also be noted that in part two the rhetoric of the poem shifts from pastoral to romance, from a world of temporal pathos to one of transhistorical steadfastness.
35. Bainbridge, *Napoleon and English Romanticism*, pp. 167–9.
36. Here, as Bainbridge points out, Southey is attempting to compensate for several disappointments, including the restoration of the 'detestable' Bourbons, the postwar fates of Italy, Greece and Spain and the possibility of civil disruption in Britain. See *Napoleon and English Romanticism*, p. 167.
37. Bainbridge considers Southey's involvement with Milton's poetics in *Napoleon and English Romanticism*, pp. 163–9, *passim*. Wordsworth explores the connection between Milton's satanic vision and Barker's panorama in a section from Book VII of *The Prelude*. See my short article ' "Mimic sights": A Note on Panorama and Other Indoor Displays in Book 7 of *The Prelude*', in *Notes and Queries*, 238 (December 1993), 462–4. See also Galperin, *The Return of the Visible*, p. 55.

Chapter 4 Coleridge: the Imagination at War

1. *F*, I, 97
2. Quotation from Sir John Suckling's *Tragedy of Brennoralt* used as the epigraph to 'The Men and the Times', II in *EoT*, I, 428.
3. *Diary, Reminiscences, and Correspondence of Henry Crabbe Robinson*, ed. Thomas Sadler, 2 vols (London: Macmillan, 1872), II, 264.
4. For further details see N. Gash, 'After Waterloo: British Society and the Legacy of the Napoleonic Wars', *Transactions of the Royal Historical Society*, 28 (1978), 145–57.
5. *Annual Register*, 1815, p. vi; quoted in Gash, 'After Waterloo: British Society and the Legacy of the Napoleonic Wars', p. 146.
6. Robert Southey, unattributed review, *The Quarterly Review*, 16 (October 1816), 225–78, p. 243.
7. Quoted in E. P. Thompson, *The Making of the English Working Class* (Harmondsworth: Penguin, 1968), p. 660.
8. Compare with Coleridge's position in 1796: '[taxation] takes [treasure] from the many, and gives it to the few; but this in truth impoverishes the whole, since all the active powers of a nation are paralyzed, and the bulk of the people become dependent on bounty instead of labour for their daily bread.' *W*, 110.
9. Patrick Brantlinger, *Fictions of State: Culture and Credit in Britain, 1694–1994* (Ithaca, NY and London: Cornell University Press, 1996), p. 90. For an interesting discussion of Coleridge's attitude to paper money and the making of 'Kubla Khan' see Kevin Barry, 'Paper Money and English Romanticism: Literary Side-Effects of the Last Invasion of Britain', *Times Literary Supplement*, 4899, 21 February 1997, 14–16.
10. See Morton D. Paley, 'Coleridge and the Apocalyptic Grotesque', in *Coleridge's Visionary Languages: Essays in Honour of J. B. Beer*, eds Tim Fulford and Morton D. Paley (Woodbridge: D. S. Brewer, 1993), pp. 15–25 and '"These Promised Years": Coleridge's "Religious Musings" and the Millenarianism of the 1790s', in *Revolution and English Romanticism: Politics and Rhetoric*, eds Keith Hanley and Raman Selden (Brighton: Harvester press, 1990), pp. 49–66.
11. Lines 300–8. Here as elsewhere unless otherwise stated I take my text from *Samuel Taylor Coleridge: The Complete Poems*, ed. William Keach (Harmondsworth: Penguin, 1997).
12. *EoT*, I, 143.
13. Kant, *Critique of Judgement*, I, pp. 112–13, section 28.
14. Jerome Christensen, *Romanticism at the End of History*, p. 12.
15. See Nicholas Roe, *Wordsworth and Coleridge: The Radical Years* (Oxford: Clarendon Press, 1988); Morton D. Paley, '"These Promised Years": Coleridge's "Religious Musings" and the Millenarianism of the 1790s' (see note 10 above); Peter J. Kitson, 'The Whore of Babylon and the Woman in White: Coleridge's Radical Unitarian Language', in *Coleridge's Visionary Languages*, eds Fulford and Paley, pp. 1–14.
16. In this respect consider Coleridge's attempts to persuade the rationalist Thelwall of the power of sublime poetry. *CL*, I, 279–81.
17. See *W*, 131–2.
18. *The Complete Poems*, ed. Keach, p. 488.
19. For this notion I must express my gratitude to Professor David Collings of Bowdoin College.
20. In his response to Pitt's Address of 20 April 1789 calling for an immediate embodying of the cavalry and additional militia and for further measures against the

'disaffected', Sheridan had argued that the possibility of French invasion outweighed mere 'party' objections. Coleridge's poem may be read, in part, as an attack on the moral shortcomings of political expediency. See *EoT*, I, lxxxii.
21. Burke used the phrase in a Latin form, 'justa bella quibus *necessaria*', in his *Reflections*. Coleridge had used the phrase ironically in the pages of *The Watchman* (1796). See *W*, pp. 48, 54, 205, 276, 310.
22. Coleridge had written in the margin of a copy of Godwin's *Thoughts Occasioned by the Perusal of Dr. Parr's Spital Sermon* (1801) that 'it is with Jacobinism as with the French Empire, we made peace just at the very time, that war *first* became just & necessary'. Erdman attributes this note to the second half of 1802 and therefore after the Treaty of Amiens. By contrast Coleridge had remarked on 3 December 1801 that the nation should resist being once again 'plunged into a war of principles'. For further details see *EoT*, I, 384; ci.
23. Charles De Paolo, 'Kant, Coleridge, and the Ethics of War', *TWC*, 16 (Winter 1985), 3–12, p. 9.
24. The distinction between the man of action and the man of art is anticipated in a lecture note from 1808: 'Hope the master Element of Commanding Genius, meeting with an active and combining intellect of just that degree of vividness which disquiets and impels the Soul to try and realize its Images – greatly increase this creative Power and the Images become a satisfying world of themselves – i.e. we have the Poet, or original philosopher ...' (*LoL*, I, 137).
25. In a lecture on *Hamlet* dating from November 1813, Coleridge warns against a corresponding overbalance of the 'contemplative faculty'. Due to his 'morbid sensibility' Hamlet becomes the 'creature of meditation, and loses the power of action' (*LoL*, I, 543–4). At the other extreme there is the character of Macbeth, a Napoleonic genius who proceeds 'with breathless and crowded rapidity' (ibid.). The political message of the lecture is clear: Wellington has just driven the French across the Pyrenees. But this should not be read as an act of revenge. The invasion is prompted by Napoleon's 'attack upon the middle classes and society' and is sanctioned by the will of a legitimate nation (*LoL*, I, 542).
26. I have adapted an argument of Jerome C. Christensen's in 'Politerotics: Coleridge's Rhetoric of War in *The Friend*', *Clio*, 8 (1979), 339–63, pp. 342–3.
27. *CN*, I, 1372.
28. Christensen, 'Politerotics', p. 358.
29. For Coleridge's representation of Napoleon as an unjust enemy see Charles De Paolo, 'Kant, Coleridge and the Ethics of War', pp. 5–9, *passim*.
30. Christensen, 'Politerotics', p. 341.
31. *EoT*, II, 157–8.
32. The quotation is cited by Julie A. Carlson, *In the Theatre of Romanticism: Coleridge, Nationalism, Women* (Cambridge: Cambridge University Press, 1994), p. 103.
33. Here, and in the discussion that follows, I have drawn on Julie A. Carlson's detailed and exacting discussion of the play in *In the Theatre of Romanticism*, p. 97. It is perhaps worth adding that the play was, somewhat surprisingly, one of only a few dramatic responses to Waterloo. The British Library, for example, holds just one play, *The Battle of Waterloo: A Tragedy* by Mary Hornby printed privately in 1819.
34. Carl Woodring discusses the question of genre in *Politics in the Poetry of Coleridge* (Madison: Wisconsin University Press, 1961), p. 212.
35. Text taken from *The Dramatic Works of Samuel Taylor Coleridge*, ed. Derwent Coleridge (London: Edward Moxon, 1852).

36. Slavoj Žižek, 'Otto Weininger, or "Woman Doesn't Exist"', in *The Žižek Reader*, eds Elizabeth Wright and Edmond Wright (Oxford: Blackwell, 1999), pp. 127–47, p. 141.
37. Carlson, *In the Theatre of Romanticism*, p. 105. See also p. 125.
38. See *F*, I, 451–54.
39. In her analysis of *Zapolya*'s treatment of sexual difference, Carlson focuses on the character of Glycine whose act of spearing her fiancé highlights the extent to which the 'Female characters – good or bad, foreign or domestic – are constantly taking matters into their "maiden hands"'. It is the overall aim of the play to diffuse this tendency and restore women to their rightful place as the 'weaker sex'. *In the Theatre of Romanticism*, pp. 115–33.
40. See the related comment on Napoleon from the *Courier* (14 May 1812): '[Napoleon has waged] the most cruel and systematic war against the source of the virtue, comforts, and increasing amity of mankind, the commercial and middle classes' (*EoT*, II, 348).
41. See 'Religious Musings', lines 200–25.

Chapter 5 Wordsworth's Abyss of Weakness

1. *The Prose Works of William Wordsworth*, ed. Alexander B. Grosart, 3 vols. (London: Edward Moxon, 1876), III, 451–2. Wordsworth who, like Scott and Coleridge, had considered himself to be fit for military leadership, argued throughout the 1810s for the maintenance of local militias. As he writes to John Scott in 1816, there is an 'identity of interests' residing in the establishment of a 'yeomanry corps': 'martial qualities are the natural effloresence of a healthy state of society'. *MY*, II, 323.
2. William Wordsworth, 'Anticipation: October, 1803', lines 10–14. Unless stated otherwise, quotations from Wordsworth's poetry will be taken from *The Poetical Works of William Wordsworth*, eds Ernest de Selincourt and Helen Darbishire, 5 vols (Oxford: Clarendon Press, 1940–9).
3. MS. B, line 913. Text taken from William Wordsworth, *Home at Grasmere*, Part First, Book First of *The Recluse*, ed. Beth Darlington. The Cornell Wordsworth (Ithaca, NY and London: Cornell University Press, 1977).
4. See René Girard, *Violence and the Sacred*, trans. Patrick Gregory (Baltimore, MD: Johns Hopkins University Press, 1977), pp. 89–103.
5. Consider also Lacan's analysis of the Freudian concept *das Ding*: 'Is the Law the Thing? Certainly not. Yet I can only know of the Thing by means of the Law. In effect, I would not have had the idea to covet it if the Law hadn't said: "Thou shalt not covet it." ... without the Law the Thing is dead.' Moreover, the 'dialectical relationship between desire and the Law causes our desire to flare up only in relation to the Law, through which it becomes the desire for death.' Yet Lacan holds open the possibility of rediscovering a relationship to *das Ding* 'somewhere beyond the law'. For the development of this idea via Kant and de Sade see Lacan, *The Ethics of Psychoanalysis*, pp. 71–84.
6. For the background to this discussion see David Collings, *Wordsworthian Errancies: The Poetics of Cultural Dismemberment* (Baltimore, MD and London: Johns Hopkins University Press, 1994), p. 13. Collings draws on Girard to explain Wordsworth's fascination with sacrificial violence.
7. Žižek, *The Plague of Fantasies*, p. 239.

8. I am influenced here by William H. Galperin's resourceful rereading of the later Wordsworth in *Revision and Authority in Wordsworth: The Interpretation of a Career* (Philadelphia: University of Pennsylvania Press, 1989). Where I differ from Galperin's deconstructive reading is in the emphasis I place on the ineluctable nature of the symbolic order.
9. Josiah Conder, unsigned review of *The Poet's Pilgrimage to Waterloo* in *Robert Southey: The Critical Heritage*, p. 213.
10. *HCW*, IV, 214–21.
11. *Shorter Poems*, ed. Ketcham, p. 178.
12. Wordsworth, *The Prelude* (1805), XI, line 47.
13. See *Shorter Poems*, ed. Ketcham, p. 16.
14. Collings, *Wordsworthian Errancies*, p. 31.
15. It is noticeable that the 'Thanksgiving' poems avoid direct mention of the 'matter of Waterloo'. As Simon Bainbridge points out (*Napoleon and English Romanticism*, pp. 172–3), Wordsworth informed Scott that 'My short Essays... cannot possibly interfere with your own work [Scott was in the process of composing his own, lengthy homage to the event], as they stand at a distance from the Body of the subject' (*MY*, II, 282). For the details of the 'Thanksgiving Ode' Wordsworth relied, for the most part, on the battle-tour described in John Scott's *Paris Revisited*. For Scott, as we have seen, the field of battle is quite literally a testing ground for the efficacy of moral and aesthetic categories. Chief among the criteria addressed by Scott is the concept of the Sublime: the battle ground is itself a sublime object, superseding the habitual distinctions between knowledge and experience, pain and pleasure, presence and absence, art and history, poet and warrior. It is little wonder that Wordsworth, eager to assert the primacy of poetic over political understanding, should feel a kinship with Scott's writing. What threatens the accomplishment of the sublime understanding of war is, of course, the matter of 'Carnage'.
16. William Wordsworth, *Concerning the Relations of Great Britain, Spain, and Portugal, to Each Other, and to the Common Enemy, at this Crisis; and Specifically as Affected by the Convention of Cintra*, in The *Prose Works of William Wordsworth*, eds W. J. B. Owen and Jane W. Smyser, 3 vols (Oxford: Clarendon Press, 1974), I, 193–415. This reference: I, 256.
17. For further discussion of Wordsworth's attitude to Wellington see Eric C. Walker, 'Wordsworth, Wellington, and Myth', in *History and Myth: Essays on English Romantic Literature*, ed. Behrendt, pp. 100–15.
18. Wordsworth, *Prose Works*, eds. Owen and Smyser, I, 255. In the *Essay, Supplementary to the Preface*, written at the beginning of 1815 to accompany his forthcoming collected *Poems*, Wordsworth inserted a passage in which he decries those critics 'of palsied imaginations and indurated hearts' who had dismissed his poetry as trite and ludicrous. Recognizing that this admission of resentment would play into the hands of his enemies the poet described himself as a fellow of Spenser and Milton, 'select Spirits for whom it is ordained that their fame shall be in the world an existence like that of Virtue, which owes its being to the struggles it makes and its vigour to the enemies whom it provokes' (*Prose Works*, eds Owen and Smyser, III, 63). In the aftermath of Waterloo Wordsworth continued to represent himself as a poet at war with his critics. In the *Letter to a friend of Robert Burns*, written towards the end of the year, Francis Jeffrey is singled out as the epitome of critical 'vanity'; characterized as 'restless, reckless, intractable, unappeasable, insatiable', he is, as Stephen Gill points out, 'the Napoleon... of

letters' (*William Wordsworth: A Life* (Oxford: Clarendon Press, 1989), p. 307). In part, this combative rhetoric was a normal consequence of the analogical scheme by which political issues were typically recast: every event taking place in the public sphere could be described in terms of another. But for Wordsworth the allusion was apposite because it captured the extent to which English society had become subtly militarized. We need only remind ourselves of the poet's ruminations on Pasley to feel the force of this statement. Where, in his critique of the military character, Wordsworth had argued that conquest should be 'bottomed' upon 'notions of justice and right' and not upon the 'vanity' and 'contempt' of a individual, so in his critique of culture he claims that poetry must embrace the pure good of Spenser and Milton and detach itself from the 'imperial vanity' of men such as Francis Jeffrey and, by extension, the Duke of Wellington.

19. Walker, 'Wordsworth, Wellington, and Myth', p. 110.
20. G. W. F. Hegel, extract from *Phenomenology of Spirit: Preface*, in *Hegel: Selections*, ed. M. J. Inwood (New York: Macmillan, 1989), p. 130.
21. *The Prelude* (1805), VI, line 526.
22. Jonathan M. Hess, 'Wordsworth's Aesthetic State: The Poetics of Liberty', *SiR*, 33, 1 (Spring 1994), 3–29, p. 28.
23. Benedict Anderson, *Imagined Communities: Reflections on the Origin and Spread of Nationalism* (London: Verso, 1983), p. 9.
24. *Parliamentary Debates*, XXXII, 310–26, *passim*.
25. Quotation from 'An Essay Upon Epitaphs', in *Prose Works*, eds Owen and Smyser, II, 53.
26. 'After Visiting the Field of Waterloo' (line 9), from the *Memorials of a Tour on the Continent, 1820*, published in 1822.
27. *The Prelude* (1805), VII, line 741.
28. Wordsworth's judgement on *The Descent of Liberty* was, to say the least, ambivalent '[Hunt's] Mask has been read with great pleasure by my Wife and her Sisters under this peaceful Roof. They commend the style in strong terms; and though it would not become *me* to say that their taste is correct, I have often witnessed with pleasure and an entire sympathy, the disgust with which in this particular they are affected by the main part of contemporary productions.' *MY*, II, 273. The *Descent*, in other words, is a work that should be considered by women, not Poets. The Laker's dismissal of the work reflects the gendered distinction between Fancy and Imagination developed in the 1815 *Preface*: Imagination is 'conscious of an indestructible dominion' (recall Hunt's 'conscious power'); Fancy is 'given to quicken and beguile the temporal part of our nature'. In Wordsworth's view, therefore, Hunt's work belongs to the sphere of the 'playful', the 'amusing' and the 'tender'; above all it is 'fleeting': it will not 'incite... and support the eternal'. See *Prose Works*, eds Owen and Smyser, III, 36–7.
29. See *Leigh Hunt: Literary Criticism*, eds Lawrence Huston Houtchens and Carolyn Washburn Houtchens (New York: Columbia University Press, 1956), p. 23.
30. Part 3, lines 153–4. Text taken from *The Poetical Works of Leigh Hunt*, ed. H. S. Milford (Oxford: Oxford University Press, 1923). All further references to Hunt's poetry will be to the versions printed in this edition.
31. Significantly, in two poems from this 1816 collection, 'Composed In Recollection of the Expedition of the French into Russia' and 'Sonnet, On the same Occasion, February 1816', Wordsworth returns to the figure of 'dread winter'. In both examples, the conversion of the 'shrunken', 'close-wrapt Traveller' into the inexorable scourge of Napoleon's army becomes a figure for the resistance to old age

and cultural marginalization. Quotations from 'Composed in Recollection of the Expedition of the French into Russia', lines 1–13, *passim*. See Wordsworth, *Shorter Poems*, ed. Ketcham, pp. 206–7.
32. *Examiner*, 425, 18 February 1816, p. 98.
33. In considering Hunt's own experiments with the sonnet form, it is possible to trace the rudiments of an aesthetic entirely opposed to the draconian sublimity identified with the later Wordsworth. With the gothic grandeur of Milton reduced to the democratic simplicity of the leafy Hampstead suburb, Hunt is able to begin the process of pacifying the high Romantic imagination. Within this space, as Stuart Curren argues, even the 'brave Kosciusko' is 'transformed from Coleridge's martial hero, as one who, faced with swearing allegiance to Napoleon or the Holy Alliance, forswears both, substitutes rhymes (spade for blade), and heroically tends to his garden: both warrior and nature are quietly methodized'. See Curran, *Poetic Form and British Romanticism*, p. 50. The 'stormier fields' of romantic excess, in other words, are replaced by the 'calm green amplitudes' of peace and humanity, a figure for the very forms of liberal understanding that Wordsworth, in his bid to establish himself as a cultural authority, has betrayed. Quotes taken from Leigh Hunt, 'To Kosciusko', lines 6 and 11. First published in the *Examiner*, 19 November 1815.
34. Bainbridge cites these references in *Napoleon and English Romanticism*, p. 233.
35. Wordsworth, *The White Doe of Rylstone*, lines 1163–72, *passim*.
36. See Theresa M. Kelley, *Wordsworth's Revisionary Aesthetics* (Cambridge: Cambridge University Press, 1988), pp. 154–6.
37. The sonnet, together with 'Intrepid Sons of Albion' and 'Oh, for a kindling touch', was sent in a letter to Scott dated 29 January 1816. See *MY*, II, 277.
38. Edmund Spenser, *The Faerie Queene*, ed. A. C. Hamilton (London and New York: Longman, 1977), VI, v, 37.
39. See Victor Brombert, 'The Happy Prison: A Recurring Romantic Metaphor', in *Romanticism: Vistas, Instances, Continuities*, eds Geoffrey Hartman and David Thorburn (Ithaca, NY: Cornell University Press, 1973), pp. 52–70.
40. *The Prelude* (1805), III, lines 279–81.
41. Josiah Conder, *Robert Southey: The Critical Heritage*, p. 213. Conder quotes from Southcy, *The Poet's Pilgrimage to Waterloo*, I, iii, 33.
42. Wordsworth, 'Occasioned by the Same Battle', lines 1–2.
43. The popular significance of Conder's opinion of the respective merits of Wordsworth and Southey is borne out in a comparison of the poets' sales figures. The first edition of 2000 copies of *The Poet's Pilgrimage to Waterloo* sold within two months, yielding Southey a profit of £215. By contrast, between 1816 and 1824 no more than 163 copies of Wordsworth's 'Thanksgiving Ode' were sold, of which only 55 were bought at the time of publication. See *A Bibliography of the Writings in Prose and Verse of William Wordsworth*, ed. Thomas J. Wise (Folkestone: Dawsons, 1971), pp. 102–4.
44. The important distinction between the public and the people is developed in Wordsworth's 'Essay, Supplementary to The Preface'. Like the power of virtue, good poetry survives because it appeals 'to that Vox Populi which the Deity inspires'. The People, like the tradition it supports, is a philosophical concept transcending time, place and party politics. *Prose Works*, eds Owen and Smyser, III, 84.
45. Ibid., 324.
46. Curran, *Poetic Form and British Romanticism*, p. 57.

47. *MY*, II, 284.
48. Carol Maddison, *Apollo and the Nine: A History of the Ode* (London: no publishing details, 1960), p. 289.
49. Curran, *Poetic Form and British Romanticism*, p. 78.
50. Ibid., p. 79.
51. Paul de Man, 'Autobiography as De-Facement', in *The Rhetoric of Romanticism* (New York: Columbia University Press, 1984), pp. 67–81, p. 74.
52. Text taken from *The Poetical Works of Edmund Spenser*, eds J. C. Smith and Ernest de Selincourt (Oxford: Clarendon Press, 1935).
53. I must express a considerable debt to Eric C. Walker for drawing my attention to this aspect of Wordsworth's Waterloo poetry. See his essay, 'Marriage and the End of War', in *Romantic Wars: Studies in Culture and Conflict, 1793–1822*, ed. Shaw, pp. 208–26.
54. See Wordsworth, *Shorter Poems*, ed. Ketcham, pp. 539–40 for details. Most recently, Eric C. Walker has proposed Wellington as a likely candidate, noting that Dion has 'fallen in magnanimity' (line 132). See Walker, 'Wordsworth, Wellington, and Myth', p. 110. Unless stated otherwise, quotations from 'Dion' are taken from Reading text 2 in *Shorter Poems*, ed. Ketcham, pp. 217–21.
55. Wordsworth refers to *Plutarch's Lives of the Noble Grecian and Romans Englished by Sir Thomas North Anno 1579*. The following quotations are taken from volume 6 of the edition edited by W. E. Henley, 6 vols (London: David Nutt, 1896).
56. *The Prelude*, X, line 272.
57. 'Dion', Reading text 1, lines 35–6. Text taken from *Shorter Poems*, ed. Ketcham, pp. 213–17.
58. 'Thanksgiving Ode', line 325.
59. See, for example, Stephen Gill's comments in *William Wordsworth, A Life*, p. 474.
60. James K. Chandler, '"Wordsworth" after Waterloo' in *The Age of William Wordsworth*, eds Kenneth R. Johnston and Jean Rouff (New Brunswick, NJ and London: Rutgers University Press, 1987), pp. 84–111, p. 98.
61. William Wordsworth, *Thanksgiving Ode, January 18, 1816 With Other Short Pieces, Chiefly referring to Recent Public Events* (London: Longman, 1816), x.
62. 'Intimations of Immortality from Recollections of Early Childhood', lines 58–63.
63. 'Invocation to the Earth' ('Elegiac Stanzas' after 1827), lines 26 and 36. Text taken from *Shorter Poems*, ed. Ketcham, pp. 200–1.

Chapter 6   'For Want of a Better Cause': Lord Byron's War with Posterity

1. *Recollections of a Long Life by Lord Broughton (John Cam Hobhouse) with added extracts from his private diaries*, 6 vols (London: John Murray, 1910), I, 307–8.
2. See E. Tangye Lean, *The Napoleonists*, p. 165.
3. See Kelsall, *Byron's Politics*, p. 163.
4. *Parliamentary Debates*, XXXII, 686–8.
5. Ibid., 653–4.
6. Kelsall, *Byron's Politics*, p. 2.
7. *His Very Self and Voice: Collected Conversations of Lord Byron*, ed. Ernest J. Lovell, Jr (New York: Octagon, 1980), p. 126.
8. *Byron's Letters and Journals*, ed. Leslie Marchand, 12 vols (London: John Murray, 1973–82), IV, 302.

9. For further information on the Whig reaction to Waterloo see E. Tangye Lean, *The Napoleonists*, pp. 106–13.
10. See *The Complete Poetical Works*, ed. McGann, II, 473.
11. See, for example, the account given by Michael Foot in *The Politics of Paradise: A Vindication of Byron* (London: William Collins, 1988), pp. 168–9.
12. Hazlitt, 'On the Connexion Between Toad-Eaters and Tyrants', *HCW*, VII, 149.
13. *Examiner*, 398, 13 August 1815, p. 512.
14. See *The Complete Poetical Works*, ed. McGann, III, 259.
15. *Examiner*, 329, 17 April 1814, pp. 258–9.
16. *Examiner*, 317, 23 January 1814, p. 49.
17. For further details see *The Complete Poetical Works*, ed. McGann, III, 492.
18. Simon Bainbridge makes a related point in *Napoleon and English Romanticism*, p. 182.
19. *The Complete Poetical Works*, ed. McGann, III, 375 and 492.
20. Lord Holland to Lord Kinnaird, from a letter quoted in Sonia Keppel, *The Sovereign Lady: A Life of Elizabeth Vassall, third Lady Holland, with her family* (London: Hamish Hamilton, 1974), pp. 217–18.
21. *The Complete Poetical Works*, ed. McGann, V, 372.
22. See Walter Benjamin, 'Theses on the Philosophy of History,' in his *Illuminations*, trans. Harry Zohn (New York: Schocken Books, 1969), pp. 253–64, p. 257.
23. Ibid, p. 270.
24. *Letters and Journals*, ed. Marchand, IV, 325. Quoted in Paul H. Fry, *A Defense of Poetry*, p. 167.
25. Terry Eagleton, *Walter Benjamin: Towards a Revolutionary Criticism* (London: Verso, 1981), p. 68.
26. *The Complete Poetical Works*, ed. McGann, II, 303.
27. Benjamin, *Illuminations*, p. 261.
28. See Paul de Man, 'The Temptation of Permanence', *Critical Writings: 1953–1978*, ed. Lindsay Walters (Minneapolis: University of Minnesota Press, 1989), pp. 30–40.
29. *The Complete Poetical Works*, ed. McGann, II, 198.
30. Ibid., 307.
31. Walter Scott, Review of *Childe Harold's Pilgrimage III*, *Quarterly Review*, 16 (October 1816), 172–208; p. 192.
32. *The Complete Poetical Works*, ed. McGann, II, 307.
33. Paul H. Fry, *A Defense of Poetry*, p. 173.
34. William Wordsworth, 'The Solitary Reaper', lines 19–20. Text taken from *The Poetical Works of William Wordsworth*, eds Ernest de Selincourt and Helen Darbishire, 5 vols (Oxford: Clarendon Press, 1947–54), III, 77.
35. Annie Dillard, 'Do We Count?', *The Observer Review*, 8 February 1998, p. 5.
36. *The Works of Lord Byron: Letters and Journals*, ed. R. E. Prothero, 6 vols (London: John Murray, 1898–1901), V, 547.
37. *The Complete Poetical Works*, ed. McGann, II, 303.
38. Ibid., II, 302–3.
39. Quotations from Andrew M. Cooper, 'Chains, Pains, and Tentative Gains: The Byronic Prometheus in the Summer of 1816', *SiR*, 27, 4 (Winter 1988), 529–62, p. 530.
40. Scott, *Quarterly Review* 16 (October 1816) p. 192.
41. I am influenced here by Milton Wilson's reading of the stanza in 'Byron and the Battle of Waterloo', in *The Mind in Creation*, ed. J. Douglas Kneale, p. 23.

42. Žižek, *The Sublime Object of Ideology*, p. 170.
43. *The Complete Poetical Works*, ed. McGann, II, 302.
44. Laurence Lerner, *The Uses of Nostalgia: Studies in Pastoral Poetry* (London: Chatto & Windus, 1972), pp. 26–7.

Conclusion

1. Sir Edward Creasy, *The Fifteen Decisive Battles of the World*, pp. 351–2.
2. Ernest Jones, *Sigmund Freud: Life and Work*, 3 vols (London: Hogarth Press, 1955), II, 189–92.
3. Sigmund Freud, 'Why War?' (1933), in *The Standard Edition of the Complete Psychological Works*, ed. and trans. James Strachey, 23 vols (London: Hogarth Press, 1961), XXII, 195–215. For an indispensable reading of Freud's theorizing on war see Jacqueline Rose, 'Why War?', in *Why War? – Psychoanalysis, Politics, and the Return to Melanie Klein*, pp. 15–40. See also Daniel Pick, *War Machine*, pp. 211–70.
4. Freud, 'Why War?', pp. 214–15.
5. Francis R. Hart, *Lockhart as Romantic Biographer* (Edinburgh: Edinburgh University Press, 1971), p. 255. The preceding quotation is from a letter sent by Maurice Fitzgerald to Lockhart on 14 May 1830. For the complete text see Hart, pp. 257–9.
6. *The Journals and Letters of Fanny Burney*, ed. Peter Hughes, VIII, 322.
7. Alison Yarrington, 'His Achilles Heel? Wellington and Public Art'. I am grateful to Professor Yarrington of the University of Leicester for allowing me to refer to this unpublished paper. The statue is discussed in the context of monuments to military and naval victory in *The Commemoration of the Hero*, pp. 217–26.
8. *Lawrence Correspondence*, LAW/3/330/1 & 2. The Royal Academy, London. Cited by Yarrington, 'His Achilles Heel? Wellington and Public Art'.
9. Colley, *Britons*, p. 258. For further discussion of the responses to the unveiling of the Achilles statue in 1822 see M. Busco, 'The Achilles in Hyde Park', *The Burlington Magazine*, 180 (1988), 920–4.
10. Jacques Lacan, quotation from 'Propos directifs pour un congrès sur la sexualité féminine' (1958), trans. Jacqueline Rose, in *Sexuality in the Field of Vision* (London and New York: Verso, 1986), p. 68.
11. Christensen, *Lord Byron's Strength*, pp. 71–2.
12. W. M. Thackeray, *Vanity Fair*, ed. Peter Shillingsburg (New York and London: Norton, 1994), p. 293. All subsequent references are to the version of the text published in this edition.
13. For Lacan, existence means integration into the symbolic order: only that which enters the order of discourse can be said to exist. Woman, insofar as she is existant, resists symbolization. She is identified with the Real, a Thing embodying impossible enjoyment, that 'impossible' object that must be excluded if the symbolic order is to take affect. For further discussion see Jacqueline Rose, *Sexuality in the Field of Vision*, pp. 68–81 and Slavoj Žižek, 'Otto Weininger, or "Woman doesn't Exist"' in *The Žižek Reader*, eds Wright and Wright, pp. 127–47.
14. For an interesting take on the theme of feminine duality see 'Brussels' in Colonel Maxwell's *Stories of Waterloo*. The innocent Lucy Davidson is in search of her wounded lover Frank Kennedy, a 'brave and chivalrous soldier' who shares his name with 'a male flirt, a professed lady-killer'. On the packet to Belgium Lucy overhears a conversation in which the evil Kennedy is denounced. She assumes, naturally enough, that her lover is not what he seems. Before long the mistake is

revealed and she arrives at the field of Waterloo a wise and penitent woman. There she discovers 'the object of her love': a noble hero, tempered by battle and thus fit for her attention. See Colonel Maxwell, *Stories of Waterloo* (London: William Nicholson, no date), pp. 281–2.
15. See the extract from Richard Barickman, Susan Macdonald and Myra Stark, *Corrupt Relations: Dickens, Thackeray, Trollope, Collins and the Victorian Sexual System* (New York: Columbia University Press, 1982), pp. 179–93, reprinted in *Vanity Fair*, ed. Shillingsburg, pp. 841–55.
16. Thomas De Quincey, *Confessions of an English Opium-Eater and Other Writings*, ed. Grevel Lindop (Oxford: Oxford University Press, 1985), p. 208.
17. Edmund Blunden, *Leigh Hunt: A Biography* (London: Cobden-Sanderson, 1930), p. 266.
18. Note to *Captain Sword and Captain Pen* in *The Poetical Works of Leigh Hunt*, ed. Milford, p. 704.
19. See Mary Favret, 'Coming Home: The Public Spaces of Romantic War', *SiR*, 33, 4 (Winter 1994), 539–48.
20. *The Poetical Works of Leigh Hunt*, ed. Milford, p. 704.
21. Ibid., p. 704.
22. James R. Thompson, *Leigh Hunt* (Boston: Twayne Press, 1977), p. 47.
23. Paul de Man, 'The Rhetoric of Temporality', in *Blindness and Insight: Essays in the Rhetoric of Contemporary Criticism*, 2nd edn (London: Methuen, 1983), p. 207.
24. *The Poetical Works of Leigh Hunt*, ed. Milford, pp. 99–100, *passim*.
25. Quotation from 'War' (N. Whitfield, B. Strong), a song performed by Edwin Starr © 1970 Jobete Music.
26. *Maud*, III, line 50 (1855) and line 44. See Ricks's footnote on p. 1092 for an account of the controversy surrounding the publication of this sentiment. Tennyson's resounding 'yes!' to Waterloo is answered in Dante Gabriel Rossetti's sardonic 'On the Field of Waterloo':

> So then, the name which travels side by side
> With English life from childhood – Waterloo –
> Means this. The sun is setting. 'Their strife grew
> Till the sunset, and ended,' says our guide.
>
> It lacked the 'chord' by stage-use sanctified,
> Yet I believe one should have thrilled. For me,
> I grinned not, and 'twas something; – certainly
> These held their point, and did not turn but died:
>
> So much is very well. 'Under each span
> Of these ploughed fields' ('tis the guide still) 'there rot
> Three nations slain, a thousand-thousandfold.'
> Am I to weep? Good sirs, the earth is old:
> Of the whole earth there is no single spot
> But hath among its dust the dust of man.

From *The Works of Dante Gabriel Rossetti*, ed. William M. Rossetti (London, 1911).
27. Žižek, *The Sublime Object of Ideology*, p. 75.

Bibliography

Primary sources

A Handbook for Travellers in Holland and Belgium. London: John Murray, 1881.
Abba. 'Waterloo' (B. Anderson, S. Anderson, B. Ulvæus). Song. 1974 Union Songs AB.
'Anniversary of the Battle of Waterloo', *Blackwood's Edinburgh Magazine*, 38 (July 1835), 112–19.
Annual Register or a View of the History, Politics and Literature for the Year 1815. London: Baldwin, Cradock, and Joy, 1816.
Battine, Cecil. 'How to Celebrate the Centenary of Waterloo', *The Nineteenth Century and After*, 77 (June 1915), 1314–19.
Battle of Waterloo: Circumstantial Details of the Memorable Event: illustrated with an Original Plan, Views. & co [. . .] *by a near observer, previous to & after the Battle*, 2 vols. London: J. Booth, 1851.
Bell, Charles. *The Letters of Sir Charles Bell, Selected from His Correspondence with His Brother George Joseph Bell*. London: John Murray, 1870.
Bentham, Jeremy. *The Panopticon Writings*. ed. Miran Božovič. London: Verso, 1995.
———. *Theory of Fictions*, intro. C. K. Ogden. London: Routledge & Kegan Paul, 1951.
Broughton, John Cam Hobhouse. *Recollections of a Long Life by Lord Broughton (John Cam Hobhouse) with added extras from his private diaries*, 6 vols. London: John Murray, 1910.
Buchan, David Home. *The Battle of Waterloo: a poem*. London: T. G. Underwood, 1816.
Burke, Edmund. *Reflections on the Revolution in France and on the proceedings in Certain Societies in London relative to that event*, ed. Conor Cruise O'Brien. Harmondsworth: Penguin, 1968; rpt 1983.
Burney, Fanny. *The Journals and Letters of Fanny Burney (Madame D'Arblay)*, 12 vols, eds Peter Hughes et al. Oxford: Oxford University Press, 1980.
Byron, George Gordon, Lord. *Byron's Letters and Journals*, 12 vols, ed. Leslie Marchand. London: John Murray, 1973–82.
———. *The Complete Poetical Works*, 6 vols, ed. Jerome J. McGann. Oxford: Clarendon Press, 1980–91.
Canning, George and Ellis, George. 'Affaires d'Espagne', *Quarterly Review*, 1 (February 1809), 1–19.
Cargill, John. *Battle of Waterloo; a poem*. Cupar, printed for the author, 1816.
Carlyle, Thomas. *Selected Writings*. ed. Alan Shelston. Harmondsworth: Penguin, 1988.
Cobbett's Parliamentary Debates: The Parliamentary Debates from the Year 1803 to the Present Times, First Series, 41 vols. London: T. C. Hansard, 1803–20.
Cobbett's Weekly Political Register. 89 vols. London, 1802–35.
Coleridge, Samuel Taylor. *Biographia Literaria or Biographical Sketches of my Literary Life and Opinions*, 2 vols, eds James Engell and W. Jackson Bate, Bollingen Series. London: Routledge and Princeton University Press, 1983.
———. *Collected Letters Of Samuel Taylor Coleridge*, 6 vols, ed. E. L. Griggs. Oxford: Clarendon Press, 1956–71.
———. *The Dramatic Works of Samuel Taylor Coleridge*, ed. Derwent Coleridge. London: Edward Moxon, 1852.

——. *Essays on His Times – in The Morning Post and the Courier*. 3 vols. ed. David V. Erdman. Bollingen Series. London: Routledge and Princeton University Press, 1978.
——. *The Friend*, 2 vols, ed. Barbara E. Rooke, Bollingen Series. London: Routledge and Princeton University Press, 1969.
——. *Lay Sermons*, ed. R. J. White, Bollingen Series. London: Routledge and Princeton University Press, 1972.
——. *Lectures 1808–1819 on Literature*, 2 vols, ed. R. A. Foakes, Bollingen Series. London: Routledge and Princeton University Press, 1987.
——. *Lectures 1795 on Politics and Religion*, eds Lewis Patton and Peter Mann, Bollingen Series. London: Routledge and Princeton University Press, 1972.
——. *The Notebooks of Samuel Taylor Coleridge*, 6 vols, ed. Kathleen Coburn. New York: Pantheon Books, 1957–73.
——. *Samuel Taylor Coleridge: The Complete Poems*, ed. William Keach. Harmondsworth: Penguin, 1997.
——. *The Watchman*, ed. Lewis Patton, Bollingen Series. London: Routledge and Princeton University Press, 1970.
'Commemoration of the Battle of Waterloo at Ipswich', *Anti-Jacobin Review*, 50 (June 1816), 572–6.
Conder, Josiah. Unsigned Review of *The Poet's Pilgrimage to Waterloo* by Robert Southey, *Eclectic Review* (August 1816), 1–18; reprinted in *Robert Southey: The Critical Heritage*, ed. Lionel Madden. London: Routledge, 1972, pp. 210–14.
Constable, John. *John Constable's Correspondence*, 6 vols, ed. R. B. Beckett. Ipswich: Suffolk Records Society, 1964.
Cornwell, Bernard. *Sharpe's Waterloo*. London: HarperCollins, 1993.
Costello, Louisa Stuart. *The Maid of Cyprus Isle*. London: Sherwood, Neely and Jones, 1815.
Cotton, Sergeant-Major, *A Voice from Waterloo: A History of the Battle Fought on the 18th June 1815*. London: B. Green, 1889.
Cowper, William. *The Poetical Works of William Cowper*, ed. H. S. Milford. Oxford University Press, 1926.
Craan, Willem Benjamin, *An Historical Account of the Battle of Waterloo... intended to elucidate the topographical plan, executed by W. M. Craan*, trans. Captain Arthur Gore. London: Samuel Leigh, 1817.
Creasy, Sir Edmund. *The Fifteen Decisive Battles of the World*. London: J. M. Dent, 1908.
Croker, John Wilson. Unattributed Review of *Waterloo, and other Poems, By J. Wedderburne Webster, Esq.*, *Quarterly Review*, 15 (July 1816), 345–50.
Davidson, Henry. *Waterloo; a Poem*. Edinburgh and London: John Murray, 1816.
De Quincey, Thomas. *Confessions of an Opium Eater and Other Writings*, ed. Grevel Lindop. Oxford: Oxford University Press, 1985.
Description of the Field of Battle and disposition of the Troops engaged in the Action fought on the 18th June 1815, near Waterloo. Privately printed, 1816.
Description of the Peristrephic Panorama, now exhibiting in the, illustrative of the principal events that have occurred to Bonaparte, commencing with the Battle of Waterloo... and ending with his funeral procession at St. Helena (Thirteenth edition). Exeter: R. Cullum, 1822.
Dryden, John. *Dryden: A Selection*, ed. John Conaghan. London: Methuen, 1978.
The Works of John Dryden, 18 vols, ed. Sir Walter Scott. Edinburgh: William Miller, 1808; revised George Saintsbury. London: Paterson, 1882–3.
Eaton, Charlotte A. *Waterloo Days: The Narrative of an Englishwoman Resident at Brussels in June, 1815*. London: George Bell, 1888.

The Examiner. London: 1814–17.
Farrington, Joseph. *The Farrington Diary*, 8 vols, ed. James Greig. London: Hutchinson, 1922–8.
Fraser, Sir William. *Words on Wellington.* London: 1889.
Harrison, Tony. *The Gaze of the Gorgon.* Newcastle upon Tyne: Bloodaxe Books, 1992.
Haydon, Benjamin Robert. *The Diary of Benjamin Robert Haydon*, 2 vols, ed. Willard Bissell Pope. Cambridge, MA: Harvard University Press, 1960.
Hazlitt, William. *The Complete Works of William Hazlitt*, 21 vols, ed. P. P. Howe. London: J. M. Dent, 1930–4.
Hegel, G. W. F. *Hegel's Philosophy of Right*, trans. T. M. Knox. Oxford: Oxford University Press, 1962.
——. *Hegel's Phenomenology of Spirit*, trans. Arnold Millar. Oxford: Oxford University Press, 1977.
——. *Hegel: Selections*, ed. M. J. Inwood. New York: Macmillan, 1989.
Hornby, Mary. *The Battle of Waterloo; a Tragedy.* Stratford-upon-Avon, printed for the author, 1819.
Hunt, Leigh. *Imagination and Fancy; or Selections from the English Poets*, ed. Edmund Gosse. London: Blackie, 1907.
——. *Leigh Hunt: Literary Criticism*, eds Lawrence Huston Houtchens and Carolyn Washburn Houtchens. New York: Columbia University Press, 1956.
——. *The Poetical Works of Leigh Hunt*, ed. H. S. Milford. Oxford: Oxford University Press, 1923.
Jeffrey, Francis. Review of *Childe Harold's Pilgrimage* III, *Edinburgh Review*, 54 (December 1815), 277–310.
——. Unattributed Review of *The Lay of the Laureate*, *Edinburgh Review*, 26 (June 1816), 441–9; Reprinted in *Robert Southey: The Critical Heritage*, ed. Lionel Madden. London: Routledge, 1972, pp. 216.
Kant, Immanuel. *Critique of Judgement*, 2 vols, trans. James Creed Meredith. Oxford: Clarendon Press, 1989.
Keats, John. *The Letters of John Keats 1814–1821*, 2 vols, ed. Hyder Edward Rollins. Cambridge, MA: Harvard University Press, 1958.
Kelly, Christopher. *History of the French Revolution*, 2 vols. London: Thomas Kelly, 1819.
Lamb, Charles. *The Letters of Charles Lamb*, 2 vols, ed. Alfred Aiger. London: Macmillan, 1904.
de Lancey, Lady Magdalene. *A Week at Waterloo in 1815: Lady de Lancey's Narrative*, ed. Major B. R. Ward. London: 1907.
Lawrence Correspondence. The Royal Academy, London. LAW/3/330/ 1 & 2.
Lewis, James Henry. *Lewis's Orations on the Battle of Waterloo and on the rise and fall of Buonaparte.* London: Macdonald, 1815.
Maxwell, Colonel. *Stories of Waterloo.* London: William Nicholson, no date.
Mercer, Cavalie. *Journal of the Waterloo Campaign.* London: Peter Davies, 1927.
Milton, John. *The Poems of John Milton*, eds John Carey and Alastair Fowler. London: Longman, 1968.
The Morning Chronicle
von Müffling, F. C. F. *History of the Campaign of 1815. Introductory observations and appendices by Sir John Sinclair*, ed. Major-General B. P. Hughes. Wakefield: S. R. Publishers, 1970.
'On the Analogy Between the Growth of Individual and National Genius', *Blackwood's Edinburgh Magazine*, 6 (January 1820), 375–81.

Paine, Thomas. *Rights of Man, Common Sense and Other Political Writings*, ed. Mark Philp. Oxford: Oxford University Press, 1995.
Peacock, Thomas Love. *The Complete Novels*, 2 vols, ed. David Garnett. London: Rupert Hart-Davis, 1963.
'Pompeii', *Blackwood's Edinburgh Magazine*, 15 (April 1824), 472–3.
Praed, Winthrop Mackworth. *The Political and Occasional Poems*. London: Ward, Lock, 1888.
Richardson, Charlotte. *Harvest, a Poem, in two parts; with other Poetical Pieces*. London: Sherwood, Neely and Jones, 1818.
Robinson, Henry Crabbe. *Diary, Reminiscences, and Correspondence of Henry Crabbe Robinson*, 2 vols, ed. Thomas Sadler. London: Macmillan, 1872.
Roe, Peter, Rev. *A Sermon, preached in the chapel of Harrogate, Sunday, July the 30th, 1815, in behalf of the sufferers by the Battle of Waterloo*. Knaresborough: G. Wilson, 1815.
Rowland-Brown, Lilian. 'Waterloo and Romance', *The Nineteenth Century and After*, 78 (July 1915), 103–4.
Ruskin, John. *The Literary Criticism of John Ruskin*, ed. Harold Bloom. New York: De Capo Press, 1987.
Scott, John. *Paris Revisited in 1815, By Way of Brussells: including a Walk Over the Field of Battle at Waterloo*. London: Longman, 1816.
Scott, Sir Walter. *The Antiquary*. London: J. M. Dent, 1977.
———. *Essays on Chivalry, Romance, and the Drama*. London: Frederick Warne & Co., 1888.
———. *The Letters of Sir Walter Scott*, 12 vols, ed. H. J. C. Grierson. London: Constable, 1932–7.
———. *The Minstrelsy of the Scottish Border, with notes and index by Sir Walter Scott*, 4 vols, ed. T. F. Henderson. Edinburgh: William Blackwood, 1902.
———. *Paul's Letters to His Kinsfolk*. Edinburgh and London: Archibald Constable and John Murray, 1816.
———. *The Poetical Works*, ed. J. Logie Robertson. London and Edinburgh: Henry Frowde, 1904.
———. Review of *Childe Harold's Pilgrimage III*, *Quarterly Review*, 16 (October 1816), 172–208.
——— *Waverley; or, 'Tis Sixty Years Since*. ed. Claire Lamont. Oxford: Clarendon Press, 1981.
Simpson, James. *A Visit to Flanders in July, 1815 Being Chiefly an Account of the Field of Waterloo*. Edinburgh: William Blackwood, 1816.
———. *Paris After Waterloo, including a revised edition of 'A Visit to Flanders and the Field of Waterloo'*. Edinburgh: William Blackwood, 1853.
Southey, Robert. *Journal of a Tour in the Netherlands in the Autumn of 1815*. London: Heinemann, 1902.
———. *The Life and Correspondence of the Late Robert Southey*, 6 vols, ed. Rev. Charles Cuthbert Southey. London: Longman, Brown, Green & Longmans, 1850.
———. 'The Life of Wellington', *Quarterly Review*, 13 (April and July 1815), 448–526.
———. *New Letters of Robert Southey*, 2 vols, ed. Kenneth Curry. New York and London: Columbia University Press, 1965.
———. *Poetical Works of Robert Southey, Collected by Himself*, 10 vols. London: Longman, 1838–40.
———. *The Poet's Pilgrimage to Waterloo*. London: Longman, 1816.
———. Unattributed Review, *Quarterly Review*, 16 (October 1816), 225–78.
Spenser, Edmund. *The Faerie Queene*, ed. A. C. Hamilton. London and New York: Longman, 1977.

———. *The Poetical Works of Edmund Spenser*, eds. J. C. Smith and Ernest de Selincourt. Oxford: Clarendon Press, 1935.
Starr, Edwin. 'War' (N. Whitfield, B. Strong). 1970 Jobete Music.
Stendhal. *The Charterhouse of Parma*, trans. Margaret R. B. Shaw. Harmondsworth: Penguin, 1958.
Swift, Edmund L. *Waterloo, and other Poems*. Place of publication unknown: J. J. Stockdale, 1815.
Tennyson, Alfred Lord. *The Poems of Tennyson*, ed. Christopher Ricks. London: Longman, 1969.
Thackeray, W. M. *Vanity Fair*, ed. Peter Shillingsburg. New York and London: W. W. Norton, 1994.
Thomson, John. M. D. *Report of Observations made in the British Military Hospitals in Belgium after the Battle of Waterloo; with some remarks upon amputation*. Edinburgh: William Blackwood, 1816.
The Times
Townsend, Eliza. *Poems and Miscellanies*. London: no publisher listed, 1856.
Walker, George. *The Battle of Waterloo*, A Poem. London: G. Walker, 1815.
Ward. R. A. James. *The Battle of Waterloo in an Allegory ... painted for exhibition at the Egyptian Hall Piccadilly [A description of the painting]*. London: no publisher listed, 1821.
Waterloo. Film. dir. Sergei Bondarchuk, 1970.
Wellington, Arthur Wellesley, 1st Duke of. *Supplementary Despatches, Correspondence and Memoranda of Field Marshal Arthur Duke of Wellington, K. G.* ed. By his son the Duke of Wellington. 15 vols. London: John Murray, 1858–72.
Wordsworth, Dorothy. *Journals of Dorothy Wordsworth*, 2 vols, ed. Ernest de Selincourt. London: Macmillan, 1941.
Wordsworth, William. *Home at Grasmere*, Part First, Book First, of *The Recluse*. ed. Beth Darlington. The Cornell Wordsworth. Ithaca, NY and London: Cornell University Press, 1977.
———. *Letters of William and Dorothy Wordsworth, The Middle Years, Part I, 1806–1812*, ed. E. de Selincourt, 2nd edn revised Mary Moorman. Oxford: Clarendon Press.
———. *Letters of William and Dorothy Wordsworth, The Middle Years, Part II, 1812–1820*, ed. E. de Selincourt, 2nd edn revised Mary Moorman and Alan G. Hill. Oxford: Clarendon Press, 1967.
———. *The Poetical Works of William Wordsworth*, 5 vols, eds E. de Selincourt and Helen Darbishire. Oxford: Clarendon Press, 1947–54.
———. *The Prelude: 1799, 1805, 1850*, eds Jonathan Wordsworth, M. H. Abrams and Stephen Gill. New York: W. W. Norton, 1979.
———. *The Prose Works of William Wordsworth*, 3 vols, ed. Alexander B. Grosart. London: Edward Moxon, 1876.
———. *The Prose Works of William Wordsworth*, 3 vols, eds W. J. B. Owen and Jane Worthington Smyser. Oxford: Clarendon Press, 1974.
———. *Shorter Poems, 1807–1820*, ed. Carl Ketcham, The Cornell Wordsworth. Ithaca, NY and London: Cornell University Press, 1989.
———. *Thanksgiving Ode, January 18, 1816 With Other Short Pieces, Chiefly referring to recent Public Events*. London: Longman, 1816.

Secondary sources

Anderson, Benedict. *Imagined Communities: Reflections on the Origin and Spread of Nationalism*. London: Verso, 1983.
Bachrach, A. G. H. 'The Field of Waterloo and Beyond', *Turner Studies*, 1, 2 (1981), 5–13.
Bainbridge, Simon. *Napoleon and English Romanticism*. Cambridge: Cambridge University Press, 1995.
——. '"To Sing it Rather Better": Byron, The Bards, and Waterloo', *Romanticism*, 1, 1 (1995), 68–81.
Barry, Kevin. 'Paper Money and English Romanticism: Literary Side-effects of the Last Invasion of Britain', *Times Literary Supplement*, 4899 (21 February 1997), 14–16.
Beiderwell, Bruce. 'Scott's *Redgauntlet* as a Romance of Power', *SiR*, 28, 2 (Summer 1989), 273–89.
Benjamin, Walter. 'Theses on the Philosophy of History', in *Illuminations*, trans. Harry Zohn. New York: Schocken Books, 1969, 253–64.
Bennett, Betty (ed.). *British War Poetry in the Age of Romanticism 1793–1815*. New York and London: Garland, 1976.
Bermingham, Ann. 'The Picturesque and Ready-to-Wear Femininity', in *The Politics of the Picturesque: Literature, Landscape and Aesthetics Since 1770*, eds Stephen Copley and Peter Garside. Cambridge: Cambridge University Press, 1994, 81–119.
Bishop, W. J. *The Early History of Surgery*. New York: Barnes & Noble, 1960.
Blunden, Edmund. *Leigh Hunt: A Biography*. London: Cobden-Sanderson, 1930.
Brantlinger, Patrick. *Fictions of State: Culture and Credit in Britain, 1694–1994*. Ithaca, NY and London: Cornell University Press, 1996.
Brombert, Victor. 'The Happy Prison: A Recurring Romantic Metaphor', in *Romanticism: Vistas, Instances, Continuities*, eds. Geoffrey Hartman and David Thorburn. Ithaca, NY: Cornell University Press, 1973, 52–70.
——. *Stendhal: Fiction and the Themes of Freedom*. New York: Random House, 1968.
Bryant, Arthur. *The Age of Elegance, 1812–1822*. London and Glasgow: Collins, 1950.
Bryson, Norman. 'Semiology and Visual Interpretation', in *Visual Theory: Painting and Interpretation*, eds Norman Bryson, Michael Ann Holly and Keith Moxey. Cambridge: Polity Press, 1991, 61–73.
Busco, M. 'The Achilles in Hyde Park', *Burlington Magazine*, 180 (1988), 920–4.
Butler, Marilyn. *Romantics, Rebels, and Reactionaries: English Literature and its Background, 1760–1830*. Oxford: Oxford University Press, 1982.
Cameron, A. D. *The Man Who Loved to Draw Horses: James Howe, 1780–1836*. Aberdeen: Aberdeen University Press, 1986.
Carlson, Julie A. *In the Theatre of Romanticism: Coleridge, Nationalism, Women*. Cambridge: Cambridge University Press, 1994.
Carnall, Geoffrey. *Robert Southey and His Age: The Development of a Conservative Mind*. Oxford: Clarendon Press, 1966.
Chandler, David. *Waterloo: The Hundred Days*. London and Melbourne: Osprey, 1997.
Chandler, James. *England in 1819: The Politics of Literary Culture and the Case of Romantic Historicism*. Chicago and London: University of Chicago Press, 1998.
——. '"Wordsworth" after Waterloo', in *The Age of William Wordsworth*, eds Kenneth R. Johnston and Jean Rouff. New Brunswick, NJ and London: Rutgers University Press, 1987, 84–111.
Charlsworth, Michael. 'The Ruined Abbey: Picturesque and Gothic Values', in *The Politics of the Picturesque: Literature, Landscape and Aesthetics Since 1770*, eds Stephen Copley and Peter Garside. Cambridge: Cambridge University Press, 1994, 62–80.

Christensen, Jerome. *Lord Byron's Strength: Romantic Writing and Commercial Society*. Baltimore, MD and London: Johns Hopkins University Press, 1993.

——. 'Politerotics: Coleridge's Rhetoric of War in *The Friend*', *Clio*, 8 (1979), 339–63.

——. *Romanticism at the End of History*. Baltimore, MD and London: Johns Hopkins University Press, 2000.

Colley, Linda. *Britons: Forging the Nation, 1707–1837*. New Haven, CT and London: Yale University Press, 1992.

Collings, David. *Wordsworthian Errancies: The Poetics of Cultural Dismemberment*. Baltimore, MD and London: Johns Hopkins University Press, 1994.

Cooper, Andrew M. 'Chains, Pains, and Tentative Gains: The Byronic Prometheus in the Summer of 1816', *SiR*, 27, 4 (Winter 1988), 529–62.

Copjec, Joan. *Read My Desire: Lacan Against the Historicists*. Cambridge, MA: MIT Press, 1994.

Cronin, Richard. *The Politics of Romantic Poetry: In Search of the Pure Commonwealth*. Basingstoke: Palgrave Macmillan, 2000.

Curran, Stuart. *Poetic Form and British Romanticism*. Oxford: Oxford University Press, 1986.

Derrida, Jacques. *Writing and Difference*, trans. Alan Bass. London: Routledge, 1978.

Dillard, Annie, 'Do We Count?', *The Observer Review*, 8 February 1998, 5.

Eagleton, Terry. *The Function of Criticism: From* The Spectator *to Post-Structuralism*. London: Verso, 1984.

——. *The Ideology of the Aesthetic*. Oxford: Basil Blackwell, 1990.

——. *Walter Benjamin: Towards a Revolutionary Criticism*. London: Verso, 1981.

Emsley, Clive. *British Society and the French Wars, 1793–1815*. London: Macmillan, 1979.

Evans, Eric. *The Forging of the Modern State: Early Industrial Britain, 1783–1870*. London: Longman, 1983.

Favret, Mary A. 'Coming Home: the Public Spaces of Romantic War', *SiR*, 33, 4 (Winter 1994), 539–48.

Ferris, Ina. 'Re-Positioning the Novel: *Waverley* and the Gender of Fiction', *SiR*, 28, 2 (Summer 1989), 291–301.

Foot, Michael. *The Politics of Paradise: A Vindication of Byron*. London: William Collins, 1988.

Foucault, Michel. *Discipline and Punish*, trans. Alan Sheridan. New York: Vintage Books, 1979.

——. 'Truth and Power', in *The Foucault Reader: An Introduction to Foucault's Thought*, ed. Paul Rabinow. Harmondsworth: Penguin, 1991, 51–75.

Freud, Sigmund. *The Standard Edition of the Complete Psychological Works*, 23 vols, ed. and trans. James Strachey. London: Hogarth, 1961.

Friedman, Barton R. *Fabricating History: English Writers on the French Revolution*. Princeton, NJ: University Press, 1988.

Fry, Paul H. *A Defence of Poetry: Reflections on the Occasion of Writing*. Stanford, CA: Stanford University Press, 1995.

Galperin, William H. *The Return of the Visible in British Romanticism*. Baltimore, MD and London: Johns Hopkins University Press, 1993.

——. *Revision and Authority in Wordsworth; The Interpretation of a Career*. Philadelphia: University of Pennsylvania Press, 1989.

Gash, N. 'After Waterloo: British Society and the Legacy of the Napoleonic Wars', *Transactions of the Royal Historical Society*, 28 (1978), 145–57.

Gill, Stephen. *William Wordsworth: A Life*. Oxford: Oxford University Press, 1990.

Girard, René. *Violence and The Sacred*, trans. Patrick Gregory. Baltimore, MD and London: Johns Hopkins University Press, 1977.
Gossman, Lionel. *Between History and Literature*. Cambridge, MA: Harvard University Press, 1990.
Grundy, John. *Thomas Hardy and the Sister Arts*. London: Macmillan, 1979.
Grundy, Reginald C. *James Ward, R. A.: His Life and Works*. London: Otto, 1909.
Hart, Francis R. *Lockhart as Romantic Biographer*. Edinburgh: Edinburgh University Press, 1971.
Hartley, J. B. 'Maps, Knowledge, and Power', in *The Iconography of Landscape: Essays on the Symbolic Representation, Design and Use of Past Environments*, eds Denis Cosgrove and Stephen Daniels. Cambridge: Cambridge University Press, 1988, 277–312.
Harvey, David. *The Condition of Postmodernity: An Enquiry into the Origins of Cultural Change*. Oxford: Basil Blackwell, 1989.
Heath, Stephen, 'On Suture', in *Questions of Cinema*. Bloomington: Indiana University Press, 1981, 76–112.
Hess, Jonathan M. 'Wordsworth's Aesthetic State: The Poetics of Liberty', *SiR*, 33, 1 (Spring, 1994), 3–29.
Hichberger, J. W. M. *Images of the Army: The Military in British Art, 1815–1914*. Manchester: Manchester University Press, 1988.
Hondt, F. De. *Promenade 1815: On Foot or by Bicycle around the Battlefield at Braine L'Alleud, Genappe, Lasne and Waterloo*. Brussels: Fédération Touristique de la Province De Brabant, 1987.
Howarth, David. *Waterloo: Day of Battle*. New York: Atheneum, 1968.
Johnson, Edgar. *Sir Walter Scott: The Great Unknown*, 2 vols. New York: Hamish Hamilton, 1976.
Johnson, Paul. *The Birth of the Modern: World Society, 1815–1830*. London: Orion, 1992.
Jones, Ernest. *Sigmund Freud: Life and Work*, 3 vols. London: Hogarth Press, 1955.
Jordanova, Ludmilla. 'The Representation of the Human Body: Art and Medicine in the Work of Charles Bell', in *Towards a Modern Art World, For Michael Kitson. Studies in British Art*, I, ed. Brian Allen. New Haven, CT and London: Yale University Press, 1995, 79–94.
Keegan, John. *The Face of Battle: A Study of Agincourt, Waterloo and the Somme*. Harmondsworth: Penguin, 1978.
Kelley, Theresa M. *Wordsworth's Revisionary Aesthetics*. Cambridge: Cambridge University Press, 1988.
Kelsall, Malcolm. *Byron's Politics*. Brighton: Harvester Press, 1987.
Keppel, Sonia. *The Sovereign Lady: A Life of Elizabeth Vassall, third Lady Holland, with her family*. London: Hamish Hamilton, 1974.
Kitson, Peter J. 'The Whore of Babylon and the Woman in White: Coleridge's Radical Unitarian Language', in *Coleridge's Visionary Languages: Essays in Honour of J. B. Beer*, eds Tim Fulford and Morton D. Paley. Woodbridge: D. S. Brewer, 1993, 1–14.
Klancher, Jon. 'Romantic Criticism and the Meanings of the French Revolution', *SiR*, 28, 3 (Fall 1989), 463–91.
Kucich, Greg. *Keats, Shelley, and Romantic Spenserianism*. Pennsylvania: Pennsylvania State University Press, 1991.
Lacan, Jacques. *Ecrits: A Selection*, trans. Alan Sheridan. London: Routledge, 1993.
———. *The Ethics of Psychoanalysis. The Seminar of Jacques Lacan*, Book VII, ed. Jacques-Alain Miller, trans. Dennis Porter. London: Routledge, 1992.
Lamont, Claire. '*Waverley* and the Battle of Culloden', *Essays and Studies*, 44 (1991), 14–26.

Lean, E. Tangye. *The Napoleonists: A Study in Political Disaffection, 1760–1960*. Oxford: Oxford University Press, 1970.
Lerner, Lawrence. *The Uses of Nostalgia: Studies in Pastoral Poetry*. London: Chatto & Windus, 1972.
Levinson, Marjorie. *Wordsworth's Great Period Poems: Four Essays*. Cambridge: Cambridge University Press, 1986.
Le Yaounc, Collete. *L'Orient dans la poésie angalaise de lépoque romantique, 1798–1824*. Lille: Atelier national de reproduction de thèses, 1975.
Liu, Alan. *Wordsworth: The Sense of History*. Stanford, CA: Stanford University Press, 1989.
Lockhart, John Gibson. *Memoirs of the Life of Sir Walter Scott*, 10 vols. Edinburgh: Adam and Charles Black, 1893.
Longford, Elizabeth. *Wellington: Pillar of State*. New York and Evanston, IL: Harper & Row, 1972.
——. *Wellington: The Years of the Sword*. New York and Evanston, IL: Harper & Row, 1969.
Lovell, Jr, Ernest J. *His Very Self and Voice: Collected Conversations of Lord Byron*. New York: Octagon Books, 1980.
Lyotard, Jean-François. *The Differend: Phrases in Dispute*, trans. Georges Van Den Abbeele. Manchester: Manchester University Press, 1988.
Maddison, Carol. *Apollo and the Nine: A History of the Ode*. London: no publisher recorded, 1960.
Makdisi, Saree. 'Colonial Space and the Colonization of Time in Scott's Waverley', *SiR*, 34, 2 (Summer 1995), 155–87.
de Man, Paul. *Blindness and Insight: Essays in the Rhetoric of Contemporary Criticism*, 2nd edn. London: Methuen, 1983.
——. 'The Temptation of Permanence', in *Critical Writings: 1953–1978*, ed. Lindsay Walters. Minneapolis: University of Minnesota Press, 1989, 30–40.
——. *The Rhetoric of Romanticism*. New York: Columbia University Press, 1984.
Manning, Peter J. '*The White Doe of Rylestone*, *The Convention of Cintra*, and the History of a Career', in *Reading Romantics: Texts and Contexts*. Oxford: Oxford University Press, 1990, 165–94.
Michasiw, Kim Ian. 'Nine Revisionist Theses on the Picturesque', *Representations*, 38 (1992), 76–100.
Modiano, Raimondo. 'The Legacy of the Picturesque: Landscape, Property and the Ruin', in *The Politics of the Picturesque: Literature, Landscape and Aesthetics Since 1770*, eds Stephen Copley and Peter Garside. Cambridge: Cambridge University Press, 1994, 196–219.
Montrose, Louis A. 'Professing the Renaissance: The Poetics and Politics of Culture', in *The New Historicism*, ed. H. Aram Veeser. London: Routledge, 1989, 15–36.
Murphy, Peter T. 'Climbing Parnassus, and Falling Off', in *At the Limits of Romanticism: Essays in Cultural, Feminist, and Materialist Criticism*, eds Mary A. Favret and Nicola J. Watson. Bloomington and Indianapolis: University of Indiana Press, 1994, 40–58.
Nellist, Brian. 'Narrative Modes in the Waverley Novels', in *Literature of the Romantic Period: 1750–1850*, eds R. T. Davies and B. G. Beatty. Liverpool: Liverpool University Press, 1976, 56–71.
Oettermann, Stephan. *The Panorama: History of a Mass Medium*, trans. Deborah Lucas Schneider. New York: Zone Books, 1997.
Osamu, Maekawa. 'The Panorama and its Subject', *Aesthetics*, 9 (2000), 37–49.
Paley, Morton D. 'Coleridge and the Apocalyptic Grotesque', in *Coleridge's Visionary Languages: Essays in Honour of J. B. Beer*, eds Tim Fulford and Morton D. Paley. Woodbridge D. S. Brewer, 1993, 15–25.

———. '"These Promised Years": Coleridge's "Religious Musings" and the Millenarianism of the 1790s', in *Revolution and English Romanticism: Politics and Rhetoric*, eds Keith Hanley and Raman Selden. Brighton: Harvester Press, 1990, 49–66.

Paolo, Charles De. 'Kant, Coleridge, and the Ethics of War', *TWC*, 16 (Winter 1985), 3–12.

Paulson, Ronald. *Representations of Revolution (1780–1820)*. New Haven, CT: Yale University Press, 1983.

Pears, Iain. 'The Gentleman and the Hero: Wellington and Napoleon in the Nineteenth Century', in *Myths of the English*, ed. Roy Porter. Cambridge: Polity Press, 1996, 216–33.

Pick, Daniel. *War Machine: The Rationalisation of Slaughter in the Modern Age*. New Haven, CT and London: Yale University Press, 1993.

Pujals, Esteban. 'La leyenda del Rey Rodrigo en el romanticismo ingles', *Revisita de la Universidad de Madrid*, 19 (1970), 259–88.

Rieder, John. *Wordsworth's Counterrevolutionary Turn: Community, Virtue, and Vision in the 1790s*. London: Associated University Presses, 1997.

Roe, Nicholas. *Wordsworth and Coleridge: The Radical Years*. Oxford: Clarendon Press, 1988.

Rose, Jacqueline. 'The Cult of Celebrity', *London Review of Books*, 20, 16 (20 August 1998), 10–13.

———. *Sexuality in the Field of Vision*. London: Verso, 1986.

———. *States of Fantasy*. Oxford: Clarendon Press, 1996.

———. 'Why War?', in *Why War? – Psychoanalysis, Politics, and the Return to Melanie Klein*. Oxford: Basil Blackwell, 1993, 15–40.

Russell, Gillian. *The Theatres of War: Performance, Politics, and Society 1793–1815*. Oxford: Clarendon Press, 1995.

Saglia, Diego. 'The Texts of Romantic Rivalry: Collaboration, Friendship, Competition and the "Don Roderick" Legend, 1810–12'. Unpublished conference paper, presented at the University of Bristol, 'Romantic Lives', 10 February 1998.

———. 'War Romances, Historical Analogies and Coleridge's *Letters on the Spaniards*', in *Romantic Wars: Studies in Culture and Conflict*, ed. Philip Shaw. Aldershot: Ashgate, 2000, 138–60.

Sales, Roger. *English Literature in History: 1780–1830: Pastoral and Politics*. London: Hutchinson, 1983.

Scarry, Elaine. *The Body in Pain: The Making and Unmaking of the World*. Oxford: Oxford University Press, 1985.

Scrivener, Michael (ed.). *Poetry and Reform: Periodical Verse from the English Democratic Press, 1792–1824*. Detroit, MI: Wayne State University Press, 1992.

Shapiro, Michael J. *Violent Cartographies: Mapping Cultures of War*. Minneapolis: University of Minnesota Press, 1997.

Philip Shaw. 'Displacing Waterloo: Southey's Vision of Command', in *Placing and Displacing Romanticism*, ed. Peter J. Kitson. Aldershot: Ashgate, 2001, 106–28.

———. 'Leigh Hunt and the Aesthetics of Post-War Liberalism', in *Romantic Wars: Studies in Culture and Conflict, 1793–1822*. Aldershot: Ashgate, 2000, 185–207.

———. 'Commemorating Waterloo: Wordsworth, Southey, and the "Muses' Page of State"', *Romanticism*, I, 1 (1995), 50–67.

———. '"Mimic Sights": A Note on Panorama and Other Indoor Displays in Book 7 of *The Prelude*', *Notes and Queries*, 238 (December 1993), 462–4.

Siborne, Major-General (ed.). *Waterloo Letters: A Selection of original and hitherto unpublished letters bearing on the operations of the 16th, 17th, and 18th June, 1815. By officers who served in the campaign*. London: Cassell, 1891.

Slater, Don. 'Photography and Modern Vision: The Spectacle of "Natural Magic"', in *Visual Culture*, ed. Chris Jenks. London: Routledge, 1995, 218–37.
Sultana, Donald, *From Abbotsford to Paris and Back: Sir Walter Scott's Journey of 1815*. Far Thrupp: Alan Sutton, 1993.
Sutherland, John. *The Life of Walter Scott: A Critical Biography*. Oxford: Blackwell, 1995.
Thompson, E. P. *The Making of the English Working Class*. Harmondsworth: Penguin, 1968.
Thompson, James R. *Leigh Hunt*. Boston: Twayne Press, 1977.
Thorslev, Peter. 'Post-Waterloo Liberalism: The Second Generation', *SiR*, 28, 3 (Fall 1989), 437–61.
Trevelyan, G. M. *British History in the Nineteenth Century and After: 1782–1919*. Harmondsworth: Penguin, 1965.
Tweedie, Neil. 'We Won the Battle of Waterloo, Says German', *Daily Telegraph*, 14 October 1999, 4.
Virilio, Paul. *The Vision Machine*, trans. Julie Rose. London: BFI Publishing, 1994.
——. *War and Cinema: The Logistics of Perception*, trans. Patrick Camiller. London: Verso, 1989.
Walker, Eric. C. 'Marriage and the End of War', in *Romantic Wars: Studies in Culture and Conflict, 1793–1822*, ed. Philip Shaw. Aldershot: Ashgate, 2000, 208–26.
——. 'Wordsworth, Warriors, and Naming', *SiR*, 29, 2 (Summer 1990), 223–40.
——. 'Wordsworth, Wellington, and Myth', in *History and Myth: Essays on English Romantic Literature*, ed. Stephen C. Behrendt. Detroit: MI: Wayne State University Press, 1990, 100–15.
Webb, Timothy. 'Byron and the Heroic Syllables', *Keats-Shelley Review*, 5 (Autumn 1990), 41–74.
Welsh, Alexander. *The Hero of the Waverley Novels*. New York: Atheneum, 1968.
White, Hayden. *Metahistory: The Historical Imagination in Nineteenth-Century Europe*. Baltimore, MD and London: Johns Hopkins University Press, 1972.
Wilcox, Scott B. 'Unlimiting the Bounds of Painting', in *Panoramania! The Art and Entertainment of the 'All-Embracing' View*, ed. Ralph Hyde. London: Trefoil Publications, 1988, 13–44.
Wilson, Milton. 'Byron and the Battle of Waterloo', in *The Mind in Creation: Essays on English Romantic Literature in Honour of Ross G. Woodman*, ed. J. Douglas Kneale. Quebec: McGill-Queen's University Press, 1992, 6–26.
Wise, Thomas J. *A Bibliography of the Writings in Prose and Verse of William Wordsworth*. Folkestone: Dawsons, 1971.
Wood, Gillen D'Arcy. *The Shock of the Real: Romanticism and Visual Culture, 1760–1860*. Basingstoke: Palgrave Macmillan, 2001.
Woodring, Carl R. *Politics in the Poetry of Coleridge*. Madison: Wisconsin University Press, 1961.
——. 'Three Poets on Waterloo', *TWC*, 18, 2 (Spring 1987), 54–6.
Yarrington, Alison. 'His Achilles Heel? Wellington and Public Art'. Unpublished paper, History of Art Department, University of Leicester.
——. *The Commemoration of the Hero 1800–1864: Monuments to the British Victors of the Napoleonic Wars*. New York and London: Garland, 1988.
Žižek, Slavoj. 'Otto Weininger, or "Woman doesn't Exist"', in *The Žižek Reader*, eds Elizabeth Wright and Edmond Wright. Oxford: Blackwell, 1999, 127–47.
——. *The Plague of Fantasies*. London: Verso, 1997.
——. *Tarrying with the Negative*. Durham, NC: Duke University Press, 1993.
——. *The Sublime Object of Ideology*, trans. Jon Barnes. London: Verso, 1989.

Index

Abba,
'Waterloo' (song), 1
Anderson, Benedict, 148
Annual Register, 3, 115
Anti-Jacobin Review, 3, 18, 21, 46, 53, 94

Bachrach, A. G. H., 220 n. 96, 227 n. 14
Bagehot, Walter, 13
Baillie, Joanna, 45
Bainbridge, Simon, 30–1, 106, 111, 220 n. 97, 223 n. 44, 231 n. 24, 231 n. 36, n. 37, 235 n. 15, 239 n. 18
Barker, Henry Aston, 83, 110, 111
  Battle of Waterloo (panoramic painting), **83–91**
  Explanation of the Battle of Waterloo, painted by Mr. Henry Aston Barker (**Fig. 10**), **87**, 88–91
  see also Barker, Robert
Barker, Robert, 80–91
  see also Barker, Henry Aston *and* Panorama
Barry, Kevin, 232 n. 9
Bataille, Georges, 196
battle tourism, 67–78, 101
Beiderwell, Bruce, 226 n. 79
Bell, Sir Charles, **39–44, 68–70**, 89, 221 n. 9, 221–2 n. 11
  watercolour sketches of wounded at Waterloo (**Figs 3–5**), **40, 41, 42**
  see also the dead and wounded body
Bell, George, Joseph, 42–3
Bellangé, J. L. H.,
  La garde meurt et ne se rend pas! (**Fig. 2**), 26, 27
Benjamin, Walter, 176–7, 178–81, 186–7
Bentham, Jeremy, 85, 90
  Theory of Fictions, 229 n. 43
  see also the Panopticon
Bermingham, Ann, 101
Blackwood's Edinburgh Magazine, 81–2, 218 n. 68
Blake, William, 131, 208

Blücher, Field Marshall, G. L. von, 96, 165, 167, 184, 207
Blunden, Edmund, 203
body, the dead and wounded
  19–29, 36, 37, **38–44**, 45, 46, 70–1, 75–6, 103–5, 107, 121, 123, 127, 149, 177–91, *passim*, 199–200, 205–9, *passim*
  see also Bell, Charles *and* Scarry, Elaine
Bondarchuk, Sergei,
  Waterloo (film), 194, 197, 226 n. 3
Booth's *Battle of Waterloo*, 70–1, 73, 74, 89, 95, 103
  Accounts of Waterloo, 206–7
Brantlinger, Patrick, 232 n. 9
Brombert, Victor, 19
Bryson, Norman, 79–80
Bunyan, John, 105
Burdett, Sir Francis, 11
Burke, Edmund, 8, 95, 120, 233 n. 21
Burney, Fanny (Frances, Madame d'Arblay), 24, 196, 197, 228 n. 38
Busco, M., 240 n. 9
Butler, Marilyn, 222 n. 13
Brontë, Charlotte, 196–7
  Jane Eyre, 199
Buchan, David Home,
  The Battle of Waterloo: A Poem, 224 n. 56
Byron, George Gordon; Lord Byron, 10, 16, 21, 53, 56, 57, 59, 76, 99, 109–10, **134, 165–91**, 193, 202, 206, 207
  Childe Harold's Pilgrimage, 21, 30, 56, 94, 97, 109, 170, 171, **179–91**, **195–6, 199–200**, 217 n. 61
  The Corsair, 191
  Don Juan, 165, **175–8, 186–7**, 200, 201
  'From the French', **172–5**
  The Giaour, 191
  'Napoleon's Farewell (From the French)', **169–70**, 173, 174
  'Ode to Napoleon Bonaparte', **171**
  Byron's cousin, Major Frederick Howard, 188–9

Byron, George Gordon; Lord Byron – *continued*
  on the dead and wounded, 176–91, *passim*
  on the Duchess of Richmond's ball, 195–6
  on the battle of Morat, 184–5
  on Napoleon, 169–75, 199
  on Walter Scott, 188
  on Waterloo and Marathon, 180–7
  on Wellington, 168, 184
  reviewed by Walter Scott, 180
  initial response to Waterloo, 167–8
  compares Waterloo with Cannae, 184
  visits Waterloo, 178–80
  contrasted with Wordsworth, 177, 178–9

Cameron, A. D., 79, 228 n. 40
Campbell's *Guide Through Belgium and Holland*, 75
Cannae, battle of (216 BC), 184–5
Canning, George and Ellis, George, 50
Cargill, John
  Battle of Waterloo; a poem, 224–5 n. 59
Carlson, Julia, 134, 136, 233 n. 33, 234 n. 39
Carlyle, Thomas, 9
Carnall, Geoffrey, 231 n. 22
Cartwright, Major, 115
Castlereagh, Lord, x, 2, 3, 4, 9, 11, 28, 148, 165, 166, 167–8, 212 n. 7
Champion, 174
Chandler, David, 218 n. 80
Chandler, James, 3, 49
Christensen, Jerome, 38, 119, 130, 135, 200, 212 n. 2, 231 n. 18, 233 n. 26
Clancarty, Earl of, 93
Cobden, Richard, 203
Cobbett, William, **11–13**, 17, 97, 114
  see also Political Register
Coleridge, Samuel Taylor, 7, 46, 95, 99, **114–39**, 168
  'A Letter to—[Sara Hutchinson] April 4, 1802' ('Dejection' ode), 126–7, 128
  Biographia Literaria, 116, 119, 127–8, 131, 132, 134–5, 137, 139
  'The Destiny of Nations', 124
  Essays on His Times, 118–19, 120, 124–5, 128–9
  'Fears in Solitude', 123–4, 126
  'Frost at Midnight', 126
  Hymn Before Sunrise, 128
  The Friend, 114, 116, 135, 137
  Lay Sermon, 115, 116–18, 139
  'The Men and the Times', 124–5, 129
  Notebooks, 125–6, 128
  'Ode on the Departing Year', 121–2, 126
  'Ode to Tranquillity', 126
  'On the Present War', 122
  'Origins of Modern Drama', 138–9
  Osorio (see *Remorse*)
  'Our Future Prospects', 128–9
  'Religious Musings', 120, 132
  Remorse, 132–3
  Zapolya, **133–9**
  on commanding genius, 127–8, 130–3
  on Imagination, 121, 125, 126–7, 131, 139
  on Napoleon, 125, 127–8, 129, 130, 132, 139
  on the National Debt, 114–19, 139, 232 n. 8
  on Shakespeare, 133, 137–9, 233 n. 25
  on Wellington, 130–1
Colley, Linda, ix, 8, 196–7
Collings, David, 234 n. 6
Conder, Josiah, 15, 29, 144, 155–6, 176, 180, 237 n. 43
Constable, John, 80
Cooper, Andrew, 188
Copjec, Joan, 7
Costello, Louisa Stuart,
  'On reading the Account of the Battle of Waterloo', 219 n. 90
Courier, 130–1, 168, 234 n. 41
Cornwell, Bernard,
  Sharpe's Waterloo, 4, 226 n. 3
Cotton, Sergeant-Major Edward, 222 n. 23, 227 n. 20
Cowley, Abraham, 158–9
Cowper, William, 108
Craan, W. M., 72–3, 108
  map of the Battle of Waterloo, 72–3, 79, 227 n. 9
Creasy, Sir Edmund, 3, 168, 192, 195, 211
  The Fifteen Decisive Battles of the World, 192–3, 210
Crimean War (1853–6), 4, 210–11

Cronin, Richard, 220 n. 97
Croker, John Wilson, 76, 92, 93, 97, 106, 220 n. 100
Cruikshank, George, *Making Decent!!* (Fig. 12), **197–9**
Curran, Stuart, 52, 60, 156, 158, 223 n. 39, 237 n. 33

D'Arcy Wood, Gillen, 229 n. 45
Davidson, Henry, *Waterloo, A Poem with notes* 18, 20, 203, 224 n. 56
De Coster, Jean, 45, 95
De Hondt, F., 227 n. 20
De Lancey, Lady Magdalene, 24
De Lancey, Sir William, 24
de Man, Paul, 159, 181, 209, 215–6 n. 33
De Paolo, Charles, 125, 233 n. 29
De Quincey, Thomas, 6, 17, 205
'The English Mail Coach', **202–3**
de Sade, Marquis, 234 n. 5
Derrida, Jacques, 177–8
Dickens, Charles, 24, 202
Dillard, Annie, 187
Don Quixote, 50
Dryden, John, 55–6
Absalom and Achitophel, 60
Duchess of Richmond's ball, 195, 201–2
Dundas, William, 148

Eagleton, Terry, 179, 230 n. 7
Eaton, Charlotte A., 67, 75–8, 104, 196
Waterloo Days, 75–6
see also Booth's *Battle of Waterloo*
Edinburgh Review, 217 n. 61
English Civil Wars (1642–6; 1648–51), 17, 56
Erdman, David, 120, 124, 233 n. 22
Examiner, 13, 16, 97, 150, 152, 169, 171, 174
see also Hunt, Leigh *and* Hazlitt, William
Evans, Eric, 7

Farrington, Joseph, 217 n. 55
Favret, Mary, 18, 22, 205–6
Ferris, Ina, 226 n. 76
Fitzgerald, William Thomas, 14, 29, 108–9, 172
'The Battle of Waterloo', 14

'The White Cockade', 172
Foot, Michael, 239 n. 11
Fox, Charles, 128, 174
Foucault, Michel, 6, 71, 73
see also the Panopticon
French Revolution (1789–94), 8, 129, 132, 134
Freud, Sigmund, 78, 193–4, 196
'Why War?', 194
Fry, Paul, 185

Galperin, William, 88, 90, 229 n. 45, 231 n. 37, 235 n. 8
Gash, N., 232 n. 4
Gaskell, Elizabeth Cleghorn, 2
Gibbon, Edward, 171
Gill, Stephen, 235–6 n. 17, 238 n. 59
Gilpin, William, 231 n. 33
Girard, René, 141, 234 n. 6
'Glorious Revolution' (1688), 8, 166, 168
Gneisenau, General, 95
Godwin, William, 120, 233 n. 21
Grenville, Lord, 166
Grundy, C. Reginald, 228 n. 24
Grundy, John, 229 n. 51

Habermas, Jürgen, 3, 17, 230 n. 7
Harrison, Tony, 22
Hart, Francis R., 240 n. 5
Hartley, J. B., 227 n. 10
Harvey, David, 80–1
Hart, Francis, 195
Haydon, Benjamin Robert, ix–x, 5, 10
Hazlitt, William, 97–9, 100, 144, 170, 178, 226 n. 76, 228 n. 23
see also the *Examiner*
Heath, Stephen, 7
Hegel, G. W. F., 5, 7, 10, 17, 85, 145–6, 164, 171
Hess, Jonathan M., 147
Hichberger, J. M. W., 22, 28, 219–20 n. 95
Hobhouse, John Cam, 165, 168
Hofschröer, Peter, 213–4 n. 18
Holland, Lord, 165–6, 168, 173
Homer, 51, 59, 170, 176, 193
the *Iliad*, 90, 197
Hone, William, 174
Horace (Quintus Horatius Flaccus), 158

256 Index

Hornby, Mary
  The Battle of Waterloo: A Tragedy, 213 n. 10, 233 n. 33
Hougoumont, 21, 41–2, 103, 180, 206
  Entrance to Hougoumont (**Fig. 11**), **104**, 105
Howard, Major Frederick, 188–9
Howarth, David, 24
Hunt, James Henry Leigh, 13, 16, 144, 150, **151–3**, **169–72**, **203–9**
  Captain Sword and Captain Pen, **203–9**
  The Descent of Liberty, 151, 172, 209, 236 n. 28
  'National Song', **16–18**
  'Ode for the Spring of 1814', 151–2
  Story of Rimini, The, 172
  'The Trumpets of Doolkarnein', 209
  'To Kosciusko', 237 n. 33
  on Byron, 169–70
  on Napoleon, 17, 169–72, 237 n. 33
  on Wellington, 16, 203, 207
  on Wordsworth, 151–2
  contrasted with Wordsworth, 237 n. 33
  see also the *Examiner*
Hunt, Henry 'Orator', 115

Jeffrey, Francis, 55, 100, 217 n. 61, 224 n. 55, 235–6 n. 17
Johnson, Edgar, 44
Johnson, Paul, 228 n. 25
Jordanova, Ludmilla, 221–2 n. 11
Juvenal (Decimus, Junius Juvenalis), 179, 180–3

Kant, Immanuel, 6, 142, 215 n. 25, 218 n. 68, 234 n. 5
  on war, 118–19, 125–6
  see also the Sublime
Keats, John, 46, 52, 56, 66, 172
Keegan, John, 213–4 n. 18, 226 n. 6
Kelly, Christopher,
  History of the French Revolution, 88–9
Kelsall, Malcolm, 167–8, 173, 174, 180, 231 n. 32
Ketcham, Carl, 145
Kitson, Peter J., 120
Klancher, Jon, 32

Labedoyere, General, 174

Lacan, Jacques, 7, 18, 32, 73, 136, 190, 199
  on feminine sexuality, 199–200, 202, 240 n. 13
  jouissance and war, 123, 126, 142, 154, 201–2, 210–11
  the Real, 7, 18, 20, 28, 32, 66, 78, 100, 130, 142, 143, 161, 190, 202; as distinguished from 'reality', 215–6 n. 33
  the Thing (*das Ding*) and the Law, 142, 143, 203, 234 n. 5
Lamb, Charles, 33–4
Lamont, Claire, 224 n. 53
Landor, Walter Savage,
  Count Julian, 223 n. 49
Le Yaounc, Collette, 224 n. 49
Lean, E. Tangye, 239 n. 9
Lerner, Laurence, 191
Lewis, James Henry 'Orator', 79, 212 n. 6
Liu, Alan, 32, 74, 78, 85, 104
Liverpool, Lord, 148
Lockhart, John Gibson, 43, 45–8 *passim*, 53, 191
Longford, Elizabeth, 35, 67
Lyotard, Jean-François, 230 n. 15

Maddison, Carol, 157–8
Makdisi, Saree, 224 n. 58
Manning, Peter J., 223 n. 44
Marathon, battle of (490 BC), 180–7, 192, 193
Marshall, Peter, 84
Marx, Karl, 180
marriage and war, 159–61, 201
  see also women and war *and* Lacan, on feminine sexuality
May, John, 98
Maxwell, Colonel,
  Stories of Waterloo, 2, 194, 240–1 n. 14
McGann, Jerome J., 131, 179, 184
Mercer, Cavalié, 72
Michasiw, Kim Ian, 231 n. 33
Milton, John, 13, 51, 55–6, 59, 100, 111–12, 120–1, 145, 151–4, 162, 193, 235–6 n. 17, 237 n. 33
  Comus, 151
  Lycidas, 190
  Paradise Lost, 89, 109, 112, 151, 153, 217 n. 64

Mitchell, Robert,
  A Section of the Rotunda, Leicester Square (**Fig. 8**), 83–4, 85–6
  see also panorama patent and design
Modianao, Raimondo, 73
Montrose, Louis A., 215 n. 33
Moore, Sir John, 52
Moore, Thomas, 167, 172
Morat, Battle of (1476), 184–5, 186, 187
Morning Chronicle, 172, 174
Morning Post, 126, 128, 172
Müffling, Major-Gen. F. C. F. Baron von, 95, 165
Murphy, Peter T., 220 n. 98
Murray, John, 44
  Murray's *Handbook for Travellers in Holland and Belgium*, 73–4

Napoleon Bonaparte, 1–4, 9, 17, 32, 66, 68–70, 83, 98–9, 100, 122, 125, 129, 130, 145, 166, 180, 196, 212 n. 6, 229–30 n. 2
  abdication of 1814, 9, 36, 54, 83, 172
  as depicted in the Panorama, 88–9
  as subject of poetry and drama, 16, 31, 36, 58–9, 98, 106–13, 134–5, 139, 150–1, 160, 169–75
  as depicted in Sergei Bondarchuk's *Waterloo* (film), 197
  'Bonaparte's Observatory' (**Fig. 6**), 68, 69, 70–1, 89, 108, 109; see also Craan, W. M., map of the Battle of Waterloo
  Byron on, 169–75, 199
  Coleridge on, 125, 127–8, 129, 130, 132, 139, 233 n. 25
  Scott on, 58–9
  Southey on, 98–9, 100, 106–13, *passim*
  Wordsworth on, 142, 151
Napoleon, Louis, 192, 210
Nellist, Brian, 223 n. 38, 223 n. 39
Nash, Edward, 96
National Debt, 37–8, 114–19, 139
Ney, Marshal Michel, 173–4

Oettermann, Stephan, 229 n. 43
Osamu, Maekwawa, 229 n. 47

Paine, Thomas, 8, 37, 115, 120, 168
Paley, Morton D., 117, 120

Panopticon (**Fig. 9**), 71, 85, **86**
  see also Bentham, Jeremy
  see also Foucault, Michel
Panoramas, 71–91, 103
  patent and design, 82–4, see also Mitchell, Robert
  explanatory 'key', 86–91.
  fold-out panorama in Booth's *Battle of Waterloo*, 74, 103
  as poetic device in Southey, 108–13.
  see also Barker, Robert and Barker, Henry Aston
Pasley, C. W., Captain, 142–3
Peace of Amiens (1802), 124, 126
Peacock, Thomas Love, *Melincourt*, 214 n. 21
Pears, Iain, 2, 212–13 n. 8
Peninsular War (1808–13), 9, 44, 49–53, 130–1, 199–200, 223 n. 44
  see also Wellington and Peninsular War
Perry, James, 173
Pick, Daniel, 215 n. 28
picturesque, 73–8, 88, 96–7, 101–05, 113, 231 n. 33
  see also the Sublime
Pieneman, Fleming, 80
Pindar, 156
Pitt (the Younger), William, 125, 133
Political Register, 94, 97
  see also Cobbett, William
Plato, 160
Plutarch, 160, 170
Praed, Winthrop Mackworth 'Waterloo', 214 n. 22
Pujals, Esteban, 224 n. 49

Quarterly Review, 50, 74, 92–3, 108, 115, 220 n. 100

Repository of Arts, 82
Richardson, Charlotte Caroline, 219 n. 90
Rickman, John, 96, 97
Rieder, John, 31
Robinson, Henry Crabb, 114
Roe, Peter, Rev., 218 n. 81, 219 n. 89
Roe, Nicholas, 120
Rogers, Samuel, 73
Rose, Jacqueline, 1, 212 n. 4, 240, n. 3, 240 n. 13

Rossetti, Dante Gabriel,
  'On the Field of Waterloo' 241 n. 26
Rowland-Brown, Lilian, 213 n. 9
Ruskin, John, 30
Russell, Gillian, 84, 213 n. 10

Saglia, Diego, 50, 223 n. 46, 224 n. 49
Scarry, Elaine, 7, 19, 22, 25, 26
Scottish border conflicts and national identity, 48–56, 61–6, 224 n. 56, 224 n. 58, 224–5 n. 59
Scott, John, 76–8, 104, 146, 154, 174, 234 n. 1, 235 n. 15
  Paris Revisited, 76–7
  see also the *Champion*
Scott, Sir Walter, 10, **35–66**, 76, 94, 98, 99, 100, 105–6, 108, 184, 203, 208
  The Antiquary, 38–9, **61–6**, 139
  'Bard's Incantation', 47–8
  'The Dance of Death', **53–5**
  'Essay on Chivalry', 50
  'Essay on Romance', 49, 51, 52
  The Field of Waterloo, 37, 53, **55–61**, 66, 90–1, 188, 191
  Guy Mannering, 61, 66
  Marmion, 54–5
  Minstrelsy of the Scottish Border, The, 48
  Paul's Letters to His Kinsfolk, 45, 57
  The Vision of Don Roderick, 36, **49–53**, 54, 55, 221 n. 4
  Waverley, 38–9, 45, 49, 53, 54, 60, 61–2, 224 n. 58, 225 n. 71
  on Wellington, 59–61, 225 n. 68
  reviews Byron, 184
  initial response to Waterloo, 10
  visits Waterloo, 35–6, 39–46
Shakespeare, William, 44, 133, 137–8
  As You Like It, 191
  Coriolanus, 144
  Hamlet, 137, 139, 233 n. 25
  The Winter's Tale, 134, 138
Shapiro, Michael J., 215 n. 27
Shaw, George Bernard, 203
Shaw, Philip, 231 n. 37
Shelley, Percy, 56, 131, 208
Shorter, R.,
  'On Seeing in a List of New Music *The Waterloo Waltz*', 214–15 n. 24
Siborne, Major-General, 226–7 n. 8
Simpson, James, 35, 60, 67, 94

A Visit to Flanders in July, 1815, 1, 67, 95
Sinclair, Sir John, 95, 96
Slater, Don, 82
Smirke, Edward, 12
Soignies, forest of, 44, 56, 191
Southey, Robert, 10, 33–4, 53, 76, **92–113**, 115–16, 133, 154, 155–6, 172, 206, 208
  'The Battle of Blenheim', 107–8
  The Curse of Kehama, 106
  Journal of a Tour of the Netherlands, 94, 96, **101–5**
  The Lay of the Laureate, 97
  'The Life of Wellington', 92, 108
  'The March to Moscow', 106
  'Ode, written during the Negotiations with Bounaparte, in January, 1814', 106
  The Poet's Pilgrimage to Waterloo, 75, 92, 96, 97, 103, **105–13**, 153, 156–7, 172–3, 237 n. 43
  Roderick, the Last of the Goths, 224 n. 49
  on Napoleon, 98–9, 100, 106–13, *passim*
  on Wellington, 92–3, 97, 108–9, 113
  contrasted with Scott, 100, 105–6
  initial response to Waterloo, 10, 98–9
  on the naming of Waterloo, 94–7
  visits Waterloo, 101–5
Spenser, Edmund, 52–3, 100, 105, 113, **153–64**, 176, 235–6 n. 17
  Epithalamion, **157–64**
  The Faerie Queene, 154
  Spenserian stanza, 51
Spenser, Countess, 197
Spenser, Earl, 197
Starr, Edwin,
  'War' (song), 209
Stendhal,
  The Charterhouse of Parma, 19–20, 200
Sublime, 6, 15, 34, 40, 60, 73, 76–7, 78, 102, 111, 114, 115, 118, 120, 141, 150–4, *passim*, 175, 202, 209, 235 n. 15
  and the Beautiful, 21, 153–4
  in painting, 21, 25, 28, 80, 86
  and the picturesque, 73–8, 88,
Sultana, David, 44, 225 n. 68
Sutherland, John, 47–53 *passim*, 224 n. 55
Swift, Edmund, 18, 203

Taxation, *see* National Debt
Tennyson, Alfred, Lord Tennyson, 4
  'The Lady of Shallot', 203
  Maud, 211, 241 n. 26
  'Ode on the Death of the Duke of Wellington', 210
  'Penny Wise, The', 210
  'Rifle Clubs!!!', 210
  'Suggested by Reading an Article in a Newspaper', 210
Thackeray, William Makepeace, *Vanity Fair*, 194–5, **200–2**
Thomson, John, 221 n. 9
Thorslev, Peter, 220 n. 97
The Times, 1, 8, 35, 81, 83
tourism, 67–78, 93
  Scott's tour, 35–6, 39–46
  Southey's tour, 101–05
  as distinguished from pilgrimage, 45, 75–6, 106–13
  see also Eaton, Charlotte, Simpson, James and Scott, John
Townsend, Eliza
  'Lines on a Stone from the Field of Waterloo', 219 n. 90
Treaty of Paris (1815), 173
Treaty of Utrecht (1713–14), 166
Trevelyan, G. M., 213 n. 15
Turner, J. M. W.
  The Field of Waterloo (**Fig. 1**), 21–4, 28–9, 80

Uxbridge, Lord, 24

Virgil (Publius Vergilius Maro), 185–6
Virilio, Paul, 229 n. 51
Voltaire (François-Marie Arouet), 109–10
Vonnegut, Kurt, 25

Walker, Eric C., 160, 212 n. 5, 229–30 n. 2, 235 n. 17, 238 n. 53, n. 54
Walker, George, 76
Ward, James, 11, 80, 228 n. 24
Washington, George, 125
Webb, Tim, 220 n. 97
Webster, James Wedderburn, 195, 220 n. 100
Wellington, Duke of, 1–2, 35–6, 59–60, 66, 76, 83, 99, 106, 130–1, 165, 166, 168, 174, 196, 207, 212 n. 6, 229–30 n. 2
  as represented in the Panorama, 86–91
  as subject of poetry, 14–15, 16, 51, 52, 58–9, 61, 98, 108–9, 145–6, 188, 210, 214 n. 22, 221 n. 4, 224–5 n. 59
  and Peninsular War (1803–13), 9, 36, 51, 52, 130–1
  as depicted in Sergei Bondarchuk's *Waterloo* (film), 197
  'Waterloo Despatch', ix, 2, 35–6, 94, 95, 212 n. 7, 230 n. 9
  and the 'Wellington tree', 76–7
  and statue of Achilles, 197–9
  attitude to writers, 60, 93–4, 230 n. 9
  on battle tourism, 93, 230 n. 4
  Byron on, 168, 184
  Coleridge on, 130–1, 233 n. 25
  Leigh Hunt on, 203, 207
  Southey on, 92–3, 97, 108–9, 113
  Walter Scott on, 59–61
  Wordsworth on, 145–6, 154, 235–6 n. 17
  Tennyson on, 210
  women's enthusiasm for, 196–99
Welsh, Alexander, 226 n. 79
West, Benjamin,
  Christ Rejected by Caiphos, 80
  Picture of Death on the Pale Horse, 228 n. 23
White, Hayden, 13
Whitbread, William, 12, 165, 166, 168
Wilcox, Scott B., 82, 228 n. 26
William III, King, 166
Wilson, Milton, 57, 220 n. 97, 239 n. 41
women and war, 21–3, 135–8, **196–203**, 204–9, *passim*, 211, 219 n. 89, n. 90, 234 n. 39, 240–1 n. 14
  see also marriage and war *and* Lacan, on feminine sexuality
Woodring, Carl R., 57, 220 n. 97, 233 n. 34
Wordsworth, Dorothy, x, 149, 212 n.1
Wordsworth, William, 30–33, 52–3, 103, **140–64**, 177, 208, 234 n. 1
  'A slumber did my spirit seal', 190
  'After Visiting the Field of Waterloo', 149–50
  'Anticipation: October, 1803', 141

Wordsworth, William – *continued*
  'Character of the Happy Warrior', 142
  'Composed in Recollection of the Expedition of the French into Russia', 236–7 n. 31
  The Convention of Cintra, 142
  'Dion', 160–1
  Essays Upon Epitaphs, 148, 159, 163, 178
  The Excursion, x, 186
  Home at Grasmere, 140
  'How clear, how keen, how marvellously bright', 150, 152
  'Immortality' ode, 31, 159, 162–4
  'Occasioned by the Battle of Waterloo', 25, 26, **148–9**, 152
  'Occasioned by the Same Battle', 15, **152–5**, 178
  The Prelude, 30, 141, 160, 162, 231 n. 37
  'Siege of Vienna Raised by John Sobieska', 152
  'Sonnet, On the same Occasion, February 1816', 236–7 n. 31
  Sonnets Dedicated to Liberty, 147
  'Thanksgiving Ode', 30, 94, **144–7**, 149, **155–64**, 178, 237 n. 43
  'While not a leaf seems faded', 150
  The White Doe of Rylestone, 153, 223 n. 44
  on Imagination, 30, 146–7, 236 n. 28
  on Fancy, 150, 236 n. 28
  on Napoleon, 30, 142–3
  on The People, 237 n. 44
  on Wellington, 145–6, 154, 235–6 n. 17
  corresponds with John Scott, 235 n. 15
  compared with Byron, 177, 178–9
  distinguishes military from poetic character, 235–6 n. 17
  relations with Leigh Hunt, 151–2, 236 n. 28
  relations with Southey, 153–7, 237 n. 43
  visits Waterloo, 149–50
Wynn, William, 92, 96, 112, 148

Yarrington, Alison, 197, 219–20 n. 95, 240 n. 7

Žižek, Slavoj, 32, 136, 215–6 n. 33, 229 n. 44

OHIO UNIVERSITY LIBRARY

Please return this book as soon as you have finished with it. In order to avoid a fine it must be returned by the latest date stamped below. All books are subject to recall after two weeks or immediately if needed for reserve.

JUN 1 6 2008

CF